The Duke of Windsor's War

THE DUKE OF WINDSOR'S WAR

From Europe to the Bahamas,
1939–1945

Michael Bloch

Coward-McCann, Inc.
New York

To Maître Suzanne Blum
guide, pupil master, and friend

First American Edition 1983
Copyright © 1982 by Michael Bloch
All rights reserved. This book, or parts thereof,
may not be reproduced in any form without permission
in writing from the publisher.

Library of Congress Cataloging in Publication Data

Bloch, Michael.
The Duke of Windsor's War

Bibliography: p.
Includes index.
1. Windsor, Edward, Duke of, 1892-1972. 2. Windsor,
Wallis Warfield, Duchess of, 1896-   . 3. Bahamas—
Governors—Biography. 4. Great Britain—Kings and
rulers—Biography. I. Title.
DA580.B53 1983   941.084'092'4 [B]   82-18265
ISBN 0-698-11177-X

The text of this book has been set in Century Expanded
Printed in the United States of America

ACKNOWLEDGEMENTS

The author gratefully acknowledges permission from the following to reprint material in this book. Maître Suzanne Blum (on behalf of the Duchess of Windsor), photo pages: 1, 2 above, 3, 4, 5, 8, 9, 10, 11 below, 12, 13, 14 above, 15 below, 16 below; Syndication International, 2 below; Stanley Toogood, Nassau, 6, 7, 11 above, 14 below, 15 above; Charles Bethell, 16 above. The three maps were drawn by Patrick Leeson.

Contents

CONTENTS

Part Three: Wars within Wars

Foreword

First and foremost I must thank Maître Suzanne Blum (Madame Georges Spillmann), French advocate of Their Royal Highnesses the Duke and Duchess of Windsor since 1946, the Duke's executrix and guardian of all the Duchess's interests since 1972, whose pupil it was my privilege to be in the winter of 1979–80, and who invited me to write this book. To say that Maître Blum made available to me numerous documents from the private archives of the Duke and Duchess, and allowed me to quote from their published and unpublished writings, is to express but a tiny part of what this book owes (and I personally owe) to her, and which its dedication is but a meagre effort to repay.

I received an immense amount of kindness and help from numerous people who were in various ways associated with Their Royal Highnesses during the war. For the period of the Duke's war service in France from September 1939 to June 1940, I was always given the most generous and enthusiastic assistance whenever I asked for it from his French friends, from former prominent members of the French Army, and from the *Service historique de l'Armée de Terre* at Vincennes. My one great sadness is that I was unable to discuss this book (as I discussed so many things) with the late General Georges Spillmann, in whose library at Echiré I did so much of the writing and research. But I had the benefit of the advice and good offices of his best friend, General Maurice Durosoy, who put me in touch with the inimitable Colonel Dutailly of the *Service historique*. General Olivier Poydenot gave me a vivid picture of the Duke's relations with General Gamelin and the French officers at Vincennes. General Pierre Billotte, one of the few Frenchmen to have been in the Duke's close confidence, told me a great many interesting things about the Duke's attitude towards the war. I am also grateful to Dr François Bédarida, Professor Jacques Valette and Professor Jean Vanwelkenhuysen for advising me on particular points of history.

When I sought the co-operation of English officers who had encountered the Duke at this period it was not, alas, always the same story. But

Colonel Gaussen of the Welsh Guards invited me to his headquarters, where Major Jones enabled me to appreciate the almost Jacobite fervour with which the Duke has always been viewed in that regiment. Among the survivors of the Duke's mess at Nogent-sur-Marne, General Sir Harold Redman, Lord Coleridge and Brigadier George Davy gave me interesting accounts of how he was regarded there both as a soldier and a man. Thanks to Larry McKinna of the Pathé Newsreel Library I had a view of the Duke at war in France which no verbal account could have given. And in Lady Sackville – once the wife of the Duke's old friend General Sir Francis de Guingand – I found not only a useful informant but a sympathetic ally.

I shall not describe here my somewhat adventurous researches into the Duke's six weeks in the Iberian Peninsula in June–July 1940. That intricate and much misunderstood episode will be the subject of another book, currently in preparation. But a work on the Duke's war would obviously be incomplete without some account of it, and so I have devoted Chapter Five to his fortnight in Spain and Chapter Six to his month in Portugal.

I am grateful to many people, particularly the Duke's former officials, who helped me in my research into his Governorship of the Bahamas, but to none more than Sir Eric Hallinan, who was Attorney-General of the Bahamas between the summers of 1940 and 1944 and saw his royal chief almost daily. He has given me the benefit of so much of his time and memory, and has read most of the book in typescript and made many valuable suggestions. I was also fortunate in being able to have a series of interviews in Florence with the late Captain Vyvyan Drury, the Duke's aide-de-camp from 1940 to 1942. Nina Drury, to whom he was married at that time, had already most generously shown me her correspondence with the Duchess and given me a vivid picture of life at Government House, a picture supplemented from various other points of view by the recollections of Mary Teegarden Holder, Mr Jason Lindsey, and the Duke's Bahamian valet Sydney Johnson. Colonel Reginald Erskine-Lindop, who as Commissioner of Police in Nassau had to deal both with the June Riots and the Oakes murder, was kind enough to answer a number of questions through his daughter. Sir James Marjoribanks, Great Britain's young Consul in Florida from November 1940, sent me a delightful memoir of his encounters with the Duke and Duchess in Miami and elsewhere.

Among wartime members of the Colonial Office, Mr Dudley Danby, Sir Leslie Monson and Sir Philip Rogers gave me some views of the Duke's Governorship as seen from Whitehall. And while soldiers of the time tended to be somewhat reticent, the same could not be said of former British intelligence officers. While the names of some of my informants cannot be mentioned here, I am glad to be able to acknowledge the help of Stewart Lack, who was in Nassau in 1943–4 as a member of the Field Security Wing of the Intelligence Corps, and of Harford Montgomery Hyde, most prolific of authors and generous of beings, who showed me the notes and correspondence of his top secret visit to the Duke on behalf of *Intrepid* in March 1941.

In February 1981 I went to the Bahamas for a few weeks to do my 'field work' – and nowhere is one more conscious of the saying that one cannot understand a place until one has experienced it with one's own senses. I am grateful to many thoughtful friends who warned me what to expect there, and in particular to Grace, Lady Dudley who predicted with remarkable clairvoyance that I would find my first few days miserably depressing and the rest of my stay boundlessly fascinating. I arrived under leaden skies which belied all I had been taught to believe about the famous Winter Climate. The best that can be said of the British Colonial Hotel, that huge crumbling lump of pink stucco which was once the pride of Sir Harry Oakes who owned it and the US Army whose wartime headquarters it was, is that its present condition accurately reflects the current standing of the British Colonial Empire. The armed guards who patrolled the establishment irked me particularly, until I heard, during an enlightening day spent at the law courts, an everyday Bahamian story of female tourists machine-gunned on account of their refusal to hand over their bags when firmly requested to do so. Indeed, it was hard to find a bar-stool in Nassau where one was not told by one's neighbour (if not the barman) about a recent entertainment provided by the arrival of gentlemen with machine-guns. Every capital has its own brand of local horror story, but none are so hair-raising as Nassau's. I discovered too, as the Duke of Windsor had done forty years before, that certain chill winds blow all the way across the Atlantic from Berkshire to New Providence Island. An agitated Governor-General refused to allow me to look at his residence which owes so much to the Duchess, with the mysterious explanation that 'I represent the Queen and I don't want no comparisons'; 'certain powerful quarters' which had promised help were suddenly silent; letters received no reply, and telephones were answered by disobliging secretaries. After two days I tore up my letter of introduction to HM Assistant High Commissioner without bothering to present it. I seemed to be on my own.

This said, it is hard for me to express adequately my gratitude for the kindness I received in the Bahamas from people of every colour and nationality. I wish I could thank them all – but life there can be hazardous at this ludicrous moment of ultra-nationalism, particularly for those dependent on Bahamian salaries or pensions but not possessing Bahamian passports. I quickly abandoned the disintegrating British Colonial for Graycliff, a delightful eighteenth-century guest-house (without armed guards!) on the hill next to Government House, where the Duke and Duchess had stayed as Lord and Lady Dudley's guests on their last visit to the Bahamas, and where Enrico and Anna Maria and their staff made the rest of my stay exquisitely comfortable. Old friends and servants of the Duke and Duchess made me very welcome. Sir Berkeley and the late Lady Ormerod received me at their house on Prospect Ridge where the Duke and Duchess first lived on coming to the Bahamas, while Alfred and Janine Legros were kind to me in many ways. The hospitality of Rick and Fiona Heyward was tremendous, as was that of Peter and Analia Whitehead. Gail Saunders, the public archivist, could not have been more helpful under the circumstances. But that my futile efforts gave way to rapid progress, and dejection to euphoria, I owe above all to the infinite moral and practical support of Mrs Roger Carron, the splendid battling editor of *The Tribune* and daughter of the most remarkable individual Nassau has ever produced, Sir Etienne Dupuch. In the middle of my stay the great man himself turned up, on one of his occasional visits from his self-imposed exile in Florida. Though Sir Etienne's relations with the Duke of Windsor were often stormy, no one is less afraid of controversy, and it was a pleasure to do battle with him and to hear his highly individual and forceful views on every subject.

It was largely thanks to Mrs Carron that I was able to meet and interview so many people who had known Their Royal Highnesses in Nassau. I have not the space here to describe the individual debts I owe to Mr Charles Bethell, Mrs Ormond Curry, Mr and Mrs Jahn Dahloff, Mrs Sidney Eldon, Mr Reginald Farrington, Sir Randol Fawkes, Mrs Leslie Higgs, Mrs Raymond Moss, Mr Norman Solomon, Mr Maxwell Thompson and Mr Stanley Toogood. It was particularly good of Mr Godfrey Higgs, the last surviving member of the Duke's Executive Council, to grant me an interview; as defence counsel in the Oakes murder trial, he has been much exposed to authors. I especially enjoyed my visits to the Bishop of Nassau, the Right Reverend Michael Eldon, who assured me that no present-day Anglican bishop would ever receive such unchristian instructions from Lambeth Palace as those sent to his embarrassed predecessor Bishop Dauglish before the arrival of the Duke and Duchess; and to Bert Cambridge, the Bahamian jazz musician who celebrated his eightieth birthday while I was in Nassau, and who during the war had been one of the handful of black members of the House of Assembly and the life and soul of many jolly evenings at Government House. No one in Nassau has fonder memories than Bert of the Duke both at work and play, and the place on the wall reserved in patriotic English households for the Queen contains a signed photograph of a grinning Duke shaking hands with Bert in morning dress after his election in 1942.

It remained for me to make a brief trip beyond New Providence to what used to be called 'the Out Islands' and have now been quaintly renamed 'the Family Islands', in which the Duke as Governor took such an interest. I have to thank Patrick Erskine-Lindop for advice on where to go, and Mitch Lowe of the Harbour Lodge at Hope Town, Abaco, where I would have cheerfully spent the rest of my life. After an idyllic few days of escape among beautiful people on remote cays surrounded by pellucid azure waters, Nassau seemed peculiarly claustrophobic and sordid. And so I quickly left the Bahamas – and many new friends – after an experience I would not have missed for the world.

I went on to the United States, where a number of the Duke's and Duchess's old friends offered me kind help and hospitality, including Mrs Morgan Schiller, Mrs Harry Pool, Mrs Thomas M. Robertson, Mrs Thomas Vreeland and the Countess of Romanones. Dr Arthur Antenucci, who was for many years their personal physician, explained to me certain interesting aspects of their medical histories. Mrs Madison H. Haythe of Greenwich, Conn., took me on a highly amusing motor-tour of Maryland and Virginia which enabled me to understand much about the Duchess that had previously eluded me, and at the end of which I stayed with my old friend John Mears and his wife Tiny on their farm near Warrenton, Va., finding myself in a county where the Duchess lived for two years in the 1920s and returned thrice with the Duke during the Second World War.

My return to Europe in April 1981 coincided with the publication of a scandalous work about the Duke in the Bahamas, which was serialized – much to that newspaper's subsequent cost – by the *Daily Express*, on pages festooned with swastikas. It would be inappropriate here to comment on the consequences of that publication, except to say that every person with inside knowledge of the subject who was approached with a view to giving evidence was willing to testify to its inaccuracy and absurdity. This book is of course in no sense a reply to that one, of the existence of which I was originally quite unaware. But if I write at length about such subjects as Axel Wenner-Gren, the June Riots, the Oakes murder and the Duke's financial problems, it is because the recent dissemination of grotesque distortions puts me under an obligation, as the authorized biographer, to lay out the facts and the evidence for them with particular comprehensiveness and regard for accuracy.

When not engaged in studying the interesting French delict of *outrage à la mémoire des morts*, I spent the rest of 1981 writing my book. My ever-patient agents, Andrew Best and Caroline Belgrave of Curtis Brown, and publishers, John Curtis and Linda Osband of Weidenfeld and Nicolson, were always ready with assistance; and Sue Burton and Martha Rothery were invaluable in helping prepare the typescript. Among the many diverting interludes of the final stages of research were my visits to the Pathé Newsreel Library in Wardour Street, where (thanks to Larry McKinna) I was able to see the Duke and Duchess disporting themselves in various ways in various parts of the globe. It was fascinating to compare the cinematographic record with the impression of one's own imagination: I had not quite realized how well she moved, or wherein lay the extraordinary charm of his brisk manners. The Library possesses not only the finished newsreels but all the original unedited footage, and the minute proportion of the ducal recordings actually released at the time is an interesting comment on the attitude of the wartime news censorship.

For use of unpublished material in Crown Copyright I must acknowledge the permission of Her Majesty's Stationery Office, and for access to or leave to quote from unpublished private papers (other than in the authorship or from the archives of the Duke and Duchess of Windsor) I am indebted to Mr Michael Colefax (Sibyl Colefax Papers), the Earl of Halifax (Garrowby Papers), the Liddell-Hart Centre for Military Archives (Alanbrooke and Pownall Papers), Mr Nigel Nicolson (Sissinghurst Papers), Mr Paul Paget (Templewood Papers) and Mr A.J.P. Taylor (Beaverbrook Papers).

I am also indebted to the Duchess of Windsor's major-domo Georges Sanègre; to my dear cousin Janek Gelbart for having done such invaluable research in Sweden on Axel Wenner-Gren; to the Public Record Office at Kew, the House of Lords Record Office, and the Bahamas Record Office; to the librarians and staffs of the London Library, Cambridge University Library, British Newspaper Library, Nassau Public Library, and the libraries of Pembroke College Cambridge and the British Institute in Paris; to Printasec Limited; to Mrs Barnett; to Mr and Mrs Harry Anderson; to Mme Marendat, and Mlle Annette Rémond; to Alain Decaux of the Académie Française; to my long-suffering mentor Mr J.A. Hopkins of Downing College Cambridge; and to those friends who helped throughout in so many ways – Andrew Baume, Peter Bloxham, Michael Dyer-Thyssen, Hugo Haig-Thomas, Betty Hanley, R.B. McDowell, Charles Orwin, Stuart Preston, and especially James Lees-Milne. To my parents I owe more than I can express.

Last but not least I must gratefully acknowledge the gracious permission of Her Majesty the Queen (communicated to me by the Royal Librarian) to consult one interesting document.

MICHAEL BLOCH
Paris – London – New York – Nassau
March 1980–March 1982

As you know Wallis and I get pretty desperate here at times and wonder how long we can stick it out, although as it is essential to have a job at the present time and we will never be offered a better one I guess we could do a lot worse, and at least we are together, which is vital and all-important to us.

The Duke of Windsor from Nassau to Mrs D. Buchanan Merryman, 24 January 1943

[The] Abdication, its inevitability, the country's reaction, the possibilities still before the ex-King – these things were discussed ad nauseam until well after the war. . . . I knew that . . . he [the Duke of Windsor] was condemned for putting private life above duty. But it was hard for the younger amongst us not to stand in amazement at the moral contradiction between the elevation of a code of duty on the one hand, and on the other the denial of central Christian virtues – forgiveness, understanding, family tenderness.

Lord Harewood, *The Tongs and the Bones*

It isn't disloyal at all is it, to like the Duke so much?

His Majesty's Consul-General at Lyons to Harold Nicolson, 11 March 1940

Part One

The Desire to Serve

1
The Return
That Never Was
September 1939

On 23 June 1939, Midsummer Eve, the Duke of Windsor celebrated his forty-fifth birthday in Paris. The next day he and the Duchess went south for the summer. Booking into a hotel incognito, they spent a pleasant few days taking the waters at Aix-les-Bains. They went sightseeing to Geneva, where they saw the newly completed Palais des Nations – the headquarters of a well-meaning organization in which the Duke did not have enormous faith. On 4 July, American Independence Day, they motored to La Cröe, their house on Cap d'Antibes, where they planned to stay until their return to Paris for the autumn season.

After the Abdication – which she had been prepared to do almost anything to avoid – the Duchess of Windsor never doubted that her mission was to devote herself to the man who had given up so much for her, and to make him happy. An excellent hostess, and possessing a talent for creating and running a house which amounted to genius, she worked hard to give him a pleasant and comfortable domestic life. Since they had taken the lease of La Cröe in May 1938 (after being ordered by the British Embassy to leave Paris before the state visit of the King and Queen), she had transformed it from an ugly, sprawling villa into one of the loveliest houses on the coast. 'There are not many women', wrote Rebecca West, who was staying nearby and called on them that summer, 'who can pick up the keys of a rented house, raddled by long submission to temporary inmates, and make it look as if a family of cheerful good taste had been living there for two or three centuries.'[1]

Once reinstalled at La Cröe, the Duchess busied herself with preparations for her summer guests. 'We have quite a house full until Sept. first,' she wrote in a letter of 20 July 1939, just before they began to arrive. 'Things look better re Poland,' she added. 'We still think there won't be a war.'[2]

It was, as everywhere in England and France, a glorious summer, not too hot and hardly a cloud in the sky. Never had the colours of the Côte

3

d'Azur looked so alive. The house party at La Cröe was a great success. The historian and wit Philip Guedalla was the first to arrive, bringing with him much amusing conversation and the proofs of his book on the Abdication,* due to be published in the first week of September. There followed three friends from the Duke's youth – Major E. D. ('Fruity') Metcalfe, Commander Colin Buist and Captain R. Amcotts Wilson – together with their wives. Another old friend of the Duke, Lord Sefton, came with Josephine ('Foxy') Gwynne, an old friend of the Duchess ; and Colin Davidson, a good-looking young Clerk to the House of Lords who helped look after the Duke's interests in London, came with his bride on their honeymoon. (Within three years Hugh Sefton and Foxy Gwynne would be married, and Colin Davidson would lie dead in North Africa.) Among the visitors who signed the red-and-gold book in the hall that summer were Somerset Maugham, Noël Coward, Lords Beaverbrook and Rothermere, Maurice Chevalier and Maxine Elliott. Leslie Hore-Belisha, the Secretary of State for War (whom the Duke would soon see again under very different circumstances), called upon his former sovereign and spent a pleasant afternoon ; and Harold Balfour, the Under-Secretary for Air, was among the later guests. Both of these Ministers of the Crown were to terminate their holidays and return to London abruptly on 22 August.

Miss Hood, who was the Duke's secretary at the time, has recalled in a memoir[3] how idyllic was that summer at La Cröe. The white house was replendent under the southern sun in its wooded grounds, with rocks and sea in the background. The gardens, at which the Duke worked every day with his hoe, were at their best. The bathing – the shore being reached by steps cut into a small cliff – was exquisite. Thanks to the vigilance of the Duchess, nothing wanted for the comfort or enjoyment of the guests; the food, prepared by the famous chef Pinaudier under her personal supervision, was delicious. Most nights they dined out of doors, at a great W-shaped table on the terrace with the sea gleaming in the distance.

The Duke was the most perfect and attentive of hosts, and enjoyed preparing surprises for his guests. One afternoon he invited over a party of Highland pipers and dancers staying at Nice, and himself led their performance, wearing his kilt and playing the bagpipes. One moonlit evening, when Grace Moore and her husband were among the dinner guests, he arranged for an accordionist to be concealed below the terrace. 'When dinner was in full swing, chords of hidden music suddenly soared up from the lawn, silencing the chatter of the guests. Presently Grace Moore took up the melody and with indescribable beauty her voice floated out into the night. For several hours she sang at intervals, holding the party spellbound.'[4]

* *The Hundredth Year.*

4

But beneath the equable façade, and in spite of his obvious domestic happiness, the Duke of Windsor was an anxious man in the summer of 1939. Two matters preyed upon his mind particularly. The first was the state of Europe and the drift to war. The second concerned the prospects for his return to England and reconciliation with his family. For, though he resolutely looked not to the past but the future, he lived in the shadow of his great act of renunciation of more than two-and-a-half years before – the Abdication.

It is beyond the purpose of this book to discuss in any detail the Abdication and the events that followed it. The Duke's critics have argued that, after he had 'voluntarily' given up the throne in favour of a reluctant and embarrassed brother of far less conspicuous gifts, and so put private happiness above sacred public duty and 'let the country down', it was inevitable and just that he should become a disgraced exile, and he was vain and foolish in failing to realize that this would be the case and in no position to complain about his subsequent treatment. (These critics invariably add, it is interesting to note, that – notwithstanding the fact that he was dismaying the country and letting it down – he was also a disastrously incompetent monarch who was doing a relieved and grateful nation a service by ceasing to rule over it.) To this, his reply both at the time and ever afterwards was that he felt himself to have had no free choice. Of course, the Abdication was 'voluntary' in the sense that, almost up to the last moment, the King retained the *constitutional* possibility of giving up Mrs Simpson and keeping the throne. But in personal and psychological terms that possibility did not exist. After twenty-five years of hard service to the State, he could no longer bear the strain of his lonely position 'without the help and support of the woman I love' – a woman the Cabinet, without consulting either Parliament or people, prohibited him from marrying while on the throne. Though there were a number of solutions other than Abdication, he rejected these as dishonourable. Some of his friends (for example, Duff Cooper) urged him to keep Mrs Simpson merely as a mistress, at least until the Coronation after which his position would be unassailable. This he considered tantamount to being 'crowned with a lie upon my lips'. Others (for example, Beaverbrook) urged him to fight the Government; this he refused to do, believing that such a constitutional struggle would harm the country.

Although he was presented with a dilemma which drove him inexorably towards his terrible decision, he later came to believe (and not without reason) that there had been those at Court and in other high places who, well aware of his dilemma from an early stage, cut off the paths of escape, hastened him to his doom and rejoiced in his fall. It was these people who (as he had cause to feel) were determined that, come

5

what may, the Duke of Windsor should never return to live in England, or ever recover any work, influence or honour. It was they (as he saw it) who directed against him an unremitting campaign of ostracism, spite and calumny, and who saw to it that he was cast out from his family, from whom he had taken his leave in a sad and emotional but not unfriendly atmosphere at Windsor on the night of 11 December 1936.*

By the summer of 1939 – when this story opens – a cruel price had already been exacted for the Abdication. The marriage for which the Duke had given up a Crown (3 June 1937) had been boycotted by the Royal Family, the Government and the Court (though several of his relations and former courtiers and ministers would have liked to have come). Their sole reaction to it had been to purport to confer upon the new Duchess of Windsor the unique privilege for the wife of an Englishman of not sharing the dignity of her husband's rank. She was conscious of the indignity only for his sake. For him, it was a terrible insult: he had given up everything for this sacred act of matrimony; he was by training deeply conscious of matters of status and precedence; and having been assured by the Government six months before that morganatic unions were unknown to English law, it was to that very fate that they had now condemned him.

Apart from being cut off from his family, the Duke was entirely deprived of the protection of the Court – that great machine which shields and advises and protects royalty in its lonely and vulnerable existence. He therefore found himself helplessly exposed – to press sensationalism, to exploitation by various individuals, to bad advice, to those myriad complications and perils which persons of his birth are not equipped to face. The target of much calumny, some of it officially inspired, he had little means of protecting his reputation either in England or abroad. The British Embassy in Paris expected him to heed its 'advice', but gave him no protection or support. He was under the (not invariably discreet) surveillance of the Secret Service, as were his remaining loyal friends in England; those of them who had held posts at Court did not (with few exceptions) continue to hold them for long under the new reign. He had been obliged to start married life in financial difficulties; not nearly as well-off as people imagined, he did not begin to receive an allowance from England until well into 1938. Whatever one's attitude towards the Abdication, it is hard to take the view that such a chastisement was well-merited. He had, after all, served his country strenuously and unremittingly for a quarter of a century, in one of the hardest and loneliest jobs in the world.

Though the Duke suffered keenly, he suffered in silence, consoling

---

* The new Queen Consort excused herself from this gathering, pleading convalescence from influenza. She did, however, send a short note to her brother-in-law, wishing him well.

himself with his new-found private happiness. He made no attempt to strike back. He never made any form of public protest; his public statements were invariably in his brother's praise and support. He did write some anguished letters to his brother and others, but more pleading than protesting. He had sworn to make things as easy as possible for his successor, and guarded himself from doing or saying anything that might upset the new reign. On one matter alone was he fixed and determined. One day, after a suitable interval, when his brother was securely established on the throne and controversy over the Abdication had died down, he meant to go back to England to live – and if possible to serve. Most British subjects indeed expected this. The Attorney-General had told Parliament at the time of the Abdication that 'no condition of exile follows a voluntary abdication'. Although in his Abdication broadcast the Duke had said 'I now quit altogether public affairs', he had immediately added that 'if at any time in the future I can be found of service to His Majesty in a private station, I shall not fail'. He still and always hoped that, with his wife, he would eventually be accepted back into his family, and be able with her to play in it a useful if subordinate role. But even if this were not to be the case, he still planned in time to return to live quietly in his own country, where the King had promised him the continued use of his much-loved and missed country house, Fort Belvedere.

It was naturally the Duke's desire that his return (first in a number of private visits of limited duration, later on more permanently) should be attended by a minimum of national controversy and royal embarrassment; and he therefore consulted the Court and Cabinet about his plans. But as the campaign against him began to develop, he made it clear that, though he would seek their advice in the matter of his return, which he was anxious should occur at the right moment, he would never allow himself to become a helpless exile. What shocked him most of all was an attempt on their part to make the relatively modest allowance promised to him by the King dependent on a new condition (which he violently and ultimately successfully resisted) that he never return to England save by their permission. As he wrote to the Prime Minister Neville Chamberlain on 22 December 1937:

> When I decided to give up the throne last December, I realized that the only dignified and sensible course for me to follow, was to leave the country for a period, the length of which was naturally to be determined by a number of considerations. But I never intended, nor would I ever have agreed, to renounce my native land or my right to return to it – for all time.
>
> If my understanding of the present situation is correct, it is now proposed that my personal freedom in this respect be linked with a private family arrangement on financial matters which my brother, the present King, made

with me the day before I abdicated, in such a way, that he would be permitted to break his private agreement with me if I were to exercise my right to visit my country, without first obtaining his approval under the advice of his ministers.

I regard such a proposal as both unfair and intolerable, as it would amount to accepting payment for remaining in exile. . . .

It is hardly necessary for me to repeat to you my loyalty to my brother as King; nor as a patriotic Englishman could I countenance any disruptive action in others. But I cannot refrain from saying, with the frankness you would expect of me, that the treatment which has been meted out to my wife and myself since last December, has caused us acute pain. . . .

The Duke hoped to make a first brief visit to England after two years' absence; and at La Cröe in the summer of 1938 he discussed this hope with Sir Walter Monckton. The shrewd and affable Monckton, an old friend of the Duke and an eminent KC, had conducted the negotiations between King and Government during the crisis; after the Abdication he continued to be the link-man between the Duke of Windsor and the powers that be. The Duke now asked him to make soundings as to how his brief return in the near future would be regarded in official circles.

Monckton duly went to Balmoral in the late summer to discuss the matter with the King, the Queen and the Prime Minister. His impressions, published in his biography, are of the greatest interest. Chamberlain showed himself surprisingly friendly, and said he wanted the Duke 'to be treated as soon as possible as a younger brother of the King who could take some of the royal functions off his brother's hands'. The King himself 'was not fundamentally against the Prime Minister's view'. The great obstacle (noted Monckton) was the attitude of the Queen, who 'then, as always' showed herself resolutely opposed to readmitting the Duke to England and giving him 'any effective sphere of work', on the grounds that he might be a threat to her husband who was 'less superficially endowed with the arts and graces that please'.[5]

Having received no encouragement to return, the Duke did not seek to do so in 1938. In the New Year, however, he made further soundings through Monckton. The result was that Neville Chamberlain wrote to him on 22 February 1939 ('in that smooth language', thought the Duke, 'of which he was master') to say that, while the Duke was not to take it 'that there is any question of postponement indefinitely', the time was not yet ripe.[6] This was bitter news for the Duke, who was by now very homesick. 'When I say I go back to England tomorrow his eye twitches in pain,' wrote Harold Nicolson after visiting him.[7] In May, however, he received a vague hint that a short visit might be possible in the late autumn.

This was the passionate prospect which filled the Duke's mind when he went south that June, and of which he never ceased to dream in the weeks that followed. He wondered with much longing whether the visit would really come off, and in what manner. Surrounded by the splendours of the French Mediterranean coast that glorious summer, by the joys and pleasures of the little lotus-land which he and the Duchess had created there, he thought only of England. The company of his English friends only increased his longing. He pined at La Cröe for his lovelier Fort Belvedere. He began to make plans. With Philip Guedalla, the faithful friend with whom he had helped found the British Council five years earlier, he discussed the possibility of obtaining the eventual chairmanship of that organization. Before leaving, Guedalla gave him a set of his books for La Cröe. 'I hope that it will not be too long', the Duke wrote thanking him, 'before we shall be asking for one for The Fort.'[8]

There was one prospect which seemed certain not only to bring the Duke and Duchess back to England for good, but also to give him the chance to serve his country once again – the outbreak of European war. This prospect, however, the Duke regarded with horror. He detested war. There was nothing pusillanimous about his pacifism. His gallant service in the First World War, his long years of high position in the State and his cosmopolitan connections enabled him to appreciate all at once the terrible suffering caused by modern warfare, its calamitous effect upon European civilization, and its general inability to achieve its original political objects. He was not the sort of pacifist who is against armies; on the contrary, he believed in the maxim 'si vis pacem para bellum', and during his reign had given (as he was entitled to do) advice to the Government in favour of re-armament. Though he optimistically preferred to believe that war could not and would not happen, he was nevertheless determined – as a private citizen who happened to have both an international reputation and a unique experience of international relations – to do what little he could to make sure of that.

Certainly, by the summer of 1939, if not long before, he was convinced that what he called 'the dictator powers' were a terrible menace to Europe; but he was equally convinced that a war in which millions of soldiers and countless millions of civilians might die, which might drag on for years, and in which it was far from certain that the enemy powers would be defeated, was not a solution to the problem. In October 1937 he had spent two weeks in Nazi Germany to see 'a dictator power' for himself. The object of his visit (his idea was to visit many other countries in the same manner, but this was not to be) was to study working and housing conditions; he was one of those who believed that the menace of war could ultimately be removed by satisfying the social aspirations of ordinary Europeans. His tour of the Reich (culminating in an interview with Hitler) left him with a disgust for the regime's brutality and vulgarity, frank admiration for its national and social progress, and a well-grounded fear that Germany was better prepared to fight a future war and to withstand its effects than the western democracies.

If he had given a cautious welcome to the Munich Agreement, the events of March and April 1939 disabused him of all remaining illusions about the European intentions of Hitler and Mussolini. 'Actually the tension is eased and there won't be a war as I always predict (touch wood !),' he wrote to the Duchess's Aunt Bessie from La Cröe on 14 April, after they had cancelled a planned holiday in Morocco on account of the international atmosphere. 'But something really has to be done to prevent these monthly incidents of agression [sic] and consequent crises, and I personally am convinced that the dictator powers can be made to behave themselves without war which is certain to destroy civilization.'

But what could be done? What in particular could *he* do? On 7 May 1939 – at the invitation of the National Broadcasting Company of America – he broadcast an appeal for peace from Verdun to the peoples and statesmen of the world. It was heard and made a considerable impression on several millions of Americans, and a copy of the text was inserted into the proceedings of Congress. Translations were broadcast over a number of national European services, including the Polish and the French. Nazi Germany refused to relay the speech, as did the BBC; but the Beaverbrook Press obligingly informed the British public how to pick it up on short-wave, and it was heard by an estimated one million of the Duke's former subjects.

He began:

I am speaking tonight from Verdun. . . . For two and a half years I have deliberately kept out of public affairs and I still propose to do so. I speak for no one but myself, without the previous knowledge of any government. I speak simply as a soldier of the last war, whose most earnest prayer is that such a cruel and destructive madness shall never again overtake mankind. . . . The grave anxieties of the time . . . compel me to raise my voice in expression of the universal longing to be delivered from the fears that beset us. . . . [Peace] is a matter too vital for our happiness to be treated as a political question. . . . [In] modern warfare victory will lie only with the powers of evil. Anarchy and chaos are the inevitable results, with consequent misery for all. . . .

It was a terrible irony that the one event likely to bring about the personal consequences for which the Duke longed – return to England, reconciliation with his family, the opportunity to serve his country – was the very happening that for the world's sake he most dreaded. He knew that 'the cruel and destructive madness' which he prayed would be averted would also be his private reprieve.[9]

The sudden announcement of the Nazi–Soviet Pact on 22 August 1939 brought the outbreak of European war immediately in prospect.

At La Cröe, the news had the effect of a thunderstorm at a garden party. Guests and servants scattered in all directions, heading for home or for their regiments. Only the Duke could not return at once to his country in this crisis, and did not have a post to take up.

By 24 August only one member of the house-party remained, the quixotic and tempestuous Major Metcalfe. Then a dashing young cavalry officer, 'Fruity' had met the Prince of Wales in India after the First World War and become the intimate companion of his late twenties. His marriage to a daughter of Lord Curzon in 1925 had interrupted the friendship, which had however been resumed twelve years later, after the Abdication. He had been the Duke's best man, and now became his self-appointed adviser, private secretary and ADC. Though given to eccentric outbursts about the apparent complacency of his self-controlled hosts, and to somewhat alarming enthusiasms for the coming conflict and eagerness to get into battle, he was an invaluable friend and aide at La Cröe during the last days of peace, and supervised with the Duchess the hurried departure of the staff and other urgent matters.

For the Duke now had his own intense preoccupations. He was trying to get in touch with the King and Government with a view to returning to England with the Duchess in the event of hostilities, and at the same time to make a desperate, last-minute appeal to the dictator powers not to go to war. Since his brother had refused to speak to him on the telephone since February 1937, he contacted Walter Monckton and asked him to consult the Palace about his repatriation. He was willing to serve the King 'in any capacity'. On 29 August, 'as a citizen of the world', he sent a telegram to Hitler, urging him not to plunge Europe into war, and another to King Victor Emmanuel of Italy, asking him 'to use your influence to prevent the catastrophe which now seems imminent'. The Italian telegram, signed simply 'David', excited curiosity in the censorship; its text appeared in a Nice newspaper the following day.

At two o'clock on the morning of Friday 1 September the Duke was woken by the excited local postmaster, who insisted on delivering personally what he described as a highly important telegram.[10] It was from Hitler, who blamed England for Europe's diplomatic tensions and alleged that if war broke out it would be her responsibility. Some hours afterwards the Duke heard – from *The Times* correspondent at Nice – that Germany had invaded Poland at dawn.

Later that morning Monckton managed to get through on the telephone to say that the King was prepared to send his private aeroplane to fetch the Duke and Duchess the following day.

At five o'clock that afternoon the Duke received a reply from King Victor Emmanuel, who said that he would do all he could to preserve peace and that Italy was remaining neutral. When Miss Hood, one of the few remaining members of staff, came to say goodbye before catching the last Blue Train for London, she found him 'in a state of happy, suppressed excitement, walking up and down the room, repeating over and over again, "Italy is remaining neutral! Italy is remaining neutral!"'[11]

In 1966, the Duke of Windsor wrote:

The instant war came in September 1939, I offered my services to my country. Notwithstanding the strained relations between me and my brother, it was unthinkable that I should sit on my hands while Britain was mobilizing. He seemed to feel as I did. . . . The King offered to send a plane attached to the King's Flight to take us to London to talk about a war job. His reaction encouraged me to believe that the common sharing that goes with war would provide a solvent of the stubborn things that divided us. But as matters turned out, I was wrong.[12]

Disillusionment came very quickly. Speaking again that night to Monckton, the Duke asked him to enquire whether he and the Duchess would be accommodated at Windsor or another royal residence. It hardly occurred to him that this would be regarded as an affront, especially since, just before the Abdication, his brother had promised that Fort Belvedere – that minor royal property near Windsor where, as Prince of Wales, he had made his beloved country house – would be kept for his use whenever he returned to England. The following morning they were up and dressed early to await the royal plane, the Duchess (who had never flown before, and whose marriage to a reckless First World War aviator had given her a horror of flying-machines) in a considerable state of nerves. But it never came. In consequence of the Duke's overnight enquiries, the King's offer of a plane had been withdrawn.

And so it was still on foreign soil that the former King of England learned, shortly after eleven o'clock the next day, that Great Britain and France had declared war on Germany.

The Duke of Windsor's reaction to the outbreak of the Second World War will already have become clear and is easily described. He regarded it as a catastrophe. Though he denied that he might have prevented it if he had remained on the throne,[13] he did believe that it could have been avoided almost up to the last moment by more adroit diplomacy. He saw that the Allies, whatever the justice of their cause, had no present means of attaining their war aims. It was not just that they had not the faintest hope of saving Poland; both physically and morally, they were weaker and more vulnerable than the enemy. Germany was ready for war, Great Britain and France were not – this was the bitter lesson he had learned with his own eyes on his German tour two years earlier, and it was to be a recurrent theme in his conversation and correspondence during the first ten months of the conflict. He feared for his country.

This is not to say that he was 'defeatist'. Since the war (terrible as it was) had now happened, there was nothing to do but to prosecute it with vigour and to try to win it. As the French said, *il faut en finir* – let's get it over with. And it was with a view to helping his country to the best of his abilities in its Herculean task that he had at once offered his services 'in any capacity' to his brother the King. He was confident that he could be useful. He was still a member of the Royal House of England, which needed all the help it could get in its difficult wartime role. He felt that he still possessed some talent as a soldier, that his long experience gave him a certain statesmanship, and that he retained a charisma which might, given the chance, have a considerable effect on Allied morale. He still hoped and believed that, with the coming of war, his family difficulties would be resolved, and that he would be welcomed back to England and given a part to play.

The offer of a royal aeroplane had raised his spirits; its withdrawal plunged him into depression. There followed several days of anguished waiting. In the tumult of the outbreak of war, it was difficult to communicate with either London or Paris. There was nothing to do save to await Monckton, who was coming out as an emissary of King and Government to inform them of their fate. Their sole companion apart from their worried neighbours remained an increasingly bombastic Metcalfe, wild and furious that the Duke had prejudiced an early return through the telephone conversation about royal accommodation, lusting impatiently after the fight.

After an adventurous air journey – including a forced landing in provincial France and subsequent arrest by local peasantry – Monckton finally arrived at Antibes on the 7th. He came in a Government, not a Royal aeroplane, a Leopard Moth. It was, intentionally, not the sort of craft in which the Duke would have cared to make the return journey; he remarked to Monckton that it looked 'as though the tyres were flat, and the plane tied up with string'.[14]

Monckton brought bad news. Not only had the Duke's modest request for royal accommodation been unequivocally refused, but it was the King and Government who were now laying down conditions. The Duke would only be allowed to return if he undertook to accept one of two posts which would be offered to him, both of very moderate importance: either that of Deputy Regional Commissioner to Sir Wyndham Portal in Wales, or of liaison officer with No. 1 British Military Mission to French GHQ under General Howard-Vyse. The Duke at once agreed to this, and offered to return immediately by any means except by air, on account of the Duchess's increasing terror of flying.

His mission accomplished, Monckton departed. Some hours later, the Duke received a mysterious telephone call from the British Ambassador in Paris, Sir Ronald Campbell, instructing him 'to start by motor for the Channel coast and to stop and telephone the Embassy again'.[15] The Duke correctly interpreted these cryptic directions as meaning that a ship was being sent from England to pick them up, but that the French port had not yet been chosen. He therefore decided to make for Vichy, which was equidistant from Calais, Cherbourg and Le Havre. They set out the following day – Friday the 8th – with Metcalfe, who had generously invited them to stay at South Hartfield, his rented country house in Sussex. Having spent the night at Avignon, they reached Vichy on Saturday afternoon and put up at the Hôtel du Parc et Majestic (which, as they could not possibly have imagined, was within ten months to become the seat of government of a shrunken and defeated France). From there the Duke rang the Embassy, only to be told to stay where he was and await further instructions.

It was from Vichy the following day that the Duchess wrote her regular letter to her beloved and redoubtable aunt in Washington, Mrs D. Buchanan Merryman – the first of well over a hundred written during the war. 'Aunt Bessie' (*née* Montague) was the elder sister of the Duchess's adored mother; and since her mother's death in 1929, the (subsequent) Duchess had looked upon her lion aunt as guardian angel, confidante and closest friend. There were few months (save when they were together) that niece did not write to aunt. The 1929–39 letters, yet to be published, form in effect a diary of her marriage with Simpson, her evolving friendship with the Prince, the first nine months of Edward VIII's reign, and her early married life with the Duke. The 1939–45 correspondence, which will be quoted throughout this book, similarly constitutes a regular journal of the Duchess's doings, feelings and thoughts during the war. The letters are written in a round, flowing, slightly chaotic hand, with erratic punctuation, and often give the impression of having been dashed out in a tremendous hurry. Sometimes they are diffuse and repetitious and tedious with domestic detail; sometimes they are concise and vivid and brilliantly descriptive; always they are spontaneous. They abound with the so-called 'Montague wit'. They show their author to be a woman who makes light of her (not inconsiderable) difficulties and lives life energetically, wasting not a minute. She is always outspoken and frank, with two reserves: she never says anything which might be in the faintest degree disloyal or disadvantageous to the Duke, and she is always concerned to dispel her aunt's anxieties and assure her that all is well. With the arrival of war a third reserve was imposed by the censorship of mails – but this, it will be seen, did not worry the Duchess unduly.

In her replies to her niece's letters, Aunt Bessie was bright, affectionate and occasionally scolding, full of good sense and solicitude and eagerness for news. Born during 'the war between the States' into an old Virginia family, she was very much a Southern lady. She was also a most delightful person. 'You couldn't help liking her,' recalled Miss Hood. 'She was white-haired, plump, kindly and easy to talk to.'[16] In September 1939 she was a mentally robust seventy-five (she would reach her century), living in circumstances of modest comfort on R Street, Washington. She loved travelling, and came quite often to Europe, where she had chaperoned her niece on holidays with the Prince of Wales and been with her constantly in the terrible weeks before and after the Abdication. Without private fortune, she had inherited a small income from a woman to whom she had been paid companion, and was now also supported by her niece and royal nephew-in-law, whom she had last seen in February 1939 after spending the winter season with them at La Cröe. She had been due to join them again in the winter of 1939–40. The Duke liked her enormously, and by this time seems to have felt for her a tenderness which he no longer felt for any member of his own family.

Writing briefly from the hotel in Vichy exactly a week after the declaration of war, the Duchess did her best both to inform and reassure her aunt:

Darling Aunt B,
We never thought it could or would happen. We have to return and left La Cröe with many heartaches on Friday afternoon, spending the night at Avignon – a very changed place. The Riviera was peaceful, but as one goes north one sees signs of war. We came here last night as it is a peaceful and safe spot – one picnics in the hotels as all the male staff has gone – it was the same at La Cröe. We leave tomorrow for the North where we will board an English navy vessel. We then go to the Metcalfes' in the country (Sussex) and the Duke will have a job – he has been offered 2 and that will have to be discussed and decided. If it can be arranged and all is well with our neighbour in the South [i.e. Italy] Lady Norman and myself would like to run our houses as convalescent homes for British officers. I am going to take it up with the army heads when I find out just what the Duke's movements will be. . . . The main thing for you is not to worry and I will write as often as possible though I can't say much. We have no news of what goes on as the papers really say nothing but fill up space with repetitions of official communiqués. Naturally the Duke wishes to do all he can for the country – quite a different point of view from what they have done for him the last 3 years. I shall miss France where everyone has been more than kind and considerate. Take care of yourself and pray for a speedy end to all this misery.

All my love,
WALLIS

It is clear from this letter that they felt they were leaving France and returning to England for a substantial period of time, perhaps for the war, perhaps for good; though if the Duke was to go off *en poste*, the Duchess would return to the Riviera in the role of hospital matron. It

The Duchess's first wartime letter to Aunt Bessie, September 9, 1939.

would have surprised them to know that they would be back in France before the end of the month, or that the wounded British army officers to whom the Duchess expected to minister would be a non-existent category in 1939.

On the morning of Monday the 11th, having received no further instructions, they continued to Paris, where the Duke called at the Embassy. 'The cloak-and-dagger atmosphere was preserved to the end,' wrote the Duchess in her memoirs. The Ambassador told them to proceed to Cherbourg, where a British officer would meet them at the headquarters of the Admiral Commandant the following afternoon. They spent a few hours in the capital, which went in fear of imminent bombardment; the Duchess found it quite deserted (she wrote to Aunt Bessie) and 'so strange to see the few people in the streets with gas masks slung over their shoulders'.[17] What saddened her most was having to abandon their house in the Boulevard Suchet, of which they had only taken the lease the previous December, and which she had spent the first half of 1939 strenuously transforming into a comfortable and beautiful residence for the Duke. It had been completed only that summer, and it seemed they would never live in it now. She wondered if she would ever see its precious and so carefully acquired contents again, as 'there is no means of transportation and nowhere to move them. We are trying to find someone to stay in the house, but no-one is keen on Paris at the moment. We shall have to take our chances on its remaining standing.'[18] But they would be back there soon enough.

Meanwhile, the fact that they were on their way back to England had become public knowledge, although their route, timetable and means of transport remained secret. On the 9th, *The Times* of all newspapers – still edited by Geoffrey Dawson who had been so hostile to the King in the Abdication crisis – published a generous leading article on the Duke, which gave him much encouragement.

> The announcement that the Duke and Duchess of Windsor are leaving Antibes for England will cause no surprise, still less any kind of contention. It has always been tacitly assumed that war would sweep away any difficulties there may have been in the way of the Duke's earlier return. . . . Now . . . the events and the hour which bring the Duke to rejoin his fellow-countrymen . . . relieve his homecoming of all possible trace of controversy and embarrassment. . . . No one could dream of the Duke's absence from England at a time in which absence would become intolerable exile, or suppose for a moment that anything would be lacking on the Government's part to speed the fulfilment of his dearest and most urgent wish.[19]

In America, identical sentiments were expressed in an editorial of the *New York Times*: 'Even in those quarters where his previous decisions were most sharply denounced it will be agreed that there is only one appropriate place for the Duke of Windsor, and that is with his own people.'[20]

Cheered by these indications, they left Paris and continued north. After a night at Evreux – staying at a hotel where the Duchess had spent a haunted night during her flight across France in December 1936 – they arrived at Cherbourg on the afternoon of the 12th. There, on the Admiral's lawn, they met Lord Louis Mountbatten, commanding the HMS *Kelly* which would carry them over the sea to England, and Randolph Churchill, representing his father who was now once again First Lord of the Admiralty. The Duke and Duchess were profoundly moved: this was the first English note of welcome they had encountered since the war began. 'The reunion in the garden at Cherbourg was heart-warming,' wrote the Duchess. 'The presence of Dickie and Randolph meant to us that Winston wanted David's return to his native land to go off well and smoothly; and David was grateful, on his account and mine, for this sign of regard.'[21] Churchill had sent a letter by Randolph, apologizing for not being able to come himself. 'We are plunged in a long and grievous struggle,' he added. 'But all will come out all right if we all work together for that end.'[22]

The Duke had cause to have uncertain feelings about Mountbatten. He had loved his handsome and spirited second cousin, who had accompanied him on his tours of Australia and New Zealand in 1920 and of India and

Japan in 1921–2. In 1922 he had saved Lord Louis' naval career from the 'Geddes Axe' by intervening personally with the King; the same year he had been Mountbatten's best man. On ascending the throne in 1936 he had made Mountbatten his personal naval ADC; Mountbatten had been loud with protestations of friendship and loyalty, not only to the King but to Mrs Simpson. During the Abdication he wrote letters assuring the King that he could rely on him as 'a friend of Wallis'.[23] But after the Abdication, he had been extraordinarily quick – skilled mariner that he was – to catch the new wind blowing from the Palace, which was a chill wind for the Duke.

Recalling what occurred in later years, Lord Mountbatten suffered from extraordinary inaccuracies of memory. He imagined – incorrectly – that he had been present at Fort Belvedere during the discussions which immediately preceded the Abdication. He also declared that he had much wanted to visit the Duke abroad and attend his wedding, but that the Duke had never invited him. The correspondence between the two men among the Duke's papers shows how far Mountbatten's memory was at fault on this point. Not only was the Duke eagerly expecting his cousin to come, but Mountbatten led the Duke to believe that he could persuade King George and the other brothers to attend the wedding too. It was in fact Mountbatten who suggested the date of the marriage – 3 June 1937 – as one likely to suit the King. But on 5 May he wrote to say that, while 'Bertie' and 'Georgie' had been willing to come, other people had stepped in to create a situation which made all the Duke's friends most unhappy – and in the event he could not even accept the Duke's kind invitation himself. That was the last the Duke had heard from his once passionate supporter. But on 12 September 1939, all this was forgotten; and he was happy and moved that Churchill had sent his old soul-mate to bring him back to England, and to be with him once again.

The party having been piped aboard, the *Kelly* sailed towards dusk. The journey took six hours on a zig-zag run in a calm sea. Darkness fell; they supped and made pleasant talk. While the Duchess remained below in the well-appointed captain's quarters, the Duke joined Mountbatten on the bridge. They talked of old times.

When the Duke returned below, the Duchess found him 'thoughtful and abstracted'.

It was not hard for me to guess what must have been passing through his mind. It was not quite three years since he had left England in another destroyer in the night. He was wondering what he would find on his return, and how his family would treat him and me, and whether it would be possible for him to find a really useful job in his country's service. The coldness which had settled down between him and his family had hurt him more than he could bring himself to admit. He had paid in full the price exacted for his choice, and now he longed to share, as he had done before, his country's perils, and to end the separation.[24]

They sat together in silence, until their reverie was broken by the sound of clattering boots and clanging metal doors. They were entering Portsmouth harbour. He turned to her and said: 'I don't know how this will work out. War should bring families together, even a Royal Family. But I don't know.'[25] He pressed her hand, turned quickly, and left the cabin.

Their arrival was dramatic. The dock was blacked out save for a single Verey light. The *Kelly* landed at the same quay from which the Duke had sailed after the Abdication. There was a red carpet and a guard of honour. The Band of the Royal Marines played *God Save the King*. The Duke was profoundly moved.[26]

Two people waited on the quayside to greet them – Lady Alexandra Metcalfe and Walter Monckton. No member of his family was there, no royal representative, not even a message. The Court had refused to take the slightest notice of his return to England. The landing ceremony had taken place on the sole initiative of Winston Churchill.

Lady Alexandra had telephoned the Palace asking if they might put a car at the disposal of the Duke and Duchess (her own car was taking their luggage). This had been curtly refused, and no royal instructions of any kind had been given regarding their reception or accommodation in Portsmouth that evening. Lady Alexandra had booked a room for them in a hotel at Southsea; but in the event the Commander-in-Chief at Portsmouth, Admiral Sir William James, acting on the personal instructions of Churchill, invited them to spend the night at Admiralty House.

The Admiral and his wife, recalled the Duchess,

... were very nice to me, almost desperately polite. However, under the politeness I became aware that it was I, rather than their former King, who was the object of their covert curiosity. When I was chatting with one, I could feel the sidelong glance of the other, charged with speculation, roving searchingly over me. In the oblique scrutiny there hovered the unasked question: *Can this really be the Mrs Simpson who caused it all? Can this be the woman who took from us our King?*[27]

The next morning the party motored to the Metcalfe residence, South Hartfield House near the village of Coleman's Hatch in Ashdown Forest, where a crowd of reporters and photographers awaited them. Though the homecoming had been shrouded in mystery, news of the arrival at Portsmouth had at once spread to London. Journalists ringing the Palace during the night were astonished to be told that the Royal Household were not aware that the Duke had returned to England.[28] But his destination had not been too difficult to discover.

The Duke beamed at the assembled correspondents, many of whom he remembered well from days gone by. 'Good morning, boys. I'm pleased to see you again.' 'Welcome home, Sir,' they replied in a chorus. 'It's nice to see you back, Sir,' said one. 'Thank you. It's nice to be back.'

The English press published large and cheerful photographs of the Duke and Duchess in their new rural surroundings; but there was little they could write. Since the leader in *The Times* only four days before, certain instructions had gone out. Subject to censorship directions from the new Ministry of Information, the papers were advised not to comment on the Duke's return, nor to provide any details of his recent past or speculations as to his future. *The Times* itself did not even mention his arrival in England. The popular dailies remarked on how happy and relaxed and well-tanned they both looked, 'smiling as happily as newlyweds returning from their honeymoon'[29]; on the Duke's undiminished youthfulness; on the fact that she wore a mustard and black tweed coat over a mustard-coloured dress, and he a double-breasted grey suit with suede shoes. The *Daily Express* noted that the travel reading espied inside the car consisted of *The Nazis Can't Win*, and *Step by Step* by Winston Churchill.

A month or two earlier the Duke's return would have created a vast public sensation and stirred great national emotion. Now, with public attention focused on the young men going out to France, the arrival from that country of the ex-King and his consort passed off quietly and calmly, without controversy or commotion. He was grateful for this, for nothing had been further from his thoughts than a hero's return, or an excess of enthusiasm which might embarrass his brother. All he had hoped for and expected was some gesture of welcome, of recognition merely, *any* gesture from his family.

Public opinion expected this too. The English press was not allowed to say so, but the London correspondents of American papers could and did. 'It is expected that the Duke will slip into the life of the Royal Family with a minimum of fuss and public attention,' wrote the *New York Times*.[30] The English novelist Mollie Panter-Downes, who had lately begun her widely read page in the *New Yorker*, wrote that the Duke and Duchess 'came home in a blaze of public apathy. No one seemed particularly glad or sorry, but everyone felt it was natural that yet another family should want to be reunited in such times.'[31]

But did they? On the evening of the Duke's arrival, they had made no sign whatever. Nor did they on his first full day in England.

Nor (with one exception) during the whole remainder of his stay. Nothing. No letters or messages, not a single visit or invitation. No royal car for him, no royal servants to attend upon him, no royal secretaries to help him answer the hundreds upon hundreds of letters from his former subjects, rejoicing at his return.

Such was their attitude (wrote Lady Alexandra in her diary) that 'he might not even exist'.[32]

His sole contact with his family (for the Duchess there was none) consisted of a single interview with his brother, which took place at Buckingham Palace on the afternoon of Thursday 14 September, his second afternoon in England.

Even this meeting had not been arranged without difficulty, and had required 'long and rather boring discussions'[33] through the intermediary of Monckton. It was only made possible by the exclusion of women. Monckton drove up to the Palace with the Duke, who had not seen London since 3 December 1936, when he had left the capital as soon as the Abdication crisis had become public.

King and ex-King were together for an hour. The meeting seemed to go well – so far as it went. The King later described it as 'very friendly' and without recriminations,[34] the Duke as 'cordial enough'.[35] They discussed the alternative war jobs the Duke had been offered. The Duke expressed a preference for the civil defence post (as Assistant Regional Commissioner for Wales) over the staff liaison post (with No. 1 British Military Mission in France). He had a deep feeling for Wales, and a modest doubt as to whether he knew enough of the changes in the art of war to make a successful staff officer. The King seemed to agree, but added that there was no hurry about making a decision. 'Let's see how things go,' he concluded vaguely. 'Meanwhile, I'll discuss your ideas with the Government.'[36] They came downstairs together. The King went over to the waiting Walter Monckton and said: 'I think it went all right.' Monckton afterwards repeated this to the Duke, who said that it had been all right because, on Monckton's advice, he had kept off contentious subjects.[37]

They were not to see each other again for more than six years. Nor did the Duke see any other member of his family in September 1939. The Duchess urged him to get in touch with his mother; but Queen Mary, who upon the outbreak of war had retired to Gloucestershire with her staff of fifty-five, had no wish to see him. He was equally unable to meet his favourite and beloved brother Prince George Duke of Kent, whom he was never to see again.

The following morning – Friday – the Duke motored to London again for a round of appointments with members of the Government. His first call was on Winston Churchill at the Admiralty, his staunch supporter in 1936, the one man in power who had done something to welcome him back to England. The Duke afterwards wrote:

I was well aware that he frowned upon my seeing Hitler and did not agree with my Verdun broadcast, though he never doubted my motives. But now he said: *'We are all in this together, aren't we?'* My answer was: 'Of course. That is why I have come back to England.' Winston's face lit up and he exclaimed: *'And we all want you back!'*[38]

21

Next he called at 10 Downing Street to pay his respects on Neville Chamberlain. This meeting was less cordial, in fact decidedly ominous.

. . . In that dour, unsmiling presence I became sensible of a shadow falling once again over my personal situation. A pile of letters lay on the Prime Minister's desk, close to his hand. No mention was made of them at first. I explained that the King had discussed war jobs with me and that I was prepared to take whatever was offered. Mr Chamberlain for his part said he would do all he could to help me. Then, with an embarrassed clearing of the throat, he suggested that I might wish to give thought to a certain unfortunate aspect of my circumstances that was troubling him. Reaching for the pile of letters, he said: 'Here, by the way, is a fair sample of the kind of letters I have been getting from people who – well – don't want you back.' He paused. 'They are mostly anonymous,' he went on.

Did he expect me to read them while he watched? Perhaps even read them back to him? I did not give them a glance. 'I get some too,' I said, 'not all anonymous.' Mr Chamberlain did not seem to hear. With the war scarcely a fortnight old, he was clearly a broken man, the first casualty of the collapse of the Munich illusion which he had fostered. He had lost out. But then, I realized finally in that famous office, so had I.[39]

At four o'clock the Duke called at the War Office to see the Secretary of State, Leslie Hore-Belisha. It was there that he became aware of the reason for the Prime Minister's nervousness.

The post in Wales for which the Duke had expressed a preference had been withdrawn overnight by the King, without explanation.[40] The Duke would therefore be sent back to France at the earliest opportunity as a member of the Howard-Vyse Mission. For the duration of his active service he would give up his field-marshal's baton and take the temporary rank of Major-General.

Earlier that day Sir Alexander Hardinge, the King's (and once – to his cost – King Edward VIII's) Private Secretary, had made it known to various members of the Government that the Duke had already agreed to this arrangement. This was untrue; but since the Duke had returned to offer his services 'in any capacity', he naturally had no choice but to accept it. As a palliative, the Prime Minister was 'making enquiries' as to whether, before going abroad, he might spend about a fortnight touring the English Commands.[41]

It cannot have been easy for Hore-Belisha to break this sudden news to the Duke. He retained much admiration for his former King, who regarded him as a friend. They had known each other at Oxford and during the First World War. As Prince of Wales and King, the Duke had admired Hore-Belisha's energy and style as Minister of Transport; after the Abdication, he had also admired Hore-Belisha's brave and often unpopular efforts at the War Office to reform the conservative army establishment. Hore-Belisha had regarded the departure of King Edward as a tragedy, and was the first member of the Cabinet to call on the Duke in exile, in Paris in September 1937. 'I don't believe in deserting friends,' he told Basil Liddell-Hart.[42] They had last seen each other less than a month before, when Hore-Belisha, enjoying a brief respite in the South of France from the tense atmosphere at the War Office, had called on the Duke and Duchess at La Cröe.

Hore-Belisha was only one of several members of His Majesty's Government who, while holding the Duke in warm personal regard, had no choice but to issue him with harsh official instructions. He did what he could to soften the blows. 'I said that everything would be done to make things easy and pleasant for him and that his chauffeur would be enlisted as a soldier.' The Duke asked if the Duchess might accompany him to the Commands; Hore-Belisha privately realized this would be difficult, but promised to see what could be done. He arranged to send the Director-General of Army Medical Services to discuss with the Duchess her plans to turn La Cröe into a convalescent home (though the Duke said he would want her to be with him in Paris). He accompanied the Duke to the door of the War Office, where they parted with a warm handshake.

The following day, Hore-Belisha had two extraordinary audiences with the King, which he recorded in his diary.[43]

16th September 1939
The King sent for me at 11 a.m. He was in a distressed state. He thought that if the Duchess went to the Commands, she might get a hostile reception, particularly in Scotland. He did not want the Duke to go to the Commands in England. He seemed very disturbed and walked up and down the room. He said the Duke never had any discipline in his life. . . .

2.30 p.m. I went to Buckingham Palace with Ironside. HM remarked that all his predecessors had succeeded to the throne after their predecessors had died. 'Mine is not only alive, but very much so.' He thought it better for the Duke to proceed to Paris at once.

Hore-Belisha now faced a heavy task.

3 p.m. The Duke came to the War Office. He expressed his pleasure at going to the Commands in England and making contact with the soldiers. I pointed out that when a soldier was given an appointment, he invariably took it up without delay. I explained that the troops were moving about, the secrecy involved, and that the Duke's presence would attract attention. It would create an excellent impression with the public, I said, if the Duke showed readiness to take up his appointment at once; that Howard-Vyse was impatiently waiting for him in Paris. The Duke appreciated all the arguments and expressed agreement. . . .

Hore-Belisha was in a state of great emotion, he wrote, as he took his former King to see General Ironside, the Chief of the Imperial General Staff, who would give him his instructions.

Once instructed, the Duke returned to Hore-Belisha to ask for three favours: whether he might have Metcalfe as his equerry, whether he might wear his decorations on his battledress, and whether he might have his Honorary Colonelcy of the Welsh Guards restored to him. 'He had ascertained that they wanted him back again,* and said he would like this.' Hore-Belisha saw no problem about the first two requests; but as for the third, he could only say that he did not appoint Honorary Colonels of Regiments, and that the Duke would have to speak to the King. When Hore-Belisha saw the Duke out, a small crowd had collected outside the War Office. 'They gathered round his car and cheered him as he drove away. He seemed very pleased, smiled and raised his hat.' The unhappy Minister than rang the Palace 'to reassure the King that the interview had been satisfactory'.

While the Duke was in Whitehall that afternoon, the Duchess was waiting for him at Lady Alexandra's London house, 16 Wilton Place, from where she wrote to her Aunt Bessie. She described their journey to England and the atmosphere of London – 'not as deserted as Paris, but gas masks and air raid shelters everywhere – an unreal world'. She continued:

> The Duke is going as a member of the British Military Mission to Paris – a very interesting job. He is temporarily dropping the rank of Field Marshal for that of Major-General for the war. We shall be here for a month while he looks at the different training centres etc – we shall go to the North and to Scotland. We will find some place outside of Paris to stay and later on I shall open La Cröe as a convalescence [sic] home as the War Office is keen on the idea I believe and the Duke can come from time to time. It is too young a war to predict what is going to happen – the main thing to hope is that it won't be a long one. . . .

She broke off, and later concluded:

> Since starting this letter the Duke has come back and we are *not* going north but are off to France. It is useless to make plans as they are unmade the next moment.
>
> All love and don't worry,
> WALLIS

The Duke had been in England for less than four days; and now he was being asked to leave the country forthwith. It was only forty-eight hours

---

* The present Commanding Officer assures the author that 'talk of this suggestion was heard from the Sergeants Mess and younger officers. Senior officers could not countenance it because it would have put King George VI in an impossible position as he had succeeded the Duke as Colonel-in-Chief of the Regiment. There is nothing about it in our archives.'

since the King had assured him that there would be no hurry about settling his wartime role. It was just a week since *The Times* had written: 'No one could dream of the Duke's absence from England at a time in which absence would become intolerable exile, or suppose for a moment that anything would be lacking on the Government's part to speed the fulfilment of his dearest and most urgent wish.' Now there was nothing in *The Times*, save for a hidden two lines some days later, far from the Court Circular, to say that he had been gazetted Major-General and would shortly be proceeding to a post abroad.[44]

In fact they stayed another thirteen days. This was the time it took for the Duke to receive what turned out to be somewhat complicated military instructions, and to sort out his staff and uniforms and other necessary matters.

Most days they motored up to London, where they set up headquarters in the dust-sheeted sitting-room at Wilton Place. 'All business is transacted from this ridiculous house,' wrote Lady Alexandra. 'Clerks, secretaries, War Office officials, hairdressers, bootmakers, tailors, with a sprinkling of friends stream in & out. They have sandwiches and tea from a thermos for refreshment.'[45] They had to return to the country before each afternoon was out, to avoid the black-out.[46]

The Duke was often cheered in the streets. He received, and somehow attempted to reply to, several thousand letters, all but six per cent of them favourable.[47] With no let-up in the silence and ice from the Palace, there were moments when the Duchess saw his face 'set itself into a mask barely concealing his deep-smouldering anger'.[48] But he was determined to make the best of things and serve so far as he could, and for the most part he radiated perfect good grace.

One afternoon they drove out to Sunningdale for a nostalgic visit to the Fort, which his brother had once promised would be his house when he returned to England. 'The lawn was overgrown; the garden in which we had spent so many happy hours together had become a mass of weeds; and the house itself, shuttered, damp and dark, was slowly decaying.'[49] It was a sad visit.

They saw a few friends. The good and kind Lady Colefax, whose table they had so often enjoyed before the Abdication, gave a luncheon for them in Lord North Street, for which she mustered Victor Cazalet, Jan Masaryk, Harold Nicolson, Bruce Ogilvie, H.G. Wells and G.M. Young.*[50] 'He is dressed in khaki with all his decorations and looks grotesquely young,' Nicolson wrote in his diary. 'I have seldom seen the Duke in such

---

* Young's impression was of 'A gentleman; a major in a not quite first class regiment, and not likely to go further than that; happily married to a devoted wife, not his equal but doing her best to live up to him.' (*Geoffrey Madan's Notebooks*, p.81.)

cheerful spirits and it was rather touching to witness their delight at being back in England. There was no false note.'[51]

That was on 27 September. Two days later, accompanied by Metcalfe and Captain Purvis of the Howard-Vyse Mission, they sailed from Portsmouth on the destroyer *Express*. They arrived in Cherbourg towards dusk after a rough journey in a heavy sea. A party of officers from the Mission were on the quayside to meet them. They headed for Paris, stopped the night on the road, and arrived the next day at their chosen residence, a hotel at Versailles, where the Duchess remained while the Duke proceeded with the others to Mission Headquarters near Vincennes, to report to General Howard-Vyse for duty.

2
Phoney War
September–December 1939

The new HQ to which Major-General HRH the Duke of Windsor reported on 30 September 1939 was situated in the suburb of Nogent-sur-Marne east of Paris, a mile and a half from the French *Grand Quartier Général* at the Château de Vincennes. It consisted of three houses standing in a park which had once been used for the breeding of tame pheasants, one containing living quarters, another offices and the third the officers' mess. These facilities were shared by two separate establishments – No.1 Military Mission responsible to General Ironside at the Imperial General Staff, consisting of some dozen officers and thirty other ranks under the command of Major-General Sir Richard Howard-Vyse, and a much smaller Inter-Service Mission, led by Lieutenant-Colonel Harold Redman, responsible to General Ismay and the Chief of Staffs Committee of the War Cabinet. The Duke, though only attached to the Howard-Vyse Mission, played a full part in the life of the common mess, and soon became well-known to all members of both Missions who frequented it.

If the Abdication had created deep differences of opinion throughout the British Army – some regarding the departing monarch with bitter resentment, others with almost Jacobite nostalgia – the Duke of Windsor appears to have aroused remarkably unanimous opinions among his fellow-officers at Nogent-sur-Marne. 'We accepted HRH at once,' writes Brigadier G.M.O. Davy, the Howard-Vyse Mission's sometime Chief of Staff.[1] Lord Coleridge, a member of the Inter-Service Mission, remembers him as 'amusing, kind, courteous and talkative' and 'wishing he were given more to do'.[2] Roland Vintras, an RAF intelligence officer who amongst other things ran the two Missions' London–Paris air service, found him 'charming, friendly as well as alert and deeply interested in his appointment'.[3] General Sir Harold Redman recalls:

> HRH was in every way friendly to us all. He was not at all 'royal', nor expecting deference, but was very much a fellow member of the mess. He talked simply and freely, of his travels when the occasion arose, but never monopolizing the

conversation. Of course we all treated him with great respect. We liked him, and he seemed to understand this, and to respond.[4]

Redman adds: 'With General Howard-Vyse there to show us the form, we could hardly have gone very wrong!' For, most important of all, the Duke got on well with his new Commanding Officer. Howard-Vyse (known on account of his large ears and Australian service as 'Wombat') was eleven years his senior, and a cavalry officer of the old school. Though certainly not one of the great military brains of the Second World War, he was charming and discreet, and it was largely his achievement that such good relations existed between the British and French General Staffs up to May 1940. Some people who happened to know both men – such as Lady Alexandra Metcalfe – predicted trouble between them. It was known that Howard-Vyse had received special instructions from the Palace on how the Duke was to be 'kept under control', and thought that the ex-King might resent such submission to a mere major-general. Vintras writes:

> Much has been made of this apparently humiliating situation, but from my own very close personal observations, I am sure the Duke was not in the least worried by it. . . . Howard-Vyse was his most perfect host and there was never any friction between them – except on one occasion when HRH took advantage of the fact that, while his Army rank was merely temporary, he was still effectively a Marshal of the Royal Air Force.[5]

In the Duke, Howard-Vyse found not only a likeable but an eager officer. 'HRH was desperately keen to make a really valuable contribution to the war effort in any way that he could be allowed to,' writes Redman, 'and he went to infinite pains and efforts to do so.'[6]

What was the purpose of the Howard-Vyse Mission? Even today, this remains something of a mystery. There is virtually nothing about it in Professor F. H. Hinsley's classic on wartime intelligence. Only a dribble of its archives are to be found in the Public Record Office. Its war diary appears to have disappeared altogether.[7] Officially it was the main channel of communication between General Ironside, the CIGS in London, and General Gamelin, the French Commander-in-Chief at Vincennes, particularly in matters of intelligence and security. It acted as the main 'behind the lines' liaison, liaison with the French armies in the field being provided by No.2 Military Mission under Brigadier J. du R. Swayne, situated twenty miles down the Marne at La Ferté by the headquarters of General Georges who directed operations at the front. The continued mystery and confidentiality undoubtedly lies in the fact that the main purpose of both No.1 and No.2 Mission was in reality to spy on the French, who were unwilling to give their allies more than the sketchiest details about their armies, fortifications and defence plans. It was the great failure of the Missions that they never made London fully aware of the great unpreparedness of the French Army – though it was not for want of trying, and they did deliver a number of important warnings which went unheeded in London, notably a report of December 1939 which bore the Duke of Windsor's signature. At the start of the war it was their task to find out how secure were the French defences on either side of the British Expeditionary Force along the Belgian frontier, and how 'impregnable' was the Maginot Line – that mysterious chain of fortifications which occupied a religious place in French military thinking and which no Englishman had yet seen – along the German frontier.

In the second week of September Howard-Vyse and his staff were wondering how on earth to go about this difficult and delicate task, when they learnt to their surprise that the Duke of Windsor was being attached to their Mission. They were not slow to realize the tremendous intelligence possibilities presented by this news. 'At last,' recalls Davy, 'we were given a heaven-sent opportunity of visiting the French front.'[8] Royalism remained strong in the French Army, and the Duke in particular remained immensely popular from 1914–18 days. Might he not be allowed to see those things prohibited to the scrutiny of other British military personnel? With his secretive nature, his reasonable military experience and his famous charm he might be well suited to intelligence work, of which, on the other hand, few would suspect him. Howard-Vyse went to London to discuss such possibilities with Ironside, who agreed to propose the Duke to the French as his personal liaison officer with the French armies in the field.

The French, indeed, suspected nothing. On 19 September, after seeing Ironside and Howard-Vyse, the French Military Attaché in London, General Lelong, wrote to Gamelin at Vincennes:

The Assignment of the Duke of Windsor to the Howard-Vyse Mission (see my telegram No. 490/S) is a matter of pure expediency. They do not quite know what to do with this encumbering personage, especially in England; but they do not wish it to be said that he is sitting on his hands. They have therefore found a way out through Howard-Vyse, who is not too proud of the fact. General Ironside has told Howard-Vyse to see you about how the Duke might be employed. He is determined to give the thing a try, even though you may eventually have to tell him frankly that the situation is absurd and cannot go on.[9]

It was an ingenious appeal to French chivalry. It was almost inevitable that the French General Staff should react: 'So the perfidious English are trying to get rid of their Prince by asking *us* to give him some work to do. Very well then! *We* shall show *them* the fit and proper way to treat such a man.' Having asked if the French might arrange for the Duke to make a series of front-line tours, Howard-Vyse reported to London with evident satisfaction on 21 September that 'General Gamelin has no objection to the Duke of Windsor going anywhere in the French zone, which is a great relief to me.'[10]

The Duke's position was now thoroughly paradoxical. The original idea in sending him off to the Vincennes Mission was to get him out of England and give him some nominal war work to do, and above all to keep his profile low. And here he was in an important secret job – in the course of which he was liable to receive considerable glamorous publicity and be made a tremendous fuss of by the French! What worried official (and especially Palace) circles most, as they observed the threatened ruin of their plans to efface the Duke, was that his front-line tours would bring him into regular contact with the British Expeditionary Force, where he might recover his old popularity with the troops. General Brooke noted in his diary that Howard-Vyse 'has instructions to guard against his endeavouring to stage any kind of "come back" with the troops out here!'[11] – and the original instructions, indeed, were to confine the Duke to visiting French forces, and prevent him from going near the British Sector at all.[12] But would this be possible? Would it not be totally ridiculous (and make an appalling impression on the French) if the Duke – the only Englishman with a free run of the French Army – were to be prohibited by his own countrymen from going near the British Army?

The powers that be had little time, those last days of September 1939, to consider the absurdity of the position in which they had placed both Howard-Vyse and the Duke. Poland having capitulated on the 28th, armed confrontation in the West was believed to be imminent. Few suspected the months of demoralizing inactivity to come. There seemed no time to lose, if one were to make use of the Duke to inspect the French armies.

The first ten days of October were busy and happy ones for the Duke. On Monday the 2nd he was formally introduced into the Mission's mess, and went off to meet Gamelin at Vincennes, which was a great success. On Tuesday he went with Howard-Vyse to see General Georges at the French Operational HQ at La Ferté; Swayne described the visit as 'very satisfactory',[13] and it was agreed that the Duke should tour part of General Billotte's First Army Group (facing the Belgian frontier) at the week-end. From Georges, the Duke heard the French view of the current military situation:[14]

(a) They are confident that their troops in front of the Maginot Line will not get pinned.

(b) If the Germans are rash enough to make a large scale attack against the Maginot Line, they would welcome it.

(c) They are still without precise indications of an attack through the Low Countries. . . .

A week ago General Gamelin seemed quite positive that a decisive battle was imminent. . . .

The next day – Wednesday – he lunched with Gamelin and his staff. 'HRH was wonderful at lunch got everything going well and everyone talking and laughing etc.,' wrote Metcalfe to Lady Alexandra. 'He really is 1st class at something like this.'[15] The success of the lunch created the best possible atmosphere for the coming tour.

Thursday – a day of hectic preparations – saw an unfortunate occurrence which indirectly brought the Duke an unexpected stroke of luck. In view of the ulterior purpose of his tours, he was to be accompanied on each of them by an experienced intelligence officer from the Mission in the guise of an aide-de-camp. The officer originally selected for this duty was Captain Purvis; but Purvis was seriously injured in a car crash that Thursday, and his place was taken by the Mission interpreter, Captain Count John de Salis – a delightful secret service diplomatist with cosmopolitan aristocratic connections who, by an extraordinary coincidence, had known the Duchess (then Mrs Earl Winfield Spencer) while attached to the Washington Embassy in the early 1920s.[16] 'One of the most amusing men I have ever met,' writes Vintras, 'and a perfect foil for the Duke, together, in their tours of the French Army, they made themselves tremendously popular.'[17] The brilliant and subtle de Salis also provided an amusing contrast to the earthy and explosive Fruity Metcalfe, who remained on the Duke's staff even though his master was unable – in spite of frequent efforts – to get him an official position either as his equerry or as a member of one of the Missions. 'Not an enormously popular officer,' recalls Lord Coleridge of Fruity.[18] Vintras found him 'fractious and eccentric', and recalled an occasion when Metcalfe, due to fly to London on the Mission plane, 'angrily refused to wear a parachute in accordance with the regulations on the grounds that to do so was cowardice, and so got left behind fuming on the tarmac.'[19] But one should not underestimate Metcalfe's loyalty, or his value to the Duke both as an aide and a friend until their final quarrel in May 1940. Though no one could accuse him of brilliance, his letters to his wife published in 1974 show him to have been a man of keen if bluff observations.

Accompanied by Metcalfe and de Salis, the Duke set out on his first tour of the front on Friday 6 October. After a visit to General Billotte, the French group commander, they called at British GHQ near Arras, where they saw the British Commander-in-Chief Lord Gort, his Chief of Staff Major-General Pownall, and his 'Chief Liaison Officer' the Duke of Gloucester.* Howard-Vyse had insisted on this call, in spite of Palace apprehensions;[20] it was brief, but the Duke of Windsor stayed to tea and made the best of impressions. Pownall wrote in his diary:

---

* In spite of its high-sounding title, this was a nominal post with minor social duties invented for the Duke of Gloucester. 'Harry' was nervous of meeting his brother and had planned to go to Lille that day, but the Duke of Windsor asked to see him and he duly turned up (Pownall's Diary).

He was nice and agreeable and spoke very intelligently. There is, for the moment at any rate, an 'inhibition' against his going round troops, indeed I believe he was not supposed to come to GHQ, but we can't help saying 'yes' if we are told he is coming.[21]

'Everyone there was delighted to see HRH and the visit could not have gone better,' wrote Metcalfe. 'It was very important to HRH as you can well imagine.'[22] Cheered by this start, they proceeded to visit the French armies on the right of the British Sector. On Saturday they toured General Blanchard's First Army occupying the central part of the front facing Belgium – a terrain which brought back vivid memories of 1914; and on Sunday they saw part of the *Détachements d'Armée des Ardennes* further to the right – later to go down in the darkest annals of French military history under the accursed name of the Ninth Army.

Like the Howard-Vyse Mission itself, the Duke's tour (indeed every one of his tours) was both a public exercise in Anglo–French relations and a secret exercise in British military intelligence. On the first count, it could not have been more successful. 'HRH was all through absolutely delightful company,' wrote Metcalfe. 'No one could have been a more lively or amusing companion. How we laughed at many incidents and at some of the French generals I'm afraid.'[23] Calling at No.2 Mission on Sunday evening, the Duke expressed himself delighted at the reception the French had given him.[24] But he had not forgotten the ulterior purpose; and back at HQ he got down with de Salis to writing his secret report.

A few words must be said about these reports, which constitute an important source in the history of the Western Front during the Phoney War. Though all bear the Duke's signature and are accompanied by a personal letter from him to Ironside, he did not compile them alone; he received expert assistance both in the investigations at the front and the writing-up afterwards. He could hardly have been expected to understand on his own all the latest developments in the art of war, or grasp the full significance of complex technical facts. Some of the prose (marked by characteristic expressions and punctuation) is certainly his own, but much of it derives from more skilled pens than his. Nevertheless, there can be no doubt that the reports represent in large measure the Duke's own observations and conclusions. He also reported orally to Swayne at La Ferté and sometimes to members of Gort's staff, and where notes were taken of these verbal accounts they are in the same sense as the subsequent written reports. He also expressed the same fears and doubts in his private conversation and correspondence of the period, and recalled them publicly after the fall of France.*

---

* For example, at a press conference in Madrid on 25 June 1940. See below p. 81.

The Duke's first report of 10 October 1939[25] was of great importance to the British Army in France (the army the Duke was not allowed to see). The long low-lying part of the Belgian frontier was considered to be the weakest link in the French defensive chain; out of deference to the Belgians (who until 1937 had been France's military allies) the Maginot Line had not been extended to cover it, and no attempt had been made to fortify it at all until shortly before the outbreak of hostilities. In the first six months of so-called war the efforts of the Allies were overwhelmingly concentrated on securing this vulnerable front, which had earlier in the century been the scene of such carnage and where it was everywhere believed the enemy would again launch their principal attack. (No attention on the other hand was paid to the mountainous frontier with southern Belgium and Luxemburg, thought to be naturally impassable.) The BEF were charged with the defence of the particularly exposed sector around Lille, and for this purpose were under the orders of General Georges, French Commander-in-Chief for the North-East. But as they worked frantically building up the defences on their part of the front, they had but the vaguest idea of what the French themselves were doing to the south-east of them. They relied on the Duke to find out.

His report confirmed the worst fears. 'During this tour, which covered approximately fifty miles of front-line sector, it was very noticeable that there was very little military activity of any kind, and very few troops indeed to be seen, only one Company of Infantry on the march being passed.' And yet the work to be done was immense. Most field works were only half-finished, and where they had been completed 'there is little or no attempt at concealment'. A minefield 'appeared to have been put there simply for show' and 'could be seen fifty yards away'. The main fortified positions had 'no camouflage of any kind' and showed 'no evidence whatever of any kind of secondary works'. Worse, 'no effort whatsoever is being made against the possibility of hostile air reconnaissance.' Anti-tank defences were utterly inadequate – 'could easily be breached at any point by a direct hit' – and anti-tank crews seemed quite untrained: one of them was asked by the Duke to demonstrate the loading of their gun and took over a quarter of an hour.

After the débâcle, the Duke spoke of one particular experience during this tour which had convinced him that there was something hopelessly wrong with the whole French military machine not only physically but morally.[26] As he put in his report: 'Wiring, against infantry, coincides in location with anti-tank obstacles, so that the same bombardment would destroy both.' When he asked why this had been done, he was told that it saved money to have as many defences as possible on the same spot. It struck him as a shocking admission, of half-heartedness as well as incompetence.

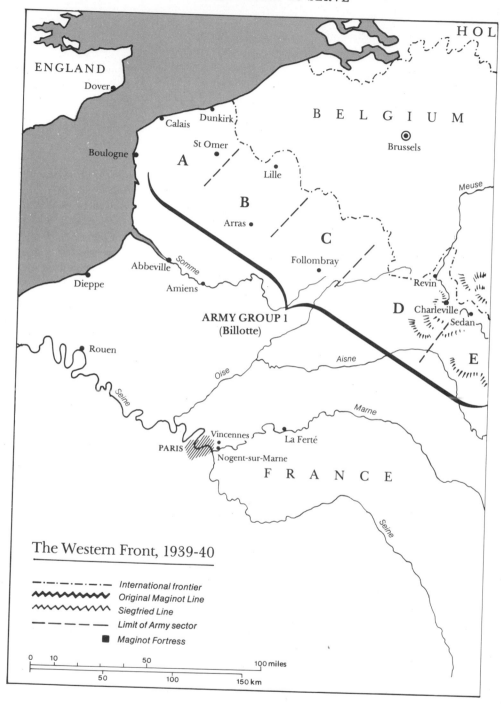

ENGLAND

Dover

HOL

BELGIUM

Calais
Dunkirk
St Omer
Lille
Brussels

Boulogne

A

B

Arras

C

Follombray

Meuse

Revin

D
Charleville
Sedan

Abbeville
Somme
Amiens

Dieppe

ARMY GROUP 1
(Billotte)

E

Rouen

Oise

Aisne

Seine

Marne

Vincennes
La Ferté
PARIS
Nogent-sur-Marne

F R A N C E

Seine

The Western Front, 1939-40

International frontier
Original Maginot Line
Siegfried Line
Limit of Army sector
Maginot Fortress

| 0 | 10 | | 50 | | 100 miles |
| 50 | | 100 | | 150 km |

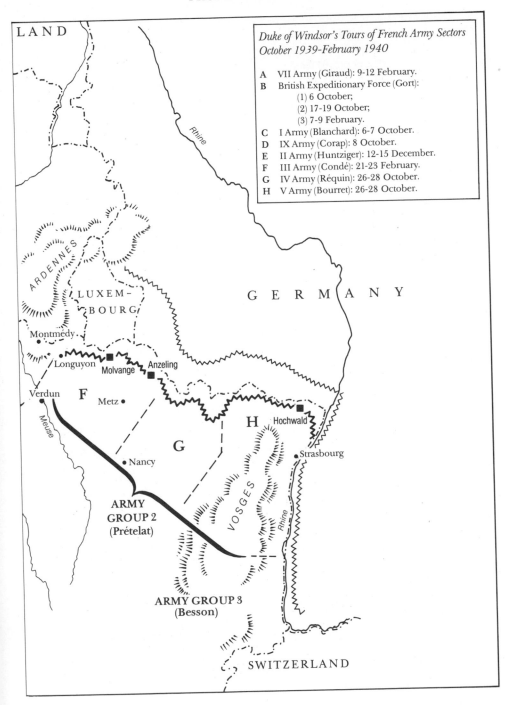

Duke of Windsor's Tours of French Army Sectors
October 1939–February 1940

A VII Army (Giraud): 9-12 February.
B British Expeditionary Force (Gort):
        (1) 6 October;
        (2) 17-19 October;
        (3) 7-9 February.
C I Army (Blanchard): 6-7 October.
D IX Army (Corap): 8 October.
E II Army (Huntziger): 12-15 December.
F III Army (Condé): 21-23 February.
G IV Army (Réquin): 26-28 October.
H V Army (Bourret): 26-28 October.

Howard-Vyse hastened to send the report to both Ironside and Gort. 'HRH The Duke of Windsor . . . has produced a valuable report on the defences, of which three copies are coming over today. . . . I am sending a copy to Swayne for transmission to GHQ.'[27] There can be no doubt of the great attention paid to it by the intelligence-starved BEF. ('Our army knew so little of the doings of the French Army,' writes Redman, 'and were really glad to get the valuable, first-hand reports that HRH was able to make of them.'[28]) As for the strategic planners in London, they sent their polite thanks. ('I am very glad you were pleased with the Duke of Windsor's report,' Howard-Vyse wrote to Ironside on 17 October. 'He took a great deal of trouble over it, and credit is also due to de Salis.'[29]) But in fact it was virtually disregarded, and its lessons were totally lost on the Imperial General Staff.

'Having made this appointment for the Duke,' thought Vintras, 'the authorities might at least have had the courtesy, if not the prudence, of listening to what he had to say.'[30] One part of the Duke's report which appears to have been of no interest to the intelligence staffs either at British GHQ or the War Office was the account of his tour of the Northern Ardennes in the vicinity of Revin:

> The main features are the high and heavily wooded ridges which form the valley of the Meuse. It was difficult to establish what was the general system of defence. . . . The wire entanglements are covered by machine gun fire, but in almost every case there is a very narrow field of fire, and the entanglements could easily be approached up to within a few yards under cover of the trees and very thick undergrowth. There are no anti-tank defences. . . .[31]

It was the voice of Cassandra.

Despite the lack of attentive official reactions, Howard-Vyse was encouraged to have further high hopes of the Duke as a military intelligence agent. He wrote to Ironside: 'It will be realized that to give the French any sort of inkling of the source of this information would probably compromise the value of any missions which I may ask HRH to undertake subsequently.'[32] The French evidently had no inkling at all, for – quite delighted by the Duke's northern tour – they at once invited him to undertake a detailed inspection of a large sector of the Maginot Line. The Howard-Vyse Mission could scarcely believe their good luck; apart from a few carefully stage-managed visits to showpiece fortresses, no Englishman had ever been able to look at the thing, let alone study it. The proposed tour – which would cover the Vosges fronts in the southern part of the Maginot, in the sectors of the Fourth and Fifth Armies – was scheduled for the last week of October.

Meanwhile, on 14 October, a great social event took place at the Château de Vincennes. At a magnificent luncheon presided over by

General Gamelin, *SAR le Général Duc de Windsor* was formally introduced as a member of the *popote* (the staff officers' mess) at the *Grand Quartier Général* – the rarest of honours. General Olivier Poydenot, then a Lieutenant-Colonel on Gamelin's *cabinet particulier* with special responsibility for Anglo–French relations, recalls that the Duke had already won all their hearts, particularly by his directness of manner. *'Il possédait d'immenses qualités d'homme et de chef. . . . Il nous traitait en camarade. Sans la moindre solennité, le Duc parlait librement, sans contrainte – pour tout dire : en ami. . . . Ceux qui, comme moi, ont eu l'honneur de s'entretenir avec SAR gardent pour lui un sincère et respectueux attachement. Cela est dû à la manière directe dont le Duc s'adressait à nous, mais avec l'exquise courtoisie du très grand seigneur qu'il était.'*[33]

The Duke (as Poydenot recalls) regarded his honorary membership as no empty privilege, and came to the *popotte* to see his fellow French officers several times a week during the rest of 1939. He often spoke to them of his regret that Great Britain had not re-armed sooner, and was only able to make a small and slow contribution to the defence of France. 'Ah! Give me a magnifying glass will you – *donnez-moi une loupe s'il vous plaît*' he would cry, as he examined the dispositions of the four solitary BEF divisions on their wall map of the front. His French (on which he continued to work until his death, as a set of extraordinary exercise books testifies) was rapid and fluent, though grammatically poor and heavily accented. He continued to attend Gamelin's lunches from time to time, and Poydenot remembers that the two men would have long discussions and sometimes disagreements on general subjects. On one occasion they disagreed about the best method of reprimanding subordinates, the Duke taking the view – which was too unsubtle for Gamelin – that the superior should always have a man-to-man reckoning with the erring subordinate in private, and state the complaint against him calmly and frankly. Gamelin's officers were much impressed by Duke's human logic, and were inclined to feel that he possessed a better understanding of men than their chief.[34]

Such was the early progress of the Duke. What of the Duchess? While he was getting the measure of his new post, she too had become deeply immersed in war work. The dynamic Lady Mendl was setting up a relief organization in Versailles called 'Le Colis de Trianon', and immediately got the Duchess to join her in running it. Based at the Trianon Palace, its aim was to send parcels of woollens and other 'comforts' to deprived

---

* 'He possessed great qualities as a man and a leader. . . . He treated us as comrades. Without a trace of condescension, he would speak to us freely, to tell us all as between friends. . . . Those who had the honour, as I did, of conversing with HRH think of him with respect and sincere affection, due to his having addressed us in so direct a manner yet with the exquisite courtesy of the great gentleman that he was.'

soldiers at the front. The public were invited either to knit for the *Colis* or provide wool for the *tricoteuses*; the finished garments – sweaters, socks, gloves and scarves – were then personally packed by the ladies of the organization together with tobacco, soap, chocolate and other *douceurs*. '*Venez vous joindre à nous et donnez un peu de bien-être au Soldat du Front sans famille ou sans ressources,*' ran the leaflet of this war-charity, which named the Duchess as *Présidente Honoraire*. '*Notre seul but est de donner au Soldat Français, malheureux dans la vie et isolé sur le front dans cette guerre, la grande joie d'ouvrir son "Colis de Trianon Versailles" – expédié par sa nouvelle, "très riche" et très nombreuse famille.*'* The Duchess threw herself with passion into the work. She put in long hours on the parcels, and thought up glamorous ways to publicize the *Colis*. She got her friends to knit or provide wool, and learned to knit herself. The women of Paris society were vying with each other in their determination to absorb themselves in good works, and the Duchess, with her energy and power of organization, did battle on the home front with gusto.

Although Paris remained deserted and in fear of imminent bombardment, the Duchess longed to give up hotel life at Versailles and return to the Boulevard Suchet, to the house where she had so recently and laboriously created a home for the Duke. In the second week of October, on his return from the front, they therefore moved into a few rooms of Suchet, 'with the dust-covers shrouding the furniture and the rugs rolled up alongside the walls'.[35] It was from there that she wrote to Aunt Bessie on 13 October:

. . . We have left Versailles and opened the house on a skeleton staff of people not yet called up or too old to answer to anything but the grave. The Duke makes trips from here and I am involved in all sorts of war work – from giving artists lunch for 1 franc at the Bal Tabarin† to wrapping up parcels in Versailles for the soldiers from there who are at the front. I lunched with Bullitt‡ and the Biddles§ which was interesting – the latter had some unpleasant experiences. So far the war does not seem to have commenced – the suspense of waiting for either peace or bombs is quite a strain – but Paris carries on with not much light and few inhabitants. Elsie Mendl entertains at Versailles every day and night, giving much cheer to both French and English billeted near Paris. Le Ritz has

---

* 'Come and join us and give some comfort to front-line troops without family or means. Our sole aim is to give the underprivileged French Soldier, isolated at the front in this war, the great joy of opening his 'parcel from the Trianon Versailles' – despatched by his new, "very rich" and very large family.'

† The night club in Montmartre, which the Duchess had helped convert into a soup kitchen for the poor.

‡ William Bullitt (1891–1967), American Ambassador to France.

§ Anthony Drexel Biddle Jr (1896–1961), American Ambassador to Poland, and his wife Margaret, an old friend of the Duchess.

La Corrigan* whom we avoid – but also Daisy Fellowes† and family – and the Bedaux‡ whom I have seen and were charming. Candé is housing some of the American Embassy staff. Constance Coolidge is working at the American Hospital. It is not so bad except that we have to live in blackness – and black curtains before the windows are *not* conducive to gaiety. Everything closes at 11 and one flash lights it home. We have only opened one floot – the banquet room, dining room and everything else is deposited in people's cellars – all the objets d'art that I searched Paris for – and the dining-room which was a real triumph with many mirrors etc – everything pasted with strips of paper in case of explosions nearby – the very preparedness is insurance against it ever happening. It is strange to be in the war this time – last time in California it didn't seem possible – but now I know how much the French have given of their soil and selves – and how one things quite differently living a secluded life. . . . One feels safe so long as the strong lines sit facing each other. . . . There is some doubt as to when La Cröe will be of use but it is accepted and I shall get it ready for January. Don't worry and I hope we will meet very soon and this war will seem a dream.

Much love

When the Duchess wrote that 'the suspense of waiting for either peace or bombs is quite a strain', she was alluding to Hitler's 'peace offer' of 6 October. In giving their only possible reply to this a week later, the Allied leaders believed – correctly – that Hitler was planning an autumn western offensive. However, if there was little sign of peace in October 1939, nor was there much sign of bombs, since for one reason or another the German attack was put off again and again until it was postponed altogether by the oncome of a severe winter. Nevertheless Allied intelligence was constantly picking up hints of German offensive preparations, and the autumn saw several false alarms of imminent battle. The first such alert had been in the last week of September at the time of the Duke's arrival; Gamelin expressed his astonishment that the Germans did not choose that moment to hurl themselves to their destruction against the Maginot Line. The second serious alarm came in the middle of October. 'Indications multiply', wrote Howard-Vyse to Ironside on the 12th, 'of the imminence of an attack on the Saar.'[36] On the 15th, Brigadier Swayne at No.2 Mission recorded in his diary that 'the great German offensive for which we have all been waiting would probably begin tomorrow'. The next day the Germans did in fact launch some minor attacks against the Maginot Line, and Swayne noted that an immediate

---

* Laura Corrigan (1879–1948), widow of an American copper millionaire and a well-known lion-hunter in London and Paris. She was notorious for her gaffes and malapropisms.
† Their old friend, the Hon. Mrs Reginald Fellowes (*née* Daisy Decazes), and her four daughters.
‡ Charles and Fern Bedaux, in whose castle in Touraine, the Château de Candé, the Duke and Duchess had been married in June 1937. Bedaux had helped organize their disastrous visit to Germany and abortive tour of the United States; they had not seen him since.

invasion was now expected of Holland and Belgium. Gamelin issued a stirring order of the day which has not gone down in history:

> Soldiers of France! At any moment the battle may begin upon which the fate of the fatherland will once again depend. The eyes of your countrymen, of the whole world, are fixed on you! Lift up your hearts! Take up your arms! Remember the Marne and Verdun!

The Duke of Windsor was not due to set out on his tour of the Vosges Sector of the Maginot Line until 26 October; but since an engagement in the north-east seemed near, it was decided to send him off at once to visit the BEF. It must be emphasized, in view of the vicious consequences this visit was to have for the Duke, that it was not just a routine inspection thought up to give him something to do. It was conceived as an important eve-of-battle tour. The four divisions of the BEF had only just finished arriving at their stations, and it was believed (as Brigadier Swayne's diary makes clear) that before the end of the month they might be engaged in bloody combat. Their morale was all-important; and no one doubted the effect of the Duke of Windsor on the morale of the ordinary British soldier. He arrived at Gort's new headquarters near Arras on the afternoon of 17 October, 'behaved charmingly'[37] in the view of Pownall, and dined with the Commander-in-Chief and his staff, including a highly nervous Duke of Gloucester. The next day, they set out early to visit the troops.

According to Dr Noble Frankland, the skilful and entertaining biographer of the Duke of Gloucester, the tour of the BEF on 18 October turned into 'something of a triumph for the Duke of Windsor, and therefore, as Prince Henry and the King obviously saw it, something of a slight, if an unintentional one, to the King.'[38] This is a very candid observation. Certainly the Duke of Windsor was in excellent form, and had lost none of his flair and charm. 'Full of go and of interest,'[39] noted General Alan Brooke (then commanding II Corps) in his diary. His appearance had a splendid effect everywhere, both on officers and men. As the Duchess wrote in her memoirs, they remembered him with affection and wanted to show him that, whatever the constitutional issues of the Abdication, they were delighted to see him back in uniform and among them once again. Here indeed was the Prince they had known in 1914 – the man of the people, still in a curious way a symbol of the youth of England, a man who knew them and was concerned for them, who inspired them by being one of them. No one he talked to would ever forget it; nor had he forgotten any man he had met in war, and there were emotional episodes as he greeted by their names ordinary soldiers he had encountered in the trenches of Flanders.

The whole performance was wonderful to witness, the Duke himself was visibly filled with almost mystical enthusiasm as he recaptured the sensations of a quarter of a century before, all who saw him were infected by the spirit – and the Court was horrified. This was the very thing it had dreaded. The Duke had been sent to France to keep him out of the way; and here he was, becoming once again the idol of the British fighting man! The fact that his was a splendid contribution to the morale of the British Army was immaterial. Such was the attitude towards the Duke that a resounding success for him could only be interpreted as 'a slight to the King'. As for the Duke of Gloucester (described by one fellow staff officer as 'greatly tiresome . . . very lazy, and very, very stupid. . . . The only part of the day in which he interests himself is when it is the hour for short drinks. . . .'), it was not perhaps surprising that this character should find himself somewhat overshadowed, uneasy as he was at having to accompany the glamorous older brother who had become branded as a family outcast. A large picture published a few days later in *The Times*[40] showed the Duke of Windsor walking purposefully along engaged in conversation with General Dill, the Duke of Gloucester vaguely visible trotting towards the back of the group. On one fateful occasion a headquarters guard presented arms as the Duke of Windsor walked by with the commanding officer, and the Duke automatically returned the salute, although Gort (who was annoyed) was the senior officer present, and Gloucester (who had fallen behind as usual) was technically senior in terms of social precedence. 'Perhaps the combination of his personal charm and the spirit of "we'll show them" left the Duke of Windsor with little option,' writes Dr Frankland of the manner in which he stole the show, 'but such antics were never again permitted.' As one soldier with Palace connections wrote: 'If Master W thinks he can stage a come-back, he's mighty wrong.'

The Duke returned to Paris delighted with his visit; here was work he loved and knew. The days passed. The anticipated German attack never came. And at Mission HQ, the Duke was astonished to receive an official reprimand for having taken a salute meant for his younger brother. He 'shrugged the incident off', wrote the Duchess in her memoirs; 'but the manner in which the rebuke was delivered, the fact that so trifling an action had been deemed worthy of notice, was petty to say the least.'[41]

It turned out that this was but the tip of a very cold iceberg. Secret instructions had gone out from Court to ensure that the Duke in future acquired no personal publicity or prestige. He was to be 'punished' by a period of inactivity, and until further notice the British sector was to be off-limits to him. But above all he was to have no publicity: war correspondents were only to be told of his appearances after they had happened. The Duchess wrote that 'we had two wars to deal with – the big and still leisurely war, in which everybody was caught up, and the little cold war with the Palace, in which no quarter was given.' The Duke had 'always had a gift for dealing with troops – the gift of the common touch and understanding. . . . It seemed to me tragic that his unique gift, humbly proffered, was never called upon, out of fear, I judged, that it might once more shine brightly, too brightly.'[42]

Unaware as yet of the extent of the intrigue to minimize his role and deny him all recognition, the Duke left Paris for Nancy with Metcalfe and de Salis on the morning of 26 October for his scheduled inspection of the Fourth and Fifth French Armies and their Vosges Sector of the Maginot Line. They covered 900 miles in three days. The terrible cold of 1939–40 was beginning, though Howard-Vyse wrote to London that 'HRH's tour was a great success in spite of the weather'.[43] At Fort Hochwald – one of the strongest *gros ouvrages** of the Maginot – four shells were fired into no man's land in honour of his visit, to the mingled strains of champagne corks and *God Save the King*. When he visited the headquarters at Ingwiller the next day, what most impressed one Colonel Vidal was that, while Metcalfe and de Salis wore crisp, smart uniforms with highly polished belts and boots, their master 'wore a rather frayed khaki overcoat, somewhat faded leggings, and well-worn shoes. . . . He did not look his age.'[44] The fact was that the Duke had taken back to France some of the same garments and uniforms he had worn from 1914–18 – all of which had been carefully preserved, darned and repaired where necessary, but rarely altered, for his physical dimensions hardly changed from the age of twenty until his dying day. It says much about the Duke's personality that he chose to wear these relics of his previous service. Clothes had a great mystique for him.

Back in Paris after this successful tour, the Duke reported to Howard-Vyse on what he had seen. He had been favourably impressed by the strength of this part of the line. The thing which had struck him most was not to do with the state of the French defences, however, but a curious incident he had witnessed involving the generals. While he had been at the headquarters of the Commander of the Fifth Army, General Bourret, a distinguished and entirely unexpected visitor had arrived – none other than the French Prime Minister, Daladier. It appeared that Bourret was a 'political' general and an ally of Daladier. This was not the case however with General Prételat, the Group Commander and Bourret's superior, whom the Duke saw later the same day. Prételat was enraged that Bourret had received the head of the Government without consulting him first. He could not conceal his fury from the Duke.[45] This scene confirmed the dark conclusions which the Duke had already drawn about the relations between the French commanders. It was not long after this that, as Lord Gort's biographer writes, the Duke produced

* The massive underground fortresses upon which the Line was based.

. . . a pungent memorandum in which he expressed the view that the generals were more actively hostile to each other than to the Germans. The French soldiers were, the Duke discovered, dedicated to political feuds. The Roman Catholics looked with horror and suspicion upon the Freemasons, for all the world as if the clock had been stopped 50 years previously.

As for the French High Command, the Duke 'was not alone, but he was among the first to decide that Gamelin was, as he put it, "a weak sister"'.[46] It was a sharp and accurate diagnosis.

An all-too-triumphant tour of the British Sector, two highly successful visits to the French Armies, two deeply perceptive reports. . . . October had been a busy and useful month for Major-General HRH the Duke of Windsor. He seemed to have made an excellent start. But if he hoped that November would bring him greater responsibilities, further interesting and important missions, such hopes were destined to be utterly disappointed. The 'punishment' decreed by the Palace now took effect. For six weeks – weeks during which the Allied High Commands, with some reason, were daily expecting a German attack – he found himself entirely ignored and given nothing of significance to do. He wanted to make a brief visit to London to discuss his position with Churchill; but Churchill put him off. 'HRH appears *now* to realize that he has no power here & is *not* to have any,' wrote Metcalfe on 20 November. 'It is a bitter blow but he's taking it.'[47]

During this period of 'disgrace' the Duke was sent off on long tours to the most desolate minor French Army zones, usually in wet and freezing weather, often living for days in a species of towed caravan. His job, according to the *New York Times*, was

> . . . to report on the men's morale. . . . Every morning he gets up at daybreak and tramps, often ankle-deep in mud, to the most out-of-the-way encampments to enquire about the men's health, asking questions about the quality of the food, the condition of sleeping-quarters, the supply of razor blades, soap, shirts or handkerchieves.[48]

Of course he acquitted himself well on these trips and always left the men much cheered; but it was depressing, insignificant, anonymous work, the most boring and routine sort of work which falls to royalty without any of royalty's comforts, public recognition or other advantages.

Indignant though she was at the tragic neglect of her husband's talents, the Duchess tried to look on the bright side of things. 'I am lucky in that I can see a lot of the Duke at the present time,' she wrote to Aunt Bessie on 28 November. 'At first Paris was deserted but now more and more people have returned as there is much to do.' She herself was busy as never before. She had thrown herself heart and soul into the *Colis*, and was helping recruit massive aid for it in America. 'Try and have a few friends help us if possible. The soldiers need warm things *terribly*,' she wrote to her aunt. 'Couldn't Anne do some alcoholic stitch and Cousin Lelia – and that dear Kitty Collins who could exchange the pen for a knitting-needle?' She had also now joined the motor branch of the French Red Cross, the *Section Sanitaire*; with her friend 'Pinky' de Ganay, she would make three-day trips to hospitals at the front to deliver plasma, bandages and cigarettes. Once, staying in a château behind the Maginot Line on one of these expeditions, she lay awake listening to an all-night bombardment, and was glad to think she had at least got within sound of the war. 'Between the *Section Sanitaire* and the *Colis de Trianon*', she wrote in her memoirs, 'I was busier and perhaps more useful than I had ever been in my life.'[49]

The Duchess had also found a new friend. 'Gray Phillips the Duke's new equerry is living in the house so when the latter is away I am not alone. He is 54 and awfully nice.' Major Phillips – who had in fact arrived on 20 October as the Duke's comptroller – had been well known to the Duke since the First World War. He was six-and-a-half feet tall and had beautiful manners. He was something of a frustrated aesthete and intellectual; he had been a brilliant classical scholar at Eton, but the Great War had projected him reluctantly into the career first of a professional staff officer, later of comptroller to such great families as the Sutherlands. He was charming, resourceful, witty and kind; everybody liked him. He was a bachelor and had a strong artistic streak. He and the Duchess got on marvellously well, and he was never happier than when helping her plan a dinner-party or arrange flowers. He was to play an important part in their lives over the next five years.

And so November passed, the Duchess fully occupied, the Duke – alternately kicking his heels at the Mission and going off to remote sectors – longing for something proper to do. In the evenings, when they were not away, they would sometimes entertain or be entertained by such friends as the Mendls and Fellowes and Eugène de Rothschilds, sometimes attend galas for war charities. More often than not they would dine alone at the Boulevard Suchet – or with Gray Phillips and Fruity Metcalfe – and then knit for the *Colis de Trianon*. Having been taught in the nursery at York Cottage, the Duke was accomplished at both knitting and crochet. The Duchess needed a little practice to become proficient, but she too was soon knitting very expertly. She even invented a new type of mitten with a zipper attachment, which allowed the soldier to use his trigger finger in an emergency.

Meanwhile, in London, the Court was deeply involved in the intrigues of military politics. Certain conservative elements in the War Office, the General Staff and the High Command were out to get rid of Hore-Belisha. They mistrusted his brilliance, were annoyed by his love of publicity, and disliked his 'foreignness' (Hore-Belisha was a Sephardic Jew). But Hore-Belisha was a popular hero; the country owed it to him that the army had been reformed and conscription introduced in time; and he had many admirers and supporters. Much intrigue would therefore be needed to dislodge the Secretary of State, and his enemies sought allies at Court, particularly in the persons of the King's Private Secretary Sir Alexander Hardinge and Assistant Private Secretary Sir Alan Lascelles. Both of these powerful men disliked Hore-Belisha; but their particular *bête noire* was the Duke of Windsor, whom they had once and with questionable loyalty served and in whose fall they had rejoiced.* When, therefore, the orders came from the Palace to keep the Duke under constant restraint and scrutiny and far from all glory, honour, usefulness and influence, there were many at the War Office who, whatever their personal feelings, would have been eager to execute these orders with particular efficiency and brutality.

By mid-November, Hore-Belisha had begun to be seriously worried by two aspects of the situation in north-eastern France – the apparent slowness with which the BEF were fortifying their sector of the front, and the security of the 'gap' between that sector and the heavily defended German frontier. He was against the idea of an advance into Belgium until that gap could be made totally secure. Such reports as the Duke of Windsor's after his visit to the First French Army showed how much the defences left to be desired. On 17 November, Hore-Belisha went on a three-day visit to France, where he toured the British Sector with Gort and saw Gamelin at Vincennes. On his return, he repeated to the Cabinet his worries about the 'gap' and, in an otherwise praising letter to Gort, wondered if the BEF were manufacturing pill-boxes as fast as they might. These complaints were resented by some and produced something of a row, which the enemies of Hore-Belisha exploited to the utmost in the effort to bring about his fall. At the beginning of December, the King was induced to go over to France at very short notice (in spite of the terrible cold) to see for himself how misguided were the 'insulting' observations of the Secretary of State. The visit began on 4 December and lasted six days.

It hardly needs to be said that the King and the Duke did not meet during the royal tour of the front; indeed, the Duke was instructed to make himself particularly scarce during this period. 'My brother-in-law arrives in France tomorrow,' wrote the Duchess to Aunt Bessie; 'but competition still exists in the English mind – so one must hide so there is no rivalry. All very childish except that the biggest men take it seriously. Anyway the Duke can leave the front and spend those days with me so

* For an extraordinary confession by Lascelles of his contempt for Edward VIII and delight in his Abdication, see James Lees-Milne's *Harold Nicolson*, II, pp.86–7.

that the cheers are guaranteed.' The King's visit was good Anglo–French propaganda, and something of a tonic to the bored BEF; but he made an indifferent impression on French officers, and the meeting with Gamelin near Metz was not a success. The King took care to express appreciation of the defences which Hore-Belisha had tended to criticize, and in this way – perhaps unconsciously – strengthened the hand of the Minister's enemies. However, back in London he sent a friendly message to Hore-Belisha, asking him to an audience so that they could compare notes on what they had seen in France. The message (which would have been entrusted to Hardinge) was never delivered. Hore-Belisha's assassins moved in for the kill.

On 12 December, only two days after the King's departure from France, and more than six weeks since he had been given any real work to do, the Duke – accompanied this time by Major Davy – was at last allowed to set out on another inspection tour of the front, his third. (Since the newspapers were full of the King's visit, which had just been made public, the Duke was unlikely to receive any publicity.) This time he was to visit the Second French Army, which held the ground between the Ardennes and the Meuse from Sedan in the West to the Luxembourg frontier in the East. It therefore included the last and weakest stretch of the Maginot Line and the first part of the 'gap' about which Hore-Belisha expressed such concern; and indeed, this was to prove one of the disastrously weak links in the French chain, where Guderian's Panzers were to break through with relative ease in May 1940. It is fascinating to observe how accurately the Duke described the weaknesses and foresaw the dangers,[50] and tragic to think how utterly his warnings were ignored.

The Duke found the officers of the Second Army living in a dream world of security.*

> I gained the general impression that the MAGINOT LINE is an effective barrier, but cannot be looked upon as impregnable. Most of the FRENCH officers with whom I discussed the strength of it seemed to consider that it was so strong that a rear position was hardly necessary. They have, nevertheless, reconnoitred a rear line some 10 to 12 kilometres in rear, and state that they are doing a little work on it. I saw no evidence of this work. . . .

In the Meuse Valley, French preparations were vague to say the least. 'There are no defences West of the Meuse. . . . In summer, the Meuse can be forded in places. . . . On the heights East of the Meuse there was no

---

* Two things must be noted about this report. 1: When the Duke talks of 'the Maginot Line', he is referring not to the original Maginot but an incomplete northern extension of it known as the Montmédy Sector. However, the mere fact that this inadequate fortification was known as part of the Line had the effect of creating a false sense of security. 2: There is no doubt that the text owes much to Davy's more skilled eye and pen, but that its opinions were also those of the Duke is shown by the fact that he repeated them in detail to Swayne at La Ferté and, the following month, to Billotte at Follombray.

SECRET.

REPORT BY

MAJOR-GENERAL H.R.H. THE DUKE OF WINDSOR,
K.G., P.C., K.T., K.P., G.C.B., G.C.S.I.,
G.C.M.G., G.C.I.E., G.C.V.O., G.B.E., M.C.

FRANCE, 17th December, 1939.

1.   On 12th December, 1939, I visited the sector of the Second French Army. The Army holds the sector between (excl.) THIONVILLE and (incl.) SEDAN.

2.   I attach at Appendix A a description of the defences of the sector, as far as I saw them. I gained the general impression that the MAGINOT LINE is an effective barrier, but cannot be looked upon as impregnable. Most of the FRENCH Officers with whom I discussed the strength of it seemed to consider that it was so strong that a rear position was hardly necessary. They have, nevertheless, reconnoitred a rear line some 10 to 20 kilometres in rear, and state that they are doing a little work on it. I saw no evidence of this work, but this was probably because I generally passed through this line in the dark. When I passed it in daylight, I saw no signs even of field defences. I was impressed by the strong natural obstacle on the frontier north of the LONGWY ironfields, which were not included within the defences of the MAGINOT system. Since the war broke out, the 3rd Cavalry Division have done especially good work in constructing field defences on this section of the frontier. The principal work being carried out at present is designed to add depth to the MAGINOT LINE itself. For this purpose, the necessary material and civilian labour has only recently become available. Work is now in full swing.

3.   I attach at Appendix B a few observations on the morale and bearing of troops I met in the sector.

4.   I attach at Appendix C my impressions of certain FRENCH Officers of the Second Army. A short sketch of the careers of other officers in the zone of the Second Army is being forwarded separately.

Edward

Major-General.

The Duke's letter to Lord Ironside enclosing his report on the Second Army, December 17, 1939.

evidence of field defences except the battery at Fort VAUX. . . .' Vaux was one of the Verdun forts – but Verdun, from where the Duke had broadcast for peace only seven months before, was little use for defence now. It was a graveyard and a museum.

The Commander of the Second Army, General Huntziger (he was to have the unhappy lot of signing the Armistice for France), appeared to the Duke as a 'striking personality' and 'a man of the world'; but the forces under him left much to be desired. The crack 3rd Cavalry Division, which had captured the Schneeberg in the September 'offensive' and whose commander, General Baron Petiet, was 'a gentleman in every sense of the word', alone made a good impression; but even they were 'not trained according to British cavalry standards'. The 1st Spahi Brigade was 'rough, tough and untidy'. The 10th Infantry Division 'seemed to be of inferior quality'. The 3rd Colonial Infantry Division was slightly better, but its transport (which seemed to be run by negroes) was 'awful. . . . Scarcely a horse would have been passed by the RSPCA or the Dumb Friends' League as fit for work, and one wheeler in the equivalent of a GS wagon was lying under the pole obviously expiring from exhaustion.' When troops were encountered on the march 'there seemed to be no march discipline as understood in the British Army'. The Duke concluded that artillery soldiers were selected for their intelligence, cavalry for their smartness, and the infantry got the rest.

The Duke concluded his report with an ominous summary:

In the minds of most of the French officers interviewed on the tour there is one dominant obsession, and that is the excellence, the impregnability of the MAGINOT LINE. Until the outbreak of war it was literally a line, and had no depth at all. At present all efforts are being directed towards deepening the position from the original and foremost anti-tank obstacle and line of works (the 'ligne de résistance') to the rearward anti-tank obstacle, not yet constructed (the 'ligne d'arrêt'). It seems inconceivable that troops out of the line should not be digging the second position, but there was no evidence of any work going on except a working party of 50 men on the march near AUDUN-LE-ROMAN. When questions were asked about this line, the answer was either 'we are beginning' or 'projeté', followed by some reference to the strength of the MAGINOT LINE.

The MAGINOT LINE does not seem to be an insuperable barrier. Given the weight of artillery, close support from aircraft, natural or artificial fog, tanks with guns capable of penetrating the armour of the embrasures, armoured trucks or tractors to carry faggots to fill up the space in the anti-tank rail obstacles, enterprising infantry with flame throwers, and sappers with explosives, it should be possible to break the crust. At present, once the crust is broken there is nothing to stop exploitation by armoured forces. But in another month the *ligne d'arrêt* should be ready. This will need a further full-scale preparation before it can be attacked, although the concrete works will be less formidable than those on the line of resistance. After that, there will be nothing but a few demolitions and troops in the open to stop an advance to PARIS.

It is perhaps fortunate that the Germans did not attack through Luxemburg and Belgium in November. . . .

It was an extraordinarily accurate forecast of what would occur, and the Duke expressed it in person when he called at La Ferté on 15 December and saw Brigadier Swayne. Yet it received practically no attention. In the War Office, for example, 'J.W.L.' sent it to 'D.D.M.O.' on 20 December with the note:

I do not think you have seen this report by HRH the Duke of Windsor. You will not I think want to read it . . . but may care to look at the covering letter. . . .[51]

Why was it ignored? Davy, who was probably responsible for most of the text, suggests in his unpublished memoirs that it was a mistake to let the Duke sign it; anything bearing his name was likely to have a brief journey on its way to the waste-paper basket. But in this case there was a very special reason for dismissing it. Quite simply, it was a total vindication of the ideas and fears of Hore-Belisha. Ironside, with the aid of Hardinge and others, was about to engineer Hore-Belisha's destruction; therefore the Duke's report had to be suppressed. Three weeks later, Hore-Belisha fell; and six months later, so did France. As the Duke and Hore-Belisha had been among the few to foresee, the Germans broke through in the Ardennes.

Though the Duke well understood why Hore-Belisha had been disliked by the conservative army establishment, he observed the departure of the unfortunate and prophetic Minister with some sadness. He had personally liked him, and been grateful for his friendship since the Abdication. He sympathized with him as a fellow-victim of the intrigues of Establishment and Court, and saw in his disappearance a further fall in his own fortunes. He was particularly disgusted by the 'dirty work' which had been used to get rid of him, and wrote to Beaverbrook (Hore-Belisha's champion) offering to communicate those sordid details which had come his way. Beaverbrook replied after a curious delay:

The envelope bears unmistakable evidence of having been opened, although there is no indicating mark of censorship whatever. I will go to see you at any time after the present political excitement dies down. . . . I would write in full about the political crisis . . . but there is no use. It will only mean delay in this letter, and possibly some interference with it in transit.

I am very weary of all the restrictions that are being imposed upon us by those who hold places under the men who hold high places. How I wish there were some control of the minor officials, the temporary clerks brought in and all

Lieutenant Colonels and others, who have uniforms but never fight, or wear wings but never fly.

I am, Sir,
Your dutiful follower
MAX[52]

The Duke was touched by this letter and of course heartily agreed with these sentiments. He had 'long suspected that my letters are prizes to the secret agents, and liable to be unofficially and ruthlessly opened.'

As Christmas approached, the Duchess worked harder than ever bringing cheer and comfort to the French troops. She and the Duke appeared at the front together, distributing parcels, putting smiles onto the faces of the men, attending troop entertainments. (Before one such expedition, the Duchess and her secretary packed 200 individual parcels themselves.) They adopted poor orphans in the French Army. In their spare moments they read a great deal; 'the present "phoney" state of the war gives a great deal of inactive time for reading,' lamented the Duke in a letter to Philip Guedalla.[53] He particularly enjoyed Harold Nicolson's *Why Britain is at War*, which he read aloud to the Duchess and thought the best account he had yet come across of allied war aims.[54] Though there was always a demoralizing tension in the air – 'It is the waiting for the war to start or to stop that makes everyone's nerves on edge' – Paris social life picked up as the year drew to a close. The Duchess wrote to her aunt:

Paris has more people than ever. Quite a lot of people come over from London on one pretext or another though not many women. . . . Elsie is still going strong – parties every week-end at Versailles – and I think she is going to remain in Paris for the rest of the winter – her first. We never dress at night – that is no evening clothes – only dinner or afternoon frocks and dark suits on those who have no uniforms.

At General Sikorski's invitation, they attended the grave Christmas celebrations of the Polish forces in France. On Christmas Eve they gave a party for thirty friends at the Boulevard Suchet. The Duke came down in his kilt playing the bagpipes, and Noël Coward was there and sang *Mad Dogs and Englishmen*.

On 30 December the Duchess wrote to her friend Lady Colefax, and summed up their war:

Everything goes on the same here except that even though the Duke wears the uniform the same Palace vendetta goes on making the job difficult and nearly impossible. I have been able to get within the sound of gunfire through joining the French Red Cross automobile section. I need not add that the British have not asked me to help them – so time and money have gone to the French. We are both thoroughly disgusted and fed up in every way but are caught like rats in a trap until the war ends. I wish you everything dear Sibyl that will make you happy in 1940 and long to see you in the New Year under happier conditions. . . .[55]

3
Sensing Disaster
January–May 1940

Winter set in. 'There is no change here and the Bore War gets more difficult each day,' wrote the Duchess to her aunt in the New Year. On top of boredom, inactivity and uncertainty there now arrived freezing temperatures to weaken morale still further. 'This awful (for Europe) cold has caused enormous suffering among the soldiers who still haven't enough warm clothing,' she wrote on 21 January. 'We send direct to the men. I am afraid some of the things sent to the distributing offices do not always reach the most needy as the old game of politics goes merrily on – and the soldiers near Paris are much more warmly clad than the men I saw near the front. You see it is an easy drive outside of Paris for the politicians. . . .' Their evenings were increasingly taken up with war charity events and troop entertainments:

> There is a series of concerts, movies etc. for different war works and shows outside of Paris, which we go to. . . . I go to Bordeaux for a night soon for a show for the SSA and then I am going off to take some things near to the front. The trips in that direction are most interesting. . . .

In the midst of all her activity, she had pangs of depression and homesickness. 'How I long to leave this dying and quarrelsome old lady Europe and come to the New World,' she wrote to Aunt Bessie. 'One gets caught up in the decay of Europe. . . . What did it prove 20 years ago? Just a reason for this one. It seems so futile to me. . . .'

The Duke took great delight in the success of the Duchess's war work and in the acclaim she received; but he was increasingly pessimistic about the progress of the war. His views had not changed. He still regarded it as a tragic mistake; but since it had happened, there was nothing to do but to get on with it and try to defeat Hitler. But he was by now profoundly doubtful of the ability of Britain and France in their present state to do so. From what he had observed of the bickerings of French generals and politicians and the poor organization of the French Army, the Allies were indeed decadent and altogether lacked the efficiency,

single-mindedness and resolution which characterized the enemy dictatorship. The half-heartedness and incompetence which he had witnessed
on his autumn tours filled him with fear. And, realizing that the situation
was critical, he was miserable at being given so little to do himself. 'The
Duke does not like his job,' wrote the Duchess in her New Year letter to
Aunt Bessie, 'too inactive – besides a lot of pressure from the Palace
which makes it impossible to do well. Even the war can't stop the family
hatred of us.' But there were consolations, and one of them was his now
massive popularity with the French Army. At the French officers'
popotte at Vincennes, recalls General Olivier Poydenot, he had been
regarded during the autumn with awe, but by the New Year he had
become accepted as a beloved comrade.[1]

He had also made a number of friends among the French generals –
notably Gaston Billotte who commanded the First Army Group stretching from the Maginot to the sea, a blunt and outspoken soldier of
unusually wide experience who knew much of England and had an
English wife. Billotte (who died tragically at a critical moment in May
1940) disagreed completely with the policy of the Allied High Command.
He thought it the height of folly to 'play a waiting-game' in the West.
Though ruefully aware of the inadequacies of the Allied armies, he
believed that further inactivity could only make their condition worse.
One had to take the offensive before the sands ran out. The Duke agreed.
'The war would have been very different', he once declared after the war,
'if Churchill had been Prime Minister of England in September 1939, and
Gaston Billotte *généralissime* of France.'[2] As it was not often that he was
asked to engage in important official conversations with the generals, the
Duke must have been particularly pleased when he was sent on a
confidential mission for Ironside to Billotte's headquarters – the Château
de Follombray near Bohain – in the third week of January 1940.

There is no written record of this visit (which probably took place on 14
or 15 January) in either the French or British public records, but there
can be little doubt as to what it would have been about. For at that
moment (the most freezing in years, with the whole of Northern France
deep in snow) the Allies had been thrown into a state of acute alarm and
alert. On the morning of the 10th a German aircraft had strayed from its
course and made a forced landing on Belgian territory; its occupants (at
once arrested by a Belgian patrol) were found to be carrying documents
(which they frantically but unsuccessfully tried to destroy) from which it
was clear that Germany planned an almost immediate invasion of France
through Belgium. That same evening a highly disturbed Gamelin was
reading this historic anthology of enemy papers at Vincennes, and
communicating urgently with Ironside through the Howard-Vyse Mission. How were the Allies to react to this startling intelligence? The

53

climate at the moment (snow blizzards) made an instant German offensive unlikely, but it was assumed that one would be launched as soon as the weather improved. The First Army Group facing the Belgian frontier was placed on top alert, while Georges, Billotte and the army commanders were hectically consulted about the possibility of a rapid move into Belgium to forestall an enemy advance. It was almost certainly in this connection that the Duke of Windsor was sent to Follombray as Ironside's emissary to liaise with Billotte. The great imponderable of those tense days was the attitude of the Belgians. They demanded assurances that they would receive help as soon as the Germans invaded – but were they willing meanwhile to abandon their neutrality and invite the Allies to take up positions on Belgian soil? On 15 January, the Allies – with Billotte's armies poised to move forward – addressed an ultimatum to the Belgian Government: either they had to accept Allied intervention immediately or they would have to take the chance of help coming in time when the crunch came. After some hesitation, the Belgians declined to open their frontier to the French and British forces. What were the Allies now to do? At Follombray, General Billotte had no doubts. They knew the current German war plan, they had the temporary protection of 'le Général Janvier', and the Belgians were vacillating; every day that passed would further aggravate the condition of creeping military paralysis; it was essential to take advantage of the situation without delay and launch some form of offensive against the Germans, with a view to driving Belgium into the Allied camp and ending the insidious condition of 'wait and see'.

That Billotte discussed these opinions with the Duke, and that the Duke agreed with them, is confirmed by a reliable second-hand witness. For, as he left the General's quarters, the Duke saw a young and familiar face – that of Billotte's son Pierre, who had a day's leave from his staff post at Montry and had come to see his father. As an honorary graduate of the French military academy at Saint-Cyr, the Prince of Wales had passed out in 1927 in the same ceremony as Pierre Billotte, whom he had also met a few years earlier at Singapore. The Duke at once recognized and warmly greeted his *camarade de promotion* (who was to become his best French friend after the war). Having seen his royal visitor off, Gaston Billotte returned to join his son.

Pierre Billotte was destined for great distinction: after an heroic escape from imprisonment in Germany he became (not yet thirty-five) General de Gaulle's Chief-of-Staff in London, commanded (as the youngest general in the French Army) a tank division in the invasion of Europe, and was instrumental in the foundation of NATO. He has served in the French Government as War Minister and Minister for Overseas Territories, and has written several books – remarkable for their clarity and detail – about events in which he has been involved. He is recognized as possessing a phenomenal memory, particularly for the spoken word; and he recalls distinctly what his father said to him just after the Duke of Windsor's departure from Follombray that snowy day in January 1940.[3]

'That man's ancestry is German and his family sympathies are German', began the General to his son, 'but for all that he is a patriot and passionately concerned for our victory – and he is miserable, because he is intelligent enough to see how far we are from it and what terrible mistakes we are making which will deny it to us.' The Duke had vigorously agreed with Billotte that, if they did not attack soon, they would be surprised and overwhelmed. He had spoken eloquently of the appalling weaknesses and unpreparedness of the Allies in the face of the German machine; he regretted bitterly that the British Army was not bigger and stronger, and that his country had not thought of re-arming sooner; he expressed relief (as he had also done in his December report on the Second Army) that the Germans had not attacked in the autumn. But for all their deficiencies, he entirely endorsed Billotte's view that now was the Allies' best chance to attack and that they simply could not afford to wait any longer. Another few months of doing nothing would render them incapable of fighting altogether.

However, the Allies did not take the offensive but continued to await the invasion which never came that winter – and which, when it did come, was now destined to follow a very different plan. The only results of the January scare upon Allied strategic thinking were a penchant for hypothetical distant ventures (such as aiding the Finns and bombing Baku), and a hare-brained scheme known as the Dyle-Breda Variant whereby the Allied armies would rush as deep as possible into the Low Countries upon a German attack – incidentally (as the Duke was soon to observe) leaving the French coast practically undefended.

Partly as a consequence of the Follombray episode, the Duke was at long last allowed a brief visit to England, to report to the CIGS. He flew to London on 21 January, and stayed for three nights at Claridges. The War Office tried to keep the trip secret; but he was persistently recognized in the street, and after he had left there was a flurry of excited comment in the press. 'The public was very pleased at his journey to London,' commented Beaverbrook's *Daily Express*. 'The wish is prevalent that he will come back oftener, stay longer, and perhaps that he will settle down here for good before too many months elapse.'[4] Naturally, the Royal Family were informed in advance of his presence in England (this time without his wife), but made no attempt of any kind to communicate with him. He saw Churchill and some other friends, and had a number of meetings with Ironside. No record is available of their military conversations, but it is known that the Duke complained bitterly that his efforts to make himself useful were constantly being frustrated. These representations were not without their effect, for Metcalfe wrote a few days later: 'HRH came back from England in great shape, seemingly everything went as he wished.' (Metcalfe was delighted to witness the joyful reunion of the Duke and Duchess – *very* true and deep stuff'.) A few days later, the Duke was at long last invited to inspect the north-eastern front again, taking in the British Sector as well as the French Seventh Army on the coast. It seemed almost too good to be true: he had effectively been banned from the BEF ever since his all-too-triumphant tour and the ludicrous 'incident' with the Duke of Gloucester in October. He was, wrote Metcalfe, 'very pleased about it', feeling it might be 'the thin end of the wedge' – the start of a new effective war role. 'I am glad for him and I also think something better will come fairly soon for HRH.'5

And so the Duke set out on his fourth major tour on 7 February. Lord Gort received him at British GHQ, and they went to look at the troops and defences on the front. Conditions were arctic. 'The second cold spell had just set in,' wrote the Duke afterwards to Ironside, 'causing renewed discomfort to troops and a further delay in the strengthening of the defences.'6 Every precaution had been taken to ensure that there would be no unduly heroic reception this time – although war correspondents (without photographers) were allowed to report upon the Duke for the first time in three months. The *News Chronicle* contrasted the visit with the King's; the same elaborate traffic arrangements were in force, but this time there were no long lines of troops at the roadside. 'Few, indeed, seemed to expect the Duke, for only at corners where traffic arrangements were sufficiently complicated to demand the presence of several men did any crowds gather. Most of them were made up of children.'7 Still, it all passed off well. He inspected the Headquarters of the RAF and the Ordnance workshops. On the 8th he visited in the rain a unit which had for him deep associations – the 1st Battalion of the Welsh Guards based at Avesnes-le-Comte, which protected the approaches to Gort's headquarters. (Why is there no mention of this visit in the otherwise well-documented regimental records?) The Prince of Wales had been Honorary Colonel of the Welsh Guards from their birth in 1915; the leading company was named after him; no institution meant more to him. He had told Hore-Belisha in September 1939 that 'he had heard that they wanted him back again'8; the restoration of his honorary colonelcy was the one military favour he craved, and it was denied to him. Throughout the war he spaced the buttons on his military tunics in the Welsh Guards fashion, in groups of five; it was thus he wore his major-general's uniform in 1940. Having lent his name and patronage to so many things, this was one of the few he felt he belonged to; and now – though it was for but a few hours, and appears to have been a deliberately low-key reunion – he was among them once again.

Early on 9 February the Duke left the British Sector – President Lebrun was coming, and it was thought undesirable that they should meet – and made his way north-west to the sector of the Seventh French Army, being received by the legendary General Giraud at Saint-Omer.[9] He found himself staying at the Château de la Motte-aux-Bois, which had been famous during the First World War for its hospitality to British officers; the châtelaine, the aged Baronne Amaury de la Grange who had known the boyish Prince of Wales so well a quarter-of-a-century before, greeted the Duke of Windsor like a long-lost son. The Duke wrote to Ironside: 'It was an added interest, and brought back many memories – both pleasant and unpleasant – to be staying in that part of France so familiar to all of us who were on Active Service last time, and so wrapped up in the traditions of our army.'

The Duke's report on the Seventh Army[10] is of unusual interest. As with the Second Army front 200 miles to the south-east, he was conscious of a false illusion of security; but this time it was a subtler illusion. Outwardly, all seemed well. The troops were as fine as he had seen – 'the general impression everywhere was one of good heart, sturdiness and health' – and the defences, largely based on the bright idea of flooding low-lying areas as the enemy poured into them, appeared at first sight to be excellent. The commander, General Giraud, struck the Duke as 'a great character . . . great disciplinarian and Spartan in his habits, possessing at the same time a pleasing personality and a sense of humour . . . dislikes politics, fears no-one . . . very popular in his command.' Yet something was seriously wrong somewhere, and the Duke found it 'difficult not to have misgivings' about various things he saw – misgivings he did not always find too easy to put into words. Two facts, however, seem to have worried him especially. The first was that the strong defences were only designed to meet an assault from the east or north-east, through Belgium. 'However strong . . . the Front System may be, it cannot be said that the Intermediate or Rear Systems on this front are as yet ready to withstand attack by armoured vehicles.' The other weakness the Duke could only refer to indirectly. He knew that, in the event of a German invasion of Belgium, the Seventh Army had secret instructions to rush forward and occupy Flanders as far as the Breda and Dyle. (This is now widely considered to have been the most disastrous single decision of the French High Command before May 1940.) But would they not therefore be abandoning the apparently excellent positions the Duke was now looking at? One of the coastal sectors, for example, 'was spoken of as being impregnable to any attack, except a long prepared major operation. No doubt, the fact that 26,000 men are available in this sector lends strength to this conviction, but . . .' (as the Duke could not actually say in this kind of report, confidential though it was), *would they be there*?

Reading this report in conjunction with his December report on the Second Army, one feels that the Duke sensed – if in part subconsciously – much of what was going to happen in May 1940. He had seen how weak and vulnerable the front south of Sedan was – far weaker than the French realized. What if the enemy were to break through *there* rather than in the north, and then head for the coast – sweeping up to the Seventh Army not from the north-east, but from the south and south-east? What was there to stop them? They would encounter no adequate rear defences – and if the French were in Flanders, they would encounter no Allied forces either. It would probably be too much to say that the Duke saw things quite as coherently as this. Through his observations, he had assembled in his brain the scattered pieces of a jig-saw puzzle; his intellect was probably too untrained for him to put all the pieces together and see the whole picture, but he certainly glimpsed enough of it to sense terrible danger. He was not the only one to have these forebodings, but since his reports were officially approved by Howard-Vyse and went directly to the desk of the CIGS, they had more chance than others of being heeded in the highest quarters. They were not. As Ewan Butler, then a young intelligence officer serving in France under Colonel Gerald Templer, wrote in his memoirs: 'The warnings which the Duke of Windsor frequently sent back from the French *Grand Quartier Général* were blandly ignored, as were our own humbler reports, and it was not long before we were all required to pay the penalty for wishful thinking.'[11]

Having completed his tour of the Seventh Army Sector, the Duke inspected the land and sea defences of Dunkirk on 10 February. He was impressed by these, and by their commander Admiral Abrial – though he wished he could have seen them closer up.[12] General Fagalde (who was to conduct the heroic rearguard action at Dunkirk) he found 'a man of resource and energy'. The Duke recognized his headquarters at Saint-Omer as that which Sir John French had occupied in 1914.[13] He had doubts, however, about the crack aerial combat group at Norrent Fontes, which mounted an exhibition of aerobatics when he stopped there the following day. The base staff he found a cheerful lot; but the weeks and months of insidious inactivity seemed to have turned the pilots – adventurous men of action that they were – into nervous wrecks.[14] It was no doubt an apt comment on the general effect of the phoney war.

When the Duke returned to the Château de la Motte-aux-Bois for the last night of the tour, his hostess had a delectable surprise for him – the Duchess. Unbeknown to each other, their war work had brought them to the same *Département*: the Duchess had been delivering blood-plasma to the military hospital of Zuydcoote near the Belgian frontier. They had not seen each other for two weeks. It was a blissful reunion.

'I am awfully busy and hope I am helping a bit,' wrote the Duchess to Aunt Bessie. As if the *Colis*, the *Section Sanitaire* and constant attendance at troop entertainments were not enough, she sought new fields of endeavour. She started an enquiry to discover which French soldiers' *foyers* did not possess a gramophone; as the information came in, she lost no time in supplying the deprived units, often at her own expense; then she launched a great campaign to collect gramophone records for them.

The Duchess's thick files of correspondence with the officers and men at the front who received her benefactions constitute an interesting contemporary document. Her grateful correspondents write of the terrible battles they are waging, not yet against the enemy, but against the cold and what they call *le cafard* – boredom, depression and the blues. Thanks to the warm clothes and other jolly things sent through the *Colis* by the Duchess, both of these scourges could be more effectively dealt with and the languishing troops could find the means to . . . the French verb most often employed is *se distraire*. The appreciation of the beneficiaries is often touching to read. Private soldiers on receiving their '*colis*' would scribble enthusiastic little notes on scraps of paper, sometimes beginning '*Chère bienfaitrice* . . .' Delighted officers would express their feelings in more literary fashion: '*Aucune plume du monde ne pourrait traduire l'expression de joie qui, grâce à votre générosité, vient de naître sur tous les visages à la réception du magnifique colis destiné à notre foyer*. . . .' Some essayed bravely into the English language: 'My Blue Devils and I thank very much your Gracious Highness for your graceful gift. . . . The pullovers are much estimated, the pipes smoked very much, and all the other objects make great pleasure. . . .'

Some wrote in romantic vein. Captain (later Major) Collière, commanding the 1st Battalion of the 423rd Regiment of Pioneers, was profoundly affected by a parcel-distributing visit of the Duchess in November; he wrote protesting the devotion of himself and his fellow-officers, and begging for a picture of her to adorn their mess. The Duchess duly obliged with a signed photograph, and asked if they wanted anything else; the Captain at once replied, asking this time if , like some damsel of the Middle Ages, she would consent to offer the Battalion a regimental banner (*fanion*) in royal blue silk. The Duchess had this made at her own expense at a shop in the rue de Rennes, and sent it off. Collière was ecstatic; he passionately enjoined her to come (perhaps with His Royal Highness) to dedicate it herself – though to do this she would first have to obtain the permission of the President of the Republic. Either because the President would not let her or for some other reason, the Duchess could not come, and her banner was inaugurated without her; the ceremony was the main item in the regimental *ordre du jour*, and many officers wrote personally to thank her. Major Collière (as he now was) had a postcard showing the banner printed in her honour. It was ready just in time for the Battle of France, and he sent it to her on 13 May assuring her of '*hommages respectueux et sentiments fidèles de vos filleuls dévoués*' – a fitting item to close the file.

In the last week of February the Duke made the fifth and last of his visits to the French armies, this time inspecting the sector of the Third Army under General Condé in Lorraine. This was a classic stretch of Maginot Line, with massive *gros ouvrages* at Anzeling and Molvange; it was the strongest and most heavily fortified section of the front the Duke had yet seen. Clearly the Germans would not get through here (as late as 14 June their First Army Group offensive would fail to make the slightest dent); but then, this was hardly where they would launch their principal attack. As always, the Duke was fascinated to notice the tensions and character differences between the generals. While General Loizeau (the Duke called him 'General Oiseau'), commanding the vi Army Corps, was hard, dry, humourless and Spartan, General Freydenberg, commanding the adjacent Corps d'Armée Coloniale, was handsome, dashing, sensual and pleasure-loving, like something out of the reign of Louis XIII, and had even organized a secret deer-hunt near his headquarters, which the highly amused Duke was invited to join, bagging a roe. The Duke wanted to have a good look at the Germans, and asked Loizeau to take him up to the advanced positions. As they stood on the Guerling Heights, looking down upon (and doubtless offering a perfect target to) the Berus Sector of the Siegfried Line, Loizeau admired the Duke's binoculars. 'Zeiss – made in Germany!' said the Duke, laughing. Loizeau showed off his own pair, which had been given to him in Moscow by Marshal Voroshilov and bore the hammer and sickle. 'But mine too are Zeiss,' he added, 'made under licence in the Soviet Union. . . .'[15] At Metz, where the Duke visited the small British relief group which helped patrol the sector, he ran into his brother, the Duke of Gloucester, who wrote to the King that 'it was the first time in years I have seen him without that worried look.'[16] Back in Paris on 24 February, the Duke of Windsor spent the best part of a week preparing the last of his secret reports on the French Army for Ironside, complete with maps and drawings supplied by General 'Oiseau'.[17] Like the others, it appears to have received little attention; and for the remaining ten weeks of the phoney war, he was given no work of any consequence.

By now the Duke regarded the war with something approaching despair. It was tragedy enough in his eyes that it had broken out at all;

but what made it infinitely more tragic, during those early months of 1940, was that the Allies seemed so determined to lose it. Having passed over their best chances during the winter, they were sinking into an ever-deepening torpor. Only two possibilities still seemed, to the Duke, to offer some hope. The first was that the Allies might somehow 'overhaul' themselves in time internally, and so be able to face the might of Germany under powerful new war governments and resolute new leaders. The second was that the German Army might eventually overthrow Hitler, and Germany and the Allies then join up (perhaps with the United States) to face the menace of Soviet Russia. Night after night, these hopes were discussed at the intimacy of the dinner-table of the Boulevard Suchet. Whereas, during the autumn, he had preferred to spend his evenings alone with the Duchess, he now longed for the company of discreet, intelligent and well-informed friends with whom he could talk about the war. Having for so long been near the centre of things with access to the best inside information, he found his remoteness from great events increasingly difficult to bear; these friends helped relieve his sense of isolation. The dinner-guests in the first days of March included people like Duff and Lady Diana Cooper, just back from America, the American political journalist Walter Lippmann, that émi-nence grise of Anglo–French diplomacy Sir Charles Mendl, and the influential historian and British Council personality Philip Guedalla.

In the second week of March, the Duke took his first leave of the war. He returned with the Duchess to La Cröe, which they had not seen since they had left it to go to England six months before. The Duchess's cherished scheme to turn the villa into a convalescent home for British Army officers had been frustrated by British official indifference on the one hand and the absence of casualties on the other. On their journey south they spent a night at Lyons, where Harold Nicolson, who happened to be passing through on a lecture tour, called on them at the Carlton Hotel on 11 March. 'They were both very startled to see me suddenly emerge at Lyons,' confided Nicolson to his diary. 'Very gracious. He has a fortnight's leave and is off to his house in the South of France. They seemed very happy.' Before leaving Lyons the Duke saw the British Consul-General, Francis O'Meara. 'He was so charming to me, as though I were the one person in the world he wanted to talk to,' O'Meara told Nicolson. 'It isn't disloyal at all is it, to like the Duke so much?'[18]

They had a happy time at Antibes, in lovely warm weather and surrounded by friends, though they were immensely saddened on their arrival to hear of the capitulation of Finland. The cause of the Finns had been especially close to the heart of the Duchess, whose friend, the American Countess de Grippenberg, was the wife of the Finnish Minister in London. The Duke inspected the French defences in the Alps along the

Italian frontier, which he was to get to know much better ten weeks later. By the end of March they were back in Paris.

Spring had arrived; and after the harshest winter in memory, it was the loveliest spring. 'Paris as you know is beautiful at this time,' wrote the Duchess to Aunt Bessie, as the chestnuts bloomed and flowers covered the Bois and the sun shone brightly day after day. 'It is hard to believe there are so many people in the world who hate each other.' They climbed back into uniform and resumed their jobs. 'We continue the same life here – endless galas for war work and talk of war.' The *Colis* was 'a really great success for such a small show as ours'; but the Duchess got little joy from her success, observing what she considered to be the rotten condition of France and the tragic waste of the Duke's talents:

> The papers are so censored that it is useless to read them and the political side I think "lousy" with everyone out for himself more than for the war. . . . The D's job is ridiculous and instead of using him where he might help the cause due to jealousy which even the death of men can't temper he has a childish job. . . . He was their best propagandist when P of W and the tax-payer gave a lot for that education and now when they might get a small return family and Government are scared to use him.

She wished she could visit America just for a while; but, as she lamented to Aunt Bessie, 'the Duke won't let me go so there is the answer and I can't honestly advise you to come here.'

As April drew to a close, the Duke, indignant at his lack of useful employment, became increasingly appalled at what he saw as the chaotic internal condition of France and England and the clear demonstration of allied incompetence provided by the Norwegian Campaign. On 3 May he wrote, in a remarkable letter to his loyal friend and supporter Philip Guedalla:

> It would seem an obvious platitude to say that in my private view, things are going very badly for us indeed at the moment, and they can't possibly go any better until we have purged ourselves of many of the old lot of politicians and much of our out-of-date system of government.
>
> We are up against a formidable foe, not only formidable in the military sense but politically as well. If we are forced to spend millions a day arming and equipping our forces to match Germany's, surely it is equally necessary to equip ourselves politically in order to match ourselves against the calculating shrewdness and freedom of action of the Nazi chiefs?
>
> The trouble with the present lot who are directing our national effort is that they are in the main too old, and are all in some degree tainted with the series of past blunders in foreign policy which are responsible for the present mess. We want new blood that is not caught up in its own bunk, men with common and not necessarily political sense, who can bring clear minds to bear on the phases of the conflict as and how they develop, and who should have greater

liberty of action than is possible with the cumbersome parliamentary and departmental machine which strangles us. Granted, there have been signs of improvement in this respect, but there are still far too many 'weeds round the propellor'.

Above all things, we need men who, while applying themselves to the prosecution of war, have an eye open as to the future; for whatever the outcome of this catastrophy [sic] of war, our problems will be infinitely more divers, complex and serious than the ones we face today.

If it were as easy to discover the giant or giants (and not too many) as it is to criticize, then I would gladly forego the pleasure just now. . . .[19]

Within a week England would find its giant; but before the end of that month the Duke would echo Oliver Harvey's cry: 'My God! what a pass those bloody old men have brought us to!'[20]

Three days later, on 6 May, the Duchess wrote to Aunt Bessie:

. . . We had a dinner last week for the British Ambassador and his wife. They are very nice, and certainly brave to come here. . . . We may have to go to London shortly for a few days and I think I will go this time just in case I have forgotten their bad manners. As the French are so well-mannered one might forget! . . . My ambulance section is doing well and it is interesting to make trips with them and better in this lovely spring weather. . . . The people are splendid – and there are very few *blessés* happily. From Norway we do not know the casualties as yet, but it is All Quiet on the Western Front.

4

Whence All
But He Had Fled

May–June 1940

On Friday 10 May 1940 – exactly a week after the Duke had written that the Allies needed strong leaders with 'clear minds' and 'common sense' – everything changed. The Germans invaded France and the Low Countries, and Winston Churchill became Prime Minister of Great Britain. The Duke looked upon Churchill as a friend, and rejoiced that his country now had a strong ruler to match Hitler. But his gloomy prognosis of the hopelessness of the Allied war machine proved all too justified as the battle proceeded. His position enabled him to appreciate all too clearly the extent of the rapidly unfolding disaster.

For the first few days of the battle the Duchess hardly saw the Duke. He left to join his Mission every morning before dawn, and returned late to snatch a few hours sleep. On the 10th and the 11th he visited French troops, and from 12 to 15 May he was responsible for the liaison between No. 1 Mission and No. 2 Mission[1] – an important job, for news was slow to reach Vincennes of the dramatic happenings at the front. On the 13th, the Duke accompanied Gamelin to La Ferté, and saw Swayne and Pownall who had been to see the King of the Belgians at Casteau. He reported to Howard-Vyse:

1. It was agreed to put the Belgian Army and . . . the BEF under General Billotte for this battle.

2. The collapse of Dutch resistance is a matter of days.

3. The Belgians have been heavily tried by bombing and machine-gunning, and will not be much good till they get back behind us. This does not apply to the left half of their army, which is in good case.

4. The DLM of General Giraud's Seventh Army is probably being drawn back.

5. The BEF have had no trouble at all in their advance and are delighted about it. Two brigades in each division are now up.

6. Air-Marshal Barratt says we have destroyed for certain 123 German machines and have lost 73 ourselves. . . .[2]

The same day he stopped briefly at the house during the afternoon, and told the Duchess that 'while the battle was serious, the main Allied forces were not yet engaged, and that therefore there was no reason for alarm.' He can hardly be blamed for this view, which accorded with the best Allied intelligence at that moment. As the official historian of the campaign writes: 'Until the night of 13 May the situation in the land battle did not appear particularly serious.'[3]

Meanwhile, the Duchess carried on as well as she could at the Red Cross and the *Colis de Trianon*. On 15 May she wrote to Aunt Bessie – her main desire, as ever, being to reassure:

> Darling – I am sure you are worrying yourself to death but please try not to – because there is nothing to be done, and if Paris should become uncomfortable I shan't stay. . . . Paris so far seems all right – and I want to stay with the Duke as long as possible and his job is here. . . . Elsie Mendl and Kitty Rothschild are still here as are tons of other people. . . . I dined with Bullitt last night. . . . The Duke is here every night leaving early in the a.m. The *alertes* are a strain. . . . We have never had such a beautiful spring – one cannot believe there is so much misery and death about. The refugees are most pathetic with their little bundles arriving from Belgium. I hope the next time I write we will have had more cheerful news.
>
> Much love,
> WALLIS

On the same day as the Duchess was penning these calm lines to her aunt, however, Reynaud was telegraphing Churchill that they had 'lost the battle'. Guderian's three deadly Panzer divisions, having crossed the Ardennes and the Meuse in the face of derisory opposition, had overcome the anti-tank defences about which the Duke had expressed such doubts and smashed through the French lines. As they raced westward, there was little to stop them from advancing either on Paris, capturing the capital, or to the sea, trapping the Allied armies in Belgium. At the British Embassy, the Minister, Oliver Harvey, wrote in his diary: 'Threat to Paris has become a reality and we are considering our plans in case of evacuation being decided.'[4]

The following day, Thursday the 16th, was one of near-panic in official and military circles. The Panzers reached the Oise; the British forces in Belgium (fortified by the stirring presence of the Duke of Gloucester) began their retreat. It was still not clear whether Guderian was advancing seaward or Parisward. Churchill, arriving in Paris by air, was horrified by the general state of abandon and despair, and stupefied by the news that Gamelin had no *masse de manoeuvre*.[5] (Howard-Vyse was largely blamed for the failure to notice and report the fatal lack of French strategic reserves.[6]) Harvey wrote: 'We are burning our archives, arranging to get the female staff away by train to Havre, packing our suitcases for a sudden flit if necessary ourselves.'[7] The Embassy typists were evacuated during the afternoon, to be followed in the night by Lady Campbell, Mrs Harvey, and the wives of all other British diplomatists and officials in Paris.

'I had *no* idea of leaving until the Duke's Mission moved if ever it did,' the Duchess wrote the following week to Aunt Bessie; but, realizing as he did the gravity of the situation, his concern for her safety was overwhelming. That Thursday afternoon – as she wrote in her memoirs – the Duke burst into the house just after she had returned from the Red Cross, and said, seizing her by the arm, 'You're leaving Paris this evening. I'll give you two hours to pack, but not a second more.' She was horrified. 'Having made one retreat through France, I was not eager to start another on such short notice. Moreover . . . my job was with the French Red Cross, and it would not be seemly for me to take to my heels the minute Paris was in danger.'[8] But he was adamant and would brook no opposition; all the British wives were escaping, and she was also urged to leave by Ambassador Bullitt and Kitty de Rothschild. So, reluctantly, she agreed to go.

He accompanied her out of Paris. The roads were a terrible sight,

> . . . crowded as I have never seen roads crowded. There were endless lines of cars, many with a mattress strapped to the roof and, I surmised, jerry-cans of gasoline hidden inside. Judging by the licence plates, all of Western Europe was on the run – Belgians, Dutch, French. We had a hard, slow trip, with many long waits in the traffic.[9]

They spent the night at Blois; it was packed with refugees, but the Duchess was recognized by a benevolent innkeeper who had put her up during her flight through France in December 1936. The following day they reached Biarritz, where the Duke installed the Duchess at the Hôtel du Palais before returning to his post in the capital.

Though she was among friends – 'Nearly everyone is here – Elsie, Kitty, Fanny and many other acquaintances' – the Duchess was miserable in Biarritz. She hated being so far from the war and starved of news; she wished she were back in Paris with the Duke. 'You must be having a terrible time glued to the radio and you probably know much more than I do,' she wrote to Aunt Bessie on 22 May.

> What I really want to do is to return to Paris as soon as possible – but one can't tell when that will be. Here it is as though one was in the US – except for the Belgian motors and the hospitals or hotels made into hospitals. The whole thing is too complicated to try so far to make heads or tails of what is happening and one doesn't dare talk – but how the rumours fly ! . . . When will one be normal again and we able to meet somewhere?

To add to her discomfiture, German wireless propaganda announced where she was staying and even gave her room number, making her 'the most unpopular guest in the long history of the Hôtel du Palais'.[10]

Back in Paris, the Duke continued to attend his Headquarters daily and follow the Allies' disintegrating fortunes, but there was maddeningly little for him to do. As the Duchess wrote to Aunt Bessie, '. . . his job ceased to exist the day the war really got started as it was to visit the French troops and they are hardly receiving at the moment.'[11] Though he had shown himself to be more prescient than most British generals in France, and was so liked by the French, he was not invited to participate in the crucial liaison conferences of this desperate time. The Panzers were now racing for the sea; nothing seemed able to stop them. As the trap closed around the BEF and French northern armies, Gamelin was sacked and replaced by the scarcely more competent but considerably less Anglophile Weygand. On 19 May – the day before Weygand took up his post at French GHQ and Guderian reached the sea near Abbéville – the Duke of Gloucester was winched out of Boulogne and flown back to England in advance of the retreating British Army.[12] Meanwhile the Duke of Windsor, whose Mission had been rendered virtually redundant by the arrival of General Spears as Churchill's personal representative, had received no instructions whatever concerning his safety or future. He was left to ponder sadly how accurate and far-sighted had been his unheeded warnings about France's military situation.

On Thursday 23 May the Duke called at the British Embassy and saw Sir Ronald Campbell.[13] He was sick of sitting uselessly in Paris, and wanted to go south where, leaving the Duchess at Antibes, he could carry out an inspection tour of the French forces drawn up along the Italian frontier. Italy was expected to declare war at any moment, and the Duke felt that the most useful job that remained to him in France was to help morale in that sector. He also wanted to find a safe hiding-place for his personal possessions at La Cröe, which included quantities of British royal souvenirs and his private archives. Both the Ambassador and Howard-Vyse (doubtless glad to get the Duke off their hands for the moment) agreed to this plan, and the Duke was temporarily seconded to the Armée des Alpes on 27 June – the day which saw the start of the Dunkirk evacuations. He set out to fetch the Duchess at Biarritz the following morning at dawn.

The Duke has been accused by his detractors of 'bolting' from Paris as soon as it was in danger, and of abandoning his post; but in fact, the capital seemed in less immediate danger when he left it on the 28th than when he had returned to it on the 18th. His destination was a corner of France which everyone believed would become a battle-front within a matter of days, and all evidence suggests that he originally intended to return to rejoin the Mission once the Duchess was safely installed at La Cröe and his southern tour of inspection completed. The Duchess refers to this intention in two of her letters. The Duke (very unusually for him) took no equerry, and told Gray Phillips to stay in Paris and expect him back within a few days; the house in the Boulevard Suchet remained running with its small staff of servants. At that moment Weygand was massing his divisions to hold the Germans on the Somme and the Aisne, Reynaud was proclaiming like Gambetta that they would fight in front of Paris and behind Paris, and it still seemed to many that the capital could resist occupation for some weeks[14]; as Harvey wrote as late as 4 June, 'the next *weeks* will decide'.

'The Duke now telephones he is arriving tomorrow and will motor me across to La Cröe *where I will again be left*,'* wrote the Duchess to Aunt Bessie from Biarritz. 'It will be much nicer for me to be in my own house as hotels are never restful for me. . . . I will wire when I arrive at La Cröe and will try and write often though there is nothing one can say except that morale is excellent.' She added in a postscript : 'We hope you in the US will hurry and send some planes etc. – we could use them.'

They reached La Cröe on the 29th, after another nightmare journey across France. 'The smell of catastrophe was in the air,' wrote the Duchess in her memoirs. 'It occurred to me that we were breasting a tide; all the traffic was headed in the direction we had left, towards the coast. We alone were pointed towards the Italian frontier.' Stopping at Aix-en-Provence to get something to eat, they were shocked to learn from an innkeeper that King Leopold had surrendered to the Germans.† The Duchess saw the Duke's face assume a hard obstinate look concealing deep emotions, a look she had only seen twice before – during the Abdication crisis and in England the previous September. 'This is the finish,' he said. 'Europe is lost. God, I wish there were something I could do. I feel so useless.'

He at once attached himself to the French Command at Nice. He reviewed troops and inspected defences, while the Duchess packed up part of the contents of the house, getting twelve cases off to a château near Aix. ('Whatever happens,' he said, 'I don't intend to let my ancestors' silver fall into Mussolini's possession.') 'The Duke is waiting here to see what Italy does *and then I suppose will return*,'* she wrote to Aunt Bessie on 4 June – the day after their third wedding anniversary, which they celebrated alone. 'The rest of the family that was in France – Gloucester – has been removed to the security of England.' She was glad to be back in her own house, 'even with all the mess about' and eating

* Author's italics.
† He had in fact capitulated on the 27th. He was the reigning monarch to whom the Duke had been closest.

with nickel knives and forks off enamel plates, though she found Antibes 'less tranquil than Biarritz' with the masses of troops and the black-out. In Paris some 'eggs' had fallen in Kitty de Rothschild's garden, only 300 yards from the boulevard Suchet; Gray Phillips whom they telephoned each day, was 'a little sour' as the electricity had been cut off and there was no ice for his drink. They had little war news apart from what they heard on the wireless. The Duchess concluded on a theme which haunted her that spring: 'It is divine but one has not the heart to enjoy the lovely weather or take any exercise when one thinks of the struggle in the north. . . . Don't worry darling – we have a great sense of self-preservation and hope for the best.'

The only civilians with whom they were in regular contact were four neighbouring villa-owners who had not yet taken flight – the singer Maurice Chevalier, a charming French couple called de Martel whose son had lost a leg in the battle, the Duchess's old friends Hermann and Kitty Rogers 'who I don't think could be bombed out of Lou Viei', and George and Rosa Wood. Captain George Wood was an old friend of the Duke; they had known each other in the army during the First World War, and during the 1930s when Wood had been at the Vienna Embassay during the Duke's several visits to Austria before, during and after his reign. Wood was rich, charming and clever, and had a beautiful Austrian wife. Their daughter had married Prince Ernst Hohenberg, son of the ill-fated Archduke Franz Ferdinand. The Hohenbergs had been seized by the Nazis in Vienna before the very eyes of the horrified Woods. Rosa Wood had never quite recovered from the experience and was desperate with anxiety for her daughter. The Duchess liked her and was deeply sorry for her, while the Duke listened gravely to Captain Wood's tales of Nazi evil and ruthlessness.

Meanwhile, the press had learnt of the presence of the Duke and Duchess in the South of France, and were indulging (since the censorship allowed them to repeat so little of the terrible war news) in much fanciful speculation about them. On 6 June various English and American newspapers reported that, according to 'informed sources' in London, the Duke had 'relinquished his post'. The Duke immediately and vigorously denied this to reporters at Nice; the story was 'wholly inaccurate'. On the 8th the Ministry of Information in London issued a statement: 'There is no foundation for the report that the Duke of Windsor has resigned his appointment. He is paying a visit to the French troops on the Italian border and will shortly return to the headquarters to which he is attached.'[15]

Those headquarters, however, were about to move; for after the miraculous news of the Dunkirk evacuations came the grim intelligence that the German armies were bursting through the Weygand Line and advancing on Paris. On the 9th the French Government fled from Paris to Tours. The same day the Howard-Vyse Mission left Vincennes with Weygand and established itself at the new French GHQ at Briare on the Loire. It was clearly out of the question now for the Duke to return to Paris, and Gray Phillips was instructed to lock up the house and get away at once – though he was only able to find a train to take him as far as Angers in the west.

The next day, 10 June, the Duke and Duchess were having lunch on the terrace at La Cröe with Maurice Chevalier, 'whom we had invited in the perhaps forlorn hope that he might be inspired to supply a flash of light-heartedness in that dismal atmosphere',[16] when the news came through on the wireless that Italy had declared war on France and England. Chevalier hurried off without finishing his lunch.* The following day the Duchess wrote Aunt Bessie a letter remarkable for its sang-froid:

> It really is becoming a most awful mess. We haven't decided what we will do exactly but will stay here for a few days anyway. You can imagine how difficult it is to make a real plan. I had just taken 2 Italian servants. . . . The Duke is with the army here for the moment but can do more or less as he likes. . . . France is having a tough time. I can't believe they will go for the Island – and I believe you will be in it before long. It is 'the old order changeth giving place to new' I am afraid. . . . The battle is supposed to start tonight here. The Duke thinks the defences in the Alps excellent. Everyone is calm and the gardeners (all Italian) are busy planting flowers for the summer. The sky is blue, the sea smooth – but the mind ruffled. . . . We have a trench, but I like the idea of the swimming pool as an abri. I hope this can get to you but since we are zone d'armée one can neither move nor breathe without much red tape.

Once again, the Duke had made an extraordinarily accurate assessment of the military situation. Having inspected the French positions, and remembering his own service with the Italian army in the winter of 1917–18, he concluded that there was no likelihood of the Italians breaking through – even though they faced six French divisions with thirty-two of their own. And indeed, when the Italians attacked on 11 June, the French line held everywhere. Even when, ten days later, Mussolini ordered a massive offensive in an extra effort to score a victory before the Armistice, it got nowhere; and Ciano wrote in his diary[17] that, had the Franco–Italian Armistice not come when it did on the 24th, the Italians would have been disastrously routed in the Alps.

Italy's entry into the war was accompanied by a mass exodus of Riviera residents; but no arrangements were made for the Duke and Duchess and for more than a week they remained where they were, confident at least that the Italian armies, though a mere twenty miles down the coast,

* According to Chevalier's memoirs, this incident took place on 1 September 1939.

would not break through.* The sudden arrival of the war on the Côte d'Azur was nevertheless dramatically apparent from La Cröe. The military airfield of Saint-Raphaël was nearby, and the sky full of planes; they seemed to form right over the villa, recalled the Duchess, as they wheeled off to bomb Italy. On 13 June the Italian Air Force retaliated by bombing the 'fort carré' at Antibes, apparently unaware that it was full of Italian internees. On the night of the 14th the thud of distant naval guns came across the water to the accompaniment of flashes on the horizon; it was the Anglo–French bombardment of Genoa, a sound the Duke 'understood and liked'.[18] But that day the Germans had entered Paris, and all France seemed at their mercy. The French Government moved from Tours to Bordeaux. Howard-Vyse had returned to England the day before with most of his staff – including Purvis and de Salis – leaving a skeleton Mission at Briare under Lieutenant-Colonel G. de Chair.

On 16 June, Pétain became Prime Minister of France and at once sued for an armistice. The Germans were now at Dijon and heading for the Rhone Valley; by the end of the month they might reach the south coast. That afternoon, the Duke managed to telephone the British Embassy encamped at Bordeaux to ask if he and the Duchess could be evacuated if necessary by the Royal Navy. He was told (with 'suave but firm politeness') that this was out of the question.[19]

Though the Duke and Duchess still refused to panic, the question of their leaving took on a new urgency over the next forty-eight hours. On the 17th Gray Phillips arrived at La Cröe after four terrible days hitch-hiking from Angers; he talked (as he fell upon food and drink) of the amazing chaos he had seen and the total collapse of French resistance. (This was the day of Pétain's 'il faut cesser le combat' broadcast, which caused most of France's remaining defenders to throw down their arms.) The next morning the Woods came round with the news that the Germans were approaching Lyons, barely 200 miles to the north. They were going to try to get away, and strongly urged the Duke and Duchess to join them; the consequences of falling into Nazi hands were too horrible to contemplate. The Duke agreed that the time had definitely come to leave.[20]

There were now only two potential escape-routes open to the Duke/Wood party – the sea passage to England (if they could get on a ship) and the overland journey into unfriendly but still neutral Spain (if they could get through). The Duke at once sought the advice of the British Consuls-General at Nice and Marseilles. Sir James Marjoribanks, who was then on the staff of the Marseilles Consulate-General, recalls that the

* For a fascinating account of the defence of the coast by General Montagne and the French XV Corps, see Max Gallo, *L'occupation italienne à Nice*, Plon 1967.

Duke was advised against attempting the sea voyage (all that was available were two ancient colliers in ballast, and priority had to be given to a thousand British troops), and urged instead to join Major Hugh Dodds, the Consul-General at Nice who, together with his colleague at Menton, Mr Dean, was about to evacuate his post and head for the Spanish frontier.[21] It was arranged that the consular convoy should pass by La Cröe the following day to pick up the ducal party. But the Consuls could not obtain visas for them, and there was a risk that they would not be admitted into Spain or even, once admitted, that the Duke might be arrested there as a serving member of the British forces on neutral soil. When de Chair, the Duke's acting commanding officer, telephoned from Bordeaux that afternoon (the 18th) to say that the rest of No. 1 Mission was embarking immediately for England, the Duke informed him of their plans and asked him to tell the Embassy (now also at Bordeaux) to arrange safe conducts for the party to cross the Spanish frontier.[22]

So at midday on 19 June, the Duke and Duchess set out for Spain with Gray Phillips, the Woods and the two Consuls. In her memoirs, the Duchess described their departure from La Cröe:

> The staff was grouped around the entrance to say goodbye. As I was about to enter the car, the gardener stepped forward to press into my arms a huge bunch of tuberoses. 'Your birthday present, darling,' David whispered. In the confusion I had forgotten the date. . . . I buried my face in the sweet-smelling mass, grateful for being able to take away with me at least this lovely reminder of La Cröe. Our staff wept as we left; and so did I.[23]

Italian planes were bombing Cannes as they passed through[24]; but after that all went well until they reached Arles, where they managed with difficulty to get rooms for the night. They set off again at dawn, hoping to reach the frontier by the afternoon. Barricades manned by veterans blocked the approaches to major towns, but the Duke, hoping they would remember him with affection from First World War days, managed to get through each time by announcing: *'Je suis le Prince de Galles. Laissez-moi passer, s'il vous plaît.'* Eventually the party arrived at Perpignan, where visas had to be obtained to cross the border ten miles away at Port Bou. Leaving the women at the hotel with Gray Phillips,* the Duke and Wood set out for the Spanish Consulate.

For some hours, they were treated like any ordinary refugees without papers. The safe conducts which the Duke had asked the British Embassy to arrange two days before had never materialized, and the Consul refused to let the party through on the grounds that the Duke might become a charge on the Spanish Government. The Duke waited

* They were evicted from the hotel in the course of the afternoon when it was requisitioned by the French Government, which planned to move there from Bordeaux in the event of the armistice talks breaking down.

and quietly remonstrated. There was a mildly comic episode when the Consul boldly asked if his royal applicant would sign his grandchild's autograph book. The Duke cheerfully replied that he would gladly exchange his own signature for the Consul's in their passports. The Consul was indignant, but the Duke signed all the same; 'Maybe the grandchild will put in a good word for us,' he said to the Duchess. Some hours later, 'only after much persuasion' as Dodds wrote in his report,[25] the Consul hesitantly agreed to issue visas to the Duke and Duchess alone. The Duke would not hear of this; it was to be all or none of them. Finally the whole party was allowed to pass, thanks to the belated intervention of Señor Lequerica, the Spanish Ambassador to France, to whom the Duke had managed with some difficulty to get through on the telephone.

They crossed the frontier around seven o'clock. At eight o'clock the British Ambassador in Madrid, Sir Samuel Hoare, telegraphed the Foreign Office to the effect that he had just been informed of their appearance in Spain, of which he had previously heard nothing.[26] After a long and rough journey with numerous mishaps, they arrived, after midnight, exhausted, at a hotel at Barcelona.[27]

Such were the circumstances in which the former King of England left France on the evening of Thursday 20 June, three weeks after Dunkirk and two days before the conclusion of the Franco–German armistice. He was the last member of his Mission and his family to quit French territory, and one of the last British generals to do so. Though the local British consular authorities had done their best to help him when flight became imperative, he had received no communication from London about his future and no instructions of any kind to return to England. The first sign of attention on London's part was a telegram sent by the Foreign Secretary Lord Halifax to the British Consulates-General at Nice, Marseilles and Bordeaux at 2 p.m. on 19 June – two hours after the ducal party had left Antibes for the Spanish frontier – asking if anyone knew of the Duke's whereabouts.[28] Otherwise, no interest was shown in the fate of the ex-King stranded with his wife in collapsing France. It was only days later that the Court and Cabinet were suddenly to realize the embarrassment of his being abandoned in disintegrating Europe, and the desirability of getting him away and giving him something to do.

It was a testing time. 'Precariousness was, of course, no stranger to me,' wrote the Duchess in her memoirs; but it was new to the Duke. 'On the whole, he adapted himself to this refugee interlude with far more resourcefulness and good humour than I might have expected from a person with no previous experience of this sort of adversity'[29] – though she was not impressed by his efforts to cope without a valet for the first time in his life. But they managed, without panic or complaining. 'You get to know people very well in the terrors and discomforts of such a trip,' Rosa Wood told Adela St Johns two months later, 'and they were – I cannot tell you how wonderful. Never a complaint, nothing but courage and trying to help others. . . .'[30]

The next morning (the 21st) the Duke went to the British Consulate-General in Barcelona and sent the following telegram to the Foreign Office for the attention of the Prime Minister:

> Having received no instructions have arrived in Spain to avoid capture. Proceeding to Madrid. Edward.[31]

The receipt of this wire threw the Foreign Office into an intense quandary. It happened that the British diplomatic and consular staffs in Italy had been temporarily evacuated to Barcelona, where the HMS *Monarch of Bermuda* was about to call to take them to England. Should the Duke and Duchess be invited to join this vessel and thus come home? H.L. Farquhar, having consulted Sir Walter Monckton, wrote in a memorandum that

> . . . the return of the Duke and Duchess to this country might raise certain complications. On the other hand if he were to remain in the Iberian Peninsula he might run a chance of being captured by the Germans and another set of equally awkward complications would arise. . . .[32]

No action was taken, because on the 21st it had not yet been decided in the highest quarters that the Duke and Duchess should return to England. So much is clear from the minutes of that afternoon's meeting of the War Cabinet. When Halifax drew attention 'to the fact that the Duke of Windsor was reported to have arrived in Barcelona', the Cabinet merely decided 'that His Majesty's Ambassador at Madrid should be instructed to get in touch with the Duke, to offer him hospitality and assistance, and to ascertain his wishes.'[33]

The decision was made the following day. Churchill telegraphed to Madrid in the morning that 'we should like Your Royal Highness to come home as soon as possible',[34] while the Foreign Office informed Sir Samuel Hoare in the afternoon that a flying-boat would be sent to Portugal to pick up the Duke and Duchess, and instructed:

> Please invite Their Royal Highnesses [sic] to proceed to Lisbon.[35]

The ducal party had left Barcelona that day (the 22nd), but not yet reached the capital. Held up by torrential storms, they spent a phantasmagoric night at Saragossa listening to the mixed strains of thunder, heavy rainfall, and the music and hubbub of the fiesta of the Virgin of La Pilar. They resumed their journey the next day, Midsummer Eve.

One must conclude that, between the 21st and the 22nd, the Palace gave their consent to the Duke's return. They did not do so enthusiastically; Farquhar was not wrong when he suggested that the Duke's return would be just as embarrassing in certain eyes as his capture by the enemy. On 24 June, Sir Alexander Hardinge, the King's Private Secretary, wrote an angry letter to W.I. Mallet of the Foreign Office[36] who was responsible for supplying him with copies of all telegrams going to Spain on the subject of the Duke. The King had noted with extreme displeasure (wrote Hardinge) that the Duke and Duchess had been referred to as 'Their Royal Highnesses'. This appellation was false and utterly impermissible.* His Majesty's express wish – that critical day which saw France's exit from the war – was that steps be taken to ensure that such an official error never occur again.

---

* The denial of royal status to the Duchess of Windsor, which has been the public policy of the Court since 1937, has an exceedingly doubtful basis in law and precedence. The immemorial custom that the sovereign's sons (and their sons) are automatically royal princes, and their wives automatically royal princesses, was confirmed in Victorian royal proclamations and officially restated on the occasion of every royal marriage prior to 1937. When, in 1936, King Edward VIII asked if he could marry Mrs Simpson morganatically (i.e. without her becoming Queen), the unanimous reply of the Government's legal and constitutional advisers was that such unequal unions were impossible under existing English law. Yet the Court subsequently regarded the Duke of Windsor's marriage as just an unequal union. Their argument was that, in abdicating, he had given up not only the throne but also his royal status, and that his successor had merely restored to him a limited form of royalty not transmissible to his wife or children. In 1938 the Duke asked a future Lord Chancellor for a legal opinion on the validity of this argument, and was assured that it was unlikely to stand up in law.

5

Spanish Interlude
June–July 1940

When the Duke and Duchess arrived in Madrid on the evening of Sunday 23 June – the Duke's forty-sixth birthday – Spain stood at the crossroads between peace and war. With the defeat of the French (who had signed their armistice the day before), the Falangist regime with its innate pro-Nazi sympathies abandoned all pretence of strict neutrality. On 12 June Spain had declared herself to be merely 'non-belligerent' – though her illegal seizure of the International Zone of Tangier two days later provided an ominous hint of belligerency. As the victorious German armies advanced towards the Pyrenees, the pro-war faction in Madrid, led by the Interior Minister Serrano Suñer, grew ever more powerful and vociferous. There had long been a huge network of German agents throughout Spain. Now, through the pro-Nazi Suñer, Berlin had virtual control of the Spanish police and official propaganda machine. Only two factors tenuously kept Spain out of the war for the time being – the ruined state of the country only a year after the end of the Civil War, hardly in a condition to fight for anything, and the unshakeable complacency of the dictator Franco, always unwilling to commit himself to the slightest decisive action.

Spain in the second half of June 1940 was an uncomfortable place for an Englishman. The pro-German tendencies of the Madrid regime were naked and endemic. Yet it was essential to England that Spain remain neutral at least to the extent of keeping the German Army out of the Peninsula. If the Wehrmacht occupied Spain and captured Gibraltar, Great Britain would lose control of the Straits – and hence of the Mediterranean, the Near East and her oil supplies. As both London and Berlin recognized these facts, Madrid became a desperate diplomatic battleground. The task of German diplomacy was to push Spain over the brink, that of British diplomacy to draw her back. Germany sought to make Suñer and his pro-war party supreme, Britain to encourage the non-interventionist elements (still strong in the Madrid Foreign Ministry) and the Spanish tendency to temporize. Above all, the Germans were out to persuade the Spaniards that Britain had no real will to carry on the fight and was all but finished, while the British had to counter this by offering proof of their country's power, confidence and determination. For there was little doubt that, if ever Franco could be made to believe that England was on the point of collapse, he would commit Spain with arms to the German cause.

The man who played this crucial game for England, and played it brilliantly, was the new British Ambassador Sir Samuel Hoare, who had arrived in Madrid barely three weeks before the Duke and had only had his first interview with Franco the day before. ('There was obviously more in him than met the eye, or how else could this young officer of Jewish origin, little influence and unimpressive personality have risen to the highest post in the State?'[1]) Hoare, though an accomplished departmental politician, had not cut a very prepossessing figure in British public life between the wars. His apparent stuffiness gave rise to the quip that he was 'descended from a long line of maiden aunts', while his reputation for evasiveness earned him the sobriquet 'Slippery Sam'. But it was these attributes, concealing shrewd and solid qualities and a first-rate brain, which made him an ideal choice for the Madrid Embassy once he had been dropped from the Government by his rival Churchill in May 1940. A straight-laced figure, and known to be one of the 'men of Munich', he was capable of putting across to Madrid's rulers that England represented no threat to 'the new Spain'. Yet at the same time he was a master of manoeuvre, quick to grasp the situation and see which quarters might be not unfriendly to England and supportive of what remained of Spanish neutrality. He lost no time in winning the confidence of Colonel Juan Beigbeder, the highly romantic Spanish Foreign Minister, whom he correctly guessed to be a secret admirer of England. 'The bull has just entered the ring,' Beigbeder remarked during one of his many private meetings with the Ambassador. 'Let's see how he fights!'

Hoare was only beginning to find his feet in his new post when, on the evening of 20 June, he was surprised to receive a telegram from which he learned that the Duke of Windsor had just crossed into Spain.[2] Curiously enough, these two men whose personalities could not have been more different happened to be old friends.[3] They had met in Italy during the First World War, and seen much of each other during the 1920s when Hoare was Air Minister and the Prince of Wales had a passion for aviation. In July 1936, Hoare (then First Lord of the Admiralty) was among the guests at the Royal dinner-party after which Mrs Simpson's name appeared for the first time without her husband's in the *Court Circular*; and four months later 'Sam' was one of the two members of the Cabinet (the other was Duff Cooper) that the King consulted during the Abdication crisis. But the ever-cautious and devoutly Anglo-Catholic

Hoare, however sympathetic, declined to support him either then or two years later when, as Home Secretary, he was asked by the Duke of Windsor to help solve the family difficulties which stood in the way of his return to England. They had met again in September 1939, and last seen each other only four months before when Hoare as a member of the War Cabinet visited the French front in February 1940.

In 1946, Hoare – by then raised to the peerage as Viscount Templewood – published a somewhat egotistical but fascinating account of his time in Madrid under the title *Ambassador on Special Mission*.[4] Naturally, there was a good deal he could not yet say about such recent events, and in particular he said nothing about the Duke of Windsor's nine days in the Spanish capital. However, ten years later he began a second book of Spanish reminiscences, *Spain in the Second World War*, in which he devoted a whole chapter to the Duke. This equally fascinating work was almost finished at the time of Templewood's death in 1958, but for some reason it was never published. Its typescript, however, may be found in Cambridge University Library among Templewood's political papers, which also contain his private correspondence of June and July 1940 on the subject of the Duke and Duchess.[5]

Both the chapter and the correspondence make one thing clear. Arriving on the board in the midst of the diplomatic game, the Duke became caught up, unwittingly but inevitably, in the Anglo–German struggle for Spain's future. The mere passive fact of the ex-King's presence on Spanish soil was capable of being exploited in numerous ways. German-controlled Spanish propaganda at once tried to spread the rumour that he had broken with the Churchill Government and was in Madrid to negotiate Britain's withdrawal from the war; Hoare had to show that there was no truth in these stories, and that the Duke was merely stopping in Madrid on his way home to help with his country's fight. The Germans wanted to use the Duke's numerous Spanish friends to persuade him to play 'a peace role'; Hoare had to protect the Duke from such influences, and wanted to use such friendships to spread pro-British feeling in Madrid. Above all, the Germans wanted to keep the Duke in Madrid for as long as possible, while Hoare sought to get him back to England as quickly as possible.

Hoare knew he could rely on the Duke's loyal cooperation and 'had great faith in his common sense and patriotism'.[6] But one thing made his task terribly difficult; even at this critical moment, the hostility towards the Duke on the part of the Court remained undiminished and bitter. They were not at all keen for him to come back. And to that extent German propaganda was right when it insinuated to the wavering Spaniards that England was disunited, and the Duke of Windsor out of tune with its rulers.

Hoare had three days to prepare for the arrival of the Duke and Duchess. He arranged for them to stay at the Madrid Ritz, where he himself had been staying up to a few days before. It was a hotbed of German espionage, and suicides and gun-battles were not uncommon in its lobby; but there was no other good hotel in Madrid, and the bare house Hoare had just rented could offer neither hospitality nor security, so to the Ritz they went. It was there that he called upon them on the Sunday evening of their arrival. Having just had a highly uncomfortable dinner in the hotel restaurant in full sight of the German Ambassador, they were delighted to see him; it was a long time since they had found themselves in the hands of an official whom they could regard as an old friend. 'Our meeting . . . came off very well,' wrote the Duchess in her memoirs, 'with the past scrupulously avoided by both parties.'[7]

Hoare proceeded to give them the first reliable news they had had about the war for some weeks. And it was appalling. France having signed an armistice the previous day, Great Britain was preparing for invasion. Her plight seemed desperate. The RAF was still much inferior in planes to the Luftwaffe, and the Army, though rescued at Dunkirk, had lost most of its equipment. With invasion impending at home, three nightmarish possibilities threatened abroad – an Italian attack on barely defended Egypt, a German seizure of the French fleet and colonial empire, and, last but not least, the dreadful possibility of Spain's entry into the war. Hoare himself later admitted that he had seen only one sign of hope at the time, the chance that if England somehow held out *for two years* she might come to possess air superiority over Germany.

What were the Duke's feelings on hearing this terrible news? There can be little doubt that he feared desperately for his country and felt the continuance of the war might only lead to further catastrophe. There can be few thinking Englishmen to whom such thoughts did not occur, however fleetingly, in late June 1940; and the Duke had far greater cause to think them than most. For he had spent almost all of the previous nine months in France, observing the French Army; apart from three very brief visits, he had not even been allowed to go near the British Army. And at Vincennes and the French front, after much intelligent observation, he had seen nothing which inspired him with the least optimism for the prospects of the Allies, even united and undefeated as they then were. On the contrary, what was tragically evident to him – as he had written to Philip Guedalla on 3 May – was the inferior will and organization of the Allies when compared to Nazi Germany; and in that gloomy assessment he had all too quickly been proved correct. In conversation with an American diplomat in Madrid on 25 June,[8] he expressed the view:

. . . that stories that the French troops would not fight were not true. They had fought magnificently, but the organization behind them was totally inadequate. In the past 10 years Germany had totally reorganized the order of its society in preparation for this war. Countries which were unwilling to accept such a reorganization of society and its concomitant sacrifices should direct their policies accordingly and thereby avoid dangerous adventures. . . .

Now that France had fallen, and England was facing the frightful situation which Hoare had described to him so graphically, the Duke could hardly be blamed for viewing England's chances with less than total optimism. At that black moment, even Lord Halifax and Mr R. A. Butler at the Foreign Office were (as we now know) seriously contemplating the possibility of mediating with Germany through Sweden. And the Duke, unlike them, was cut off from his country, and so unaware of 'the Dunkirk spirit', of the tremendous surge of defiance which was arising in England, of the lighting metamorphosis of the system into a powerful war dictatorship under the single-minded genius of Churchill. The British machine *was* altering itself to match the German machine, but of this he knew nothing. Though he knew that Churchill was determined to carry on the struggle, he had heard or read none of the stirring speeches in which this determination was being conveyed to the people.

Much of the Duke's mind was therefore filled with the desire for an end to an apparently hopeless struggle. And yet there can be little doubt of his personal admiration of Churchill, or that there was something in him which responded passionately to Churchill's cry that 'we shall defend our island, whatever the cost may be'. His realistic pessimism was tempered by a stubborn patriotic pride. When his Spanish friends and relations talked of the certainty of German victory, the Duke listened coldly and refused to accept that his country would be defeated. 'There's still the Channel to cross, remember that,' was his only reply to a vivid discourse on Nazi might by his cousin by marriage, the Infante Alfonso Maria. 'Hitler doesn't know Winston – and Winston will never give up.'[9]

However black their view of the situation, and whatever their private feelings and hopes, there was one thing which could be said both of the Duke of Windsor and Sir Samuel Hoare. So long as England survived and was determined to resist, they would serve and support their country's struggle with all their might. 'Even if the Duke felt that his influence might have averted war,' wrote Hoare, 'and that a world war was a horrible calamity, there could be no question of his embarrassing his King and country when once the war had started.'[10]

Nowhere was it more important for the Duke to be seen to be supporting the cause of Churchill's England than in Spain. German propaganda was trying hard to persuade the wavering Spaniards that the ex-King was hostile to that 'hopeless' cause. As Hoare wrote to Churchill on 27 June:

Before he [the Duke] arrived, every kind of rumour was spread by the German Embassy. Under the pressure of the German machine the Spanish press declared that you had ordered his arrest if he set foot in England, that he had come to make a separate peace behind your back, that he had always disapproved of the war and considered it an even greater mistake to go on with it, etc, etc. I did my best to ridicule these stories and since he has been here I have gone out of my way to show to Madrid that there is not a word of truth in them. I have had him constantly in and out of the Embassy and to luncheon and dinner. This has all meant a good deal of additional trouble when my hands are very full, but I think that it has been worthwhile. . . .[11]

The Duke for his part put himself entirely under Hoare's guidance and made it clear that he was the Ambassador's friend. He sought and followed Hoare's advice on all matters concerning public statements and the press. When American correspondents clamoured for a press conference, the Duke refused to see them in his spy-haunted room at the hotel, and instead held a conference for both British and American journalists at the Embassy, with the Ambassador in the chair.[12]

This took place on the afternoon of Tuesday the 25th.[13] He described their flight from France and how he had perceived early the chronic weaknesses of the French Army. He spoke of his conviction that England would survive and win, and of his eagerness to return home to help in the struggle. It was the correct and patriotic thing to say, and he said it. But the conviction was one he did not entirely feel; and his eagerness to return, though undoubted, was qualified by very complex circumstances.

When Hoare met the Duke and Duchess at the Ritz on Sunday evening he had shown them the telegrams (despatched only the previous day) which revealed to them for the first time that they had officially been asked to come home, and with all speed. Further, he was able to inform them that they were to be fetched from Lisbon by flying boat, and that the Duke of Westminster's house near Chester, Eaton Hall, would be placed at their disposal as a residence. Why, then, did they not set out for Lisbon the following day? Why did they stay for all of nine days in Madrid – in spite of the generally unfriendly atmosphere in Spain, and the evident determination of the enemy to make mischief over the Duke's presence? The answer is given very neatly in a telegram sent by Hoare to Churchill on Monday the 24th, the day after the Duke's arrival. 'He is ready to leave Madrid', writes Hoare, 'provided his stay in Lisbon does not overlap with the Duke of Kent's.'[14]

For it so happened that, on that same 24 June, the Duke of Windsor's youngest and favourite brother, Prince George Duke of Kent, arrived in Lisbon as head of the British delegation to the week-long celebrations commemorating the 800th anniversary of Portuguese independence.[15] This visit was of great importance. It was a gesture on the part of both

London and Lisbon to show that the ancient friendship of England and Portugal had not been unduly affected by the critical war situation. It meant a great deal to the Anglophile (but strictly neutralist) dictator Salazar, who was concerned that the thunder should not be stolen from the Duke of Kent's official presence by the sudden unofficial appearance of the Duke of Windsor. On the 21st Salazar had written to the Portuguese Ambassador in London:

> I received today the British Ambassador, who had expressed a desire to see me before the arrival of the Duke of Kent's mission. In the course of our conversation on this subject the current rumour was mentioned of the possible arrival in Lisbon of the Duke of Windsor, who at the moment is in Barcelona. I indicated to Selby that the presence of the Duke of Windsor at the same time as that of the Duke of Kent would be inconvenient and undesirable for several reasons. . . . If the Duke of Windsor does come while his brother is here, I shall let him know by all means that we should be grateful if he retired for that period to another part of the country. With regard to the Duke of Kent, I told Selby how pleased we were that the mission should be headed by His Highness, and how well we understood its high significance. . . .[16]

There can be no doubt that the Duke of Windsor longed to see again the brother he loved and had not seen for three years. There is equally no doubt that he was prepared to do nothing that might interfere with or detract from the Duke of Kent's task in Portugal. Since it was obviously out of the question that he should go to Portugal while his brother was there without seeing him, he resolved not to set foot on Portuguese territory until his brother had left. The Duke of Kent was due to leave Lisbon on Tuesday 2 July; and that was the day the Duke of Windsor planned to (and did) leave Madrid.

If the matter of the Duke of Kent was the delaying factor in the Duke's journey from Spain to Portugal, it was not the only obstacle in the way of his return to England.

The Duke remembered with pain his return to England in September 1939. On that occasion he had been motivated entirely by two ideas, service to his country and reconciliation with his family. On both counts, he had been spurned, and ever since he had been kept down and denied the chance to serve his country well. For any success or kudos he achieved he had paid dearly. The Duke would not have been human if he had failed to be emotionally affected in some way by this experience. As he wrote some time later to his brother the King, 'ever since I returned to England in 1939 to offer my services and you continued to persecute me and then frustrate my modest efforts to serve you and my country in war, I must frankly admit that I have become very bitter indeed.'*

* See p. 296.

Now, once again, the Duke was allowed to come home. The fact that the decision had been taken belatedly and reluctantly, that it had so obviously been forced on an unwilling Palace by the catastrophic turn of the war, only served to emphasize that he could expect no better treatment than before. All he knew about the future was that a house had been found for him a convenient 200 miles from London. But one thing led him to hope that things might be better now. Churchill was in charge – Churchill who had been his friend and supporter during the Abdication crisis, who had welcomed him warmly in September 1939 and January 1940 and praised his desire for real service. Surely Churchill would persuade his family to come to terms with him and the Duchess, and give him work worthy of his training, if not status worthy of a prince? What the Duke did not know was that the Court and Royal Family had been opposed to Churchill as Prime Minister, preferring Halifax; and Churchill now depended upon the support of his former opponents – and none more than the King.

Since the Duke could not return home for at least ten days on account of the Kent Mission in Portugal, he took advantage of the opportunity to ask certain questions. On 24 June he sent Churchill the first of a series of long telegrams. There were two things he wanted to know. Would he be given a post in England? And would his family give some recognition, however nominal, to the Duchess? The Duke discussed the telegram with Hoare, who fully backed him up on the matter of the post. 'The Duke of Windsor is most anxious to have a reply to his personal wire before leaving here,' Hoare telegraphed Churchill the same day. 'He does not want to appear to be returning as a refugee with nothing to do. I hope you can help him with a friendly answer as soon as possible.' Churchill's reply the following day was laconic and avoided all questions. 'It will be better for Your Royal Highness to come to England as arranged, when everything can be considered.'[17]

What happened now is well known. The Duke responded on the 26th that, before coming home, he wanted to be assured that he would be given a war job of some consequence in which there would be recognized status for his wife. Churchill was unable to give this assurance. For two days – days indeed which were critical to the future of England – the Prime Minister and the ex-King conducted a fierce argument by telegram. Churchill begged the Duke to come back without conditions, and not to argue about matters which could be settled later. The Duke unyieldingly declared that he would not return to England unless his condition was met, though he was willing to serve anywhere overseas in the British Empire.[18]

Much has been written about the rights and wrongs of the Duke's ultimatum, and the emotions which inspired it. Any examination must begin with the accounts which the Duke and Duchess themselves have given of the episode. This is what the Duchess wrote in her memoirs in 1956:

What followed now seems fantastic and even a little silly. But David's pride was engaged, and he was deadly serious. When, after some time, he felt it necessary to tell me what was going on, he put the situation in approximately these terms: 'I won't have them push us into a bottom drawer. It must be the two of us together – man and wife with the same position. Now, I am only too well aware of the risk of my being misunderstood in pressing for this at such a time. Some people will probably say that, with a war on, these trifles should be forgotten. But they are not trifles to me. Whatever I am to be I must be with you; any position I am called upon to fill I can only fill with you.'

It was characteristic of him to hold such a view. It is one of the reasons why I know that he is a finer person than I can ever hope to be. But his stubbornness worried me as it had worried me on earlier occasions.

I tried as hard as I could to make him see the matter in another light: the importance above everything else of his not allowing his gallantry towards me to interfere with his returning to England in a war job. The question of my position as his wife, I said, could be dealt with later, if it had to be dealt with at all. But, as on more than one earlier occasion in our association, David turned a deaf ear to my argument. And in truth, all that he ever specifically asked for was a fairly simple thing: that I be received, just once, by the King, his brother, and the Queen, in order to erase by that single gesture of hospitality the stigma attaching to my never having been received since our marriage by the Royal Family, his family.

For me to suggest that I did not desire that recognition would be hypocritical. I felt almost as much as did David that I deserved it. But not, however, from a mere desire for social status. Rather, I wanted it for the reason that I dreaded being condemned to go through the rest of our lives together as the woman who had come between David and his family. Yet I felt, deep in my conscience, that it was scarcely seemly for us to make an issue of so private a matter when the rest of Britain was fighting for its life; and, while David agreed that it was undoubtedly a poor time to stand on a point of pride, he nevertheless insisted that it was also a time when old quarrels should be put aside and by a single action be buried for ever. Therefore he would not yield.[19]

In 1966, the Duke wrote:

. . . His [Churchill's] personal advice to me was not to quibble about terms, but to come home and wait patiently while he 'worked things out'. But I could not in honour take this line. The year before, while we had been in England, the presence of the Duchess at my side had never been acknowledged, even perfunctorily. Before going back I wanted an assurance that simple courtesies would be forthcoming. Winston could not manage this. From a distance, what I insisted on may look to be of small value. But the perspectives of my life had changed, and the matter loomed mighty large for me.[20]

However, the Duke subsequently admitted to friends, and even in certain interviews, that, looking back, he considered his insistence under the circumstances to have been mistaken.

How one judges these actions and motives must naturally be a personal matter. In the eyes of the Duke's harshest critics, his attitude amounts almost to blackmail and treason, as well as causing a criminal waste of the premier's time at a moment when he had little to spare. But one thing must not be forgotten. If the Duke was persistent and obstinate in laying down his condition, the Palace was equally persistent and obstinate in turning it down. And the condition was not onerous. The Duke asked for no specific privileges for himself, and the merest gesture towards his wife. He did not raise the subject of the Duchess's royalty. If he was unreasonable in advancing such a limited request, it is hard to avoid the view that the Court was unreasonable in refusing it. Intransigence is a two-edged sword.

One man who believed at the time that both sides were being thoroughly unreasonable, and that it was essential for them to come to terms, was Sir Samuel Hoare. Nothing better illustrates the fairness and sagacity of this remarkable and much-maligned figure than his attitude towards the telegraphic battle which took place beneath his Embassy roof between 26 and 28 June. On the 24th, he had supported the Duke's desire to be guaranteed a job. 'He does not want to appear to be returning as a refugee with nothing to do.' On the 26th–27th he wrote to Halifax, Churchill and Beaverbrook vigorously urging a post for the Duke. 'I am certain that somehow or other Winston must find him a job,' he wrote to Halifax. 'I know how difficult this is. Nevertheless I feel that there will be a great deal of trouble unless he does.'[21] If all else failed with the Palace, Hoare suggested a naval command of some kind. 'He still loves the sea better than anything else.' But if Hoare believed that it was perfectly legitimate for the Duke to wish to be assured of work, he thought it pure folly for him to lay down any condition regarding recognition of the Duchess. He wrote to Churchill that he had argued with the Duke for hours on end that this was not the moment for bargaining over such details. The Duke had replied that he agreed – provided both sides in the controversy behaved in the same way.[22]

It was not just what he saw as the relative merits of Duke and Palace which concerned Hoare. He considered the mere fact of continuing enmity to be a national danger. The existence of division and bitterness in Britain's Royal Family would have been a liability to the country at the best of times. In war it was dangerous, and under the prevailing circumstances it threatened to be very dangerous indeed. For England, it was a moment when unity (and the appearance of unity) was all. It was madness for the Royal Family to continue to cast the Duke and Duchess out into the cold, and equal madness for the Duke to stand upon his pride and make conditions for return. 'I do feel strongly that this is the moment to get them both back to England and to clear up the situation,' Hoare wrote to Churchill.[23] What worried him most of all was that the Germans would get to hear of it. Hoare did not imagine that the Duke's estrangement from his family would affect his patriotic feelings towards his country. But there was no telling what diabolical plot the Germans, with their habitual ignorance of the British mentality, might not hatch to exploit the quarrel to ensnare the Duke, or to persuade the Spaniards that England was a house divided against herself and therefore doomed.

It was only seventeen years later, when the German Foreign Office documents were made public[24] and the memoirs of the German spy chief Walter Schellenberg published,[25] that Lord Templewood was to realize just how justified his fears and suspicions had been.

It is not intended to give a detailed account here of the German plot against the Duke in late June and July 1940, such as Templewood gives in his *Spain in the Second World War*. This will be dealt with in a future publication based on the Duke's archives. What has been frequently misunderstood is the aim of the plot as revealed by Schellenberg and the German documents. Its object was not to get the Duke to 'change sides', or to use him as a quisling – though there was a vague idea of tempting him with an offer of restoration to the throne. The Germans did not imagine he would simply 'turn traitor', but they thought he might be persuaded or tricked – or if necessary forced – into serving German ends and putting himself under German control. Their purpose was to use him as an instrument to further England's collapse by attributing 'peace' statements to him which might cause confusion in his country and weaken its resistance, and using him if need be as an eventual hostage. German intelligence knew that he had always considered the war a tragedy, and they also knew (as Hoare feared) about the deepening rift with his family. The plot rested on the assumption that, given the war situation, these two circumstances would suffice (with a certain amount of subtle encouragement) to incline the Duke against returning to England and to induce in him the appropriate mood of uncertainty and disillusionment. As a first step it was hoped to persuade him to 'retire' from the service of wartime England and take up permanent residence in 'neutral' Spain. Installed there under German eyes, he might be cajoled into disassociating himself publicly from the Churchill Government and England's continuing struggle, and hence into proposing peace solutions. If he refused to co-operate at any stage, the plan was to abduct him and the Duchess by force.

The plot was launched even before the Duke's arrival in Madrid. The German Ambassador telegraphed Berlin on the 23rd reporting that they were expected that day, and wondering if 'we might be interested in keeping the Duke of Windsor here and eventually getting into communication with him'. Ribbentrop replied: 'It is possible to keep the Duke and Duchess of Windsor in Spain for at least some weeks before granting them a further exit visa?'[26] At the same time, through the offices of Serrano Suñer, the Spanish press began to spread the rumours that the Duke was coming to make peace and had broken with Churchill and the British Government.

The Duke had failed to rise to the bait, categorically denying these rumours and putting himself under the wing of the British Ambassador. At the same time he did not have the faintest inkling of a plot. As he wrote to Templewood on 14 August 1957, in a letter relating his utter astonishment at the German documents which had just been published:

> Although we were conscious of considerable anti-British feeling in Madrid in June 1940, little did we suspect that we were the innocent targets of sinister Nazi intrigue. . . . We will always be grateful for the advice and guidance you gave us at that difficult and dangerous, if exciting, time.[27]

Of course, the Duke and Duchess did not actually meet (so far as is known) a single German during the summer of 1940. Nazi intelligence did not seek to approach and influence them openly and directly, but very subtly and indirectly, through Spanish connections.

For the Duke had many Spanish friends and relations. He loved and understood the Spaniards in a way he never did the French. He was closely related to the Spanish Royal Family; Queen Victoria's granddaughter Victoria Eugénie of Battenberg – 'Ena' – had married the deposed King Alfonso XIII, whose cousin, the Infante Alfonso Maria, had married another Victorian grand-daughter. The Duke had visited Spain on several occasions before the overthrow of the monarchy in 1931, and had been very popular there. He had numerous Spanish friends, particularly in diplomatic circles and among such conservative noble families as the Romanones and Primo de Rivera. He spoke fluent Spanish, having picked it up on his South American tours. The Duchess too had some Spanish associations: she had once been much in love with a member of the Spanish Embassy in Washington, Felipe Espil; and a sometime member of the Spanish Embassy in London, Javier 'Tiger' Bermejillo, had been a friend both of Ernest Simpson and the Prince of Wales. Both Espil and Bermejillo were now high officials of the Madrid Foreign Ministry. Bermejillo and Miguel Primo de Rivera were the principal (and possibly subconscious) agents upon whom the Germans and their Spanish stooges relied in the plot – and they were to play their parts with (perhaps deliberate) maladroitness.

Hoare 'neither wished nor was able to prevent [the Duke] from renewing his old friendships or making new ones'[28]; and the Duke and Duchess saw many Spaniards socially during their nine days in Madrid. A number of these certainly encouraged the ex-King to stay on in Spain, to play a role for peace, to recognize that England was finished. Given the mood of Spain and the position of England at that moment, such suggestions would have sprung fairly naturally from the most Anglophile and well-intentioned Spanish lips; but a few of the hopeful persuaders had been primed in some more or less direct manner (for all Spaniards went in fear of Serrano Suñer). The Spanish Government showed its hand more directly when, through Primo de Rivera, it generously offered to provide the Duke with a permanent residence (the Caliph's Palace in Ronda) if he chose to stay.

It would be idle to pretend that all these suggestions made no psychological impression on the Duke and Duchess. They certainly shared no certainty that England would be victorious, and there must have been moments when they thought wistfully of the dream of escaping from the nightmare of dying Europe to the peace of some remote and romantic Spanish castle. But the Duke was always alive to the dangers of indiscretion; he wore the loyal mask, and if it slipped occasionally, it never slipped dangerously. He consulted Hoare constantly, and heeded his warnings about what he should not say and whom he should not see. But if he did not allow himself to be unduly influenced by his Spanish friends, he himself had an undoubted influence on them. Overnight, he recovered his old popularity. His presence put heart into Spanish monarchists, reminding them that their Pretender too was a great-grandson of Queen Victoria. In a matter of days, all Madrid was mildly in love with the former King of England. Curious groups gathered round him in the street. At a moment when England's stock in Spain seemed about to be wiped out, he was his country's best possible advertisement. The fact that his country's plight tortured him with uncertainties made a deep impression on the emotional Spaniards, such as a front of confident bombastic loyalism could never have done. With the Duke's arrival in Madrid came a sudden gust of long-forgotten Anglophilia. It came just in time; for England's critical moment in the Peninsula had arrived.

The historic event which British diplomacy had been dreading occurred on Thursday 27 June. Sweeping down from the French Atlantic coast, the German Army reached the Pyrenees. Would it stop there? As Hoare wrote to Halifax:

Will it mean the passage of German troops through Spain to Portugal or Africa? Will it mean even more, and bring about the German occupation of strategic points in Spain and the setting up of a puppet goverment in German hands? Will it mean, at least for the time being, a continuance of the present precarious position of non-belligerency with constant German pressure, but with no overt act of German domination? I can no more answer these questions than you can answer the bigger questions about the future of the Empire and the world. . . .[29]

At the same moment, the propaganda machine started up again on the subject of the Duke and peace. 'Spanish Press is circulating German propaganda of peace negotiations being carried on by Duke of Windsor and myself,' wrote Hoare in an urgent telegram to the Foreign Office. 'It is important to deny them on the radio and in the press as vigorously as possible.'[30]

On Saturday the 29th, an anxious Hoare gave a great party at the Embassy for the Duke and Duchess, to which was invited practically everyone in Madrid who knew them or whose influence might be useful in helping to keep Spain out of the war, including the Foreign Minister Beigbeder. Almost a thousand people came. 'The Duke and Duchess rose in every way to the occasion,' wrote Hoare in his memoirs.[31] 'They could not have been more helpful to Lady Templewood and me. So far from making any defeatist remarks, they went out of their way to show their belief in final victory.' The party was the talk of Madrid. There was to be nothing like it again for over three years. For nothing short of the presence of the Duke and Duchess of Windsor could have persuaded the cream of the Spanish nobility and a sizeable part of Madrid's official world to congregate in the British Embassy at a time when Britain was despised by the Falangist regime and appeared to be close to defeat.

The following day marked the crisis of Hoare's ambassadorship and of all British wartime diplomacy in Spain. At the invitation of the local Spanish commander, a detachment of German troops crossed the frontier and paraded itself in San Sebastian. 'Fraternal' visits by the German Army to other Spanish towns were simultaneously announced. It looked like the start of the German military occupation of the Peninsula. With great difficulty (for it was a Sunday in midsummer), Hoare managed to get hold of the Foreign Minister and his staff – men who included the Duke's friends, who had been at the Embassy the evening before. That night, the cross-border troop movements were stopped, and the commander who had authorized them was sacked. Spain's non-belligerency was preserved by a hair's breadth.[32]

On Monday 1 July, just after the resolution of this crisis, Hoare wrote to Halifax that the Duke and Duchess would be leaving for Lisbon the following day.[33] They had, he said,

behaved admirably during their stay here. They have made themselves extremely popular with the many Spaniards whom they have met and apart from the family row in which once again I have been unwillingly involved, they have been both easy and affable. We have seen a good deal of them, having them to dinner and luncheon and at a big party we gave at the Embassy . . . the biggest cocktail party that there has been for years. . . . Several hundred came and it was generally adjudged to be a great success. You can imagine what a trouble it is to have this kind of thing on one's back when the world is crashing. I think, however, that it can be said that we have already created a great body of good will here that may stand us in good stead if real trouble comes. . . .

The obliging Beigbeder, who had just chased the Germans out of Spain, did everything to facilitate the journey of the ducal party to Portugal. Indeed, the Duke and Hoare can hardly have realized what a good friend they had in the Spanish Foreign Minister. To the German Embassy, who had requested him to keep the Duke in Spain even if it meant denying him an exit visa, Beigbeder gave the false report that the Duke and Duchess would soon be back in Madrid and had only gone to Lisbon to see the Duke of Kent (who had already left for England!).[34]

And so on 2 July Hoare telegraphed to announce their departure to the Foreign Office. 'Their visit has stimulated German propaganda but otherwise it has done good in extending our personal contacts. They have both been very discreet and have made a good impression on the Spaniards. They took my advice on several points, e.g. interview with press.'[35] But he added in a simultaneous telegram (i.e. not for the file) that he did not think they would return to England without further assurances.[36] And once again he pleaded with Churchill to get the Duke a job and come to some general accommodation with him. A gesture had to be made to end the family row, and if it was not ended soon it would become deep and dangerous.[37]

On Tuesday 2 July – nine days after their arrival in Madrid and the day the Duke of Kent returned to London from Lisbon – the Duke and Duchess of Windsor, still accompanied by Gray Phillips and the Woods, set out by car for Portugal. Having stopped on the way to see the ruins of Toledo, they spent the night as guests of the Spanish Government at Mérida and reached the border the following morning. They were met there by Neil Hogg, the Second Secretary of the British Embassy at Lisbon and a son of Lord Hailsham who had been Lord Chancellor at the time of the Abdication crisis. Hogg recalls:

I met the Ducal party at the Badajoz/Elvas frontier on a blazing day in July. . . . Both posts had been informed in advance that the Duke would be coming, so the formalities were brief; even so, I was left at the Spanish post to tie up loose ends, while the party went on towards Lisbon in two cars and a trailer. As they did not know their way, they went right into the fortified town of Elvas instead of round it, and found themselves unable to turn in the narrow streets. They were quickly recognized by the enthusiastically pro-British inhabitants, who manhandled the cars into the right direction and showered the party with boxes and boxes of the preserved fruits for which the region is famous. When I caught up with them, I found them facing the right way, astonished, gratified and somewhat bewildered.

I had arranged for lunch at the country house of an old-established English family in the neighbourhood of Vila Viçosa, but they would have nothing of it. Instead we picnicked under a cork oak in the middle of the burning Alentejo plain known to the Portuguese as Africa. There we sat, eating sardines from the tin with our fingers and making the kind of conversation that you hear at Embassy luncheons. You could not have guessed that Europe was falling in ruins at the time. . . . Fortunately, to my utter astonishment, there proved to be a copious spring nearby; this, in a notoriously waterless region, still seems to me nothing short of a miracle. To his great credit, the Duke insisted on washing his dogs himself.

The onward journey to Lisbon was uneventful. I conducted the party to a fine house outside the city, that had been made available by the well-known banking family of Espiritu Santo, and withdrew to my office.[38]

There was nothing secret about their arrival, which was front page news in the official newspaper *O Jornal do Comércio*. But no unpleasant official propaganda was weaved about them, as in Spain. They breathed a different air in Portugal. Though the German secret services were active there, the popular feeling was strongly pro-British; the dictator Salazar too was a profound secret admirer of England. As David Eccles, a young British agent then in Lisbon, wrote to a friend at the Foreign Office in June 1940:

> You ought to know that something extraordinary and unforgettable is happening here. Dr Salazar has made up his mind that, whether we are victorious or defeated, Portugal shall stand by England. He has dropped all show of neutrality. The more difficult the allied position becomes, the more resolutely he supports our cause.[39]

The highly successful visit of the Duke of Kent had reinforced pro-British feeling in the country. The extended unofficial stay of the Duke and Duchess of Windsor was to do the same.

The accommodation which had been obtained for them was the villa of the banker Dr Ricardo de Espiritu Santo e Silva, a friend of the Duke of Kent, a man with connections both in London and Berlin and well known to British Intelligence as 'Mr Holy Ghost'. It was situated at Cascais, a fashionable fishing village some miles west of Lisbon. It was there that the British Ambassador to Portugal, Sir Walford Selby, greeted them on their arrival on the evening of 3 July.[40]

Once again, the Duke found himself under the wing of an old friend. They had got to know each other well in the 1930s, when Selby was Minister to Vienna and Edward had made that series of visits which (as Selby later attested in his memoirs) were a factor in relieving German pressure on Austria.[41] George Wood had also been a member of Selby's Legation staff in Vienna, so that the meeting at Cascais was something of a reunion. But there was a note of urgency about the occasion. Two flying-boats of RAF Coastal Command had arrived in Lisbon to take the party back to England; they were due to return within the next forty-eight hours.* The greetings over, the Duke and Selby disappeared for private discussion.

It is important to establish as precisely as possible what happened at this point. Unfortunately the only published memoir – which is that of the Duchess – is not very accurate, and does less than justice to the Duke.[42] Writing of those hectic days fifteen years later, without notes or witnesses to correct her memory, the Duchess can hardly be blamed for getting events in the wrong order. There is one thing she writes, however, which is probably correct, and which would go some way towards explaining the inaccuracy of the rest. She says that the Duke never actually repeated to her his private conversation with Selby, and that she was not 'fully in the picture' at the time; it was only 'after some time' (she says) that the Duke actually told her 'what was going on', presumably showing her the telegrams.† If this is accepted, it becomes clear that the Duchess is not speaking as a first-hand witness when she suggests:

(1) that, having arrived in Cascais on 3 July, the Duke persisted in his attitude (of which she was not yet fully aware) that he would not return unless his condition was met;
(2) that there 'began a day and two nights of what must have been one of the oddest and least satisfactory exchanges in the history of the British monarchy, with Winston firing away from 10 Downing Street, in the midst of his other distractions, and David countering from Cascais';
(3) that, the Duke's demands still being refused, he resolutely declined to return, but repeated his offer to serve anywhere in the Empire;
(4) that 'he requested Sir Walford to have the flying-boats sent home immediately'.

None of these statements appears to be quite correct. What the Duchess almost certainly had in mind were events which had in fact taken place the previous week in Madrid, when the Duke was having traumatic interviews on the subject of his return not with Selby but with Hoare. The really frantic exchange of telegrams with Churchill had taken place from 26–28 June, and that is probably the 'unsatisfactory exchange' lasting 'a day and two nights' to which the Duchess refers. Certainly,

* Selby was accompanied by two men whom the Duchess imagined to be the captains of the flying boats, but who were in fact members of the Embassy.

† The Duchess certainly appears to have had no doubts at first that they would be returning to England. On 30 June she told Alexander Weddell, the US Ambassador to Madrid, that they would be leaving for Lisbon on 2 July and flying at once from there to London.

after their arrival in Portugal, the Duke did not engage in a thirty-six hour communications battle with London. Things were to happen much more quickly than that.

What, then, did the Duke and Selby talk about that evening of 3 July? The details of their private conversation may never be known; but two important facts about it are revealed by the sources. First, Selby handed the Duke an extraordinary telegram from Churchill dated 1 July, which had been addressed to him in Madrid but just missed him there and been sent on to Lisbon.[43] In this telegram Churchill insisted that the Duke return to England immediately without conditions, and hoped it would not be necessary to send military orders forcing him to come home on pain of court martial. This message distressed the Duke terribly. As he wrote to Churchill the following October:*

> I used to have your support until you reached the supreme power of PM since when you seem to have subscribed to the Court's hostile attitude towards me. Due to the negligence of both our military and diplomatic authorities in France I got lost in the shuffle of war and, left to my own devices to avoid capture by the enemy, I duly informed you when I had reached a neutral country. You thereupon summoned me back to England, and when I felt bound in my own interests to make my compliance with this summons contingent upon a simple and fair request which my brother evidently turned down, you threatened me with what amounted to arrest, thus descending to dictator methods in your treatment of your old friend and former King. . . .

The second fact which is known is that the Air Ministry in London received a message from Lisbon the following morning to say that the Duke would after all be leaving by air that night for London. In other words, it would appear that Churchill's 'court martial' telegram, distressing as it was, did succeed in resigning the Duke to an immediate return without conditions. Realizing that his requests, however fair, were hopeless, he gave in.

That message, however, crossed with another telegram from Churchill,† which the Duke received when he went to the British Embassy on the morning of Thursday the 4th.[44]

> I am authorized by the King and Cabinet to offer you the appointment of Governor and Commander-in-Chief of the Bahamas. If you accept, it may be possible to take you and the Duchess there direct from Lisbon dependent on the military situation. Please let me know without delay whether this proposal is satisfactory to Your Royal Highness. Personally I feel sure that it is the best

---

* For the rest of this letter and the circumstances in which it was written, see pp. 144–8. The Duke's typed draft is corrected in both his hand and the Duchess's; the Duke originally wrote 'gangster methods' which the Duchess changed to 'dictator methods'.

† The Foreign Office copy of the telegram contains the following hand-written note: 'A message has just been received by the Air Ministry to the effect that the Duke will leave Lisbon tonight by air for England. The above telegram may, possibly, affect his decision.'

open in the grievous situation in which we all stand. At any rate I have done my best.

The Duke immediately telegraphed back:

I will accept appointment as Governor of the Bahamas as I am sure you have done your best for me in a difficult situation.

To which Churchill replied:

I am very glad Your Royal Highness has accepted the appointment where I am sure useful service can be rendered to the Empire at the present time. . . . Sincere good wishes.

One must pay close attention to the chronology, which gives the lie to so many stories. On 2 July they left Madrid; on the evening of the 3rd they reached Cascais; on the morning of the 4th the Duke both received and accepted the offer of the Bahamas.

To the Duchess, the Duke said:

Governor of the Colony of the Bahamas – one of the few parts of the Empire I missed on my travels. It's a small governorship and three thousand miles from the war. Well, Winston said he was sorry, but it was the best he could do, and I shall keep my side of the bargain.[45]

To President Roosevelt, Churchill wrote:

The position of the Duke of Windsor in recent months has been causing His Majesty and His Majesty's Government some embarrassment as though his loyalties are unimpeachable there is always a backwash of Nazi intrigue which seeks to make trouble about him now that the greater part of the continent is in enemy hands. There are personal and family difficulties about his return to this country. In all the circumstances it was felt that an appointment abroad might appeal to him, and the Prime Minister has with His Majesty's cordial approval offered him the Governorship of the Bahamas. His Royal Highness has intimated that he will accept the appointment.[46]

To Sir Samuel Hoare, Lord Halifax wrote:

I dare say it is quite a good plan that they should go to the Bahamas, but I am sorry for the Bahamas. . . .[47]

To Aunt Bessie, the Duchess wrote:

The St Helena of 1940 I hear is a nice spot. At least the British have got the Duke as far as possible. We refused to return to England except under our own terms, as the Duke is quite useless to the country if he was to receive the same treatment as when he returned to offer his services wholeheartedly in Sept only to suffer one humiliation after another. Once bitten twice shy, and they would guarantee him no different treatment – so he asked for something out of England and he got it ! . . . Can you fancy a family continuing a feud when the very Empire is threatened and not putting every available man in a spot where he would be most useful ? Could anything be so small and hideous ? What will happen to a country which allows such behaviour ?[48]

6

Leaving Europe

July–August 1940

Why had the Bahamas been chosen?

The appointment was unprecedented and utterly extraordinary. It must be stressed that the Duke of Windsor is the only member of the British Royal Family ever to have served as Governor of a Crown Colony. Such a post would normally be unthinkable for royalty, who are brought up (especially if born to be King) to avoid all political responsibility and all controversy, and who at that time did not expect to be criticized in public and certainly not to have to reply to criticism. A colonial governor (before responsible colonial government began to be introduced in the 1950s) was not just the King's representative in an overseas territory; he was the chief political executive responsible for all administration. There was nothing remote, neutral and protected about his position. He *was* the Government (and as such constantly exposed to local criticism), combining the duties of Sovereign, Prime Minister and Commander-in-Chief all in a single office. He was required to account to London for the running of his colony; he was usually only appointed after long field experience in colonial administration. No more bizarre job could have been conceived for one who had trained and served as constitutional monarch. The Colonial Office always felt the anomaly acutely. How were they to issue instructions to take potentially unpopular local action to one in whose protected name they had not long before issued all instructions?

Royalty, it is true, had served as Governors-General in the Dominions. Queen Victoria's third son the Duke of Connaught had been Governor-General of Canada, and his son, Prince Arthur, Governor-General of South Africa. The Earl of Athlone (Queen Mary's brother, the Duke of Windsor's Wodehousian Uncle Alge) had also occupied Government House in Durban, and was now the King's representative in Ottawa. The Duke of Kent had been designated Governor-General of Australia, although kept in England by the outbreak of war. But the Dominions, as the Statute of Westminster had formally recognized in 1932, were entirely self-governing; all authority rested with cabinets responsible to

95

parliaments; and the Governors-General merely exercised the role of the Sovereign at home – so that princes, if they could be spared, were ideal. In July 1940 both Australia and New Zealand were awaiting new Governors-General; the incumbents had to postpone their retirement until suitable successors could be found during the war. Why not choose the Duke of Windsor for one of these posts? The Government of New Zealand had not opposed itself to the King during the Abdication crisis, while in Australia the Labour Party, now about to come to power, had strongly taken his side.[1] No Dominion, especially during the war, would have opposed the advice of the Crown to accept the Duke of Windsor as Governor-General; and his single wartime Dominion visit (to Canada in September 1941) was to show that his public popularity was undiminished. But that was the very trouble in certain eyes. The Duke remained excessively popular. There was a terror of reviving the legend of the Prince Charming who had toured the Dominions in the 1920s to such rapturous acclaim. The whole idea was to efface him; so a colony, against all reason and precedent, it had to be. But which?

In 1940 there were some thirty-five territories with governors under the control of the Colonial Office in London, graded in careful pecking order from the star possession of Malaya down to the remote (if evocative) islet of St Helena. The Bahamas Colony came very near the bottom of the list. It was just above the Seychelles and the Falkland Islands, but below Fiji and Mauritius. Of the nine colonies under the wing of the West Indian Department of the Colonial Office,* only one (British Honduras) was less important. But one factor distinguished the Bahamas from other minor colonies. It was incredibly hard to govern.[2] It was regarded as a kind of punishment station in the Colonial Service, combining a minimum of importance with a maximum of frustration. Sir Philip Rogers, then Private Secretary to the Permanent Head of the Colonial Office, recalls that it was 'notoriously difficult politically'.[3] Sir Leslie Monson, who was in the West Indian Department in 1940, describes it as 'a bloody awful job, a job for a man on the way out'.[4] If it was intended to give the Duke a post that was both minor and difficult, nothing could have been more so than the Bahamas. It was traditionally a grave of reputations.

Extraordinary as it was, the Bahamas offer was not the result of a frantic and hasty decision made at a desperate moment of the war. On the contrary, it emerged from several days of careful discussion between 10 Downing Street, the Colonial Office and the Palace, albeit at a terrible time.

On Churchill's coming to power in May 1940, Malcolm Macdonald had

* Jamaica, Trinidad and Tobago, British Guiana, Barbados, Bermuda, the Windwards, the Leewards, the Bahamas, British Honduras.

been replaced as Secretary of State for the Colonies by George, 1st Baron Lloyd of Dolobran, a romantic and forceful character who had been the last powerful British ruler of Egypt in the 1920s and a staunch supporter of Churchill and re-armament in the 1930s. Lloyd had viewed the passing of Edward VIII with mild regret. (It is interesting that the anti-appeasers – Lloyd, Eden, Duff Cooper, Amery, Vansittart, Churchill – were relatively sympathetic to the King in 1936, the appeasers solidly against him.) But Lloyd, like Churchill, was a man of power, and he regarded an ex-King at large in collapsing Europe, boycotted as he was by his successor, as a grave embarrassment. Dudley Danby, then Lloyd's Private Secretary, recalls being telephoned in the last week of June by John Martin, the Prime Minister's Private Secretary, to be asked, 'Are there any spare governorships going? We need one quickly for someone big. . . .' Though the Colonial Office was at that moment burdened by two immense problems – how to deal with the French colonies and how to safeguard the British position in the Middle East – Danby recalls that a list of vacant or soon to be vacated governorships was duly drawn up.[5] But the Bahamas was not on it; and the decision was not to be taken at the Colonial Office, nor even at 10 Downing Street.

On 14 July – ten days after the appointment had been offered to the Duke and five days after it had been gazetted – Lord Lloyd lunched with his best friend Sir Ronald Storrs, that other romantic proconsul who had become Military Governor of Jerusalem in 1917 at the age of thirty-five. Storrs recorded in his diary:

G [George Lloyd] told me that *the Windsor appointment in the Bahamas is the King's own idea, to keep him at all costs out of England.* G never thought it would come to him to submit to H.M. his proposal for appointing his late sovereign to serve under him in a small governorship. W inclined to be Bolshie and accepted the governorship on condition 'that the family did not interfere'. *G hopes he will not do well* as that may make him eager for promotion somewhere more important, and altogether does not like the thing very much . . .[6]

Here all is revealed.* The choice was the Palace's. They had chosen a place which was small, far from England and the war, and in which it was very hard indeed to 'do well'. It promised neither glory nor peace. In one sense alone the Duke might have been considered well-suited to fill it. Both of the previous Governors – Sir Bede Clifford (1932–7) and Sir Charles Dundas (1937–40) – had been the sons of English peers and married to American wives; these facts had lent a certain glamour to

---

* The Duke was never fully aware of the true background to his Bahamas exile. Three days later Storrs happened to meet George Wood at Mrs Keppel's. 'He told me that W is delighted with the appointment and pumped me for its origin, of which I affected ignorance, gathering in exchange that they think it was Winston.'[7]

their baleful role as mascots of a winter tourist playground.[8] Sir Bede (an old equerry of the Duke who was well known at Court) was in fact in London in July 1940, on leave from his governorship of Mauritius; it is very possible that he was consulted. As for Sir Charles, he was in mid-term in Nassau; he suddenly found himself transferred to Uganda (then Britain's model African protectorate) to make way for his royal successor. The Colonial Office were not sorry to move him, for his governorship of the Bahamas had been nearly disastrous – an object lesson in how much heartache and how little kudos was to be found in the post. He took his reposting not with the best of grace. 'I don't see why I should be moved to make way for him,' he said to a local notable[9]; while in his memoirs he later wrote: 'I have told of the vicissitudes that befell some of my early predecessors and of how unceremoniously certain of them were evicted from their offices. My own term of governorship was cut short in startling manner. . . .' But Dundas went on to write: 'As for my Royal successor, I wondered if for him the Bahamas colony was the best choice. . . . I feared the worst. . . .'[10]

The Duke was offered and accepted the Bahamas on Thursday 4 July. He set out across the Atlantic exactly four weeks later, on Thursday 1 August. Much nonsense has been written about the reasons for this four-week delay, and how the Duke occupied himself during it. The detailed history of those weeks must await another publication; a summary of the facts is given here.

Once the decision had been taken, the Duke was condemned to kill time in Portugal until the necessary arrangements could be made to take him out to his post. As it was top secret to begin with, he could do little until it was officially announced. Meanwhile, on the 5th, he sent Gray Phillips to London as his emissary with the returning flying-boats, to get his Colonial Office briefing and deal with all those matters colonial governors (not to mention royalty) must deal with before going abroad. After Phillips' departure, the faithful George Wood offered to become the Duke's aide-de-camp and follow him with Rosa for the rest of the war, an offer which the Duke gratefully accepted. Then it was merely a matter of waiting until the announcement was made.

They bathed and went sightseeing. They saw a great deal of Selby and their hosts the Espirito Santos. They made a predictably good impression on the Portuguese, and many friends among them. The Duke paid a formal call on General Carmona, the President of Portugal, and attended a bullfight, where he was recognized and given a standing ovation by the crowd. But they never ceased to be aware of the tense atmosphere of Lisbon, a city in terror of invasion and swarming with refugees and diplomats seeking evacuation. Amidst this chaotic and tragic human swirl they saw many of their old friends – William Bullitt, Tony and Margaret Biddle, Suzanne Blum, Daisy Fellowes – whose related experiences did little to improve their spirits.

The appointment 'leaked out' in London and so was announced slightly earlier than planned, on the BBC news at 8.45 p.m. on the 9th. The War Cabinet was concerned that the Duke should be conscious of a pleasurable public reaction. Churchill telegraphed that the news was 'received with general satisfaction here and with delight in the Bahamas',[11] while Lord Lloyd (who privately hoped the Duke 'would not do well') wrote: 'I very much hope you will find both interest and enjoyment in your time in the Bahamas.'[12] *The Times* (doubtless prompted by 10 Downing Street) devoted a leading article to the appointment, describing the Bahamas as

> . . . one of the oldest and most honourable of appointments under the Crown. Others no doubt rank higher in formal dignity and in the extent of the jurisdiction. Even if that measure be applied, the greater the honour now done to a historic colony and the greater the credit due to the DUKE himself.

Following the announcement, Gray Phillips in London (who was joined there by Wood on the 14th) set about making the preparations for the Duke's departure. Since the posting of a member of the Royal Family to a small governorship was unique, these were numerous. In particular information about the new post had to be obtained; a few known and trusted personal attendants had to be found; the sending out of uniforms and countless other necessary items had to be organized; and many questions of protocol had to be settled. Faced with these complicated tasks, Phillips and Wood received only moderate co-operation from the Colonial Office and almost none from the Court. 'Feel sure you do not know red tape we are up against as regards new appointment,' the Duke telegraphed to Churchill on the 18th.[13]

Meanwhile, on 11 July, Selby had telegraphed the Foreign Office to say that the Duke had heard nothing as yet about his journey to the Bahamas and was becoming impatient.[14] He wanted *'decision to be taken soon as possible and arrangements made'*. The reply came that the Duke should try to make his own travel arrangements from Lisbon; but this was difficult. The normal route from Europe to the Bahamas was by sea via the United States; and the American Export Steamship Company, which ran the weekly service from Lisbon to New York, was unsure whether it would be able to carry the Duke owing to United States neutrality legislation. On the 14th, however, the Duke wrote to Phillips that he had managed with difficulty to make provisional reservations on the SS *Excalibur* leaving for New York on 1 August.[15] On the 17th Selby telegraphed saying the Duke was having further difficulty getting these tentative bookings confirmed, and asking if the Foreign Office might be able to arrange this through the State Department.[16]

This proved to be the start of an anguished saga. For that same day the Foreign Office received a telegram from Lord Lothian, the British Ambassador in Washington, suggesting that it was undesirable for the Duke and Duchess to pass through America on their way to the Bahamas, as their presence might generate 'harmful publicity' and also somehow interfere with the campaign for the presidential election in November.[17] The next day Phillips reported to his master that the plan to travel by way of New York had been vetoed in Whitehall. This was too much for the Duke, who telegraphed bitterly to the Prime Minister:

> Understand . . . that Colonial Office have raised some objections to my sailing in American ship to New York. . . . As I was requested to make my own plans for reaching my post and I knew it was your desire that I should not unduly prolong my stay in Portugal, I have had great difficulty in securing reservations in vessel of American Export Line sailing . . . August 1st. . . . Have been messed about quite long enough and detect in CO attitude the very same hands at work as in my last job. Strongly urge you to support arrangements I have made otherwise may have to reconsider my position.[18]

After a delay of almost a week, Churchill replied on the 24th that 'His Majesty's Government cannot agree to your landing in the United States at this juncture. This decision must be accepted.'[19] The Foreign Office were now arranging with the State Department for the *Excalibur* to be re-routed via Bermuda, whence the Duke would be taken directly to the Bahamas in another boat without having to tread on American soil. On the 26th the Duke answered:

> I agree to arrangements you have made for journey to Nassau via Bermuda. Regarding not landing in the United States, I take it that this only applies until the events of November. May I therefore have confirmation that it is not to be the policy of His Majesty's Government that I should not set foot on American soil during my term of office in the Bahamas? Otherwise I could not feel justified in representing the King in a British Colony so geographically close to the United States if I was prevented from ever going to that country.[20]

'As regards your visit to the United States,' Churchill replied cautiously on the 27th, 'we should naturally wish to fall in with Your Royal Highness's wishes. It is difficult to see far ahead these days . . . but we should naturally do our best to suit Your Royal Highness's convenience.'[21]

The re-routing of the *Excalibur* involved immense complications.[22] Lothian saw Under-Secretary Welles about it on the 20th, and was told that all would depend on the compliance of the shipping-line. The American Export Steamship Company was thoroughly unenthusiastic, as was the International Communications Division of the State Department.

Commissioner Max Truitt expressed the view that the diverted liner would be 'a sweet morsel' for seizure by German or Italian submarines; but this did not deter the British Embassy in Washington. As late as 26 July, less than a week before the sailing, the Company stalled, pointing out that the diversion would greatly increase the ship's war risk and insurance and would be very expensive – at least $17,500. But the necessary assurances were given, and the operation went ahead.

This was not quite the end of the matter. In Lisbon, there had as yet been no cancellations from the *Excalibur*. It was full to the brim with desperate refugees and urgently returning diplomats. The Company's agent explained these difficulties to the British Embassy and recommended that the Duke leave a week later, on 8 August. On the 25th Selby telegraphed this news to the Foreign Office, adding: 'In the absence of any sudden development in the situation here I see no objection to the postponement.'[23] On the 27th Lloyd telegraphed the Duke that the diversion had now been agreed to, the places were being obtained, and that 'at this late hour it would be very difficult to alter all the arrangements made'.[24] On the 29th the Duke telegraphed Churchill that 'I agree to sail August 1st as you have arranged'.[25]

It is sometimes said that the Duke tried to delay his departure from Portugal, while the British Government kept pressing him to leave. Quite the reverse was the case, certainly up to the last week of July. Selby's telegram of the 11th made it clear he was keen to be off without delay. But the Government, far from taking the initiative in getting him away, simply left him to make his own plans. As soon as he was able (after the announcement on the 9th) he began his efforts to get on to the first passenger vessel on which it seemed he would be able to leave – the *Excalibur* sailing on 1 August. It might have been thought that London, with a view to his departing for his exile in the best possible frame of mind, would have made matters easy for him. But in fact, as the Duke wrote to his trusted London solicitor George Allen on the 20th, he and the Duchess were

. . . encountering every conceivable form of governmental obstruction and red tape in the making of our arrangements for the voyage and the taking up of this wretched appointment. Any keeness [sic] that I had at first been able to evoke has been completely knocked out of me, and both the Duchess and I view the prospect of an indefinite period of exile on those islands with profound gloom and despondency. However, as I refuse to accept an appointment in England under the conditions which prevail, I suppose that there is no alternative but to go.

In this letter, the Duke asked that a large sum of money be transferred from his account with Coutts and Co. in London to the Royal Bank of Canada in Nassau.

In the second half of July, the German plot, of which he was wholly unconscious, proceeded against the Duke. Various Spanish and Portuguese friends of the Duke and Duchess – notably Bermejillo who stayed with them at Cascais from the 8th to the 13th, and their host Espirito Santo – were supposed to persuade them not to go to the Bahamas but to return instead to Spain. These agents seem to have been somewhat half-hearted to say the least; Bermejillo was of course working for Beigbeder who was secretly trying to help the Duke, while Espirito Santo appears to have been a double agent working for British Intelligence. However, their reports, which proceeded to Germany by stages via the Spanish Embassy in Lisbon, the Spanish Foreign Ministry, the Spanish Interior Ministry and the German Embassy in Madrid, certainly suggested that the Duke was all eagerness to break with the British Government and go to Spain. On the strength of these reports, the German spymaster Walter Schellenberg was sent out to Lisbon to bring the plot to fruition. But on arrival he discovered that the reports had been either fabricated or wildly exaggerated; that the Duke had no intention of returning to Spain; and that the only way to get him there would be to abduct him. This, indeed, Schellenberg was ordered to do, on the personal instructions of Hitler. Schellenberg prevaricated, tipped off the Portuguese police who strengthened the Duke's guard, and contented himself with staging a series of incidents designed to frighten the Duke and Duchess.[26]

A week before the Duke's scheduled departure, with no sign that he would be deflected from his purpose, a new stratagem was used. The Germans had now realized that Beigbeder was not playing their game, and so were relying exclusively on Suñer.[27] A Spanish acquaintance of the Duke, Miguel Primo de Rivera Marqués de Estella, was sent out to Cascais on behalf of the Spanish Government to warn him that there was a plot to kill him in Portugal and that he would be well advised to return to Spain immediately. Having lived for weeks in a tense atmosphere of spies, refugees and armed guards, and deeply disillusioned by the course of his preparations for the Bahamas, the Duke hardly knew what to make of this extraordinary information. He at once passed it to Walter Monckton, who (as arranged a little while earlier) joined him on the 28th for his last few days in Portugal, sharing an official plane with Gray Phillips. Monckton recognized the possibility of an abduction plot, and arranged for a Special Branch detective to accompany the Duke on his voyage.[28] But he 'never doubted that the Duke would leave to take up his appointment in the Bahamas'[29]; and even before his arrival the Duke had 'unhesitatingly refused' Primo de Rivera's offer of a Spanish 'sanctuary'.[30]

On the 31st the Duke and Duchess gave a large farewell party at the

Aviz Hotel in Lisbon. Before sailing the following day, the Duke paid a friendly call on Dr Salazar. The Germans, through the Spanish Ambassador in Lisbon, tried to get Salazar to put last-minute pressure on the Duke not to leave Europe[31]; but it is safe to assume that the benign and Anglophile dictator did nothing of the kind, and they sailed that afternoon at three o'clock on the *Excalibur*, the ship upon which they had always intended to travel.

On 7 August, shortly before their arrival in Bermuda, the Duchess wrote from the ship to her Aunt Bessie.

SS EXCALIBUR
Wednesday the 7th

Dearest Aunt B,

I am so furious I can't see you as we are not coming to NY but that bloody Govt won't let us come to the US until after the elections – as if we had anything to do with American politics. Naturally we loathe the job but it was the only way out of a difficult situation – as we did not want to return to England except under our own conditions. . . . I have awful reports of the house – small, hideous, hardly any furniture – all unsatisfactory. It is very hard to have just finished two houses and now going to one with nothing in it and I was unable to get *anything* from either of the French houses. The Biddles are on the boat and Phillips from Rome. . . . We have a veranda to ourselves and have our dinner etc there and sit on the Captain's bridge so it has not been difficult. The Biddles seem certain of Roosevelt being re-elected. . . . We are staying at Govt House Bermuda until 13th and then by some boat to Nassau. We are quite a party, but none exciting. These boats are very nice – very clean and food good. The weather has fortunately been kind. . . . I see a black 1940. Let's hope for better things after December – the stars promise better things.

All love,
WALLIS

P.S. I miss my houses so terribly and can only think of returning to the irritating French. I could kiss them all now – including Fernand, the butler you never saw.

Part Two

Governing the Pirates

———

7

The Worst Post
in the British Empire

1717–1940

According to tradition, Columbus was the first European to reach the Bahamas; his first American landfall was on San Salvador on 12 October 1492. Thrilled to have reached dry land after thirty-three days in unknown seas, he sent a glowing report to the Catholic Kings in whose name he claimed the islands. But the Spaniards were profoundly unimpressed by their first transatlantic acquisition. The Bahama Islands (from the Spanish *bajamar*, the shallow seas) consist of a long coral archipelago lying to the north of Cuba, stretching some 400 miles from Florida in the north-west to Hispaniola in the south-east. Thirteen of the islands are more than fifty square miles in extent; there are countless smaller islands, cays and rocks; and the whole group is ringed by a pattern of shoals, reefs and lagoons – picturesque to the modern tourist, but a nightmare to the seafarer of yore. Apart from these scenic offshore waters and a pleasant winter climate, the territory is singularly cursed by nature. Unlike the lush, volcanic islands of the Caribbean group, the Bahamas consist of harsh, porous limestone and are flat, dry, stony and infertile. Their landscape has aptly been described as 'almost lunar'.[1] There are no mineral resources; the natural vegetation is poor, and agriculture difficult. Small wonder then that Spain, having carried off the native Arawaks as slaves, simply abandoned the arid isles. Bypassed by history, they remained abandoned for 150 years, known only as a peril to navigators. The first part of the New World to be discovered by Europeans, they were the last to be settled by them. Since they supported human life with difficulty, they were destined to be settled eventually by desperate men.

In 1629, the English Crown laid almost accidental claim to the islands. Charles I wanted to reward his trusted Attorney-General Robert Heath with the right to colonize the Carolinas; and since the Bahamas occupied the same latitudes, he threw them into the grant for good measure. Though Heath is still commemorated as the 'father' of the Bahamas, he

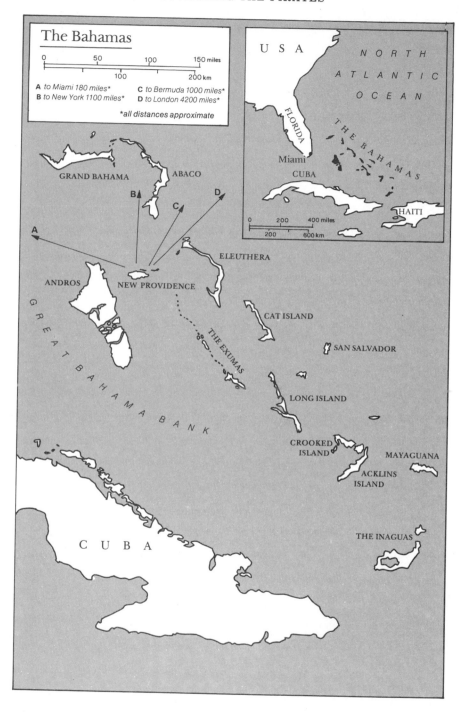

The Bahamas

0   50   100   150 miles
0   100   200 km

A to Miami 180 miles*   C to Bermuda 1000 miles*
B to New York 1100 miles* D to London 4200 miles*

*all distances approximate

USA

NORTH ATLANTIC OCEAN

FLORIDA

Miami

THE BAHAMAS

CUBA

HAITI

0   200   400 miles
0   200   600 km

GRAND BAHAMA   ABACO

B

A

C

D

ELEUTHERA

ANDROS   NEW PROVIDENCE

CAT ISLAND

SAN SALVADOR

THE EXUMAS

GREAT BAHAMA BANK

LONG ISLAND

CROOKED ISLAND

MAYAGUANA

ACKLINS ISLAND

CUBA

THE INAGUAS

never entertained the notion of founding a colony there; he did not even settle the fertile Carolinas. But the Bahamas thus acquired a tiny niche in English overseas topography, and by 1648 they were sufficiently heard of to be selected for quite another colonizing venture. A group of free-thinkers from Bermuda, stirred by the Roundhead victory in the English Civil Wars, went off to found an Ideal Republic on the island of Eleuthera. The Company of Eleutherian Adventurers met with utter disaster. Having quarrelled amongst themselves and lost their stores, they found they could not live off the land and had to plead for rescue in dire distress. Most returned to Bermuda; of the miserable remnant who stayed, most eventually moved on to a more hopeful island they called New Providence, establishing a tiny settlement on the site of Nassau. In 1668, Charles II – continuing the economical Stuart policy of rewarding loyal subjects with desert islands no other nations wanted – granted the Bahamas to a company of eight noblemen known as the Lords Proprietors, who sent out a Governor to rule the settlement on New Providence. But that settlement, to the Proprietors' horror, soon began to flourish as a pirate station, with the Governors well to the fore in supporting and even organizing the exploits of the pirates.

For fifty years, the Jolly Roger fluttered over the shallow seas. Hardly better able to survive than the original Adventurers, the New Providence settlers took all too naturally to a life of waylaying the laden Spanish treasure ships that plied the hazardous Bahamian channels, bound for the rich colony of Cuba. By the 1690s the Bahamas had become the world's main pirate ground, Governor Cadwaller Jones maintaining a reign of terror in Nassau on the pirates' behalf. London, seven weeks distant, had no control, and reprisals, starting with the Spanish sack of New Providence in 1684, were frequent and terrible.

In 1706 a French raid wiped out what remained of the proprietorial settlement of Nassau, leaving the pirates in sole control of the Bahamas. In 1714, when George I came to the throne, the British Government at last began to take a worried interest in the disreputable isles. Not only were they a disaster zone for trade, but the pirates sympathized openly with the Jacobite Pretender. In 1717, most reluctantly, the Crown took charge. The first Crown Governor, a rough ex-privateer named Woodes Rodgers, set out with a small fleet to subdue the pirates and bring them under the King's sway. He seemed to be successful. After brief resistance, the New Providence pirates accepted the Royal Pardon and settled down (albeit sullenly) under the flag. As a motto for the new Crown Colony Rodgers chose '*expulsis piratis commercia restituta*'. It has always been a good Bahamian joke that the real version runs the other way – commerce expelled, the pirates restored. Blackbeard might be dead, but his soul lived on.

So began the Bahamas' two-and-a-half-centuries-long colonial career. From start to finish, it was a problem colony. The ex-pirates proved almost impossible to govern. If things had seemed reasonably under control in the first few years, the establishment of an elective House of Assembly in 1729 led to trouble which was to become all too familiar. Led by the Speaker John Colebrooke, the House proceeded to obstruct the whole business of Crown Government. 'Such a headstrong set of simple, ungovernable wretches were never convened in legislative capacity,' complained Rodgers' successor, Richard Fitzwilliam, in 1734. A ghastly power-struggle began which was to continue right down to the 1960s, between the Governor on the one hand, striving to bring order and good government to the most desolate of territories and the most difficult of subjects, and the proud, independent and avaricious settlers on the other, at heart pirates still, who sought fiercely to uphold their 'privileges' and rather resented being ruled at all. Holding the purse-strings, the House exercised power without responsibility, and withheld funds for the most essential functions of government, especially defence. In 1736 the Nassau garrison mutinied, unpaid and practically unsupplied by the House. 'It will be impossible for me to answer to the Ends of my being sent hither', the exasperated Fitzwilliam wrote home, in language to be echoed by all his successors, 'without Your Lordships' Interposition in Favour of this miserable Place.'2

In the mid-eighteenth century the Colony experienced a brief renaissance, as the series of great naval wars in the West Indies enabled the settlers to return to true form as privateers. This licensed form of piracy brought great prosperity, notably under the brilliant governorship of General Thomas Shirley, sent to Nassau in 1758 as a punishment for military failure in Canada. But the Peace of Paris in 1763 brought privateering to an end, and with it the truce of the Nassuvians in their relations with the Government. (It was usually the case that the Bahamas did well out of wars and predatory pursuits, and badly out of peace and ordinary trade.) As the Colony lapsed back into poverty and apathy, the House became ever more obstructionist, again refusing to provide for the proper defence of the island. Nemesis came during the American War of Independence. In March 1776 a Yankee raiding-party under Captain Taylor landed in the east of New Providence to find the forts practically undefended. Having been assured that their property would be respected, the Nassuvians promptly gave in to the raiders and handed over Governor Browne as a hostage. After the eventual resumption of Crown Government, Nassau enjoyed a few happy years privateering against the American rebels until in 1782 the Bahamas were captured by the Spaniards. But the conquerors had no use for their valueless old colony, which they contemptuously restored under the Peace of Versailles the

On the Duke's forty-fifth birthday, June 23, 1939.

Above and below, with Lord Louis Mountbatten on board the HMS *Kelly*,
September 12, 1939.

In Whitehall:
a cartoon showing
the Duke on his way
to the War Office.

Arriving at Buckingham Palace with Walter Monckton,
for his interview with the King.

With English and French officers at Vincennes, October 1939. Left to right: the Duke, General Gamelin, Colonel Petibon, General Howard-Vyse, Captain Huet, Colonel Redman.

The Duchess and Lady Mendl knitting for the *Colis de Trianon*.

Christmas with General Sikorski and the Poles.

On the Maginot Line in the snow.

At a hospital near the front with the *Section Sanitaire*.

Inspecting troops at Nice, June 1940. "There is no foundation for the report that the Duke of Windsor has resigned his appointment."

Arrival in Nassau, August 17, 1940. On the gangplank, the Duke allows the Duchess to pass ahead of him. Coming down the steps of the *Lady Somers*: Leslie Heape (Colonial Secretary), Rosa Wood (obscured), Captain George Wood, Lieutenant Oppe.

Nassau. The Royal Victoria Hotel is in the foreground, the British Colonial Hotel is in the background, and the public buildings are center right.

In the Public Square. Colonel Erskine-Lindop, Commissioner of Police, stands behind the Duke.

In the Council Chamber. The Chief Justice (in full-bottomed wig) administers the oath. Kenneth Solomon stands in the center with his back to the camera.

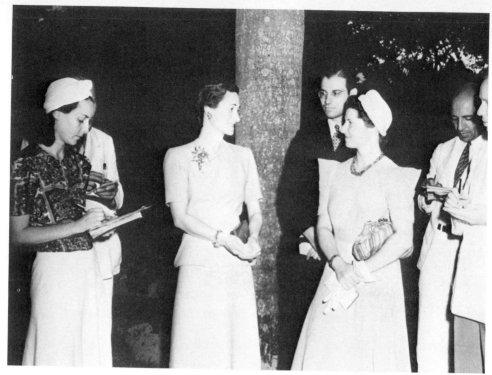

Miss Teegarden meets the Duchess, August 18, 1940.
Behind her (taking notes) is Etienne Dupuch.

The "colored people's welcome," August 23, 1940.

following year. It was a great humiliation for England that, of all the territories she had lost, the Bahamas was the only one she got back.

In the wake of American Independence, numerous fleeing Loyalists settled in the Bahamas with their still more numerous slaves. The population of the Colony shot up, reaching about 15,000 by 1800 (over 10,000 of them negroes). The new settlers mostly colonized the Out Islands (islands other than New Providence); they were a vigorous breed of planters who, using intensive slave labour, achieved fair initial success, getting sugar and even cotton to grow in the acarpous Bahamian soil. Like future immigrants, they tried to get the old settlers to change their piratical ways; but in vain. Various electoral and administrative devices preserved the hegemony of the old Nassau whites; and the Out Island plantation settlements, after a brief flourish, began their long decline into the marginal existence from which the Duke of Windsor and others were to make such determined efforts to save them in the 1940s.

The Yankee victory also brought to the Bahamas the worst (but not the least colourful) of the governors. As the last Royal Governor of Virginia, Lord Dunmore had been a disaster to the British cause. In other times he might have hanged; in the progressive climate of the 1780s it was considered enough to send him to the Bahamas. In him, the Bahamians at last found a ruler as corrupt and unscrupulous as themselves. He filled places with the husbands of his mistresses; he speculated in Crown lands; he built recklessly. His extravagance put him at the mercy of the House, who made him sign a bill giving them the sole right both to levy taxes and supervise expenditure. Then war broke out with France. Recalling how his predecessor had been carried off by the Americans in his night-clothes, Dunmore was determined that Nassau should be prepared. He built vast barracks, which all the British forces in the West Indies could not have filled. He constructed great shore batteries and two massive forts, destined never to fire a single shot. These bizarre and superfluous fortifications bankrupted the little Colony. Dunmore was recalled in disgrace.

Nevertheless, the Revolutionary and Napoleonic Wars were quite a happy time for the Bahamas, providing as they did the last resurgence of privateering. This too was the heyday of 'wrecking' (ships being lured onto the rocks with false lights), a livelihood which came naturally to the Bahamians, profiteers from the world's disasters. The resumption of peace in 1814 revived the usual state of political conflict in Nassau, made especially bitter by the burning issue of the day – the future of slavery. It need hardly be said that the settlers were passionately opposed to any reforms tending to bring an end to that institution. In 1817 the House tried to arrest an Attorney-General who was striving to relieve the condition of the blacks (as they were again to do in the Duke of Windsor's

time in 1942). So hysterical became the temper of the House as Eman-
cipation approached that it was dissolved in 1831 and did not sit again
until slavery was abolished throughout the Empire in 1833. That,
however, would be the last time a Governor was able to dispense with a
difficult legislature.

Abolition instilled anew in the local whites a passionate distrust of the
British Government and a lasting determination to resist all its progressive actions in the colonies. Even such an apparently obvious imperial
measure as the introduction of lighthouses (which threatened to put an
end to the lucrative pursuit of wrecking) provoked fierce local opposition
and was delayed for many years. Above all, the House was resolved to
maintain – if not increase – its privileges and independence, at a time
when London was trying to consolidate its grip on the colonies by
replacing uncooperative elected assemblies with subservient nominated
councils. In Nassau, as elsewhere, a nominated Legislative Council
('LegCo') was set up in the 1840s as an upper chamber, while the leading
members of the House were drafted along with the principal officials onto
the Governor's Executive Council ('ExCo'). The idea was to emasculate
the House by reducing it to a tame organ of government, until such time
as the wholly controlled LegCo might replace it as the source of legislation and taxation. This indeed happened in most colonies; but in the
Bahamas the opposite happened. LegCo dwindled into powerless insignificance, while ExCo became a sort of Politburo whereby the local
establishment controlled the unfortunate Governor. Local power was
consolidated by a system of administration by boards, which were in
practice always filled from the House which so tightly controlled their
expenditure.

Thus it was that, from the middle of the nineteenth century until the
1940s, almost all the local actions of the Governor were controlled by a
caucus of powerful local politicians, the cabal of tough, avaricious and
mostly related white merchants known as 'the Bay Street Boys' (Bay
Street was and is the main thoroughfare of Nassau running parallel to the
shore). They were rough, hard, unscrupulous men, venomous towards
their rivals (a new man in business would find his premises burnt down)
and arrogant in their pretensions of social superiority (the colour bar was
always enforced more rigidly in the Bahamas than in any other British
Colony). But they were the true heirs of the pirates, and there was
something bold and daring about them. Above all, they were independent. 'Who is the Secretary of State for the Colonies ?' one Speaker of the
House of Assembly demanded to know. 'He has no standing in this
House.'[3]

In the mid-nineteenth century, the Bahamas enjoyed one brief period
of extraordinary prosperity. During the American Civil War (wars

always tended to be good news for the Bahamas) New Providence flourished as the main neutral destination of the adventurers – many of them Bahamian – who ran the Northern blockade of the Southern ports. For three glorious years, most of the world's cotton was sold in Nassau instead of Charleston. But it was all too typical of the Bahamian pirate mentality that they were content to rely on such predatory windfalls while neglecting all steady and productive pursuits; and with the collapse of the Southern Confederacy in 1865, the Colony sank back into its usual state of depression. The economic vacuum was gradually filled by a commercial protection racket, based on the total economic dependence of the now impoverished Out Islands on the Bay Street merchants. 'Bay Street' ran the islands as a great inefficient peasant estate, providing the desperate Out Islanders with the means of making a marginal living (loans, boats, agricultural implements, fishing-tackle) and controlling the sale of their erratic produce (fish, sisal, pineapple, sponges). In return, Bay Street used the Out Island vote (cast, or rather bought, in elections reminiscent of *The Pickwick Papers*) to sustain their total power in the House of Assembly; for while New Providence came to have over a third of the Colony's population, twenty-one out of the House's twenty-nine members – all rich white Nassuvians – continued to represent the depopulated Out Islands. Through their control of the House (and hence of all politics), Bay Street was able to ensure – right up to the 1940s – that the Out Islanders (as well as the coloured population of New Providence) remained in a state of poverty, ignorance and dependence, never in a position to improve their condition or develop their settlements or organize their own economic life. Since agriculture was thus kept in a primitive state, and the Bahamas never produced enough to be remotely self-sufficient, the hungry townspeople were obliged to buy the American produce which Bay Street imported, which attracted heavy customs duties, which in turn provided the House with its revenues, and which the all-powerful Finance Committee disbursed with miserly vigilance, always in such a way as to uphold Bay Street interests and tighten the operation of the System.

With Bay Street in control and determined to keep the Colony backward, the governorship of the Bahamas ceased to have any real importance. After 1904 it no longer even carried the customary knighthood. It was a post to be filled by an incompetent or eccentric official who could not be got rid of on account of his personal connections – such as William Grey-Wilson, a cousin of Earl Grey, whose career consisted of ten years governing St Helena, seven years the Falkland Islands, and eight (1904–12) the Bahamas. But it was certainly no sinecure. At least in St Helena and the Falklands the Governor's word was law, whereas the Governor of the Bahamas had practically no authority, 'only the power of veto and such executive powers as he can exercise without money, or with such sums of money as he may be trusted with by a reluctant and suspicious legislature', as a work on colonial administration put it.[4] And yet he was still the chief executive and had somehow to administer the languishing Colony, with the aid of other unhappy British officials who were paid miserable salaries and treated with contempt by the House and attacked for their slightest reform or effort to help the mass of the population. It is hardly surprising that Nassau came to be regarded in the Colonial Service as the worst post in the British Empire. As a former Colonial Secretary of the Bahamas recalled:

> It was in the Bahamas that I realized, more than in any other Colony in which I served, the local hostility to the imported official. . . . The House of Assembly refuses to increase the salaries of higher officials, hoping that if they are kept low enough no one will want to accept the appointments. . . . This policy places the civil service at the mercy of the legislature. . . . The Secretary of State has the greatest difficulty in filling these posts in the Bahamas. . . . If in the circumstances one half of the officials prove to be successful in their posts, the Colony is more lucky than it deserves. . . .[5]

With the rigidity of the local establishment and their economic system, and the impossibility of reform or even efficient administration, the Colony sank into ever-greater poverty and insignificance in the fifty years before 1914. In spite of its key position next to the United States, it ceased to be of the remotest importance to imperial strategy or trade. The development of nearby Florida in the last years of the century, far from stimulating similar progress in the Bahamas, merely resulted in a mass emigration of impoverished Out-Islanders to find work in Miami. It was Britain's forgotten colony, an unruly place which London hardly bothered to rule. After a hopeless struggle in the late 1860s to prevent the disestablishment of the Anglican Church – yet another broken link with royal authority – the Government all but gave up trying to govern, virtually confining itself to administering justice, running the postal and customs services, and providing the white quarter of Nassau with a minimum of policing and sanitation. But all that would change in the second quarter of the twentieth century, as London began to insist on reform throughout the colonies.

The First World War was a grim time for the Bahamas. With the U-boat campaign in the Atlantic, the Colony's main trade- and supply-lines were completely cut off; the war killed most of what remained of Bahamian agriculture. Nassau knew real hunger, and once flourishing settlements in the Out Islands became ghost towns. By the end of hostilities (to which the Bahamas had contributed a surprising number of volunteers) the Colony was crippled with debt and seemed to face further hard times. The population had dropped to 50,000. The time was ripe for a new form of piracy; and at the end of 1919 the Bahamian pirates (steadfast in their allegiance to their Bay Street captains) came into their own again. Nassau's salvation was the Eighteenth Amendment. The heir to buccaneering, privateering, wrecking and blockade-running was bootlegging.

Huge quantities of imported 'booze' suddenly materialized in the Bahamas, quickly disappearing again as they were deftly smuggled off to the dry mainland. Poor, sleepy Nassau became a rich gangster town, a miniature Chicago. To the names of the old Bay Street fortunes – Sands, Bethell, Higgs, Solomon – were added some new ones – Christie, Collins, Murphy, Symonette. . . . Washington protested violently to London; but what could London do? Crown Government in Nassau was as weak as ever. Had it wished to, the Colonial Office had not the means to suppress this new piracy. As it was, with the Bahamas Government levying £1 a bottle on imported liquor, the Colony's revenues shot up fourfold between 1919 and 1924, thus enabling Nassau to be provided with the basic amenities of a modern town. The Foreign Office coldly informed the State Department that, if the United States was incapable of enforcing its own laws within its own territory, His Majesty's Government could hardly be expected to interfere with a trade which was perfectly lawful within the British Empire. But like all the great predatory windfalls of the Bahamas, this one came to an end with a vengeance. The election in 1932 of President Roosevelt who had pledged to end Prohibition threatened to leave the Colony once again without revenue or exports. But this time there was a path of escape. As the new Governor Sir Bede Clifford put it to his Executive Council: 'Well, gentlemen, it amounts to this: if we can't take the liquor to the Americans, we must bring the Americans to the liquor.'[6]

And so an astonishing change came over Nassau in the 1930s. Having for fourteen years been a rough place full of gangsters, it suddenly transformed itself into a sophisticated winter haven catering to the rich from the mainland. Bay Street stores smartened themselves up with wares for the American tourist; horticultural experts using flower-pot techniques somehow fashioned lush tropical gardens out of the scrub; an institute was founded to train blacks to be domestic servants. For all its barrenness, littleness and provincialism, Nassau had quite a lot going for it in its new role – an agreeable climate for three months of the year, the absence of any form of direct taxation, and an alluring atmosphere of sin. It had the nostalgia of a wild west town which did not seem to have quite submitted to the sheriff's authority. Three men were needed to complete the dream – a brilliant land-agent to sell it, a fabulously rich man to set an example by going to live in it, and an engaging aristocrat to preside over it. The first was provided by the ex-bootlegger Harold Christie, the second by the Canadian gold millionaire Harry Oakes, the third by Governor Clifford himself.

Among the Bay Street Boys, Clifford was undoubtedly popular. Rollicking nobleman that he was, they came to venerate him as a sort of Pirate King. For his part, he sought to charm them but never to tame them or to have any reckoning with a still obstructionist legislature. He made no effort to stimulate languishing trade and agriculture. He discouraged London from social reform, believing that the Bahamas' role as an élite resort depended upon the blacks being kept firmly in their place. His overriding aim was to give Nassau the top winter season in the western hemisphere, and in this he largely succeeded. His policy indeed brought a steady flow of wealth into the Colony, in which most classes shared. But that it was storing up trouble became clear under his successor, Sir Charles Dundas, whose disastrous governorship began in 1937.

Sir Charles had the best of intentions. With the full support of the Colonial Office, which was now sick and tired of Bay Street, he arrived determined to reform the Bahamas and alter its whole unsatisfactory character. He ought to have known better, for he had once been Colonial Secretary in Nassau. But apart from that interlude (in the last days of bootlegging) his career had been spent in East Africa. His dream was to turn the Bahamas into a kind of West Indian equivalent of colonial Kenya or Southern Rhodesia. He thought it appalling that a British territory should rely on the largesse of pleasure-seeking foreigners and produce nothing.[7] Nassau, a slave to Bay Street tourism, was beyond redemption. He therefore turned his attention to the penurious and neglected Out Islands, their populations drained to serve the tourist trade on New Providence. Dundas had no illusions that the natives could revive their declining settlements. Inspired by the example in another continent of Delamere and Rhodes, he sought to parcel the islands out on easy terms to vigorous white settlers from England and America, whose enterprise and energy might transform them in time from empty spaces of flat rock into verdant and productive paradises.

Given the local hostility to him and how short a time he had, it is remarkable how much Dundas actually achieved. London backed him up. He managed to find a number of 'pioneer investors' of the type he was looking for: Levy and Davis, rich American residents of Nassau, who started large farms on Eleuthera; the Ericksons from Maine, who revived the salt industry on Inagua; an extraordinary Swede, Axel Wenner-Gren, who set up important operations on Hog Island and Grand Bahama – all names which were to loom large in the Duke of Windsor's governorship. These projects achieved much success, and attracted new communities of European settlers. Dundas also persuaded the eminent female travel-writer, Rosita Forbes, to start a 'manorial settlement' on Eleuthera and write about it in a series of popular romantic works[8]; given time, such publicity might have had considerable effect. But Bay Street was horrified. It was anathema to them that their captive constituencies should achieve productive lives of their own; deriving much of their wealth (and the House its customs revenue) from the importation of American food, the last thing they wanted was the self-sufficiency of the Bahamas. The Legislature became increasingly obstructionist, and even ExCo was rebellious. Dundas, used to colonies where the Governor had no opposition, did not have the tact to deal with this serious situation. 'Clifford might take some controversial action and only afterwards tell ExCo,' recalls a member of one leading Bay Street family. 'Dundas would consult them, hear their advice, and then do exactly the opposite.'[9]

The political climate in Nassau now deteriorated rapidly. Always contemptuous of rich American pleasure-makers in Nassau, in the winter of 1938–9 Dundas succeeded in antagonizing some of them to such an extent that the Colonial Office was flooded with petitions for his removal.[10] Then the sponge crop failed, a deadly virus sweeping the sponge-beds; the Bahamas lost its principal remaining export; and the House refused to co-operate in the relief measures proposed by the Governor. Dundas went over to the offensive; with a view to breaking Bay Street's electoral stranglehold, he demanded the introduction of a secret ballot to replace the corrupt system of open voting. He threatened to dissolve the House if they would not agree to this. Eventually, in a mood of violent resentment, they passed a limited measure introducing it in New Providence for only a term of five years. It was now war between Government House and the local establishment; and when international war broke out in September 1939, the House distinguished itself by refusing to pass the Trading with the Enemy Act and other vital legislation which had to be brought into force by Order in Council. In the months that followed, protests to London about the 'dictatorial methods' of the Governor grew ever louder. Then, in May 1940, came the final straw. In ExCo, Dundas proposed an income tax to raise wartime revenue; the protests became hysterical. Then came news of the disaster in Europe. Dundas lapsed into a state of numb shock.[11] Now that the Bahamian situation had become critical, his nerve failed him. Sir Charles was promptly removed to Kampala. The Duke of Windsor was sent to Nassau.

The news of the appointment stupefied the Bahamas. It hardly seemed possible that the man born and trained to be King and Emperor should be coming out to rule (if rule he could) a barren colonial backwater with a population of 70,000. Apart from brief stops of the Kents and Athlones in the 1930s to see their friends the Bede Cliffords, no one could remember when royalty had ever set foot in the Colony – until some venerable person recalled that the ill-fated Prince Albert Victor had once landed there in the 1880s on the HMS *Bacchante*. When astonishment subsided, local reactions were mixed. Awestruck blacks awaited with Messianic fervour the coming of the great-grandson of the Great White Queen who had liberated the slaves. Among the local whites, most felt flattered and excited; some disapproved of the Duke for having abdicated, or of the Duchess for having been 'the cause of it', or had strong views on divorce. But all, without exception, were aware of one thing. Nothing would have a more splendid effect on the tourism upon which the Colony (even in wartime) depended than the reign of the ex-King and his American Duchess at Government House. Nothing would do more to draw American money to Nassau.

It was this realization more than anything else which, much to the relief of the Colonial Office, defused the politically explosive state of affairs in Nassau before the Duke's arrival. Bay Street, aware from motives of self-interest of the need to give a good welcome to the Royal Governor, suspended its mortal struggle with the Government. The House went so far as to vote a totally inadequate £2,000 towards the renovation of the collapsing structure that was Government House. They were reassured to learn that the Duke was an old friend of Sir Bede Clifford; they hoped that, like the popular Clifford, he would confine himself to promoting Nassau as a top tourist resort, and show none of the frightful mania for reform which had been the undoing of the detested Dundas. But the knives were only sheathed, and Bay Street was ready to resume the bitter fight as soon as it felt its interests to be endangered, royalty or no royalty.

The impending arrival of the Duke and Duchess created vast public interest in the United States. Hardly had the *Excalibur* left Lisbon than a bevy of tourists (unheard of in summer) and a regiment of (mostly female) journalists materialized in Nassau. All the big papers and news agencies were represented; there were 'big names' like Joan Younger and Inez Robb. There was a gang of newsreel men and photographers from the illustrated magazines. Even some minor provincial journals sent reporters – such a correspondent was Mary Teegarden of Albany, NY, representing her local newspaper the *Knickerbocker News*.[12]

Miss Teegarden was a young tennis star for whom, as with most American girls of her age and background, it was a youthful dream to go to Nassau to meet the Duke and Duchess. Reading her bright columns on the front page of the *Knickerbocker News*, it is hard not to be affected by the romantic enthusiasm she evidently felt for her task. Arriving in Nassau on 7 August (on the boat, as she excitedly noted, which was to take Sir Charles and Lady Dundas to New York), she found the date, means and route of her heroes' arrival shrouded in mystery. Taking rooms above Dirty Dick's liquor store on Bay Street, she proceeded to explore the little town. She wondered what the Duke and Duchess would make of such a bizarre and tiny place, and how they would take the terrible summer heat and humidity. Nassau languished in sweltering idleness; occasional indications that it was part of an Empire at war were provided by blacked-out ships, censored telegrams, the arrival of rich refugees and the departure of young volunteers. In the intervals of playing tennis in the scorching heat, she watched the meetings of the House of Assembly; she heard them vote the £2,000 for Government House, and was amused to see the wives of Members knitting in the gallery. She asked all Bahamians she met for their views on the Royal Governor. The coloured population seemed wildly enthusiastic; most of them referred to the Duke as 'de King'. The local whites too seemed much in favour of him, particularly on the ground that he would be a magnet for American tourists. Certainly there had never been so many Americans in Nassau in the terrible month of August.

On the 11th the local papers reported the arrival of the Duke and Duchess in Bermuda.* When and how they would get to Nassau remained secret, but hectic preparations now began for the great event. The Legislature rehearsed the Inauguration. There were desperate efforts to make Government House look less of a wreck, while its gardens were hastily tidied up with convict labour. Government buildings were repainted inside and out, streets festooned with pennants and Union Jacks. Messages of greeting appeared everywhere: 'Welcome Sweet Papa HRH', proclaimed one of them. Soldiers drilled; bands practised; the Nassau Garden Club thought up elaborate floral tributes. Finally, at dawn on Saturday 17 August, Miss Teegarden hurried down to Prince George's Wharf in time to see the Canadian cargo ship MV *Lady Somers* swing into the deep-water channel between Nassau and Hog Island, shadowed by a grey cruiser. The cruiser vanished; accompanied by a little flotilla of gaily-decked local craft, the ship proceeded slowly up the harbour. At precisely seven o'clock, it docked.

For an hour, the ship gave no sign of its eminent passengers, but on shore, a great crowd was gathering. It grew until it numbered some 16,000 of New Providence's estimated 20,000 people, all gazing at the *Lady Somers* as if it were some space-craft from which would emerge they knew not what. On the wharf, a more select and privileged group of local notables and white-uniformed officials and their wives were nervously lining up, and the Colonel trying to get the guard of honour into some sort of order. They waited. The sun rose higher in the sky. The

---

* They arrived there on the 9th and left on the 15th.

temperature shot up from the eighties to the nineties. To the unaccus-
tomed, the heat and humidity and the odour of the crowd were almost
unendurable. Around eight o'clock the ship gave signs of life. A Buick and
a trailer of luggage were swung ashore. Someone emerged with three
cairn terriers and took them for a walk. There was a shuffle on the wharf,
and the Colonial Secretary went on board with a young Canadian naval
equerry left behind by the retiring Governor – then a further wait.
Finally, on the stroke of nine, came the sight for which all had been
waiting. The Duke and Duchess made their appearance on deck. Down
the ship's steps they came – first the Duke, then the Duchess, followed by
the Colonial Secretary, Rosa Wood, George Wood and the equerry.
When they reached the gangway (out of sight of the crowd), the Duke let
the Duchess pass in front of him, and so she preceded him onto Bahamian
soil.

Eyes opened wide; shutters clicked; reporters scribbled in notebooks.
Not even the most disapproving could deny that their début was
impressive. They moved with the easy elegance common to royalty and
film-stars. They looked very gracious, and they had chic. The Duke wore
the heavy khaki uniform of a major-general* with suede shoes, the
Duchess a blue coat over a pink-and-blue printed silk frock and a
mother-of-pearl cap with a *chou*. Only those close by could see how
affected they were by sudden exposure to the heat, which hit them like
the blast from an opened oven. There was a long ceremony on the wharf,
as the officials and notables were presented and the Duke inspected the
guard; before he was halfway down the line, dark, damp patches began to
appear on the back of his tunic. To the cheers of the crowd, they crossed
the Square to the Council Chamber; by the time they got there, their
clothes were wringing wet. There were 150 people packed into the
stifling room. The oath was administered by the Chief Justice; sweat
poured from the Duke's right hand as he laboriously wrote his signature.
There were formal addresses of welcome from both Houses to which the
Duke replied, saying 'how delighted I am that the Duchess is with me to
share in the pleasure of my first visit to these islands. We can assure you
that we are very touched by the warmth [sic] of our welcome in Nassau.
. . .' The anthem was played, while they faced the crowd from the
balcony. Then they drove up to Government House, where a thought-
fully-arranged mass of bright, odourless tropical flowers briefly concealed the fact that the pillared wooden dwelling was falling to pieces.

That afternoon, as the Duchess gloomily inspected their new residence,
the Duke managed nine holes of golf at the Bahamas Country Club. They
retired early. The next morning (it was a Sunday) the Duchess was said

* He had in fact, after some argument, reverted to being a field-marshal, the major-generalship having
been a temporary rank created for his service in France.

to be 'literally under the weather', but the Duke caused some surprise by attending divine service at the Cathedral. He sweated profusely, fanned himself and dropped the fan. Both the Bishop and the Dean were mysteriously absent from the Colony; the service was conducted by the Senior Canon, who prayed for the Duke and read the text: 'And the devil said unto him: "If thou therefore will worship me, all will be thine. . . ."'

Outside the Cathedral, Mary Teegarden chatted amiably to the Duke's Special Branch detective, Sergeant Holder.* That afternoon, she and all the other journalists were received in the lower gardens of Government House. For a patient hour the Duke and Duchess posed for photographs and answered questions. Would they visit America soon? They certainly hoped to. The renovation of Government House? No time yet to think about it. The Duchess's wardrobe? Non-existent. Did the Duke hope to be Britain's goodwill ambassador in the western hemisphere? 'While I have been employed in this role by Great Britain in the past', he replied, 'I doubt if the British Government intend that my present official activities should extend beyond the confines of these islands.'

It was a rotten sort of garden, the Duke reflected afterwards to a friend[13]; nothing but a disused swimming-pool on a terrace and some imported palm trees on a parched lawn; a tribute to the shortcomings both of the Government that was supposed to look after it and the people who had lived there. While he was there, he would try to make a better one. He was going to have plenty of time.

* Whom she was later to marry.

8
Making the Best of a Bad Job

August–November 1940

'Many thanks for your message of welcome and good wishes on my arrival in the Bahamas,' telegraphed the new Governor to Lord Lloyd, Secretary of State for the Colonies (who had privately 'hoped he would not do well'.) 'The Duchess and I have been most cordially welcomed here, and we look forward to helping Bahamians in their various problems and industries.'[1] In the first days of the governorship, they gave every impression of applying themselves to their new tasks. The Duke quickly absorbed the details of his job, and expressed the desire to do something for the people; the Duchess took up the presidency of the recently formed local branch of the Red Cross, and began to interest herself in infant welfare. In the first fortnight, they visited together all the government offices, and gave a series of dinners for the main officials and local figures. Few failed to be won by their charm, zest and interest in the Colony. On 23 August, six days after their arrival, there was a great open-air public welcome from the coloured people, with thousands massed on a hillside at Fort Charlotte. Choirs sang *Rule Britannia, Bahamian Sons and Daughters*, and a specially composed *God Bless the Duke and Duchess of Windsor*; the Duke made a speech and inspected veterans; the Duchess was presented with flowers; and there were three deafening cheers. They saw off young men who were going to join the forces, and welcomed the children of an English preparatory school which had been evacuated to the Bahamas. The Duke consulted everyone about local conditions, presided over the first meetings of his Executive Council, and on 2 September closed the current session of the Legislature with a speech of his own which, though necessarily brief, was agreed by all to be excellent.[2]

In those first days of the new governorship – of the first-ever royal governorship of a Crown Colony – the Duke and Duchess proved that, at least as far as the routine was concerned, they were well up to the job. They did all that was expected of them; they strove vigorously to make a good impression; they gave not the slightest hint of being bored, depressed or disappointed. But smiles, charm, a sense of ceremony, an absorbing interest in everything – these are the commonplace accomplishments of colonial governors and their wives, if they are any good. Such is the public façade, and underneath it lie private moods, feelings and thoughts. What official does not have private feelings about his post, which he takes care (if he is competent and sensible) never to show in the exercise of it? If this is true of governors, it is even more true of princes. Royalty, both by training and experience, wears a mask. It is always on show. It must never take sides, or give offence. It must be interested in everything, and radiate patience, charm and goodwill. In the life of a prince there is, there must always be, a gulf between the public and the private face. Since he was a prince, it was not perhaps unnatural that the Duke should excel at the external business of being a governor – the first royal colonial governor; and his wife, though without the advantages of such a training, proved as good as he. But this was the public face. What lay behind the mask? What were the inner feelings of the smiling and charismatic couple who, during those last scorching days of August 1940, beamed at the welcoming crowds, dutifully performed before the international press, charmed local society across the dinner-table, and delighted all by driving around democratically in a Land Rover?

The truth may be told in a few words. Though touched by their welcome, they were appalled by Nassau.[3] From the moment of their arrival they were filled with anguish and dismay. They had to struggle psychologically against intense depression, and physically against acute discomfort. But above all, their reactions were ones of shock and incredulity at their new surroundings. They could scarcely believe them, let alone adjust to them yet. They could not have been more aghast and stunned if they had taken command of what they had imagined to be a sea-going ship, only to discover belatedly that it was in fact a space-ship, in which they were already hurtling (with indefinite prospects of return to earth) through the uncharted reaches of outer space.

In order to understand the precise nature of these emotions, one must go to Nassau. No one who has not been there can realize what a bizarre, unreal and isolated little place it is. Arriving there for the first time is like landing on the moon. Even today, four decades later, with the face of the town hideously transformed by gleaming bank buildings and high-rise hotels and the huge American motor-cars which Bahamian youth require to zoom round the narrow streets of their tiny isle, it is hard for the European or American visitor not to be uncomfortably startled by the smallness and barrenness of the place. Of course, in terms only of its dimensions and lay-out – the commercial street, the harbour, the square of (imported) palm-trees containing the government buildings, the little ridge on which stands Government House and other (now rotting) colonial mansions, the sprawling shanty-town – it is not so very different from the principal towns of other small West Indian islands. But in the Caribbean the drabness of the settlements themselves is compensated for by a certain volcanic lushness in the surroundings, the sight of richly vegetated hillsides, the sense that all around ripe fruit is dropping off the trees. In Nassau there is none of this. One is always conscious of treading a harsh, coral landscape, that waterless, reliefless landscape which the principal historian of the Bahamas describes as 'lunar', a landscape which sustains next to nothing. To the newcomer's eye, Nassau is not so much a town as a combination of ugly buildings, a meagre flower-pot horticulture, and an alternately tough, petulant and apathetic local population (in 1940 it numbered less than 20,000), set down upon a limestone desert of pine and scrub. It is like an oasis without the pond and the fruit trees. For worshippers of sun and sea in search of ten days' holiday, or those who will live practically anywhere to escape paying income tax, it no doubt is and was a pleasant place. But to the outsider conscious of his environment, used to a temperate climate and to life in the city or in green open spaces, the sensations are stifling, overwhelmingly claustrophobic.

Under the best of circumstances, it was inevitable that the Duke and Duchess should have been (to say the least of it) somewhat taken aback by the Bahamas. But, as it was, the circumstances of their arrival were calculated to make their mental and physical discomfort worse in every way. They had come straight from the war, from the chaos of collapsing France and the inferno of spies and refugees that was Lisbon. After the sound of gunfire and the drama of disintegrating Europe, there seemed something shocking about the isolation and 'nothingness' of the Bahamas. The Duke longed for war service, but governing the Bahamas he felt more like a prisoner of war: after the terror and excitement of the battle he suddenly found himself removed to a drab, cut-off backwater, a place of dismal routine, all the while knowing that the conflict was continuing to rage in the world outside. And yet, arriving on this remote and petty stage, the Duke and Duchess at once had to get into the ceremonial act – not only for the Colony, but also for the massed regiments of the American press. They had all the strain of being on show before the eyes of the world. And worst of all, they underwent the experience during the very hottest part of the Bahamian year, a time of searing humidity and mind-destroying temperatures. Nassau during August, as one of the journalists covering the arrival wrote, 'fitted exactly into Dante's description of the inferno. . . . Your clothes are a sodden mass five minutes after you put them on, and your brain feels much the same way. . . . By 9 o'clock the sun was unbearable. The town lay sweltering and sweating and stinking under it. . . .'4 The Duke and Duchess had no experience of tropical climates, and only had their heavy European clothes with them. Any lingering capacity they may have had to fall in love with the Bahamas at first sight, or even to view it with some equanimity, was instantly dispelled by the heat and humidity. In time they grew to tolerate the Bahamian climate – but never to get used to it. In those first days in August 1940, it drove them to the verge of delirium.

As they gasped and wilted under these unfamiliar conditions, it only remained for them to discover that their new residence was a derelict building. Though it occupies one of the best sites in Nassau (on an eminence 200 yards from the shore, looking down at the great pink lump of the British Colonial Hotel), Government House has never been one of the architectural splendours of the British West Indies. It was part of Lord Dunmore's 1790s town-plan – and Dunmore did not imagine that any Governor of the Bahamas would ever care to live in Nassau. In nineteenth-century drawings, it looks like a Nissen hut with a pediment and a veranda; 'a chocolate-box affair' is how one twentieth-century observer has described it.[5] The main problem, as always in the Bahamas, was that the House of Assembly were determined never to spend any money on it. (All the more so since, being the seat of government, it represented 'the enemy'.) In 1929 the decayed and neglected structure had finally blown down in a hurricane.[6] Here was the long-awaited opportunity to erect some more solid and suitable edifice; but the opportunity was missed, and the 'reconstructed' Government House – built of timber on the shoe-string budget allocated by the Legislature – proved even more precarious and uninhabitable than its predecessor. Nor were its interiors a model of elegance and style: when Sir Bede Clifford arrived as Governor in 1932 he found not a stick of furniture inside it, and had to borrow from rich American residents.[7] By the late 1930s the building was riddled with termites and visibly crumbling; Frederick van Zeylen, the Belgian Director of Public Works, thought it positively unsafe[8]; but such were the stormy relations between the Legislature and Governor Dundas that not a penny was voted to improve it. Only when Dundas was removed to make way for the Duke did the House of Assembly grudgingly disperse a wholly inadequate £2,000. But no work was done before the appearance of the Royal Governor and his wife. Adela Rogers St Johns saw Government House the night before their arrival. Plaster was falling from the ceiling. Huge patches of humidity were everywhere. The ladies of Nassau were doing their best to decorate it with flowers, 'but no miracle of flowers could make it anything but the most thoroughly hideous house I have ever seen. In the drawing-room were bevies of large, over-stuffed sofas upholstered in a shade of salmon pink rarely used in household decoration. . . . No doubt it would have been possible for His Royal Highness and the Duchess of Windsor to live in Government House as it was. It would also, no doubt, be possible for them to wear hair-shirts. . . .'9

The Duke and Duchess put up with Government House for exactly a week. Then, momentarily, their courage failed them. In a long telegram to Lord Lloyd the Duke wrote enthusiastically about his new post, but complained that it was 'impossible to occupy Government House in its present condition and it will take at least two months to make it habitable.'10 Meanwhile, official entertaining was impossible and the heat was intolerable. He therefore wondered if he might be allowed to retire for a few weeks to his ranch in Canada, until the worst of the heat had passed and the rebuilding was completed. As it happened, this request was not regarded entirely without sympathy by the officials at the Colonial Office. It was in fact normal for Governors of the Bahamas to 'go north' during the terrible months of August and September, and Sir Alan Burns, the civil servant onto whose desk the Duke's telegram first fell, was a former Colonial Secretary of the Bahamas who understood how hard conditions must be for him.11 Whitehall went so far as to seek the views of Lord Lothian in Washington. Lothian, however, repeated his view that it was essential to keep the Duke out of North America at least until after the US presidential elections in November.12 Lloyd therefore replied to the Duke that there was 'great difficulty in Your Royal Highness's proposal to leave your post so soon after you have assumed office'.13 He added that the Duchess could go to Canada alone if she wished; but this (as he surely knew) was something which neither of them could countenance, and they accepted the verdict philosophically. They had now moved out of Government House into a comfortable villa on Prospect Ridge some three miles outside Nassau, loaned to them by Frederick Sigrist, the creator of the Hurricane fighter, who had just been appointed Director of British Aircraft Production in America. (But soon Sigrist and his wife would be returning from the United States, and the Duke and Duchess would have to find somewhere else.) Every morning, however, they returned to their offices at Government House (the Duke often making the trip by bicycle), where – waging an hourly but invisible battle against the heat and the strain – they supervised the renovation of their disintegrating official residence, and studied and attended to their numerous official duties.

There was one other factor which contributed to the depression and tension of those first days – though while it largely concerned the Duchess it was paradoxically the Duke who suffered most from it. Going through the files of previous correspondence between Government House and the Colonial Office, the Duke was astounded to discover a series of telegrams, for the eyes of his predecessor Dundas and the senior Government House officials, relating to how he and the Duchess were to be treated in the Bahamas (presumably they were intended to be destroyed but had not been so). In particular there was Telegram 134 Secret and Personal of 24 July, which contained the following message from the Lord Chamberlain:

> You are no doubt aware that a lady when presented to HRH the Duke of Windsor should make a half-curtsey. The Duchess of Windsor is not entitled to this. The Duke should be addressed as 'Your Royal Highness', and the Duchess as 'Your Grace'. Ends.

To the Duke the discovery of these telegrams was profoundly humiliating and distressing, the rubbing of salt into an open wound. It has been seen how he regarded the stigmatization of his wife as the only woman in British history not to share the dignity of her husband's rank as a terrible insult. He had learned to live with this insult, but what shocked him now was that, at the critical moment of the war, and after he had made the grand gesture of accepting a petty governorship, the Government and Court should have gone out of their way to issue such instructions to the very men who were about to become his subordinates. His family had promised 'not to interfere',[14] yet here were their persecutions, following him across the Atlantic! But now he was Governor, he would make sure that she received all the honours that were due to her. For her part, the Duchess was indifferent as to her title, save to please the Duke; she asked to be addressed as 'Duchess', and never expected royal honours – particularly from the British officials and their wives, who would have suffered keenly for it. But she could not help being uncomfortably aware, in the days just after their arrival, of the deep impression made upon the small, narrow, reactionary white community in Nassau (with its purita-nical attitude towards divorce, and still-lingering resentment of the Abdication) by the difference in rank of the Royal Governor and his lady, impressed upon them so officially such a short time before.[15]

As the weeks and months passed, and they became familiar with their Colony, the Duke and Duchess were to have many other reasons for failing to love the Bahamas; but these were their private first reactions. Did the Duchess write of them in that intimate journal of her doings and thoughts, her letters to Aunt Bessie? It has been observed that, in these wartime letters, the Duchess was always torn between the desire to tell all, the discretion imposed by the censorship (not usually much restraint), and her concern not to alarm her aunt. The first Bahamian letter was written from Government House on 31 August, exactly a fortnight after their arrival. Most unusually, it is a letter dictated to a secretary, and perhaps because of this (and the fact that, as the Duchess says, she is 'almost knocked out') it lacks the usual frankness and aplomb. But reading between the lines it would not have been hard for Aunt Bessie to divine the crushing sense of disappointment, the struggle against discomfort, the sense of isolation.

Darling Aunt B

I am completely ashamed not to have written before, but I have been almost knocked out by the heat which is enough to make everything the most terrific effort. Also by the house, which is impossible. . . . We have taken Mr Sigrist's house for a couple of months while we try to make government money do more work than is going to be possible for it. . . .

As you have been to Nassau I don't have to describe it to you. In fact you described it to me and you were right ! It will be very difficult for us to come to America. . . .

I can't get used to being so far away from the war. Although one has to go where one is told in wartime, I really would have preferred air raids in England and helping more closely with the fight to feeling so absolutely far away. . . . Strangely enough, after having had a taste for it for six months one gets wrapped up in the war. To come to a place which gives no idea of war makes me quite restless. I even miss air raid sirens – the nearest thing here is the twelve o'clock whistle.

I hope you have had a cool summer as it is *so* hot here and people tell me that it has been even hotter than is usual. . . . You can imagine how keen both the Duke and myself are to have you here, and the minute the great guest-room is arranged I will let you know.

All love
WALLIS

In the months that followed, the Duchess's less than ecstatic first impressions of the Bahamas did not greatly improve. In her intimate, hand-written letters to Aunt Bessie over the autumn she expressed herself briskly and with increasing freeness on the subject.

[*16 September :*] The heat is *awful*. I long for some air that isn't caused by electric fans. . . . I hate this place more each day.
[*7 October :*] Where did you stay when you came to this dump and why did you come here ?
[*25 October :*] One might as well be in London with all the bombs and excitement and not buried alive here.
[*21 November :*] We both hate it and the locals are petty-minded, the visitors common and uninteresting.

Such were the feelings and thoughts which the Duke and Duchess confided to a very few intimate correspondents such as Aunt Bessie, and to that tiny band of friends which had come out with them to the Bahamas and now formed their little entourage – their comptroller Gray Phillips (who now doubled as the Duke's Private Secretary), the ADC George Wood and his wife Rosa, and the additional equerry and public relations officer Captain Vyvyan Drury, a First World War comrade of the Duke and General Howard-Vyse's brother-in-law, who arrived on 28 August, to be followed by his wife Nina. However, it must not for one moment be thought that the Duke and Duchess wallowed in these anguished emotions, or that they in any way betrayed them to the people of the Bahamas or to the world at large. The private face of dismay and depression was entirely concealed by the public face of cheerfulness and enthusiasm. It was fairly obvious that they found it hard to take the heat (what newcomer did not?), but apart from that they hid the strain perfectly. It required a tremendous effort of self-control – but they managed it. It was a team effort; singly, neither of them could have held out for long under such conditions. Physically, she was the one who suffered more; psychologically, he was the more dismayed. But he possessed the experience and stamina of royalty – the suave public appearances, the smooth personal contacts – and she had the buoyancy, the resilience. Each made up for what the other lacked. Together, they were strong; and they had never felt closer to each other than in this adversity.

The general impression shared by those who met them during those first days, and suggested by the innumerable photographs and newsreels of the time, was of graciousness and enthusiasm. They appeared really interested in the task which confronted them, difficult though it evidently was. The Duke spoke of his post with keenness and optimism; this was also the main theme of his personal correspondence as Governor those last weeks of summer. 'The role of Colonial Administrator is a novel and unfamiliar one,' he wrote to Lord Beaverbrook on 30 August, 'but I do not believe that it will prove too formidable.'[16] They seemed all eagerness to get to know the Colony. 'The Duke accompanied by the Duchess every day visits some place of Government activity,' wrote the American Consul John Dye in an early report to the State Department on the new Governor. 'The Duchess is active in Red Cross work and both are becoming popular with all classes of the population with the exception of a few die-hard English.'[17]

Was this hypocrisy? How could it be that, while the Duke was writing to members of the British Government about how deeply interested he was in his appointment, the Duchess was scribbling to her Aunt Bessie that they both hated it more each day? Was their enthusiasm mere cynical pretence?

Here again, one comes back to the curious dichotomy of the public face and the private face. This is not merely a matter of images; in a circumstance such as the present one, it amounts almost to schizophrenia. Perhaps one day someone will write a book about the psychology of royalty – and of those people (colonial governors, film-stars, presidents, etc.) whose role is in some respects similar to royalty. Their predicament is of a kind which affects all who are prominent in public life; but royalty is the highest and most complex form of public life. It therefore finds itself existing on a whole series of virtually independent levels. Royalty in the boudoir is a different person from royalty talking politics with ministers; surrounded by its family, it is not the same thing as when it is surrounded by its courtiers; royalty presiding over a garden party is different again, as is royalty taking part in pageantry, royalty making a speech, or royalty waving to cheering crowds at home and abroad. Like an actor playing many parts, royalty can only succeed in its many guises by keeping them as separate as possible in its mind, in effect by splitting its personality. It is in this light that one must place the attitude of the Duke – the King's representative in a Crown Colony and once a king himself – and the Duchess, who understood him and sought to follow his example. The exhausted, near-exasperated couple who cursed their fate and struggled against their melancholia in the privacy of Sigrist House on Prospect Ridge were simply not the same people as smiled across the dinner-table, got down to things at Government House, studied the Colony's problems and were so very interested in everything. The Duchess was sincere when she confided to her aunt that they did not care for the Bahamas; but they were both equally sincere when they declared that they were keen on their jobs and meant to make a success of them. Far from contradicting each other, these two 'sincerities' rather complemented each other. They saw success as a way out of their difficulties, bringing the satisfaction of achievement in a near-impossible task and the possibility (as they still and always hoped) of a better post once they had won their laurels. Their anguish merely reinforced their determination. And, after all, what choice did they have but to make the best of a bad job, the only one which had so far been offered to them? As the Duke wrote from Nassau to Aunt Bessie two-and-a-half years later* (but expressing what had been their feelings from the beginning):

As you know Wallis and I get pretty desperate here at times and wonder how long we can stick it out, although as it is essential to have a job at the present time and we will never be offered a better one I guess we could do a lot worse, and at least we are together, which is vital and all-important to us.

That the Duke (when he put on, as it were, his governor's clothes) was perfectly serious about his job, that he was determined to learn it quickly and do it well, that he was genuinely concerned for the people under his rule, and that he was eager for some form of rapid personal achievement, is abundantly clear from his attitude to Bahamian politics at the outset of his governorship.

It was seen in the last chapter that the principal theme of Bahamian

* See below, p. 288.

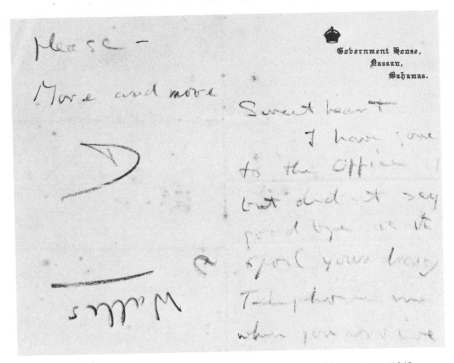

Love note left by the Duke for the Duchess to find on waking, autumn 1940.

colonial history was the perpetual friction between the local white ruling-class – the 'Bay Street Boys', tough merchant heirs of the original pirate settlers – and the Governor and his officials. Theoretically it was the Governor who 'governed', with the assistance of his Executive Council, and during the war the Defence Regulations also gave him almost dictatorial powers to use in an emergency. But in practice the Governor could do nothing without the consent of the House of Assembly, which held the purse strings and thus exercised power without responsibility, and which was absolutely controlled by the obstructive oligarchy of Bay Street and dedicated to the narrow interests of that powerful class. The House had been in continual conflict with the Duke's reformist predecessor Dundas, and were only now prepared to tolerate the Duke on condition that he abjured Dundas's policy of economic and social reform and devoted himself instead to promoting Nassau as a resort. They wanted him to be a glamorous but a passive governor, a charming yes-man. As one important observer close to Bay Street put it:

He will learn if he hasn't learnt already that the best way to govern the Bahamas is not to govern the Bahamas at all. If he sticks to golf he will be a good Governor and they'll put up statues to him. But if he tries to carry out reforms or make any serious decisions or help the niggers he will just stir up trouble and make himself unpopular.[18]

What were the Duke's first intentions as Governor? Certainly he did *not* intend to 'stick to golf', and one extraordinary fact is clear from his earliest telegrams and public statements – within two weeks of his arrival, he had a policy. Though he never imagined that he would be staying in the Bahamas for almost five years, he followed the same policy throughout that time, and succeeded in it to the greatest extent that he could have done. It was a policy with two central aims; the first was a continuation of Dundas's policy – the development of agriculture in the Out Islands; the second was a cause of his own – the systematic relief of native unemployment.

The Duke had naturally studied upon arrival the political legacy bequeathed to him by his predecessor, and while he was anxious – particularly at so critical a moment of the Empire's fortunes – not to risk 'rocking the boat' by controversial reform, he found himself totally in agreement with Dundas's economic policy. He resolved to press ahead with this; it was lamentable that the Colony should rely on so predatory and fickle a pursuit as tourism while the islands languished and produced nothing. On 23 August, only six days after his arrival, he declared while addressing the crowd at the public welcome for him at Fort Charlotte: 'While these islands are in one respect most richly endowed by nature, no one today can afford to rely exclusively on resources that have proved most profitable in the past.'[19] In his speech proroguing the Legislature on 2 September he said: 'It is my intention to visit the Out Islands before venturing to reach any conclusions as to the needs of the community as a whole.'[20] It was a surprising statement to throw at Bay Street; apart from the hated Dundas, no previous governor had considered it particularly necessary to visit the Out Islands at all, nor was it considered the role of the Governor to cater to 'the needs of the community as a whole'.

The Duke's concern about native unemployment is not to be wondered at. As Prince of Wales and King he had been gravely concerned for Great Britain's unemployed; 'Something must be done,' he had told the unhappy people of the Welsh valleys in November 1936; and now he found himself the chief executive of a territory with a decided labour problem. Much of the black population of Nassau was idle and impoverished, or only worked for the four months of the tourist season; in the Out Islands – as the Duke was told by John Hughes, the sympathetic little Welshman who was Senior Commissioner for the Out Islands – the situation was tragic. As before, the Duke resolved that something would have to be done; but this time, he felt he was in a position to do something himself. The first thing to do was to appoint a Labour Officer to study the problem. The Duke asked Hughes (to whom he had taken a liking) if he would combine such a role with his present one; Hughes agreed with great enthusiasm.

But alas, the Duke had reckoned without Bay Street. A Labour Department would cost money, and the Governor was assured that the House (which was horrified by the whole scheme) would never even consider providing funds for such a purpose. Thus obstructed, the indignant Duke did something which illustrated his keenness but also his ignorance of colonial administration. Not yet fully aware that colonies operated on a fairly rigid principle of self-sufficiency,* and that governors were expected in all but very exceptional cases to raise the funds for their administration locally, he telegraphed the Colonial Office in the second week of September asking for the use of Crown funds to set up the local Labour Office. They refused. 'I am of course aware of the attitude the House of Assembly has adopted in the past,' wrote Lord Lloyd on the 14th in a consoling telegram, 'but am confident that as time goes on Your Royal Highness's personal influence with the House will steadily wax and that by watching your time you will get them to agree.'[21] The fact that the Duke found himself checked in this way is less significant than the extraordinary fact that the whole matter had been proposed, examined and made the subject of this correspondence all within a month of his taking office.

As well as taking these political initiatives, the Duke made it clear at the outset that his would be 'a new style of government'. He would not be a remote and desk-bound governor; he wanted to get acquainted with the Colony and its problems at first hand. Hence his desire to visit the Out Islands. 'Unlike career governors with whom I worked', writes Sir Eric Hallinan, 'the Duke did little writing in official files. He preferred to discuss matters personally with those whose views might help, officials and non-officials. . . . He would seek and attend to advice from different points of view and then form an opinion.'[22] As when he had come to the throne, he wanted to 'open the windows', to do away with those administrative customs which in his view were outmoded and hampered good government.

Something must now be said about the people who were associated with the Duke in his administration. He was ably assisted by three senior overseas officials of the colonial service, of whom the most remarkable was Eric Hallinan, who as Attorney-General represented the Government in the Courts and was the Governor's legal and constitutional

---

* This principle was about to be modified by the Colonial Development and Welfare Act – though it may be noted that the Bahamas was not eligible during the war for assistance under the Act owing to its undemocratic character, a fact which much exercised the Duke in the later stages of his governorship.

adviser. Hallinan – who was to play a large part in the story of the Duke's governorship, and has given much help and information to the present writer – was then thirty-nine years old. Rosita Forbes described him as 'a very charming person, not devoid of guile'.[23] He was a barrister of King's Inns, Dublin, and Gray's Inn, London. His Irish Catholic family had long traditions in British service (his grandfather, an Indian Army general, had been an equerry to Queen Victoria), but had also suffered under the Protestant Ascendancy and supported the constitutional struggle for Home Rule. This background deeply coloured Hallinan's colonial service career.[24] Much as he loved the British Empire, he believed that its overwhelming purpose (which was indeed its declared purpose) was to prepare its peoples for self-government, and that the main duty of its servants was to improve the condition of its less fortunate subjects. He hated the Colonial Office system of 'indirect rule', which so often left the people to languish in ignorance and misery under oppressive local regimes. From Northern Nigeria, where the emirs were left to exploit the peasants, he came to the Bahamas, where Bay Street was left to exploit everyone else. It was inevitable that such a man – charged as he was with constitutional issues in a situation of growing constitutional crisis – should come to blows with the corrupt, reactionary local establishment. The Duke, whom he admired, did much to protect him, and relied heavily on his advice. He was to go on to achieve distinction in the colonial judiciary, ending his career as Chief Justice of the short-lived West Indian Federation.

The Colonial Secretary, responsible for the day-to-day running of the Colony, was W. Leslie Heape; he was forty-four and had previously held the same post in Grenada in the Windward Islands. 'Leslie had the temperament of a soldier,' recalls Hallinan, 'loud-voiced, conventional, conscientious and hard-working with absolute integrity.'[25] He was a dedicated and practised administrator who, as Rosita Forbes who was always at loggerheads with him recalled, 'adored correspondence'[26]; but a leg injury sustained during the First World War had affected his general health, and made him rather short-tempered and slow. He was an excellent colonial secretary, but was to find himself in difficulties when the Duke was away and he, as Acting Governor, had to take decisions in a crisis. But he did not lack courage; like Hallinan, he wanted to 'do something for the people', and so found himself a target for the unscrupulous forces of Bay Street.

Unfortunately for the Duke, Hallinan had only preceded him to the Bahamas by one month, and Heape by three; they were therefore not much able to put him wise as to the Bahamian *status quo*, which they were still in the painful process of discovering themselves. However, the third senior official, the Receiver-General Robert Taylor, a large, jolly, experienced man of fifty-seven, had been appointed four years earlier during the reign of Edward VIII, and so was able to enlighten his then sovereign as to what now lay in store for him.

The Governor's Executive Council ('ExCo') was composed of these three senior officials together with five 'unofficial' local men, all of them Bay Street Boys and members of the House of Assembly. In 1940 the 'unofficial' contingent consisted of a pompous dypsomaniac, 'a lawyer without much knowledge of the law', two ex-bootleggers and a grocer.

The senior member of this distinguished gang was Walter Moore, an aged merchant who controlled the Bahamas sisal trade and had taken to the bottle. He is remembered as 'a miserable man, a real sycophant'[27] who possessed 'the meaningless solemnity of an alderman'.[28] Moore made little contribution to ExCo and had no influence. The real power among the non-officials was a dour, sharp, reserved little man called Kenneth Solomon, who was the archpriest of Bay Street and held the rank of 'Leader for the Government in the House of Assembly', a key position in Bahamian politics. Hallinan records:

> He was the contact-man between the Governor and the House of Assembly (i.e. the Bay Street Boys). . . . As Leader for the Government he introduced legislation and was supposed to fight the Government battles in the House. In practice he supported what he, as captain of the Bay Street Boys, approved, and saw to it that any Government measures which met with his disfavour were defeated. He was a lawyer without much knowledge of the law, and quite without culture. But he was clever, forceful and assured in the control of his own small world. Through him, Government could always discover what the reaction of the House of Assembly would be to any proposal, for he *was* the House of Assembly.[29]

This humourless, narrow reactionary was to become the Duke's *bête noire* in the Bahamas. It was he who had told the Governor that his plans for the relief of unemployment stood no hope of success (which meant that he, Solomon, would never allow them to succeed).

The third member of the local group was the grocer R. W. Sawyer, a complete nonentity who made his only memorable remark on ExCo when, arriving at a meeting after an air journey, he declared that he was 'glad to be back on terracotta'. The remaining two members were both men who had made their money bootlegging in the old rum-running days of the 1920s and early 1930s. ('One was always conscious', writes Hallinan, 'that the smooth exterior of these people concealed the moral character of the thug, whose ancestors had lured ships onto the rocks with false lights and, still further back, indulged in piracy.'[30]) One of the former bootleggers, a Mr Collins, was of little importance, but the other, Harold Christie, was a central figure in the Bahamas, being the principal promoter of real estate in the Colony and controlling a strong family group in the House. 'Harold was a strange creature,' says Hallinan, 'squat, thick-set, with the slit-eyes, flat face, high cheek bones and sallow skin of the Carib. . . . He had a genuine flair for interesting rich clients in luxury homes, in starting exclusive clubs, and generally in the development of the Bahamas. He was not a glib salesman; you were told about a property and its potential in a slow, disjointed utterance that came from the depths of his being, a declaration of his utmost faith in future possibilities.'[31] While Solomon chose to do battle with the Duke from the outset, and was to become his arch-enemy, Christie's policy was to pose as the Duke's friend and meet his wishes as Governor as far as possible. As the property tycoon principally responsible for developing New Providence as a resort, he knew that the Colony would never get a better advertisement than from the Duke of Windsor's governorship.

The Duke presided over his council of three officials and five non-officials 'with patient good humour and without a trace of condescension'.[32] ExCo (which generally met once a week, usually on a Wednesday) was a consultative body – orders were made 'by the Governor-in-Council' – but in practice it was left to decide most issues of purely local significance (excepting such matters as security) which required the Governor's verdict but did not involve legislation. Hallinan recalls that they discussed 'a wide range of topics, from such a serious matter as whether the Governor should exercise the Royal Prerogative of mercy to commute a death sentence, to such trivia as whether Sally Rand, who danced naked but for the clever manipulation of a fan, should be allowed to perform in the Colony.'[33] Judging by the minutes,[34] it was the trivia which predominated, and the discussion was on the level of an English parish-council. At the Duke's first meeting, on 21 August, the first item on the agenda was whether the duty should be refunded on an imported church bell. On 18 September the main issue was the endowment of a public library and reading-room for Ragged Island (population 208); on 23 September it was overcrowding in the Nassau prison (average population 146). Such were now the counsels of the former King of England. But beyond the frequent triviality of its own business, ExCo played a wider role as the liaison between Government and local establishment, and the Duke was generally obliged to consult and seek the support of the local group before making or announcing any policy decisions. On most questions, it was difficult for him to act without them. They therefore (especially under Solomon's determined leadership) possessed considerable power to thwart him.

On the other hand, the Legislative Council ('LegCo'), forming the Upper House of the Legislature, had long been a superfluous and unimportant body, to which Bahamians who had been helpful to the Government were appointed as an empty civic honour. It was presided over with unction by the bibulous Moore, but in reality controlled by Hallinan who represented the Government on it. Its main function was the rubber-stamping of legislation sent up from the House of Assembly (it could not initiate legislation); but it had the (rarely used) power to veto bills and to pass resolutions, both of which, under Hallinan's guidance, it was going to do in the course of the struggle between the House and the Duke's administration.

Of the eight members of LegCo, one was a black man – Alfred Adderley, a coal-black, Cambridge-educated lawyer with something of the air of an African potentate. He was the leader of a mere handful of coloured men who played some role in Bahamian public life.* The economy of the Colony was entirely under 'white' control. Of the twenty-nine members of the House of Assembly, only five (three out of the eight New Providence members, and the two Dupuch brothers in the Out Islands) were coloured. A tiny number of 'advanced' coloured families had produced doctors and lawyers; more often than not these families were not Bahamian at all but of Caribbean origin, such as the Callenders and Pitts. Other men of colour who had some sort of education became priests or primary schoolteachers or clerks in government offices; the summit of black ambition was to become local commissioner on one of the more depopulated of the black Out Islands. The highest-ranking coloured official in 1940 was Sidney Eldon, who after thirty years in the Treasury Department had risen to be Accountant to the Receiver-General.

The virtual exclusion of non-whites from the public life of the Colony was the conscious policy of Bay Street, who did everything possible to keep them poor and ignorant and uneducated, to prevent them setting up in business, and to deny them any positions of importance. To this end, the House of Assembly consistently refused to vote funds for public secondary education, or for any measures designed to promote the social or economic improvement of the people. The opportunities presented to coloured people in the Bahamas were therefore considerably less than in such British colonies of the Caribbean as Trinidad and Jamaica, where a

---

* The colour scheme of the Bahamas, then as now, was extremely intricate. The 'pure' extremes of black and white were more often found in the Out Islands than in Nassau, where most of the population had some mixture of blood. Even 'Bay Street' was largely composed of very pale mulattoes. The mass of the population who were not pale enough to qualify as 'white' were divided amongst themselves, in the words of Dupuch, into 'groups determined entirely by degree of colour, starting with black at the bottom, through to off-black, dark brown, brown, light brown, "high yaller" and near-white'; but these divisions only had meaning amongst themselves, and 'both the official group and the local whites classed all coloured people as one'. (*Tribune Story*, pp.37–8.) The local 'whites' were 'colonials', whereas coloured people (of whatever hue) were 'natives' – though of course the first white settlers had come before the first black slaves. The lighter-coloured population tended to be looked down upon by both 'blacks' and 'whites' – though it was mostly they who produced the priests and clerks, and such remarkable individuals as Dupuch and Symonette.

sizeable non-white middle class was developing. And while it was possible (though extremely difficult) for a black or coloured man in Nassau to become a Member of the Legislature or a minor official, the social colour bar was absolute, and had been reinforced by the new dependence of the Colony on American tourists who expected to find abroad the rigid segregation they practised at home. A man like Adderley might thus sit on LegCo and have excellent professional relations with white lawyers, clients and officials, but would never be seen in a white house or admitted to any of the major hotels.

With Bay Street dominating the economic and political life of the Colony, the Governor and his officials had no choice in the short term but to accept this social system. Their long-term aim (and the policy of the Colonial Office) was to change it gradually by bringing about social and economic reform and so bettering the condition of the blacks. There can be no doubt that the Duke – with his immediately declared policy of developing the Out Islands and relieving unemployment – was in warm personal sympathy with this object, and genuinely concerned to promote the welfare of the coloured people. It will also be seen that he was one of the few to recognize the dangers of keeping them in poverty and subjection. However, it must also be said that, never having had to work with them before, he did not always feel at ease with them as individuals; the coloured politicians in particular he often found petulant and aggressive. But it would be absurd to say that the Duke was what one would now call 'racist'. By the standards of colonial governors of the time his personal treatment of 'non-Europeans' was perfectly acceptable and normal, and he was considerably more enlightened in his attitudes than the majority of Bahamian whites, or either of his predecessors, Clifford and Dundas. He had an excellent relationship with such negroes as the jazz musician Bert Cambridge (whose election to the House of Assembly in 1942 delighted him), and he took away with him from the Bahamas a young coloured valet, Sydney Johnson, whom he kept to the end of his life and loved as a son. It is true that the Duchess – who was to found and run three highly successful clinics for black babies – saw nothing strange in Nassau's colour bar, being a Southern lady. But even had she and the Duke wished to ignore it, it would have been impossible for them to do so. Bay Street – the local ruling-class without whose cooperation the Duke could not govern – would never have stood for it. As late as 1953, Bay Street was to engineer the recall of a governor who, in a very small way, had begun to invite blacks socially to Government House.

For their part, the ordinary black people of the Bahamas adulated the Duke and Duchess. They expressed their feelings at the tumultuous public welcome at Fort Charlotte. As the great-grandson of 'Queen Vicky' who had liberated the slaves, the Duke was invested in their eyes with near-divine status. To them he was still 'de King', or even 'de Lawd'. The story of how he gave up his throne for love had passed into Bahamian folk legend – and into the lyrics of the songster Blind Blake (which always drove the Duke into fits of laughter):

> On de tenth of December he gave a talk
> An' he gave de trone to de Duke of York:
> It was love, love alone
> Dat cause King Edward to leave de trone.

The people hoped for 'great things' from the Royal Governor. They trusted and looked up to him. The one serious civil disturbance of the governorship, which began during his absence from the Colony, was to cease at a word from him.

This awe and adoration was not, however, reflected in the columns of the principal black newspaper of the Colony, the *Nassau Daily Tribune*. The proprietor and editor of this lively journal, Etienne Dupuch, was – and is – a remarkable character. Of mixed French and negro ancestry, he had built up the single-sheet newspaper inherited from his father into an important local institution. He achieved this in the face of the bitter opposition and obstruction of Bay Street, whose interests were represented by the dull and official *Nassau Guardian* run by the white Moseley family. Dupuch had astonishing energy and verve, and his journalism was always stimulating. He was practically the only coloured member for the Out Islands in the House of Assembly (he represented Inagua), and did great public service by harnessing the power of the *Tribune* to such projects as the shipping of scrap-metal to England in aid of the war effort. The motto of his paper was 'Being Bound to Swear to the Dogmas of No Master', and by character the highly-opinionated Dupuch was indeed nothing if not defiant. Violent criticism was his *forte*. A staunch believer in the freedom of the press, he criticized everything. He set himself up as a sort of one-man opposition party in the Bahamas. He attacked Bay Street and the Governor's administration with equal vehemence. Today, when the Bahamas is a liberal black republic, Dupuch – as engaging and energetic as ever in his eighties – is still the thunderous critic of the establishment. All this is of course splendid – nothing is more important to the political development of societies (particularly corrupt societies) than intelligent and effective opposition – but Dupuch's opposition occasionally verged on the intemperate or the personal, and he admits candidly (he is always candid) that, even before his arrival, he had a down on the Duke of Windsor. He thought (and had said so at the time) that Edward VIII had behaved contemptibly in abdicating. As a Catholic, he disapproved of divorce, and he regarded the Duchess as a low woman. Always brave and outspoken to the point of rashness, Dupuch did not dissimulate his animosity in order to curry favour with the new Governor. The *Tribune* adopted a patronizing and critical tone towards his governorship from the beginning.

When the Duke attempted to tell Dupuch that one did not publicly criticize royalty, Dupuch replied that he was criticizing him not as a member of the Royal Family but as Governor of the Bahamas.[35] Dupuch made no allowances for the fact that he had no experience of political criticism and that his training made it hard for him to reply to it. In time the two men achieved an uneasy working relationship – they even came to respect one another – but Dupuch was always liable to attack without warning, and the Duke in return was not beyond puncturing Dupuch's enormous ego with one of those snubs which royalty knows so well how to administer. In the first weeks, however, the Duke was affronted and bewildered by the *Tribune*'s assaults, which both his entourage and his senior officials agreed were going much too far. It was therefore with their support and encouragement[36] that he issued in late September the following press statement, of which the draft among his papers is corrected in his own hand. It is an extremely interesting example of his style, and says much about his reactions as Governor during that early period. The last paragraph carries his own solution of how best to deal with press attacks:

A certain section of the local press has chosen to adopt a policy of consistently endeavouring to misinform their readers about the activities of the Government. A constant and vituperative stream of criticism has been directed against not only the Government, but also against almost every prominent public figure on the Island. Whilst informed, impartial and fair criticism is the duty of the Press, ignorant attacks made in a newspaper without knowledge of facts, can only be inspired by spite, or by an attempt to increase circulation by the methods of what is known as 'The Gutter Press'.

This would be despicable enough at any time, but at this juncture, when the Empire is passing through the greatest crisis in its history, and at a time when utmost unity of effort is required, and the fullest support should be given to those in responsible quarters, it is intolerable.

An endeavour to create dissatisfaction in these days is a treasonable act, and should be treated as such. The Press in this Colony has been fortunate so far, in that it has up to date escaped the strict newspaper censorship which has been imposed in England, and nearly every part of the Empire. The Press in this Colony may, however, at a moment's notice, be subjected to similar censorship, for the Government has the fullest powers and, if an attempt is made in certain quarters to spread disaffection during time of war, it will perhaps be the best solution.

In the hope, however, that this will prove unnecessary, we offer the suggestion that a Press conference should be instituted from time to time, at which the fullest information that is consistent with security and policy could be given out to the local papers, who would then have no excuse for issuing false information, or for making unwarranted attacks on public characters without any true knowledge whatever of what is being done, or what efforts are being made in responsible quarters on behalf of the people of this Colony.

The Governor's press conference was a new idea and a clever one, and for a time this announcement had the desired effect. But the *Tribune* was not the only newspaper to which the Duke found himself exposed that autumn – there was also the American press to be reckoned with. Of the regiment of reporters who had been in Nassau to greet the Duke and Duchess on 17 August, a determined battalion stayed on to keep them under siege. They followed them everywhere and clamoured daily for interviews. Naturally, all had to be refused. Starved of information, they resorted to invention. No governor in the history of the British Empire had had to go about his duties in such an atmosphere of press sensationalism, and it added to the strain of the early weeks. Finally the Duke decided to adopt a similar solution to that which he had employed in the case of the *Tribune*. With a view to quenching the American thirst for news of them, he made it known that he and the Duchess would allow one reputable reporter to be attached to them for a week for the purpose of writing a comprehensive series of articles about them. During that week, the favoured writer would live with them, have total access to them, accompany them on their official round, and be able to talk to them on any subject. They would not censor the articles, provided the general tone was acceptable. In order to achieve the widest possible circulation of this series designed to kill further publicity about them, they approached William Randolph Hearst, who nominated the female romantic novelist Adela Rogers St Johns, authoress of such heart-throb productions as *The Skyrocket*, *A Free Soul* and *The Single Standard*. Mrs St Johns duly arrived in Nassau to take up her new love-story assignment at the beginning of October; out of trepidation possibly she declined the honour of staying with them, but otherwise took full advantage of her opportunities to observe them.

It is hard to know how much value to put on the series of no less than fourteen articles which Adela duly churned out under the title *The Windsors' Own Love Story*, and which appeared in newspapers all over the Union in the second half of November 1940. It is gushy, romantic stuff directed towards a lower-middle-class audience. In her memoirs,[37] published almost thirty years later, Adela revealed that – although she had not actually put anything false into the articles – she was not sure she had really liked the Duke and Duchess, and felt that the Duchess had not liked her either. (In this Adela was quite mistaken. On 7 October the Duchess wrote to Aunt Bessie: 'Mrs St Johns is here writing a Windsor story. She seems very nice and well above the average.') In this later account, Adela says she found them charming but superficial in their manner towards her; she thought there was something tough and hard about the Duchess, and something pathetic in the Duke's total adoration of her. This does not come through in the articles, which are certainly not a source of great value on the personality of the Duke and Duchess. On the other hand, during their first year in the Bahamas, Adela St Johns was the only journalist who saw them and talked to them every day for a period, and published a substantial account of their life. Her articles are therefore of interest for what they reveal of their daily doings, the circumstances of their existence, and, above all, their reported remarks on various subjects.

In fact, Adela almost captured the paradox of their life in the Bahamas. She saw that they both took a hard-working and serious view of their jobs. The Duke eagerly discussed with her his plans for the improvement of native conditions. She accompanied the Duchess every day to the Red Cross, where 'it was plain to see that she had won all their hearts, and with them she was simple and direct and eager'. (This was seven weeks after their arrival.) But at the same time – although they guarded themselves from discussing their private feelings with her – she sensed something of their dissatisfaction. At their dinner-table, the principal theme of their conversation was the distant war, which seemed to occupy their minds constantly. Everything they said was correct and patriotic; they never seemed to doubt that Britain would win – though when the Duke toasted the King, it sounded like a passionate prayer for his embattled country. But when they turned from the war to the subject of their appointment, it sounded to Adela like a wartime sacrifice. 'He had offered himself "in any capacity" for service to the King, and the service chosen was governorship of the Bahamas. Like a good soldier and a good subject, he had obeyed.' In one unguarded moment the Duchess revealed herself with disarming frankness, exclaiming:

> How can you expect me to wish him to stay here? . . . I, too, wish us to do our duty. But is there scope here for his great gifts, his inspiration, his long training? I am only a woman, but I am his wife, and I do not believe that in Nassau he is serving the Empire as importantly as he might.

In Washington, Lord Lothian was aghast to read this in the *Times Herald*, and telegraphed it immediately to London. He considered trying to have further publication of the series stopped, but concluded that this would be impossible.[38]

Although Adela later wrote that she had felt obliged to take a somewhat cynical view of the Duke and Duchess, she admitted that there was one moment when they had moved her very deeply, and made her feel that they were real people whose romance was indeed beautiful and true.[39] It was at an evening party at the Emerald Beach Club in aid of air-raid relief. She found the setting magical – tropical flowers, soft lights, gentle breezes and the strains of a dance orchestra. It was hard to think that war existed anywhere. The Duke and Duchess arrived to the strains of the National Anthem. There was something fairy-tale about their diminutive elegance and grace. The orchestra struck up with *Stardust*, a popular romantic melody of the period; after a brief word with an ADC, the Duke and Duchess swept onto the dance floor. They danced enchantingly. Watching these two small people, moving perfectly together in perfect rhythm, Adela had reluctantly to admit to herself that this was a tale of perfect love. But there was a touch of melancholy about them. Afterwards she learned that it was the first time they had danced in public since the outbreak of the war. She wrote: 'I came to believe that it was almost a harder thing to do – to dance that night, to laugh and be gay, to help the people of the Bahamas to raise money for air-raid victims – than to stand beneath those air raids in London in uniform. . . . Almost, for a moment, under the magic of this man and woman, you were living again in a safe and beautiful world where people had a right to be happy.'

Adela also remembered the extraordinary energy with which the Duchess – in the intervals of her official entertaining, her Red Cross work, and her almost daily tours of inspection with the Duke – managed to supervise and direct the reconstruction and redecoration of Government House. It has been seen that they arrived to find this residence in a near derelict state, and had moved out after the first week. However Frederick van Zeylen, the Director of Public Buildings and Works, calculated that merely to make the building sound and habitable would cost at least £5,000. Grudgingly, the Legislature (which had previously voted a mere £2,000) rose to this sum. 'There was an idea that it was done only for them,' van Zeylen remarked in an interview some years later, 'but it would probably have been done had anyone else been governor.'[40] The interior redecoration the Duke and Duchess paid for themselves.

On 16 September – exactly a month after their arrival – the Duchess wrote to Aunt Bessie: 'Isabel Price [Mrs Winthrop Bradley, a well-known New York decorator] came down here and together we are going to dish this shack up so that at least one isn't ashamed of asking the local horrors here.' (In order not to infringe exchange control regulations, they gave Mrs Bradley enough sterling to buy a small villa in the Bahamas.) The Duchess explained to Adela:

Don't you see, I must make a home for him. That's why I'm doing this place over, so we can live in it with comfort as a home. All his life he has travelled, and a place to come back to is not always a home. The only one he ever had he made for himself at Fort Belvedere. He had to leave it – you don't know what that meant to him. I must make him a home. . . .

Mrs Bradley was joined by the fashionable American architect Sidney Neil, and from a small, whitewashed office, the Duchess directed both building and decorating operations in the manner of a general waging a campaign. She involved herself closely with the work, spending hours with the workmen explaining how she wanted things done; a secretary was astonished one day to walk into a bare room to find the Duchess, dressed in a simple dirndl skirt and surrounded by awestruck labourers, stooping down to mix paints in a pot to get the exact shade she wanted.[41] She found a useful and unexpected aide in the person of Gray Phillips, who shyly revealed that he harboured an aesthetic urge and had always been interested in interior decoration.

In the middle of October, as the work on Government House continued, the Duke and Duchess (now free of Adela) moved out of Sigrist House, whose owners were about to return, and took up residence at 'a shack by the sea' called Westbourne, one of the several New Providence mansions belonging to the richest man in the Bahamas, Sir Harry Oakes, Bart. (He was to be murdered there three years later.) On the 25th, the Duchess wrote to her aunt from Government House that 'things are going slowly here and I am not interested enough to push very hard. . . . I see no chance of being in before the middle of December.' She enlisted Aunt Bessie's help for various purchases in America.

Please could you send Ernest Hemingway's latest book about the Spanish War and Anne Lindbergh's last book and if you know of a few more good ones send them too. . . . If you have any silver you do not use, would you *lend* it to me? There is nothing but tin here. But remember, I don't want *anything* you ever use, no matter how seldom you need it. . . . Would you like a warm coat for Xmas, or money? Perhaps you would consider spending it here in these sordid Nassau surroundings. It would be fun to have you but it won't be La Cröe.

What the Duchess refrained from saying was that the Duke now found himself in a terrible nervous crisis.

It was two months since they had arrived. During that time the Duke had shown himself to be astonishingly active and enthusiastic, and had established both a style and a policy. But now, quite suddenly, he was plunged into the depths of despair. It was not an uncommon feeling among those officials exiled to the Bahamas. Hallinan, whose whole time in Nassau was intensely unhappy, recalls: 'The venom engendered by the political situation, coupled with wartime tensions and a claustral climate, made it hard to keep one's balance.' The weather in October is particularly dreadful. It is the hurricane season; the awful summer heat hardly seems to abate at all, and there is a constant hint of thunder in the air.

Under these trying conditions, the Duke found himself almost crushed beneath the weight of three terrible problems.

The first was the matter of his constitutional position. It has been seen that the Duke of Windsor is the only member of the British Royal Family this century to have had to take political responsibility and expose himself to political criticism. His role as Governor of the Bahamas – of the Colony where perhaps more than in any other the Governor was liable to be attacked by local politicians – was one for which his training as a neutral, protected constitutional monarch had in no way prepared him. He had tackled his unfamiliar and perilous job with confidence and courage – 'I do not believe it will prove too formidable,' he had assured Beaverbrook – but now, with the onslaughts of the *Tribune* on the one hand, and the dire warnings of Bay Street on the other, he began to feel the anomaly and strain of his position acutely. 'Hallinan, I feel so *exposed*!', he cried in a moment of anguish to his deeply sympathetic Attorney-General.

As if having to take political responsibility was not enough, the Duke now also began to realize (and this was the second problem) that he exercised his executive functions from a position of considerable political powerlessness. Since he required the consent of the House for almost all measures, he saw that he was at the mercy of a rough and hostile gang; and he began to wonder – like every governor before him – whether he was ever going to get them to agree to anything at all. The vehemence with which Kenneth Solomon and his cronies had denounced the Labour Department scheme and other proposed reforms had alarmed and momentarily disheartened him. 'As regards these islands, we have already discovered a host of problems which require immediate attention,' he wrote to Philip Guedalla. 'Unfortunately the House of Assembly, which votes the money, is in the hands of the unscrupulous merchants of Bay Street, and they are a very tough nut to crack.'[42]

Clearly, Bay Street was determined not to allow the Duke to play the part of a reformer. The part they did envisage for him dispirited him utterly, and was the third cause of his distress. Being the mascot of a winter tourist playground would have been undignified enough in peacetime for the former King of England. In wartime it was a horrible fate, and made him all the more aware of how far he was from the conflict in which he longed to serve. Of course, since the Bahamian economy depended on tourism, it was the Duke's duty to support it; but he deplored the fact that the Colony should rely on such a source of income and produce nothing.

The Duke spoke with great frankness of these odious and apparently ineluctable problems, and of the near-despair with which he, at that particularly gloomy moment, viewed his job, in a long personal letter written to Winston Churchill to mark the first two months of his governorship.*

Dear Winston,

In time of war and more especially just now that Great Britain is subjected to intensive bombing-attacks and threatened with invasion, and when the fortitude and behaviour of her populace in the face of these onslaughts are the admiration of the whole world, I would generally regard it as a man's duty to accept without complaint whatever the appointment he was given. There are, however, even in moments of national danger, always exceptional cases where a man would be doing a disservice to his country's cause were he not honest enough to bring to the notice of the Government the fact that he is a 'square peg in a round hole', or sufficiently frank in giving his reasons for such a state of affairs. . . .

As a member of the Royal Family, I have been raised under the protective wing of successive British Governments. Now I find myself in a post in which the tables are reversed for, as one of my officials explained to me the other day, he had been brought up by the Colonial Office to regard the position of Governor as one of protection for the Secretary of State in all matters of policy affecting the colony to which he was appointed administrator.

That in itself at once constitutes a problem for me, for having been taught all my life to avoid controversial matters, I am now expected to hand out the instructions of the S. of S. as if they were my own orders and to take all the local blame for them. Needless to say, the American newspapers have made full use of this embarrassing position, for whereas an order issued by the Governor of the Bahamas was not even news, one by the Duke of Windsor is a headline. But the most disagreeable feature of all in this place is the fact that I am open to being exploited in all manner of ways.

Take the colour problem, for example, which is an outstanding one in the British West Indies and the subject of an exhaustive report by the Moyne Committee in 1939. It is particularly acute in the Bahamas due to these islands' close proximity to America and the fact that local politics are controlled by reactionary lawyers and merchants, for while they will not let up an inch, the Governor must be conciliatory without queering the pitch for the native European element. This is by no means easy to achieve and ever since my appointment was made known in July the two rival local coloured newspapers have each used me as a stick to beat the other, the one proclaiming that my coming here heralded a new era of miracles for the negro population, while the other pursues a policy of criticism regarding my smallest administrative action or any slight change that I have considered it in the Colony's interest to make. This feud, which is meat to the American press, has assumed proportions which have needed drastic indirect attention, and although I think I have it in control for the moment, I could never guarantee it as fool proof.

* A typed draft, with handwritten corrections of both the Duke and Duchess, is among the Duke's papers. It is undated, but refers to the fact that he had completed two months' service. It is very possible that the letter was never sent. The Duke quite often drafted such letters merely to gather his thoughts and relieve his anguish.

Then another thing which makes me vulnerable for exploitation purposes is that the revenue of the Bahamas as you know depends entirely on three or four months' tourist traffic from America in the winter. It is unfortunate but it cannot be helped. For one good reason after another various attempts at raising, canning and exporting such climatically suitable agricultural produce as pineapples, tomatoes, sisal and sponges have all failed, and for better or worse the Bahamians have literally to rely on the tourist for a livelihood. For worse as it has turned out, for it has had the effect of inculcating a spirit of indolence amongst the coloured people who now prefer to exist for eight months on what they have been able to make off the visitors in Nassau in the winter than to work reasonably hard all year round in the Out Islands and as likely as not earn less.

What with the Exchange and Import Control operating adversely in countries not in the sterling block it is of course going to prove increasingly difficult to maintain this source of revenue up to the normal level in war time, and local interests have already quite naturally begun to use both the Duchess and myself to boost the American tourist trade for the coming winter season. I will not go so far as to say that they have as yet done so in an undignified manner, and as Governor I have a certain amount of control. But it does not require much imagination to see how we are the draw in this down at heel place, and enquiries have already come from American tourist agencies as to how they can advertise to their clients the assurance that they will get a good look at us if they go to Nassau on the cruise from New York.

Here again is a definite snag, for if we do not allow ourselves to be used to a certain extent to encourage American tourists to visit the Bahamas we shall be doing the Colony a bad turn ; on the other hand it goes against the grain to play the part of 'greeter' amidst all the horrors and misery that this war inflicts and which we have seen with our own eyes, a role that has never been in our make up and a form of publicity that, while helping these islands, would obviously react very badly on ourselves at this time.

The truth of the matter is that the place is far too small to carry anyone who has been the subject of so vast an amount of publicity, good and bad, that I have. While the situation created by my being sent here is merely very unpleasant in so far as I am concerned, it is in my opinion reacting to the detriment of the Colony's interests as a whole, and they will never, poor people, be able to take the fierce glare of the spotlights that have quite accidentally been suddenly switched on to them. . . .

Finally the Duke protested bitterly about the continuation of 'the mean and petty humiliations in which a now semi-Royal Family with the co-operation of the Government has indulged itself for the last four years'. The fact that their arrival had been preceded by special Palace instructions about the Duchess's treatment struck the Duke as symbolic of the desire to carry the campaign against them across the Atlantic. 'Somehow I felt that in view of the gravity of the war situation, this chronic insult to my wife might well be overcome if not entirely lost in the vast changes that are taking place before our eyes. But NO ! . . .'

It seems amazing that, during the Battle of Britain, the Court should have devoted time and effort to carrying on the harassment of the Duke of Windsor, shut up safely in a remote colony as he was ; but such was not a figment of the Duke's imagination, and came on top of all the other heartaches which contributed to his depression that October. Some of the acts against him were no more than mean little pin-pricks. He donated a canteen for London air-raid relief, to be called 'The Duke and Duchess of Windsor's canteen' ; he was told that 'it would be a mistake at this stage to give publicity to personal gifts', and the canteen remained nameless.[43] But there were more serious intrigues afoot. Vyvyan Drury – the Duke's second equerry who acted as a kind of public-relations officer – had been to America (where he had good personal connections) to visit the newspaper bosses and sound out their attitudes towards the Duke and Duchess.[44] He now reported that most of them were personally very favourable, but that their editors acted upon persistently slanted and critical accounts supplied by the press section of the British Embassy in Washington. Moreover, the weekly summaries of American press comment sent to Whitehall by the British Press Service in New York were utterly biased when it came to the Duke and Duchess. Only the most adverse comments were repeated – and the most minor and out-of-the-way newspapers had been searched in order to find them.[45]

In an access of bitterness at this news, the Duke wrote on 15 October to his loyal friend and supporter Philip Guedalla, whose highly romantic and pro-King book on the Abdication, *The Hundredth Year*, had recently been published in England in spite of a great official effort to prevent it coming out.*

. . . We do hope 'The Hundredth Year' has sold well for your sake as well as ours, though the Court and Government 'fifth-columnists' must have been hard at work damning it from the day it was published.

I say this because we have ample evidence of their activities on this side of the Atlantic, and the persecution of the Windsors goes on relentlessly. We know from reliable sources that they more or less control news regarding ourselves in America, and that they go so far as to encourage any lousy publicity, and that disgraceful and libellous lies are rife even in Washington. I have good reason to believe that the latter emenate [sic] from the FO; at any rate, the British Embassy has taken no steps to deny them.

I am only now beginning to realize the virrulence [sic] of the campaign that Official England launched against me the day I ascended the throne, and how, with Macchiavellian cunning, it used the fertile soil of the American press in the fabrication of sufficient evidence against me to justify its ultimate aim of having me out. However, who knows that this appointment in the Bahamas, in itself

* See my article 'Philip Guedalla Defends the Duke' in *History Today*, December 1979.

148

the end so far as we are concerned, may, on the other hand, prove to be the first opportunity we have as yet had of really doing something to frustrate their game and change the unfavourable atmosphere that over four years of intensive pernicious British propaganda has created for us in the United States. . . .

The last sentence shows a dramatic change in the Duke's mood. The latest evidence of his 'relentless persecution' had roused him out of his depression in a tumult of wrath; it was a call to action. 'They' had exiled him to the most ungovernable place on earth, doubtless expecting it to be the grave of his reputation. Very well then! He would prove them wrong. He would overcome the monstrous difficulties which beset him. He would succeed where all his predecessors had failed. His was only a narrow stage, but he would bestride it like a Colossus. He was filled all of a sudden with a terrible determination.

The chance for him to announce his vigorous intentions as Governor came very soon, with the opening of the new session of the Legislature on 29 October.[46] He wrote his opening speech himself; indeed, he wrote all such speeches himself, and they are characteristic of his oratorical style – slightly patronizing and platitudinous, but always well-reasoned and trenchant.*

It was largely a war speech. He spoke of 'the mighty conflict in which the British Empire is engaged, and in which this Colony is more than playing its part. Our thoughts are always with Great Britain, thoughts full of admiration and understanding for all that her people are living through. . . .' He spoke of the need to improve local defence arrangements; he spoke of possible American bases in the Bahamas. Then he turned to domestic matters. 'In his speech to you on the occasion of the last opening of the Legislature . . ., my predecessor stressed the importance of increasing local production, a policy I heartily endorse.' It was a brave thing to say, seeing that this policy had won Sir Charles Dundas the lasting hatred of Bay Street; but the Duke was adamant. Agriculture in the Out Islands had to be developed; he spoke of 'the admirable private enterprises' which he was soon going to visit; he wanted to encourage such private farming schemes by exempting agricultural machinery from tariffs. These remarks thoroughly alarmed the House, whose interest it was to keep the Out Islands poor and subservient. But the greatest shock was to come. Towards the end of his speech, the Duke declared (in language which left no doubt that he was

---

* Dupuch in his memoirs gives the Duke his due. 'There is no doubt about it, the Duke was a man of letters. It was said that he wrote all his own speeches for the Legislature. I believe this because, for a couple of days before the Legislature opened or closed, anyone who asked for an interview was told that the Duke was not available because he was working on his speech. And he wrote a good speech, among the finest delivered from the throne. . . .' *Tribune Story*, p.84.

expressing his own ideas rather than those of his officials or of the Colonial Office):

> Since I last addressed you I have been giving special thought to a problem which confronts all governments, namely unemployment. . . . [I]t would be foolish to adopt an attitude of complacency in this matter and a policy of hoping for the best. . . . In my opinion it is essential that some form of central organization be set up which will be ready and equipped to take care of any serious shortage of employment the moment it arises, and with this in mind I hope after careful personal investigation to submit a concrete scheme for you to consider during the forthcoming session. In the meantime I am taking steps to appoint an Advisory Board to consider wages in relation to the cost of living.

A 'central organization' to 'take care' of employment for the negroes! A government agency poking its nose into wages and prices! Such wild socialistic plans had never before been heard in the House of Assembly, and Bay Street regarded them with horror. Clearly the Duke was going to have a battle on his hands; but he had now nailed his colours to the mast. His speech unmistakably carried the message 'Something must be done!' He was *not* prepared to be a mere tourist magnet and the yes-man of Bay Street. In spite of all the difficulties which confronted him, he was determined to do something to improve the lot of the black people of the Colony.

One man who listened to the speech in the Council Chamber with profound interest was John Dye, the United States Consul in Nassau. He at once realized its extraordinary significance, and hastened to send a copy of it to the State Department with the following despatch:

> . . . This speech is one of the most sensible and business-like that has been delivered by a local Governor for many years.
>
> It contains no important proposals for new legislation but it does recommend a number of vital amendments to existing laws and in general indicates that the Duke is already familiar with local conditions and has a determination to improve those conditions. . . .
>
> It is the first time a Governor has suggested a study of wages of labour in connection with the cost of living.
>
> It may be true that he and his Duchess were sent out here to get rid of them, so to speak, but he is taking his job seriously and is showing a keen interest in the welfare of the Bahamas.[47]

Having declared his policy, the Duke got down to action. The first thing he wanted to do was to visit the Out Islands. Strangely enough, the idea that a governor should leave New Providence to tour the rest of his fief was a very new and unfamiliar one for the Bahamas. There was a well-established tradition in the colonial service of administering territories one never saw (an idea particularly alien to the Duke's conception of government), and most previous governors had only been taken beyond

Nassau by the occasional fishing-trip. The man who had broken the ice was the Duke's predecessor, Dundas. Determined to implement his ambitious plans for large-scale agricultural development in the Out Islands, he had visited the more important ones by air. The Duke wanted to go further than this and to visit all the inhabited islands by sea, taking the Duchess with him. He was no desk-bound governor; he believed it was impossible to understand a problem until one had witnessed it with one's own eyes. He wanted to set out on his first tour of the islands immediately after opening the House. But there was stormy weather and some trouble finding a boat, and it was only on 10 November that he, the Duchess, the Woods and the Senior Out Island Commissioner, John Hughes, finally left Nassau on a mail-boat, the MV *Content*.

The trip lasted six days. Most of that time was spent visiting the island which, next to New Providence, was then the most important of the Bahamas – the long, serpentine isle of Eleuthera, scene of the disastrous English settlement of 1648, but more recently of the most successful of the ambitious land projects which Dundas had encouraged. Three days were devoted to inspecting two unusual enterprises run by ingenious Americans – the aluminium millionaire Arthur Vyning Davis, who owned the Rock Sound estate in the south (where the *Content* landed), and Austin T. Levy, a Jewish 'cotton king' from Providence, Rhode Island, who had developed 5,000 acres at Hatchet Bay in the north. By blowing up solid rock to create a soil, and encouraging settlers to come out from the United States, these enterprising tycoons had achieved near-miracles in the barren Bahamas. Rock Sound was a flourishing citrus plantation in full production. Hatchet Bay was a model dairy and poultry farm, which already supplied Nassau with almost all of its fresh eggs and milk (rare commodites in the Bahamas); Levy was particularly unpopular with Bay Street because his milk sales interfered with their rum trade! The Duke was fascinated by these two estates and their proprietors (both of whom were to become frequent and popular visitors to Government House). Why, he asked himself, was their example not being followed everywhere? He would do his best that it might be so. . . . Certainly the rest of the tour showed the great necessity for such projects. The (largely white) native settlements they visited at Governor's Harbour, and on the nearby cays of Spanish Wells and Harbour Island, were old and picturesque, but tragically backward and impoverished and unproductive. And so the Duke returned to Nassau more determined than ever to change the economic system of the Bahamas, having seen for himself both what needed to be done and what could be done.

As for the Duchess, she was moved to pity by the sights of poverty they had witnessed, but frankly she had been rather bored by the tour. 'We had a week's trip to the other islands in a mail-boat,' she wrote to

Aunt Bessie on 21 November. 'They are worse than here if possible.' The passing weeks did not make her love the Bahamas, but rather resigned her to the vicissitudes of life there. 'The climate is better – that is, it is cooler – but the coolness is caused by continual *wind* – so you can take your choice – sweat or be blown to pieces. . . . We never see anyone – it's safer to keep on very formal terms – and as the staff is nice we can have a laugh or two.'

By the 'staff' the Duchess meant their little court of five – the Woods, the Drurys and Gray Phillips – who gave them their unfailing loyalty and friendship, and did everything to help them endure the first difficult weeks. But in spite of their support, and the essential company of each other, they had moments of loneliness; for theirs had been gregarious lives, and they were used to being surrounded by people they knew. Having to keep their distance from local society, they felt isolated; and they longed to see a few familiar faces. The Duchess anxiously scanned the lists of British evacuees coming into the Colony in the hope of seeing the odd familiar name; when she found one, it was always exciting news to be repeated at once to Aunt Bessie. 'Do you remember a friend of Katherine Galbraith called Mrs Leech in London? She is here. . . .'[48] 'Yvonne Holt, a girl I knew in London, is refugeeing here – but depressed, so not a great addition.'[49] In the course of the autumn two old acquaintances of the Duke also turned up in Nassau, to be greeted by the Royal Governor with much enthusiasm – Major Frank Goldsmith,* a sometime Conservative MP who had acquired a European reputation as a hotelier, and Captain Alastair ('Ali') Mackintosh, a First World War flying-hero who now lived in New York and had business in the Bahamas. These two lively and civilized Englishmen were received almost in the manner of Stanley greeting Livingstone, and were afterwards to become 'regulars' at the as yet uncompleted Government House.

The couple's isolation was not eased by their problematical social relations with the two principal categories of non-local resident in Nassau. There was the villa-owning community of (mostly American) winter visitors, due to descend in December and stay till March. The Duke and Duchess dreaded their arrival, but were resigned to having to preside over the Nassau season in the midst of world war. And there was the growing and more permanent class of (mostly elderly English and Canadian) tax exiles, whose focal point was the exclusive Emerald Beach Club and whose acknowledged social leaders were Sir Frederick and Lady Williams-Taylor. It was from these people that the Duke and Duchess at first encountered some hostility: in the early weeks the Williams-Taylors and others made a sport of snubbing the Duchess. It is

* Father of Edward and James.

interesting to note, however, that almost all of this society was eventually won round to the Duchess, Lady Williams-Taylor in particular bringing herself to curtsey to her and sing her praises with all the rapturous enthusiasm of a convert.

In the autumn of 1940 there were only two pairs of British residents whom the Duke and Duchess got to know fairly well – and these were naturally the owners of the houses in which they stayed. Sigrist and Oakes were not dissimilar characters – both self-made men, both un-affected pioneer sorts, and both therefore belonging to a type calculated to appeal to the Duke. Fred Sigrist was a blunt and kindly Yorkshire-man. As the aeronautical engineer who had created the Hurricane and was now directing the desperate production of it in America, he provided a link with the Duke's devious old supporter Beaverbrook, who had become Minister of Aircraft Production in London. Sigrist's wife Beatrice was noted for her beauty, insouciance and charm. Sir Harry Oakes was a more complex and eccentric character, the son of a good family in Maine who had abandoned middle-class American life to become a rough, globe-trotting gold-digger, finally discovering in Canada – after a long and bitter struggle – the second richest mine in the world. 'He was a small, energetic, rugged man,' recalls Hallinan, 'never happier than when driving a bulldozer. His appearance and style although rough was not vulgar; he had a natural dignity. He did an immense amount of good with his great wealth. Money had not spoiled him: he remained essentially the plain, single-minded man who had roamed the world in search of gold and, when he found it, gave most of his wealth away.'[50] It was inevitable that the Duke should have much to do with Sir Harry, who apart from being the proprietor of Westbourne, and indeed the greatest property-owner on New Providence, was also the richest resident of the Bahamas and the biggest backer of local enterprise. But he also liked him for himself. Oakes's popular Australian wife was quite different from Sir Harry – sensitive, beautiful and calm. The Duchess was to become very fond of both Bea Sigrist and Eunice Oakes.

Apart from Oakes, there was another fabulously rich resident of Nassau who was interested in the development of the Bahamas. He was a Swede, and his name was Axel Wenner-Gren. Something must be said about this unusual character, whose history – and in particular his relations with the Duke of Windsor – has been the subject of grotesque distortions. The first thing to be said is that, when the Duke and Duchess arrived in Nassau, Wenner-Gren was not there, being temporarily absent in South America. However, they much looked forward to his return. For what has not until now been revealed is that they already knew a great deal about him – and had in fact planned to meet him exactly three years before.

Who was Axel Wenner-Gren?* Born in 1881, he was a brilliant Swedish engineer-industrialist who had founded the Electrolux Company in 1919 and made a fortune in the 1920s from the world-wide exploitation of two great domestic inventions – the electric vacuum-cleaner and the solid-state refrigerator. As the Electrolux vacuum-cleaner swept the globe, Wenner-Gren became master of a huge industrial empire, based in Sweden but with major interests elsewhere, especially in the United States. Like many powerful international businessmen of this period (Charles Bedaux is a strikingly similar example) he felt that, having created so successful an economic activity which transcended frontiers, he could help in bringing nations together and so play a role as a sort of world statesman. He idealistically believed that, if only the ultimate catastrophe of war could be averted, the world would move towards economic and finally political union; he felt that his own mission in this majestic process was to help unify the nations of northern Europe.

Wenner-Gren was at first horrified by the coming to power of the Nazis in Germany, with their brutal militarism, virulent economic nationalism, and hatred of 'international' tycoons such as himself. By 1936, however, it appeared that Hitler was there to stay and would have to be reckoned with; at the same time the international situation was rapidly darkening, and Wenner-Gren came to believe – with amazing naivety, but perfect sincerity – that he might be able to persuade the Nazi bosses to make their odious internal and foreign policies more 'acceptable' to other powers, and act as a kind of diplomatic intermediary to help avert the final calamity. He knew Goering slightly from the time when that baroque individual had been briefly married to a Swedish noblewoman, and on 11 September 1936 he paid the first of two visits to the Reichsmarschall at Karinhall to explain his views. The interview was cordial, but nothing whatever resulted from it. Wenner-Gren duly reported their conversation to the Swedish Prime Minister Albin Hansson, and then crossed the Atlantic to discuss the international situation with President Roosevelt; the President was outwardly polite but inwardly suspicious. In 1937, Wenner-Gren expressed his ideas in a curious Utopian tract, published in several languages, entitled *An Appeal to Everyman*, in which he called for international disarmament, the establishment everywhere of democratic governments and the abolition of trade-barriers, and advocated the rapid improvement in all countries of education, wages, and working and living conditions.

---

* There are two important Swedish biographies, the official life by Gunnar Unger (*Axel Wenner-Gren: En Vikingsaga*, Bonniers, Stockholm, 1962) and *Dansen kring guldkalven* (*The Dance Round the Golden Calf*) by Ragnar Boman and Ingrid Dahlberg (Askild & Kärnekull Förlag, 1975), a highly critical left-wing account. It is interesting to note that one of the few points on which the two books agree is that Wenner-Gren was unjustly accused of being actively pro-German during the war.

It was around this time that the Duke of Windsor – only a few months after his Abdication – was brought into curious indirect contact with Wenner-Gren. While at Candé preparing for his marriage, he received a long letter dated 28 April 1937 from Rochester, N.Y., from his old acquaintance Oscar Solbert; Colonel Solbert was a retired Swedish-American staff officer who had been Military Attaché at the US Embassy in London just after the First World War, and had accompanied the then Prince of Wales on his United States' tour of 1924. Recalling the brilliant public qualities he had then witnessed, Solbert now begged the Duke to 'head up and consolidate the many and varied peace movements through-out the world. . . . I am not a pacifist, as you know, but I do believe that the one thing the world needs more than anything else is peace. . . .' He added that he had 'talked this matter over' with 'Mr Axel Wenner-Gren, the most successful captain of industry in Sweden', who was 'very enthusiastic about the idea' and 'prepared to put a considerable sum of money behind the plan. What is more, he felt he could vouch for the participation in it of the people from the Scandinavian countries, Sweden, Norway, Denmark and Finland.' What Solbert and Wenner-Gren prob-ably did not know was that similar ideas were being suggested to the Duke by many other influential people – notably by his host at Candé, the enigmatic time-and-motion tycoon Charles Bedaux. It was in fact Bedaux who, at the Duke's request, replied to Solbert four months later in the following terms:

> . . . The Duke of Windsor is very interested in your proposal that he lead a movement so essentially international. We all know that as Prince of Wales and King he has always been keenly interested in the lot of the working man and has not failed to show both his distress and his resolve to alter things whenever in that field he has encountered injustice. . . . He is determined to continue, with more time at his disposal, his systematic study of this subject and to devote his time to the betterment of the life of the masses. . . . He believes it is the surest way to peace. For himself he proposes to help soon with a personal study of housing and working conditions in many countries. From you he desires to receive the detailed draft of a workable plan. He is happy to learn that Mr Wenner-Gren stands ready to help. . . .[51]

The result of this request was that the Duke received one of the first copies of Wenner-Gren's *Appeal to Everyman*, which likewise put forward the notion of promoting peace through an international move-ment to improve social conditions. As Prince of Wales he had already heard something of Wenner-Gren's international and social ideas during his state visit to Sweden in October 1932. He was now fascinated by them, and began to correspond with Wenner-Gren with a view to their meeting that autumn. But the meeting never materialized, for two reasons.* After the disastrous mistake of beginning his international study of workers' housing conditions with a visit to Nazi Germany, and the subsequent traumatic collapse of his plans for a similar tour of the United States, the Duke felt obliged to withdraw for the time being from all public activity. And in the meantime a deeply disillusioned Wenner-Gren had decided to give up Europe as a doomed continent and make his future in the New World. In the autumn of 1937 he purchased the magnificent yacht *Southern Cross* and set out in it for America by way of the Far East. He aimed both to consolidate his interests in the United States and create a new economic empire in the great unexploited terrain of Latin America. (But he reckoned without the hostility of the State Department, which saw him as a threat to American economic hegemony on the continent.) After a year's sailing and travelling around the Americas, he finally decided to make his base in Nassau. He was attracted to the Bahamas by the non-existence of income tax, the challenge of contributing to the development of a barren territory, and the easy accessibility to both North and South America. He quickly became a friend of Governor Dundas, and was uneasily tolerated by the Bay Street Boys on account of his great wealth. He acquired a splendid residence in the form of the secluded estate founded by Edmund Lynch on Hog Island, the large cay just off Nassau which forms the harbour; hoping it would be an ideal haven from a world in turmoil, he named it 'Shangri-La'.

In May 1939 Wenner-Gren returned to Europe on the *Southern Cross* to wind up his interests there. With almost incredible simple-mindedness (but undeniable good intentions) he now made one final dramatic effort to avert the Second World War.[52] (This too was the moment when the Duke of Windsor was making his international broadcast for peace.) Learning, from the Hungarian Frederic Szarvasy, that Neville Chamberlain was looking for neutral intermediaries to assist in Anglo–German discussions, he dashed across to Germany where, on 25 May, he had the second of his interviews with Goering. The Reichsmarschall was sceptical about the chances of Anglo–German *détente*, but nevertheless drafted for Wenner-Gren a memorandum of 'points which might constitute a basis for future negotiation'. Armed with this document, Wenner-Gren rushed back to Sweden where he showed it to none other than King Gustav V, who was sufficiently impressed to give him a hand-written letter of introduction to Chamberlain. The British Prime Minister duly received the Swede, but told him that Great Britain could not come to terms with Germany unless

---

* Gunnar Unger, basing himself on their correspondence, writes in his official biography that the Duke and Wenner-Gren did in fact meet in Paris in October 1937. This appears to be an error. Wenner-Gren wrote proposing such a meeting, but his Paris dates clashed with the Duke's already-planned visit to Germany. He did however meet up with Bedaux.

Hitler gave convincing proof of his honest and peaceful intentions. Wenner-Gren (who had had no contacts with the Nazi leaders apart from his two interviews with Goering) declared that he would try to obtain such proof. Locking himself up in his castle at Häringe in Sweden, he drafted an amazing series of detailed proposals to lay before the Führer, including a second disarmament of Germany, an amnesty for political prisoners, restoration of rights to Jews and the abolition of the concentration camps. But Goering, to whom he sent this somewhat sanguine programme with a request to transmit it to his chief, brusquely declined to do so, saying that it was utterly unacceptable to the regime and would only excite Hitler's fury and scorn.

Despondently, Wenner-Gren set sail for the Bahamas on the *Southern Cross* at the end of August 1939. The war broke out while he was at sea, and he picked up the survivors of the torpedoed SS *Athenia*. Back in Nassau, he discussed with Dundas ways in which he could help the Governor's plans for the economic development of the islands. He set up an ambitious crayfish-canning plant on the island of Grand Bahama, and began various agricultural and drainage works on Hog Island (of which he came to own four-fifths). In Washington, he told the Secretary of State, Cordell Hull, of his European peace endeavours. In February 1940 he briefly returned to Europe to follow the American peace mission of Sumner Welles.

The presence of a rich, cosmopolitan and highly peripatetic Swede in a British colonial territory during the war inevitably posed something of a security problem. To Dupuch, with whom he was always on friendly terms, Wenner-Gren lamented that he was 'so international a figure as to be considered a spy in any country'. As the most eminent foreigner in parochial and xenophobic Nassau he excited intense local suspicion, and war hysteria led to incredible rumours – such as that he had actually led the U-boats to the *Athenia*. In May 1940, as the battle burst out in Europe, Dundas wrote to London asking for security guidance on Wenner-Gren. The reply showed that British Intelligence had no clear evidence that Wenner-Gren was dangerous but were nevertheless uneasy about him:

> Opinion is that Wenner-Gren is probably susceptible to German propaganda and not particularly pro-Ally being mainly interested in his own future and in inter-Scandinavian cooperation. Security service regards him with some suspicion . . . and thinks that his return to Bahamas might not be undesirable as it would enable him to be kept under observation.[53]

The author has talked to former members of the Secret Service involved in the watch on Wenner-Gren, who say that there was never any proof that he was an enemy sympathizer or worked against Allied interests (except perhaps certain United States economic interests). It was, however, not unnatural in war that he should have been suspected.

Meanwhile, Wenner-Gren's Latin American projects were germinating, and in the spring of 1940 he had set out on a six-month business tour of Mexico and South America. He was in the midst of this when, in July, he learnt that the Duke of Windsor was to succeed Dundas as Governor of the Bahamas. Wenner-Gren's reactions to the fate in war of the man he had once hoped would secure international peace are interesting. On hearing the news, he is said to have exclaimed to his colleagues: 'How can they deport such a fine man to so uncivilized a place, where one needs a hide of steel to survive? How can they expect him to stand up to the pirates?'

Pitying the Duke, Wenner-Gren sent instructions to Nassau that Shangri-La with all its privacy and comfort should be placed at the disposal of the new Governor and his wife until his own return in the autumn. The Duke was advised against accepting this offer, and followed this advice; but there can be no doubt that he was immensely looking forward to meeting the man he had so much hoped to meet three years before. Lonely and friendless in Nassau, surrounded by a village society with village ideas, by the tough and narrow Bay Street world of grocers and ex-bootleggers, by a Ruritanian official world, he longed for the company of an independent, cosmopolitan figure of lively intellect and wide culture, for a man of vision and ideas who shared something of his *Weltanschauung*. He had studied the Swede's security file, which was a mass of rumour and suspicion. What he knew for certain was that Wenner-Gren had, like himself, made a sincere effort to prevent the war, and that in his *Appeal to Everyman* he had expressed ideas about peace and social justice identical to his own. He also knew that Wenner-Gren understood the Bahamas, and had been invaluable to his predecessor Dundas for his help and advice over a whole range of political and economic issues. Furthermore, Wenner-Gren happened to have an American wife. The Duke therefore awaited his return with her to Nassau with interest, if not impatience.

The *Southern Cross* arrived back in Nassau on 17 October. The following day Wenner-Gren called on the Duke at Government House. It was a curious fate which had finally brought them together in this God-forsaken place, so far from the fallen Europe which they had once tried to meet to try to save. The tall, energetic, silvery-haired Swede (he was fifty-nine, but had the air and stamina of one half that age), with his handsome features and charming manners, evidently did not disappoint the Duke, who on the 25th, together with the Duchess, inspected Wenner-Gren's projects on Hog Island and dined with him and his wife Marguerite at Shangri-La. Four days later, on the 29th, the Wenner-

Grens were present in the Council Chamber to hear the Duke deliver his speech to the Legislature; and on the 31st they dined with the Duke and Duchess at Westbourne, together with the Fred Sigrists. The Duke and Duchess saw them frequently over a period of nine months – after which they were never to see each other again.

What were the relations between the Duke and Wenner-Gren during those nine months? According to a Swedish intimate of Wenner-Gren who later managed his Bahamas enterprises,* they 'seemed to strike up a real friendship, though there was always a clear distance on both sides. They had many and long meetings during which they discussed the economic and political problems of the Colony. . . .' For it was no mere coincidence that Wenner-Gren had been present to hear the Duke's important policy speech of 29 October – nor can one doubt that the Duke had first discussed it with Wenner-Gren. The Swede had acquired a wide understanding of the Bahamian situation; he had enthusiastically collaborated with Dundas in his valiant efforts to transform that situation; now he sought to do what he could to help the Duke. His original feelings of pity aroused by what he called the Duke's 'exile to this pirates' nest' were now replaced by admiration for the speed with which the Royal Governor had grasped the local problem and formulated a policy. He invited the Duke to visit his great Out Island project, the crayfish cannery on Grand Bahama. But what interested the Duke most of all was the work on Hog Island, in which he saw an ideal solution to the local unemployment problem. As Wenner-Gren's Swedish friend (who was to direct the post-war continuation of that work) recalls:

Wenner-Gren was always fascinated by the development of raw land. On Hog Island he had some 700 barren acres. Near the house he managed to plant banana and citrus and start a great garden. . . . The Western portion of the Island was a huge, mosquito-infested swamp, which in 1939 he had started to dig out and turn into a lake. One day the Duke of Windsor asked him whether he might not accelerate and expand these operations to create more work in Nassau. Wenner-Gren readily agreed and immediately started a huge project for the development of the Island. He landscaped the gardens. He finished the lake, and excavated a network of shallow canals connecting it with the Ocean to the North and the Harbour to the South. He constructed a 'Hurricane Hole' (now a yacht marina) and made an agreement with the Government enabling this to be used as a refuge by local boat-owners. . . . On these schemes he employed hundreds, sometimes over a thousand labourers, all the work having to be done by hand as there was no machinery available at the time. . . .

At its height, in the spring and early summer of 1941, the Hog Island project employed over fifteen per cent of Nassau's total workforce. It was a triumph for the Duke's employment policy; he often went with

* He has asked me to withhold his name, which however will be familiar to many in the Bahamas.

Wenner-Gren to inspect the work and did all he could to help it along – he personally saw the 'Hurricane Hole' scheme through ExCo. But it is incredible what war hysteria can do to the human mind, and the rumour was eventually heard that the canals (designed for yachts six feet at their deepest) and the Government-sponsored 'Hurricane Hole' (freely usable by local craft, and destined to save Nassau's marine craft in the hurricane of October 1941) were in reality intended for a fleet of German submarines . . . which were on their way (according to some versions) to establish Wenner-Gren as Nazi Governor of the Bahamas. At first this story was treated as a joke, but later, when Wenner-Gren had been discredited and exiled from the Colony, it was actually begun to be believed, and even elaborated into an amazing tale of intrigue in which a variety of sinister roles were reserved for the man originally responsible for the Hog Island project – the Duke.

Apart from Wenner-Gren's advice and practical help to the Duke in local politico-economic affairs, the Duke and Duchess also much enjoyed the society of the Wenner-Grens, who were excellent hosts and guests. Wenner-Gren advised the Duchess on her good works in the Bahamas, and provided funds and materials to help her set up two infant welfare clinics in Nassau. The Duchess also got on well with her fellow-countrywoman Marguerite Wenner-Gren, who was as lively and colourful a personality as her husband and also interested herself in sculpture and poetry. In verses such as these she demonstrated a fine appreciation of the atmosphere of the Bahamas which the Duchess doubtless shared:

> Gigantic blossoms,
> trees dripping teardrops of humidity,
> armies of vicious land crabs
> rising on their spindly hind legs,
> with round, vindictive, goggling eyes,
> vice-like claws ready for attack;
> the coral snake poised for the kill. . . .[54]

Often – at Westbourne, at Shangri-La, at Government House, or on board the *Southern Cross* – the Duke and Wenner-Gren would talk alone over their cigars late into the night. Did they talk much of the war? It is more than likely. But all one can say is that, if the Duke confided to Wenner-Gren his private views about the international situation, Wenner-Gren was the perfect confidant, and never seems to have repeated them to anyone, even in his intimate circle. They were likewise discreet in their correspondence, which mostly concerns invitations, their habit of lending each other periodicals which were hard to obtain, and (on an official level) Wenner-Gren's economic projects.

What one cannot doubt is that the Duke had longed since his arrival to be able to discuss the state of the world with some well-informed friend of broad views. The war and the fate of England never ceased to haunt him that late summer and autumn. He had followed the Battle of Britain day by day in fear and hope. 'You must be having a very anxious time in Great Britain,' he wrote to Beaverbrook at the end of August, 'but from all accounts the RAF seems to be on top though still numerically inferior.'[55] That autumn the public task which he regarded as most sacred was his farewells to the young volunteers (mostly sons of Bay Street) who were off to join the forces (there was no conscription in the Bahamas). He gave orders that the Union Jack over Government House was no longer to be lowered at dusk – 'for this is no time to be pulling down our banners'.[56]

He longed to do something to contribute to England's struggle; and an opportunity – albeit minor – had come in the first days of the governorship. On 2 September the Anglo–American agreement was signed whereby the United States offered Great Britain fifty destroyers in return for the right to lease air and sea bases in a number of British West Atlantic territories – including the Bahamas. 'Responsible opinion appears to be entirely favourable to leases of bases in the Bahamas,' the Duke had hastened to telegraph to the Colonial Office on the 4th.[57] (There were few other colonies of which this could be said.) The Agreement struck both him and the Duchess as a crucial occurrence, worth far more than the fifty ships; it was the decisive commitment of America to the Allied cause. 'When is the US going to tell the people they are at war,' wrote the Duchess to Aunt Bessie on 16 September, 'because you can't deny that you are already.' The Duke (with the able assistance of Heape and Hallinan) threw himself wholeheartedly into making the formal arrangements for the bases and studying the possible sites; when Admiral Greenslade of the US Navy came to Nassau for secret discussions in early October, he found that the Royal Governor had already collected a mass of information and formed particular views. The Americans especially wanted bases on the islands of Eleuthera and Mayaguana; the Duke was opposed to Eleuthera, where both the historic settlements and the important new agricultural projects might be endangered by a military presence, but was in favour of leasing the whole of the small southerly island of Mayaguana.[58] He opened his speech to the Legislature on 29 October by declaring himself 'confident . . . that the House will be prepared to approve measures . . . to meet the requirements of the United States.' Thanks largely to the Duke's role, the bases in the Bahamas were arranged with far less trouble than in certain other colonies, notably Bermuda.[59]

The bases negotiations – secret as they were, and concerning as they did the future presence of a 'non-belligerent' military power – did little to remind the Bahamas of the existence of the Second World War. That was achieved by two startling local occurrences which took place in November

1940. Both concerned the arrival of men in boats. Tapscott and Widdi-combe – the only survivors of the torpedoed HMS *Anglo-Saxon* – reached Eleuthera after drifting 3,000 miles for ten weeks in an open eighteen-foot lifeboat. They were taken to hospital in Nassau, where they were treated as heroes, made good use of for Allied propaganda purposes, and much visited by (and photographed with) the Duke and Duchess. The other arrivals were less welcome – convicts from Devil's Island off French Guiana, who had been cast adrift when it had become impossible to continue the penal colony after the fall of France. For weeks the problem of what should happen to them aroused heated debate in ExCo; the Duke took up a neutral position between the contending strong opinions; eventually it was decided to cast them adrift again, with provisions.[60]

The fuss caused by these two peripheral episodes merely served to stress, however, how remote the Colony was from the real war, and the Duchess undoubtedly spoke for both of them when she wrote that she 'would rather be in London with all the bombs and excitement and not buried alive here'. The Battle of Britain was narrowly and heroically won; the Blitz followed; German tanks rumbled into Bucharest; huge Italian armies crawled into Greece and Egypt. . . . And in Nassau the Duke continued to preside weekly over his Executive Council – the alcoholic Moore, the mean and hard little Solomon, the bootleggers and the grocer, the three officials – which gravely considered (when not considering the fate of French convicts) whether Armistice Day should be a public holiday,[61] whether a census should take place in 1941,[62] whether fireworks should be allowed to be sold,[63] whether the Royal Victoria Hotel should be permitted to import a string orchestra for the coming season. . . .[64]

England and Europe seemed far behind them now; they felt cut off, isolated. In front of them, America floated like a mirage. Only 200 miles from Nassau – but how far! They longed to go there; but would they ever get there? 'It will be very difficult for us to come to America,' the Duchess had written to Aunt Bessie on 31 August, and her words were truer than she could have known. It was now over seven years since she had been in her native land; it was of course unthinkable for her to return there without the Duke – and would they ever let him leave? Writing to Aunt Bessie on 20 September she sounded fairly hopeful: 'We hope to try to come [sic] to New York the first part of Dec. I must have a few things so would stay a short time in NY and then . . . visit my family which I haven't seen for years.' But a month later she despaired of making any such trip:

And I don't think there is a hope of the US before the spring. . . . I begin to think we are fated never to go to America. Gt Britain hates the idea of us going, because you know the Duke is an independent thinker and they don't want him to open his mouth. Also Lothian is controlled by Nancy Astor – as you know, an arch-enemy of ours – and L. will advise against coming on account of the press. That will be the excuse. . . .

In Lisbon that July, the anguished Duke had been told – curtly – that he could not travel out to his post by way of the United States as his presence there would interfere with the presidential election campaign; and he had received vague assurances about the possibility of going to the mainland once the election was over. On 5 November 1940, Roosevelt was elected for a third term by a massive majority. Would they now be allowed to make the longed-for trip? They doubted it. They would have been surprised to know that they would indeed be in America before the end of the year – and even more so that they would indirectly owe their visit to the personal intervention of President Roosevelt himself.

9
Pax Americana
November–December 1940

___

On 24 November 1940 – less than three weeks after Roosevelt's election victory – Lord Lothian, the British Ambassador in Washington, was called to the White House for an important discussion with the President.[1] What the President had to say thoroughly alarmed the Ambassador. Roosevelt announced that he would be spending the first half of December on a West Indian cruise on the USS *Tuscaloosa*, during which he wanted to inspect some of the proposed sites for US naval bases under the Destroyers–Bases Agreement on the coasts of Jamaica, Antigua, St Lucia and the Bahamas. While in Bahamian waters – where he planned to be on 12 and 13 December, looking at the proposed base sites at Mayaguana and Eleuthera – the President particularly wished to meet the Duke of Windsor. He could not, alas, stop at Nassau, as his doctors permitted no shore visits; but he hoped the Duke would join him on board the *Tuscaloosa* for lunch. That was not all. Now that the election was over, Roosevelt also hoped the Duke and Duchess would soon be coming to America, where he looked forward to giving them lunch at the White House. Lothian remarked frostily that 'His Majesty's Government wanted the Duke to remain at his post for as long as possible before coming to the United States of America'. To this, Roosevelt replied that *every* Governor of the Bahamas visited the United States in winter, almost as a matter of formality, and he did not see how the Duke could be prevented from doing so.*

Lothian lost no time in reporting this highly disturbing conversation to the Foreign Office. The reply came back on 29 November, couched in urgent terms which left no doubt as to London's attitude 'regarding a

___

* This was not the first time Roosevelt had talked to Lothian about the possibility of meeting the Duke on a cruise of the base sites. He had raised the subject in a more tentative manner as early as mid-September (FO 371/24249/353), and since then had been left in no doubt as to British official hostility to the plan. Just after the re-election Lothian had in fact made it known to the White House that 'unless the President is very anxious to do so His Majesty's Government would be inclined to suggest that he should not go to the Bahamas . . . on the ground that it might make inevitable a visit to the United States of the Duke of Windsor' (FO 371/24249/373). Yet the President persisted.

possible meeting between the Duke of Windsor and the President'.[2] It was a meeting which the Government *'was not anxious in any way to encourage'.** The Colonial Office had telegraphed the Governor of Jamaica about the President's itinerary, but had said nothing about the proposed meeting. Lothian was to consider what action might be taken 'to discourage [the President] from pursuing his idea about meeting the Duke of Windsor, *who has been left in ignorance of the suggestions***'.

Why did London object so violently to the idea of the meeting at sea? Such hostility at first sight seems amazing. Under normal circumstances, any Governor of the Bahamas would have been expected to join a President of the United States in the Colony's waters, as a matter of ordinary courtesy. The Governors of Jamaica and the Windward and Leeward Islands were naturally going to see the President as he sailed round their territories, and in the case of the Bahamas the President had *expressly desired* that the Governor do so! The fact that the Foreign Office were ready to run the risk of displeasing Roosevelt by thwarting his wishes, and denying him a customary honour, shows the extraordinary lengths to which the Government (under perpetual pressure from the Palace) were prepared to go to frustrate any event which might contribute to the Duke's popularity or prestige, or which might lead to his playing a wider and more useful role than the narrow and frustrating one to which he was strictly confined. The fears inspired by the proposed *Tuscaloosa* meeting were exactly the same as those which had been aroused by the Duke's visits to the British Army in France a year before. It was bound to be a glamorous occasion, and to stimulate sympathetic public interest in America and much world-wide publicity. Worst of all, judging by the President's ominous remarks to Lothian, it might prove to be the prelude to a successful and well-publicized tour of America by the Duke and Duchess, and that the Foreign Office wished to avoid at all costs.† And so the Duke was 'left in ignorance of the suggestion' (indeed of the fact that the President was coming to the Bahamas at all), while some means was sought 'to discourage the President from pursuing his idea'. Unwittingly, it was the Duke himself who now provided officialdom with an unhoped-for solution to the problem.

Towards the end of November, Hugh Johnson, the Nassau dentist who was treating the Duchess for a gum infection, announced that her condition had become serious and surgery was now imperative. He recommended that she be operated on by Dr Horace Cartee, a surgeon in Miami; the Duke therefore sent off a telegram to London asking for a few days' leave to accompany her to hospital there. The Colonial Office were

---

* Author's italics.
† 'I rely on you', Halifax wrote to Lothian on 3 October (FO 371/24249/360), 'to dispel any erroneous ideas about our view of a visit by His Royal Highness to the United States.'

not slow to recognize this heaven-sent opportunity to get the Duke out of the way during the coming presidential stop in the Bahamas (of which he was as yet unaware). The *Tuscaloosa* was due on 12 and 13 December; the Duke was told that he could leave the Colony from the 9th to the 14th![3] The Foreign Office wrote to Lothian with undisguised relief and satisfaction that there was 'now presumably no physical possibility of a meeting'[4]; the Duke would leave for Miami without even knowing that the President would be passing through. Meanwhile, in Nassau, the Duke and Duchess were both delighted and puzzled; they could hardly believe their good luck; they had almost despaired of ever going to the mainland together. But it was not long before they learned – by accident – of the highly ulterior motive for London's indulgence.

It still remained to break the disappointing news to the President that the Duke would not be there to meet him. On 2 December the *Tuscaloosa* sailed from Charleston with its eminent passenger, escorted by the destroyers *Mayrant* and *Trippe*; it was due off Jamaica on the 6th. On the 5th the Colonial Office sent the following telegram to the Governor of Jamaica (who was naturally going to join the President):

> Please inform President on arrival that Governor of Bahamas has been granted leave from December 9 to 14 to visit Miami owing to necessity Duchess undergoing dental operation there. He will thus be absent from Colony at time of President's prospective arrival at Mayaguana.[5]

By some extraordinary error (or perhaps the intervention of a friendly soul in the Colonial Office) this telegram was repeated to Nassau, and so the Duke tumbled to the whole noble scheme. 'The Governor of the Bahamas has got to hear of it!', wrote Scott of the Foreign Office to Burns of the Colonial Office – the start of a long and furious correspondence between the two ministries about the responsibility for the indiscretion.[6] Lothian was telegraphed in a panic to try to get the President's Bahamas stop cancelled in mid-voyage – but then it was learned with relief that it was too late for the Duke and Duchess to change their plans, and they would be leaving on the 9th as envisaged. Their feelings may be imagined, but they swallowed their anguish; it was the kind of treatment with which they were all too familiar. There was nothing to do but to make the best of 'tooth week' – their first brief trip, mere hospital visit that it was, across the Florida Channel.

The news of the impending royal visit threw Miami into intense excitement. It was in vain that the Duke expressed the desire 'to shun all possible publicity', to refuse all invitations and avoid public appearances. The Mayor of Miami, Alexander Orr, declared with delight that the whole city 'was longing to get acquainted with them', and that their arrival would be celebrated as a great civic event, with an official reception committee, bands, and the entire Miami police force. At this moment a new British Consul arrived in Florida to take up the post at Jacksonville. James Marjoribanks was only twenty-nine, and it was not without trepidation that he learned that almost his first task would be to receive the Duke and Duchess of Windsor on their first visit to America as man and wife. 'Within two weeks of my arrival in the United States for the first time,' writes Marjoribanks, 'I was faced with the prospect of meeting and greeting my former King, whom so many, including ecstatically myself, had loved and respected, and whose sudden departure from the throne (I was in Peking at the time) had left so many of us desolate.' He threw himself vigorously into the arrangements. 'There was a lot to organize – transport (which always goes wrong somewhere), security (in the hands of the excellent city police chief), the sifting of those who were entitled to be included in guest lists from those whose main motive was commercial advancement. . . .'[7]

At the last moment, a hitch occurred. The *Munargo*, the only regular passenger boat between Miami and Nassau, suddenly cancelled its forthcoming sailings. As the Duchess was averse to flying, it was hard to see how they were to make the journey. British officialdom was thoroughly alarmed at the prospect of their remaining after all in the Bahamas during the danger period of the presidential visit; and it was with some relief that the Colonial Office learned that Axel Wenner-Gren had generously offered to take them across on the *Southern Cross*. Says Marjoribanks: 'Wenner-Gren, I knew, did have some connections with Germany – few Swedes did not – but the vessel seemed to me merely an excellent vehicle for a royal visit since war-time exigencies ruled out any reasonable alternative passage by sea.'[8]

They sailed with the Wenner-Grens (it was an overnight trip) on the afternoon of Monday 9 December, accompanied by Captain Drury and a maid, valet and detective. Drury was enchanted by the voyage (rather turbulent though it was); a keen yachtsman, he had never travelled in so luxurious a vessel in thirty years of seafaring. The crew (which was large and extraordinarily international) was filled with excitement when it learned the identity of the passengers, and the Duke moved simply among them in his famous way (as one of them recalls to the author), charming them utterly.[9]

The yacht docked in Miami at ten o'clock the following morning, 10 December 1940 – exactly four years to the hour since Edward VIII had signed the Instrument of Abdication. An expectant crowd of 12,000 waited on the quayside. The Duke and Duchess appeared at the rail to tumultuous cheers and applause; then the reception committee – headed by the State Governor and four mayors – went aboard, followed by a horde of photographers and journalists. Sir James Marjoribanks recalls :[10]

> It was a lovely day. . . . I heard a clear, strong English voice emerging from a group of white-uniformed officers on the yacht's quarter-deck and there emerged a very small, sunburned man with a kindly, good-humoured expression who shook hands with me at once, without introduction. 'Ah! You are the Consul from Jacksonville. How good of you to spare the time to come aboard.' As the French say, *'j'étais bouleversé'*! I was immediately impressed by his quickness of expression and movement. Despite his 'pocket' size, he was at once in charge of everything, but with a humour and good nature which were positively disarming. . . .

This is what Marjoribanks remembers of the visit which followed.

> To be frank, there had been some doubt in official circles about how things would go. Britain was at war; the US was not. Would the American press highlight the Duke on the golf course? I think he, as an ace operator, may have had a round or two during the hurried official schedule. But the pictures I remember from this and other visits were of conversations with factory hands, visits to RAF trainees. He never missed a chance to perform some act of public relations in aid of the British war effort. On one occasion I remember him addressing in Spanish a group of fifty South American businessmen whom he ran into by chance in the company of Mr Orr, Mayor of Miami – whose obvious delight in his guests contributed to the general euphoria. The Duke and Duchess took everything in their stride. A holiday atmosphere prevailed; Britain's stock soared with the advent to Miami of our former monarch. I remember recording in my despatch to the Foreign Office that the visit had been 'a success from every point of view'. This was no exaggeration.

As for the Duke himself,

> . . . he gave one an intensely youthful impression. He had the capacity to spread around him immediately an atmosphere of gaiety and zest for life. There was never anything stand-offish or remote, an insistence on physical fitness, not a trace of the morose, alcoholic impression that some accounts of the Abdication crisis had spread about. He was like a young, quickly intelligent naval officer of the best type, with a boyish vocabulary and a strong sense of fun. But if anything went wrong, the Royal indignation was not far from the surface, and the object of his wrath would be told where he got off in no uncertain terms. . . .

Such were the impressions of Great Britain's young diplomatic representative in Florida. It is heartening that, within the Foreign Office machine generally so unfriendly to the Duke, there were good men like James Marjoribanks, who admired and respected him for his qualities and wanted to do their best for him; and he never forgot the attentions of such men.

After an hour of chatting to the journalists and notables who had come to meet them, posing for photographers and waving to the madly cheering crowds, the Duke and Duchess drove off – in an open car escorted by eleven police motorcycles – to St Francis' Hospital, where the Duchess was operated upon by Dr Cartee at one o'clock. Two hours later Aunt Bessie in Washington received the following telegram: 'Operation successful. Patient comfortable. Will keep you informed of progress. Love Edward.' However, the true facts were that the state of the Duchess's jawbone had been even more serious than imagined, and for the next twenty-four hours she was in pain and some danger. During that time, the Duke was plunged into anxiety and concern; those who saw him found him nervous and abstracted. Finally, on the afternoon of the 11th, she was declared out of danger (though still confined to hospital for three days of convalescence), and he breathed again.

It was on the afternoon of the following day – Thursday 12 December – that the Duke was astonished to receive, almost simultaneously, two extraordinary items of news. The first was the report of the sudden death earlier that day of Lord Lothian in Washington. The second was a wholly unexpected telegram from Roosevelt, inviting the Duke to fly out on a US Navy seaplane to join him after all on the *Tuscaloosa* off Eleuthera. Both of these messages came as a great surprise to the Duke, and together they gave him much food for thought. The fact that they had come on the same afternoon was the purest coincidence – though one which did not lack a certain dramatic irony, as the Duke was quick to appreciate.

It is worth considering carefully what happened at this point, for nothing shows more clearly the lengths of absurdity to which the Duke's detractors are prepared to go than their common interpretation of this episode. At least three recent writers have suggested, firstly, that the *Tuscaloosa* meeting was entirely the Duke's idea, reluctantly agreed to by a polite but exasperated Roosevelt; and, secondly, that the Duke seriously hoped to succeed Lothian at the Washington Embassy, and, imagining for some reason that this post lay in the gift of the President of the United States, he flew out to the *Tuscaloosa* on his own initiative to ask for it. As regards the first of these assertions, it has been seen that the meeting at sea was not only Roosevelt's own idea, but one which he had been advancing for no less than three months, with the greatest determination in the face of repeated British objections. The Duke for his part had known nothing whatever about the plan (thanks to the delicate precautions of the British Government) until just before his departure for Miami, and had had no communication of any kind with the President about it; the invitation which he now (and much to his pleasure) received was something which he had not anticipated and which took him quite unawares – he had no proper clothes, for example. As for the curious notion that the Duke, having to his chagrin become the first royal colonial governor, now hoped (with the President's help) to become the first royal British Ambassador, there is no evidence whatsoever for this view. Vyvyan Drury, who was constantly at the Duke's side during those days and in his confidence, clearly recalls the reactions that were expressed to him by the ex-King.[11]

Drury is quite clear that the Duke never imagined himself a likely or even a suitable candidate for the ambassadorship itself. (This is confirmed by Sir Berkeley Ormerod, who was then starting his distinguished career with the British Information Services in New York and was later to become a friend of the Duke's.) This is hardly surprising. It was quite bad enough that the Duke, with his training as an apolitical constitutional monarch, should have been charged with the executive government of a politically complicated Crown colony. It has been seen how bitterly he had complained that autumn – notably in his long October letter to Churchill – about having to take political responsibility and expose himself to criticism. How much worse would it have been for him in the most politically sensitive and exposed of all foreign postings! It was in fact one of the Duke's strong personal beliefs that royalty and heads of state should never undertake the *political* representation of their countries overseas; he told Adela Rogers St Johns how shocked both his father and he had been when President Wilson went in person to the Versailles Conference, where he duly (as George v had predicted to his son) lost all prestige in the affray of international political negotiation. So it is absurd to suggest that the Duke longed for the ambassadorship and was disappointed not to have it. In the event it was almost inevitable that the post should go to a senior member of the Government; and it is noteworthy that Halifax, who eventually received the appointment, retained his seat in the War Cabinet.*

But the Duke and Duchess (as they had just to their satisfaction discovered) were very popular in America. Thousands of letters, telegrams and petitions from Americans influential and humble flooded into the White House, the State Department and the offices of newspaper editors, declaring enthusiasm for the idea of the Duke as British Ambassador. A senator announced: 'They couldn't pick a better man.' The *Miami Herald* even reported that the Duke had already been offered first refusal of the post. All this has been described as the Duke's 'campaign' to secure the job for himself – as if he had some kind of organized political machine working for him in America. In fact the show of support was quite spontaneous. Drury confirms that the Duke did nothing either to encourage or to discourage it. But he was grateful for it

---

* On 19 July 1945 Halifax wrote in his diary that the Duke 'has evidently given up the idea of being Ambassador here, if he ever had it, and was very emphatic about the importance of having a non-career diplomat with political background' (Garrowby Papers).

– and it filled him with an idea and an ambition, a noble idea and a worthy ambition which he was to hold on to for the next eight years.

What the Duke longed from this moment to do was to represent Great Britain in America in the field of public relations. In other words, he wanted to perform the role abroad that royalty normally performs – and which he in particular had performed *par excellence* as Prince of Wales. On his great tours he had been brilliantly successful as England's 'goodwill ambassador'. Now more than ever before his country needed men to play this vital part, and the reception the Duke (and indeed the Duchess) was getting in Florida in December 1940 showed that he had lost none of his tremendous flair for it; if anything, his charisma was greater than ever. It was only a brief private visit with a medical purpose; and yet – as Marjoribanks recalls – his presence in Miami gave a massive fillip to the British cause there. How much more might he not do if he had a mission in America! He liked and understood Americans, and Anglo–American relations was a field he had long adored and understood. As Harold Nicolson had written of the Prince of Wales only a month before he had come to the throne: '. . . He talks a great deal about America and diplomacy. He resents the fact that we do not send our best men there. He knows an astonishing amount about it all. . . .'[12]

What exact job might the Duke do in the context of Anglo–American relations? It seemed unlikely that the King would despatch him as a formal representative of royalty. But might some kind of government job be created for him? Throughout the war, the Duke never ceased to hold on to this hope. It pervaded his correspondence with friends. 'I feel confident that I could serve my country best in some untechnical appointment in America,' he wrote to Beaverbrook in April 1942; while to his trusted London solicitor, George Allen, he wrote as late as May 1944:

. . . A created job in America . . . is the war assignment for which I consider myself best qualified. . . . I have made some very useful contacts, both official and private. And I could make many more which would be of value to Anglo–American relations were I given a whole time job to do so, a sort of roving commission, in close co-operation with the British Ambassador of course, but not resident in or tied down to Washington. The job would have to be defined, but I would insist on handling it in my own way. . . .

The idea of such a position was not as odd as it might seem. In the autumn of 1940 it had been proposed to appoint exactly such a kind of 'roving ambassador' to handle British public relations in South America; the Duke was interested in that job too (he had a great amateur interest in Latin America), and wrote sadly to Guedalla that 'the very fact that it would most certainly be more interesting wartime employment for us and probably more useful, is just the reason why they would never send us to South America'.[13] (The job went eventually to Eugen Millington-Drake, the famous British Minister to Uruguay – a charismatic figure whose allure was not wholly unlike the Duke's.) The Foreign Office was also considering whether the Duke of Kent might not be used to boost Britain's cause in America, seeing (as R. A. Butler wrote to Churchill in March 1941) that he had 'many good qualities as a roving Ambassador of goodwill'.[14] In December 1940, the Duke of Windsor did not have it in mind to ask for any specific post; but he hoped and believed that, as time passed, his popularity and Anglophile influence in the United States would become more and more apparent, so that eventually London would be glad to make use of him as an instrument of public relations. Alas, this hope was destined to be utterly disappointed. His American popularity (and indeed hers) would indeed grow, but it induced in what he called 'Official England' nothing but suspicion and alarm. Far from wishing to capitalize upon it, British policy was to try to destroy it – to conspire by all means against the Duke and Duchess achieving a resounding public success in America. This policy was (as the Duke and Duchess believed) directed by the Court, which – determined to keep the Duke, not to mention the Duchess, forever out of England and in disgrace – recoiled at the idea of their accumulating great prestige across the Atlantic. Their argument was that the Duke had to be 'restrained' so as not to overshadow the hesitant public image presented by the King. Churchill was saddened by this policy, but dared not oppose it as he relied on the King's support. Thus keeping the Duke 'in check' in the United States became an over-riding priority, pursued even at the expense of Anglo–American relations.

The Duke was all too aware of the forces against him. For his part he sought allies, and there can be little doubt that, when Roosevelt unexpectedly asked him out to the *Tuscaloosa*, he hoped to find the President friendly towards his plans for helping his country's cause in America.

What lay behind the President's invitation? This is an essential question. Right through the autumn, he had striven to bring about the *Tuscaloosa* meeting with a persistence which was almost childlike. It had been made clear to him by the now sadly departed Lothian that the British Government were utterly opposed to it; still he persisted. The Governor of Jamaica had informed him that, the Duke being away from his Colony, it was no longer on the cards; in spite of this further and final hint, he had gone out of his way to make sure that it happened all the same. Most surprising of all, he had done so in the end without consulting or informing the British authorities in any way. On 12 December the Foreign Office were happy in the thought that the dreaded encounter had definitely been averted. By the time they learnt that it was to take place after all, it had already happened.[15]

This determination is in fact susceptible of a very simple explanation. Like so many of his fellow-countrymen, Roosevelt was fascinated by the Duke and Duchess. As Beaverbrook wrote, he was utterly perplexed and intrigued by the Abdication of Edward VIII. 'He could not understand it.'[16] He became increasingly obsessed by the personality of a man who could give up a throne for love, and the allure of a woman who could inspire such a sacrifice. This later became clear to the Duke himself when, after their subsequent official meetings in Washington, he found himself detained by the President for hours on end, and subjected to curious and probing conversations. As the Duke wrote afterwards:

> To this day [1966], I haven't a clue as to what he really wanted of me. But from his questions about my life, my experiences as King, I rather suspect it was because he, a man who had achieved on his own the highest summit of political power in a man's reach, was curious about the motives and reasoning of a man who could give up an inherited position of comparable renown. . . .[17]

They were not in fact total strangers to each other. 'When I was in America for the first time as Prince of Wales in 1919,' recalled the Duke, 'he had been my gay and witty companion as Assistant Secretary for the Navy when I visited the Naval Academy at Annapolis.' Roosevelt was all too aware that he had to tread carefully where the Duke was concerned, given the British official attitude; but this made him all the more keen for a friendly private meeting at sea, safely within the boundaries of the Duke's colonial territory; and being told the Duke was in Florida, he promptly ordered the US Navy to fetch him.

The Duke and Drury flew out from Miami Coast Guard Air Station on the morning of Friday the 13th.[18] The Duke would have liked to be in uniform; but as the visit was unexpected and his current wardrobe was for a week's stay in neutral territory, the only uniform he had with him was that of Commandant of the Royal Yacht Squadron at Cowes, which he duly wore with yachting cap and binoculars. They landed by the *Tuscaloosa* around eleven o'clock, and boarded the 35,000-ton cruiser in a rainsquall; the Duke stood bareheaded as a band played *God Save the King*; he inspected a guard, and there were hearty greetings. Then the Duke and Roosevelt retired alone to the President's cabin for an hour of private conversations. Afterwards there was a jolly luncheon under awnings on the top deck in the bright winter sunshine; the President had the Duke on his right, and on his left Drury and Harry Hopkins; the principal dish (doubtless a witty touch on somebody's part) was kingfish. To begin with, the conversation was about the Bahamas and the Out Islands and deep-sea fishing: Roosevelt knew the islands well. The

President then asked the Duke about George V's stamp collection, which the Duke said had been placed at the disposal of the Empire; and the President remarked: 'Your father was a sailor king with a sailor's heart and a sailor's vocabulary, and when he got on the subject of the Germans he used some good old Anglo-Saxon monosyllables with deep conviction', which made the Duke smile. The Duke hoped Nassau would one day boom and prosper like Miami, and Roosevelt explained that the United States was interested in developing the whole of the West Indies in co-operation with Great Britain. After lunch, they all discussed the bases. Roosevelt said he regarded the proposed Bahamas bases as of immense importance, as they might be required to guard against an attack upon the United States. The problem was where to put them; Mayaguana, which the Duke favoured, was uncertain as an all-weather harbour. Before the visit came to an end, the President said how much he was looking forward to the Duke visiting America; and the Duke remarked that he was particularly hoping to see some of the Civilian Conservation Corps camps which Roosevelt had set up to relieve unemployment, which the President promised to arrange. The Duke and Drury left at about four in the afternoon, with much ceremony and hearty handshaking. The guns of the *Tuscaloosa* boomed out a friendly salute as they took off on their way back to Miami.

It was the first of about a dozen meetings of the two men during the war. Of the President's personal liking for the Duke there can be no doubt. 'It was indeed good to see you again after all these years,' he wrote on New Year's Eve, 'and when an airbase is finally decided upon, you and I will have to make an "inspection trip" to see it.' But what had they discussed during their private hour? The Duke had very probably expressed his great desire to help promote Anglo–American relations; and he had probably also wanted to know Roosevelt's views on the state of a war-torn world. For it has been observed that the Duke of Windsor, throughout his long exile but particularly during the war, had a passion for good information on current affairs, for the opinions of the best-informed people. Having once been 'on the inside', he longed to know the true stories behind public announcements and newspaper reports. There was one subject in particular which they almost certainly touched upon – a subject which the Duke, talking of Roosevelt, mentioned to an interviewer six days later. This was the idea of *Pax Americana*, which had come to obsess the Duke in the last months of 1940 – the idea that America would eventually impose a peace settlement on Europe. More will be said about this shortly.

Back in Miami, the Duke was mobbed by reporters who asked if it was true that he had been offered the British ambassadorship in Washington; he replied that it was not. When asked if he would accept it if offered to him, he replied: 'I would certainly accept it if I thought it was in the interest of our two countries.' Much has been read into these innocent words.

The day after the *Tuscaloosa* meeting, the Duchess came out of hospital, and they moved to the Miami Biltmore for the remaining three days of their stay. It was during these three days that they appeared in public and made such a splendid impression on the people of Miami, contributing so significantly (in the words of Marjoribanks) to pro-British feeling there. They left on the *Southern Cross* on the 17th amid tearful scenes. 'Now that we have found our way to America,' declared the Duke, 'we look forward to an early opportunity for another visit.' A band played *Auld Lang Syne, There'll Always Be An England* and *God Save the King*.

A few days later the Duke gave some of his impressions of America to a visitor at Government House:

> I had a wonderful time in Miami. It was the first time I had been in the United States in 16 years and the first time my wife had been there in 8 years. Our visit did us the world of good. There is something so stimulating no matter where you go in America. American vitality – it is a tangible quality. You can feel it in the air. You absorb it. . . . To go to the United States is like going to the big city. Your blood begins to tingle; you come back . . . strengthened and reinvigorated. I have always admired the great natural energy of you Americans. Think of a city like Miami – 40 new hotels going up this year! What town in history ever had 40 new hotels in one year? Where does the money come from? It is a good thing, anyway, for everybody profits when there is such a boom. . . .[19]

The *Southern Cross* did not return directly to Nassau. Wenner-Gren suggested a forty-eight-hour cruise of the Western Bahamas, to which the Duke and Duchess agreed with much pleasure. They were introduced to the sport of deep-sea fishing, which Roosevelt had recommended to the Duke, and landed on the island of Grand Bahama (then possessed of a stark natural beauty, now the site of a horrendous industrial complex) to inspect Wenner-Gren's operation for the fishing and canning of crayfish. This fascinated the Duke; it was the sort of enterprise he wanted to stimulate throughout the islands. Wenner-Gren talked of the problems he was encountering – the hostility of Bay Street, the dishonesty of native fishermen who sold their catch on the side – and explained that once he had surmounted these he hoped to do much more on Grand Bahama. He dreamed of a great agricultural development embracing half the island; the Duke much encouraged him in this idea. The two men also talked much and sadly of the state of the world; and with his subsequent letter thanking Wenner-Gren for the use of his yacht – 'I think you know all that its comfort and privacy meant to us under all the circumstances of that visit' – the Duke enclosed a signed copy of his Verdun peace speech of May 1939, 'which in my humble opinion makes as much sense now as it did at that time'.[20]

They were back in Nassau on 19 December. To their delight, the Woods in their absence had got Government House ready for them to live in, and so (though much work remained to be done) they at last moved back into their official residence. The Duke went down to the House that evening, where he made a short speech about the *Tuscaloosa* meeting and signed the Bill which enabled the United States to acquire bases in the Bahamas. Then they went about all the Christmas duties which fall to colonial governors and their wives – presiding at various celebrations in aid of charity, visiting government offices to tender good wishes, organizing children's parties at Government House. On Christmas Day they attended church, reviewed the local militia and visited the sick. Then they faced, with a heavy heart, the unenviable task of presiding over Nassau's tourist season in war.

The last days of 1940 were, for the Duke, a time of agonizing reflection upon the fate of England, the progress of the war and the condition of the whole world. He had never ceased to think during the autumn of his country's survival and the plight of its people and its cities. 'Life must be hell in London now, and I can well imagine how difficult it must be to carry on your business,' he wrote to Allen on 11 October. 'And it will become increasingly so unless something more effective is found to deal with enemy bombers in the winter.' He felt terribly isolated – cut off from England, from real service, from information as to what was really happening in the corridors of power and on the battlefields.

Assiduously performing his duties as a wartime colonial governor, he was a perfect and inspiring representative of his King and his country's just cause. But behind the public face was the private face; and beneath the tireless, irreproachable service lay his secret personal convictions. Though he admired and understood Churchill – more so perhaps than his brother – the Duke (like all the rest of his family) was too cosmopolitan, too passionate for peace, too concerned for the survival of the imperilled civilization of which the institution of monarchy was a part, to share Churchill's conception of a fight to the death. He detested war, and from the start had thought the Second World War a second world disaster. Whenever he reflected upon it, the Duke (so like his brother, as George VI's wartime diary reveals) was plunged in misery and depression. 'The outlook for the world really gets blacker and blacker,' he wrote from Nassau to Aunt Bessie, 'and I can see no ending to it all let alone a victorious one. The whole of mankind is going to suffer bitterly for the folly of this conflict, and one can only thank God that one is not of those who are responsible for its prosecution.'[21] He feared above all for his country. Her survival was magnificent, American support was tremendous, but how long could Great Britain carry on against such seemingly massive odds? He had witnessed at first hand the fall of France. Alone, England resisted. Narrowly, she remained unconquered. But did it seem likely, at the end of 1940, that she would eventually conquer Germany? What were her war aims? Who thought now of Poland? If the war could not be won, all one could hope for was its indefinite prolongation – and the longer it went on, the greater the suffering and destruction, the greater the certainty that what remained of civilization would fall and Communism lay its cold hand on a shattered Europe. Holding these pessimistic, but hardly unreasonable, ignoble or uncommon views, the Duke, like most of his family and fellow countrymen, longed for an honourable end to the war. The problem was – what honourable end could there be? Surrender was indeed unthinkable; and, given the case of France, it seemed unlikely, in December 1940, that negotiation with the enemy could result in much less than surrender. The Duke, however, harboured one great private hope – that a powerful and prosperous America, Roosevelt's America, might eventually impose a just solution on an exhausted Europe.* He foresaw very clearly that only the United States or Soviet Russia could replace Nazi Germany as dominant power on the continent. Understandably, his preference was for American rule.

This was only his private hope. But did he express it to Roosevelt during their secret discussion on board the *Tuscaloosa* on 13 December? It would have been surprising if he did not. Only six days later, just after his return from Miami, he hinted at it in a remarkable interview with the influential American magazine *Liberty*, which was to cause a considerable stir when published the following March.[22] Speaking of his meeting with the President, he said America should give as much help to England as she could – without expecting any return, for one did not lend money to a close friend. England for her part must have a proper reverence for America; it was essential (said the Duke without mentioning names) that England be represented by the right people in America:

> It is just as blatant for an Englishman to believe that he is superior to the rest of mankind as for Hitler to preach racial superiority. . . . The insufferable snobs who accept your hospitality and then insult you by a fatuous pretence of superiority ought never to be allowed to leave England. . . . That sort of thing is especially maddening when one considers the terrific sympathy and aid America is giving my country in her hour of trial.

Turning to the war in Europe, the Duke threw out a great many

---

* At the time of Dunkirk, Churchill had declared that if Britain were 'subjugated and starving', the Empire would hold out 'until, in God's good time, the New World, with all its power and might, steps forth to the rescue and the liberation of the Old.'

rhetorical questions. At one point he said: 'Is there such a thing in modern war as victory?' But at another point he declared that Hitler had failed, because he had promised the Germans a short war 'and with all his control of press and radio he cannot deceive his own people into believing the war is finished – they know damn well it is still going on and that they have to make sacrifices for it.' The Duke asked: 'Do you think the President has any idea of intervening for peace?' The Duke himself seemed doubtful; he agreed with his interlocutor (the eminent Baltimore novelist and current affairs broadcaster Fulton Oursler) that a peace by conciliation might for Great Britain amount to a capitulation. But of one thing he felt certain – that when peace eventually came to Europe, it could only be a *Pax Americana*. As he put it:

> When the war is over, many strange things are going to happen – and one of the strangest is that America will no longer be called the New World. It will be the Old World and Europe will be the New World.

America (concluded the Duke) had been the principal force behind the last European peace settlement, but had then disastrously failed to play her part in it; this time it would be a settlement she would have to implement, enforce and guarantee. She would be the dominant member of a new League of Nations with police powers; she would rebuild a devastated Europe with her gold. It was a fair prediction of the UNO and Marshall Aid.

The Duke was invited to broadcast a Christmas message to America. It was a piece which demanded some tact. Since he would be addressing a neutral country he had just privately visited, it would have been a mistake to deliver an outright Allied propaganda speech. In not doing so, the Duke very nearly expressed his private thoughts:

> Great Britain has again become entangled in the strifes and quarrels of the Old World. . . . Yet on the continent of America . . . there are two peoples that for decades have lived peacefully side by side, with a frontier several thousand miles long, unguarded by a single fort or a single soldier. . . . However, this is no time for retrospection, for as members of the British Commonwealth of Nations we in this colony are engaged in Britain's conflict, at the same time confident in the strength and character of our race and that their endurance and tenacity will bring this tragic war to a successful conclusion. . . . Our admiration for the gallantry of the fighting forces knows no bounds, but our special sympathy goes out to all who have become the innocent victims of modern warfare. . . . May the end of hostilities be not too far distant, and may God grant to those in power wisdom and vision to provide . . . a settlement based on justice, sanity and goodwill.[23]

He was thinking of an American settlement.

10
The Play Ground
January–August 1941

The winter tourist season of 1940–1 was the best Nassau had ever known. In spite of mild wartime restrictions, and the increasing difficulty of getting over from the mainland, rich Americans and Canadians flocked over as never before to enjoy the local sun, sin and sport. Regular winter residents reached their houses early. The hotels were packed, the clubs crowded, the harbour filled with magnificent yachts. As many as 20,000 people came over from the mainland, as compared to 14,000 the season before; the amount of dollars spent in the Colony went up by fifty per cent.[1] The merchants, shop owners and property developers of Bay Street did roaring trade for three months, while native unemployment all but ceased. The society column of the *Nassau Guardian* was filled with names from the *Social Register* and *Debrett*. There was a glittering calendar of social and sporting events, mostly in aid of war charities; there were dances and fairs, golf tournaments and yacht races. But the presence of the Duke and Duchess dwarfed all other attractions. All conversation was about them; great crowds attended their public appearances; the abiding ambition of everyone was to meet them, or even (the social *nec plus ultra*) to be entertained at Government House. The jolly, aristocratic governorship of Sir Bede Clifford had started Nassau off as an élite tourist resort ten years earlier. Now, the charisma of the Duke and Duchess caused it to flourish as never before.

How did they look upon their task in wartime as the 'first family' of a tourist paradise? Enough has been said in the preceding chapters to provide the answer to this question. Though they realized that it was their public duty to help the tourism upon which the Colony depended, their role left them disgusted, bored and appalled. The Duchess wrote that it was like being 'buried alive', that they would far rather be in London facing the Blitz; while the Duke had told Churchill that

> . . . it goes against the grain to play the part of 'greeter' amidst all the horrors and misery that this war inflicts and which we have seen with our own eyes, a role that has never been in our make up and a form of publicity that, while

helping these islands, would obviously reflect very badly on ourselves at this time. . . .

Now that the dreaded season was upon them, how were they to deal with it, and perform the role required of them while preserving their dignity? During the late autumn they had given much thought to this question, and – with the aid of their five faithfuls, Gray Phillips the Drurys and the Woods – they had worked out a four-point plan along the following lines:

1. They would fulfil their public duties with all elegance, cheerfulness and style.
2. They would accept no social invitations whatever – whether to public functions or to private parties – except in the case of events designed to benefit war charities.
3. They would entertain – in a formal and modest manner – at Government House.
4. They would not allow the season to interfere with their ordinary work, and would continue to devote themselves to improving the lot of the people of the Colony.

Such was their plan of campaign, and they stuck to it unswervingly throughout that long winter.

They did not isolate themselves from the season. Whenever there was an occasion of a public or a charitable nature they were there, presiding over fairs, bazaars and exhibitions, attending 'benefit' theatre, concert and cinema performances, opening new hotels, clubs and golf courses, presenting the prizes after tennis, golf and yachting competitions. It was a royal programme and they fulfilled it royally, putting on their best act and rarely failing to charm the crowds. But they did not attend any parties that season; they refused even to dine in other people's houses. Hostesses approached them in vain, even those who cunningly tried to make cocktail parties look like fund-raisers by demanding a fixed contribution from each guest. On the other hand, they did offer hospitality at their own official residence. 'It was much to the Colony's advantage', writes Hallinan, 'that eminent winter visitors should be entertained in a style that, although not lavish, was elegant and maintained the reputation of the Bahamas as an élite resort.'[2]

Many people have borne witness to the Duchess's talents as a hostess. She had a large, Southern conception of hospitality, and possessed two remarkable gifts – an unusual social facility for putting people at their ease and making them give the best of themselves, and an absolute mastery of the arts of household management. She knew about comfort, and how to achieve it. She knew about food, and at her table it was always delicious. With the aid of Gray Phillips, who was a perfect head of household, she selected and organized her staff brilliantly. She had the services of a French chef of genius, Pinaudier, and a Jeeves-like English butler, Marshall. Apart from her French maid and the Duke's guardsman valet, the rest of the indoor staff were mostly coloured, and she trained them herself to the highest standards. Moving on noiseless feet, they sustained an aura of quiet elegance – for there was nothing remotely 'fast' or ostentatious about either the style of entertaining or the physical surroundings at Government House. In refurbishing the building, the Duchess had contrived an atmosphere which was unobtrusive, slightly formal, and (a fact remarked upon with surprise by numerous visitors) undoubtedly royal. With its chintz patterns and pastel colours, its economy of space and snug corners, its family portraits, its deft touches of local colour (for example, the excellent bamboo work), its consoles full of bibelots and framed photographs, its mere hint of grandeur, this new residence was not unlike most of the other houses in which the Duke had lived. But it was far more comfortable, and far better run.

Who dined at Government House that winter? Naturally there were the Colony's main rulers and leaders – the senior officials, the police and security chiefs, the Bishop (now getting on tremendously with the Duchess), the members of ExCo and LegCo and other local notables. There were the few people in the Colony with whom the Duke and Duchess had so far struck up friendly relations – the Oakeses and Sigrists and Wenner-Grens, Austin Levy and Arthur Davies, Captain Mackintosh and Major Goldsmith, the United States Consul John Dye. Occasionally there were some of the British residents – though that was still a distant quarter, and there were no invitations for the Williams-Taylors and others who had snubbed the Duchess (but who were soon to change their tune in view of this awful exclusion). And then, the Duke and Duchess invited – as they were expected to – a carefully chosen selection of the rich and prominent North Americans who had descended upon Nassau for the season. Some of these they came to like very much and asked often – a Mrs Donahue and a Mrs Vanderbilt, the delightful New York naturalist and antique dealer Arthur Vernay, the famous explorer (who was involved in collecting small arms for Britain) Suydam Cutting, their lively Canadian neighbours the Killams (whose house Graycliff is still the most beautiful in Nassau), and the Detroit motor magnate Alfred P. Sloan.

Apart from these, any really interesting or celebrated person who happened to be passing through could expect an invitation to Government House and a warm welcome there. One such was the authoress Rosita Forbes, who briefly stopped at Nassau in January on her way to her estate on Eleuthera. In her memoirs, she left an interesting account of her first meeting with the Royal Governor and his wife, with whom she was to become very friendly:

DATE OF ARRIVAL		NAME		DATE OF DEPARTURE	
1940 –	41	GOVERNMENT HOUSE, BAHAMAS.		1940 –	41
September	16th	E. Fraser Phillips.		April	11th
December	6th	Alastair Mackintosh		December	9th
January	28th	Bessie L. Merryman		March	9th
January	30th	Jack Warner		February	10th
February	13th	Alastair Mackintosh.		February	18th

The Duke and Duchess took with them to the Bahamas a visitors' book, bound in red morocco, the first entries in which hailed from Fort Belvedere in 1935. But they had few guests during their first year at Government House.

That evening, drinking my iced tomato juice in the clever resetting of the Government House rooms which are now singularly charming, the Duke asked for news of his English friends. I could not give much. . . .

The Duchess made me feel very welcome. That is one of her gifts. She has a remarkable talent for housewifery, as the great ladies of earlier centuries conceived it. Cooking, decorating, flowers, clothes all come into her idea of home-making, and are part of the hospitality for which she has genius. . . .

At Government House we talked about England. With his intimate knowledge of Europe it was impossible for HRH to underrate the gravity of the situation.

The Duchess listened, putting in an occasional apposite comment. She looked very young. I think she is the only woman whom the Bahamian winds cannot dishevel. Her smooth dark head looks as if it had come out of a Persian miniature, where the Princesses are impervious to time and weather. The Duchess . . . has definite ideas how to help the Bahamas. . . .

Both the Governor and the Duchess talked that evening with amused perspicacity of Bahamian complications – human and social – which I doubt if Gabriel and Solomon in partnership could solve. 'We Southerners', said the Duchess laughing, 'always flatter ourselves we know best how to deal with coloured people . . .' Perhaps they do. . . .[3]

Another Southern lady who was dearest of all to the Duchess came to Nassau that January. Her beloved Aunt Bessie, whom she had last seen in Europe for the Christmas season of 1938, arrived to spend six weeks with her niece at Government House. It is hardly necessary to write of the Duchess's emotions on being reunited with her worldly, witty and wise closest relation, to whom she poured out her heart in her letters, whom she had so sorely missed, and to whom she had written in December 1935: 'You are all that is left to me in the world.' The seventy-six-year-old but amazingly lively aunt became popular with everyone in Nassau, and made herself useful by helping in the final stages of the redecoration of Government House, where she, Alistair Mackintosh and the Duchess's old friend Jack Warner were the only house-guests that winter.

Aunt Bessie also followed with keen interest her niece's efforts to set up a proper infant welfare service in Nassau. The Duchess had been shocked on arrival to learn of the high infant mortality rate among the coloured population, largely due to the prevalence of congenital syphilis. Alice Hill Jones, the excellent coloured nurse who until then had been trying to cope with the problem without funds or facilities, later recalled:

> Soon after she came to Nassau, the Duchess heard I needed a car to make the rounds. I met her for the first time when she came to my house herself to say she had found one for me, a 4-door Plymouth sedan. She was very kind, and very, very interested in the work. A few days later she came round to the Western Junior High School, where I tried to hold a weekly clinic for the mothers and babies. She was awfully distressed to see what a terrible problem we had to deal with and how bad the facilities were. There and then she said she was going to set up a proper clinic, and that very night she rang America to arrange it all. . . . When it was finished it was so complete that it even had ink in the wells! And then she started another one. . . . Soon there were three excellent clinics a week for the children. The Duchess came every week to the Wednesday afternoon one, armed with a pile of layettes. She was very observant, and asked me to 'investigate' any children she thought needed special help; and she would always receive me very kindly at Government House to hear my reports. . . .[4]

The Duchess was helped in this work by the generous benefactions of Wenner-Gren, and the constant support of Rosa Wood, Nina Drury, Anne Heape and Monica Hallinan. The white ladies of Nassau, horrified that the Governor's lady should spend an afternoon a week helping to weigh and wash black babies, tended to confine their good works to the Red Cross and the (exclusively white) 'Independent Order of the Daughters of the Empire', both of which were concerned with war work to the exclusion of local relief. The Duchess played an active role in all this too, but not with the heartfelt enthusiasm she gave to the clinics. The only war work as yet to be done (apart from looking after Tapscott and Widdicombe) was the raising of funds and the sending of parcels, at both of which activities the Duchess was by now expert.

March, the last month of the season, turned out to be the busiest for the Royal Governor and his lady. On the 1st there were St David's Day and on the 17th St Patrick's Day celebrations. For the Red Cross there was a puppet show on the 4th, a concert on the 19th, a cabaret on the 25th. On the 10th there was a *musicale* organized by the Duchess at Government House in aid of her clinics. On the 7th they attended the last day of the races, on the 20th and the 22nd the Yale v. Nassau Rugby Match. On the 15th and the 16th four professional golfers, including the legendary Walter Hagen and Tommy Armour, played a 'benefit competition' in Nassau at the invitation of the Duke, who joined in for a round. On the 21st the world première of Gabriel Pascal's film *Major Barbara* took place at the Savoy Theatre in aid of air-raid relief. On the 23rd there was a National Day of Prayer. They presided over all these events, went about their daily routine, and continued to entertain in the manner expected of them. Aunt Bessie left on the 9th, to be followed by other house-guests, including the Duchess's widowed cousin Lelia; though as the Duchess assured her aunt, 'your place in the household and in the hearts of Nassau was not threatened for a second!' And so, hiding their exhaustion from an enchanted world, they dutifully danced the season out.

It was the last season of its kind – though few were to realize that as yet. It had been remarkable for the numbers of tourists and the amount of money brought into the Colony, the amazing sums raised for war funds, and the glamour and perfect style which radiated from Government House. It was a triumph for the Duke and Duchess – though the very last they had sought. It is not enlivening to be cast in the part of tourist mascot in time of war; but they had bravely played the role that had been required of them, smiling among the teacups.

The season had been exceptional in another and less happy way. It was the first since 1919 during which the Governor had spent practically no time in America. Since the Nassau season was largely an American season, it was traditional (as Roosevelt had told Lothian in November 1940) for the Governor to make several brief formal trips to the mainland, and to exchange a series of visits with the Mayor of Miami. Such visits had taken place even during the days of Bahamian bootlegging and American Prohibition; after the outbreak of war they became especially important, since Florida was enthusiastically pro-British and much occupied with British war-relief work. In accordance with the usual practice, the Duke was invited in the New Year of 1941 to the President's Birthday Ball in Miami and the running of the Bahamas Handicap Races nearby, both in aid of suitable war charities. But London prohibited him from accepting these or any other American invitations, on the grounds that it might excite controversy while the Lend-Lease Bill was before Congress.[5] The Duke and Duchess found this reasoning hollow (during 'tooth week' had they not boosted pro-British feeling in America?), and told the press that they 'had been looking forward to going to Miami as a gesture of gratitude for the magnificent response of the American people to the call for relief and comfort for the people of Great Britain'.

In fact, the Duke did spend all of two hours in the United States that winter. In the second week of January he and the Duchess had gone cruising for a few days with Alfred Sloan on his yacht *Rene*; on Cat Cay, a little Bahamian islet close to the Florida coast where they stopped on Saturday the 11th, an aviator suggested that he fly over that afternoon to watch the Miami Air Races; yielding to a sudden adventurous impulse, he had accepted. 'So far as the crowd was concerned, the Duke was the show,' commented the *New York Times* in their report of the Races.[6] He stayed just two hours, signed autographs ('For boy scouts? Any time.'), said hello to the Duchess's dentist Dr Cartee, then flew back to rejoin her on Cat Cay. When the Foreign Office found out about this trip, it was furious. 'We would be most grateful if we might be consulted whenever a Governor, *and particularly the Governor of the Bahamas*,* proposes to pay any visit to foreign territory,' it wrote to the Colonial Office in the driest of notes. 'There may be political questions involved, and in any case we should like to be in a position to warn our mission in advance.'[7]

But was London's travel ban *just* for the season? With the season's end, would the Duke and Duchess be allowed to leave the islands? Alfred Sloan offered them the *Rene* for the spring; the Duke asked London if he might sail it to the mainland in April and spend two weeks there. 'The Duchess and I wish to visit her family in Baltimore and I would also take the opportunity of studying some CCC Camps for administrative reasons and for which I have the President's verbal approval.'[8] Both the Foreign Office and the Colonial Office were for once inclined to see no harm in the idea. Lend-Lease had passed Congress. Sir John Balfour minuted that 'any publicity would harm the Duke more than our national interests' – most satisfactory – while R. A. Butler wrote, 'I can't think there will be any objections from the US point of view'. But the veto was imposed all the same. 'We can *not* come to the US in April,' wrote the Duchess to Aunt Bessie. 'W.C. wishes us to wait awhile. The Duke is in a rage. I am used to "no", so am calm. We shall now try for August and September. Only when the war stops will we regain our independence from HM Govt. . . .'[9]

* Author's italics.

The season had highlighted the security problems of a colony which had hardly been touched by the war. In the third week of March a young intelligence officer then stationed in Bermuda, Captain H. Montgomery Hyde, called at Nassau in the course of a security inspection of West Indian colonies.[10] New Providence, as the future biographer of Oscar Wilde quickly discovered, decidedly did not come up to scratch; one would hardly have known it was part of a battling Empire. Large numbers of people were coming and going without any passport formalities or attempts to identify them; the censorship was perfunctory; enemy aliens were leading a fairly unrestricted existence; and the local security files were not in the Colonial Secretariat where they should be, but (as a result of a decision of the Duke's predecessor) locked up in the Governor's private office at Government House. In the list of guests at the British Colonial Hotel, Captain Hyde discovered the name of a well-known female agent of the German Consulate in New York. The brother of the President of Mexico arrived with a large entourage, and called on the Duke; Captain Hyde saw no harm in that, but later discovered that one of the retinue was on an American blacklist. Most alarming of all, the island was practically undefended; the latest defence works had been Dunmore's eighteenth-century forts. The sole effective measure which the House had been prepared to sanction had been the appointment of thirty 'coastal-watchers' to detect the appearance of 'suspicious craft'. As Montgomery Hyde wrote in his secret security report, 'the development of the tourist trade . . . is of much greater importance in local eyes – and incidentally to local pockets – than any measures of defence or security, no matter how desirable these may be on imperial grounds.'

At Government House, Captain Hyde found the Duke expressing 'a very ready appreciation of security problems generally' and resolved to do something about so unsatisfactory a state of affairs. Hyde made the point that 'a U-boat suddenly appearing off this island could easily shell the cable and wireless station and carry off the entire occupants of Government House before anyone realized that this island was being attacked.' The Duke was genuinely alarmed, and walked meditatively over to the window, where he looked out with Hyde over the 400 undefended yards to Bay Street and the shore. Personally fearless though he was, the Duke was to be haunted from that moment by the vision of a kidnap from an enemy submarine. In the next few months, he took what extra security measures he could, in the face of the grumbling of the House. When war came to the western hemisphere, he would do much more.

While Captain Hyde's profession made him particularly conscious of 'the unprecedented character of the head of the government', he found the Duke helpful and charming. The Duke asked him what he had done before the war; Hyde replied that he had been Lord Londonderry's private secretary; and the Duke remarked that, if the war had had one good effect, it was to stop women like Lady Londonderry entertaining in their characteristic style.

In his report on the internal security of the Bahamas, Montgomery Hyde had mentioned Axel Wenner-Gren as 'the most conspicuous among the aliens residing in the Colony'. Was Wenner-Gren a security risk? 'There is no doubt that his schemes for the development of Hog Island, where he resides, and the Grand Bahama, are benefiting the Colony considerably by their outlay of capital and the employment of local labour,' wrote Hyde, 'and it may well be that his other activities are likewise perfectly innocent.' Just in case, Hyde suggested that he be kept under strict censorship and security surveillance; but no incriminating facts were found. Other people were keeping a close eye on Wenner-Gren too, and finding nothing to confirm that he might be dangerous. John Dye, the charming and vigilant United States Consul in Nassau who had become very friendly with the Duke, wrote in a despatch:

> I know him and Mrs Wenner-Gren quite well and we have exchanged luncheons etc. with them. During our several conversations . . . we have discussed the war and even the rumours that he is pro-Nazi. I could detect nothing to confirm such rumours, and some of the important things he has done and said would tend to disprove the rumours, but I am still of an open mind. I can see why he would not dare come out strongly anti-Nazi on account of feared reprisals. I do believe he is friendly to and an admirer of, the United States. . . .[11]

In spite of such reports, however, the hostility towards Wenner-Gren in the State Department had grown to near-hysterical proportions. The reasons were based not so much on security as economics. Having abandoned a Europe he saw as doomed, Wenner-Gren's aim was to exploit the great untapped resources of Latin America. He had already established strong business bases in Mexico and Peru, whose governments were much in favour of his activity. In State Department eyes, the growing ascendancy of this resourceful European posed a threat to the United States' economic hegemony in Latin America. Wenner-Gren was a victim, not of Roosevelt's 'all aid short of war' policy towards the Allies, but of the Monroe Doctrine.

Meanwhile, the Duke had continued to see much of Wenner-Gren. He admired increasingly the Swede's practical genius, while Wenner-Gren for his part marvelled at 'how the young man is standing up to the pirates'. Their correspondence that winter and spring was mostly about Wenner-Gren's two major enterprises in the Colony. The Hog Island Project, which the Duke had so encouraged in the autumn, was proving a great success; by the spring of 1941 it employed 1,000 men, over ten per cent of the working male population of New Providence. On the other hand, the crayfish cannery on Grand Bahama, which the Duke had visited on the *Southern Cross* in December, was not doing well; but in spite of this, the Duke vigorously urged Wenner-Gren to press ahead with his ambitious plan for a large and important agricultural development on that island. He set great store by the ultimate realization of this scheme, and encouraged Wenner-Gren to apply with his support for the purchase of a large tract of Crown land on Grand Bahama.

For the Duke's thoughts were turning once again to the absolute necessity to revive agriculture in the Out Islands. The season had been an economic success; but how many more could there be like it during the war? Now more than ever, it seemed to him madness for the Bahamas to rely so entirely on fickle tourism – and unhealthy that the natives should live off three months' seasonal income in Nassau, while the Out Islands produced next to nothing. As Rosita Forbes, who shared his views, wrote in 1944:

> The Out Islands, which are the real Bahamas, carrying the main population with unlimited space to cultivate, are neglected and ignored by the politicians of the capital. With few exceptions, Nassuvian interests are concerned with shopkeeping and land values. Agriculture means nothing to the merchants of Bay Street. They would rather import canned goods from America than encourage difficult local production. Yet the only lasting prosperity for the Bahamas is in farming. Miracles do not last. . . . Tourists are always uncertain. . . .[12]

Since their mainland trip was off, the Duke and Duchess set out in the *Rene* on 27 March on another tour of the Out Islands. This time they were to visit the remoter Bahamas, many of which had never been visited by a Governor before. They took with them only Sergeant Holder and John Hughes, the sympathetic Welshman who was Senior Out Island Commissioner and much liked by the Duke.

The 234-foot yacht headed south-east, where its first stop was San Salvador, 200 miles from Nassau. This was the island upon which Columbus had made his first American landfall in 1492. Bay Street was full of plans to exploit the 450th anniversary for the next season; but the island itself was barren and impoverished, inhabited by barely 1,000 struggling negroes. 'Almost as primitive as it appeared in those far-off days when the great explorer first set foot on its shores,' wrote *Nassau* magazine, 'San Salvador has a strong flavour of the past.'[13] Yet it seemed assured of a more prosperous future; for Sir Harry Oakes, great benefactor that he was, had bought several thousand acres on the island, cleared the land, brought out an agricultural expert from Jamaica, and then offered to turn the estate over to the islanders if they would farm it under his supervision. There was already a herd of sixty cattle, and over 400 sheep. The Duke was profoundly interested; here was an initiative which ought to be followed everywhere, with official encouragement.

Next they stopped at Inagua, the most southerly of the Bahamas and the home of the pink flamingo. Unlike San Salvador, Inagua had once been prosperous; in the first half of the nineteenth century it had flourished in the salt trade, exporting as much as one and a half million bushels a year. But the trade had been killed by United States tariffs, and the settlements became ghost towns, with a population on the edge of starvation. But in Inagua too there was a new age of hope. The Ericksons, a remarkable family from Maine, had successfully revived the salt industry in the teeth of fierce Bay Street opposition, and were now keeping most of the island busily employed. The Duke admired their enterprise, the Duchess what she called their 'covered-wagon spirit'.

They stopped briefly at Crooked Island, Long Island and Cat Island – desolate places where people lived the barest of existences – and finally came to Abaco, the lush, large and beautiful island jutting into the Atlantic in the north-east of the archipelago, first settled by loyalists who had set out from New York in the 1780s. In those early days it had thrived with cotton and sugar; now the land was poor, unproductive and neglected. They saw the historic all-white settlement of Hope Town on Elbow Cay, with its candy-stripe lighthouse and seafaring tradition, and inbred but curiously beautiful people, all speaking the American accents of the eighteenth century, all descended from the loyalist widow Malone. But they were saddened by the neglect, and the apparent inability of the people to help themselves.

They had meant to sail on to Grand Bahama (then so idyllic, now so horrible) to see the site of Wenner-Gren's proposed development, but in the early hours of 3 April the yacht ran aground in rough weather off Hole-in-the-Wall Light, and they had to be rescued.

The Duke returned to Nassau stimulated and full of reformist intentions. The Oakes project on San Salvador, the Ericksons' enterprise on Inagua, showed what could be done, what ought to be done throughout the islands – what Wenner-Gren also wanted to do. But the Duchess's first reaction to the trip was one of gloom. The sights of poverty and abandon aroused her pity, but also reminded her in a sudden upsurge of bitterness how primitive, backward and hopeless was the fifth-rate territory her husband had been sent out to govern. 'We have made quite a tour of these islands, each one worse than the last in dreariness', she wrote to Aunt Bessie from the *Rene* on 31 March; and she described how they had sat for whole hours in the burning sun listening to addresses of homage slowly read out by stammering, inbred, backward people – 'all because of a woman's jealousy and a country's fear his brother wouldn't shine if he was there !' But the Duchess was a woman of action. She had seen people in desperate need and, back in Nassau, she set at once about relieving their condition. The problem was that all charitable funds were going to war purposes, and local relief had therefore become entirely neglected. Feeling that here was a case where charity might begin at home, the Duchess set up a Bahamas Assistance Fund, to which the Duke made over the income from a charitable trust he had founded as Prince of Wales. The Duchess busily corresponded with the commissioners for the Out Islands, and consulted priests and doctors who knew the islands. Her speed and power of organization were extraordinary. Almost at once shipments of tinned milk went out to parts where malnutrition was most serious, medical supplies were sent to settlements in desperate need of them. And all the time the Duchess continued her work for the Red Cross, her infant welfare clinics – and the various duties which fell to a governor's wife.

During April Sir Edward Peacock, the Canadian financial adviser to the Royal Family who had helped negotiate the Abdication Settlement and remained on friendly terms with the Duke, was in America as head of the British Purchasing Commission. He offered to meet the Duke in Florida to discuss his private business affairs. The Duke's financial situation was very complex, and he possessed nothing like the great fortune some people imagined. In December 1936 he had given up to his brother absolutely everything he had inherited from his father (including his private family estates of Sandringham and Balmoral) in return for an annual income of about £21,000, part of it liable to tax, and which the Court later tried to make dependent on a condition, which the Duke fiercely resisted, that he never return to England. The Duke's capital, upon which he had drawn heavily since the Abdication, was tied up in low-yield government securities and did not bring in much more. On top of this he had his Governor's salary of £3,000. (The Bahamas was naturally near the bottom of the list of governors' salaries.) All this might be thought to add up to an income which was not inconsiderable for 1941 ; but the charges upon it were very heavy. The Duke's position demanded that he personally keep a large retinue; throughout the war he ran his two houses in France and the unprofitable ranch in Canada; and as former King-Emperor (who in the Bahamas especially was expected to keep up standards) he had to live, entertain and travel in a certain style. Above all, the Duke was anxious for the future, for he realized that, once the war was over, he would probably be in a position neither to earn his own living nor to call upon his family for any kind of support. He was therefore keen to see Peacock to discuss how to organize, in wartime, his limited material resources, as well as to have news of his family and home. London reluctantly agreed to let the Duke spend just a week-end in Palm Beach; and so, on 18 April, he and the Duchess arrived back on the mainland for the second of their brief, private visits.

Florida had not changed in its enthusiasm for the Duke and Duchess.[14] When they arrived at Miami docks on board the last seasonal passenger vessel to leave Nassau, they found – as in December – a huge cheering crowd, and a reception committee headed by the ecstatic Mayor Orr. 'Welcome Duke and Duchess, Miami's Beloved Visitors', read an immense sign. In Palm Beach they stayed (it was a brief secret) at the Everglades Club, where they were soon under siege. When not in conference with Peacock that week-end the Duke managed some golf, while the Duchess went shopping, amid crowds of gapers, to buy some cool summer clothes to replace what she called her 'refugee rags'. Though the season was over, they were inundated with invitations, most of which they refused; but they did see some of their friends – Ali Mackintosh who was now *'ami de la maison'* at Government House, the Duchess's old friends Gordon and Mai Douglas, 'Doc' Holden who had been a Fort regular, and a few agreeable Americans they had met in Nassau such as the Harold Vanderbilts and Mrs James P. Donahue, a Woolworth heiress who had an amusing son. On Sunday the Duke and Duchess inspected the US Army air-base nearing completion at Morrison Field; the Duke praised the arrangements made for the comfort of the men. On Monday they visited the local branch of the British War Relief Society, from where the Duke broadcast, expressing 'the deep appreciation which the Duchess and I feel for the diligent and ceaseless efforts of the Palm Beachers in support of the British cause during the past months'. The young British Consul James Marjoribanks was again delighted by the public effect of the visit. 'Everyone found the Duke a delightful and exciting person to meet,' he remembers. 'He was someone whose personality inspired affection as well as respect.' The seas were rough and they could not find a boat to return on, so they travelled on Harold Vanderbilt's private aircraft. Two thousand people saw them off. The Duchess had never flown before; she put on a brave face for the crowd, but was terrified and kept her eyes shut for the whole hour of the flight, only opening them once, at the Duke's insistence, to look at the lovely aerial view of the blue-green lagoons. In sympathy with her sufferings, the three cairn terriers which had accompanied them kept up an ear-piercing, non-stop din. It was a memorable journey, about which they laughed a good deal later.

Back in Nassau, the Duke had much work to do. After months of negotiation in which he, along with the governors of the other 'bases colonies', had played a minor role, the Bases Agreement had finally been signed in London on 27 March. 'I have today signed the document implementing the agreement of September last for the leasing to the United States of bases in the Bahamas and elsewhere,' telegraphed the Prime Minister, 'and I wish to express to you my strong conviction that these bases are important pillars to the bridge connecting the two great English-speaking democracies. You have cause to be proud that it has fallen to your lot to make this important contribution to a better world.'[15] A steady stream of important service personnel, British and American, now began to call on the Duke, to discuss what the American bases were to consist of and where they were to be. The callers naturally expected to stay at Government House, and so the Duchess assumed a role she was to play for the next four years, that of hostess to generals and admirals who were liable to turn up in numbers without any notice at all. Her official guests, like her social ones, rarely failed to be charmed. But even in the war-spared Bahamas, housekeeping was not without its problems. On 16 May the Duchess wrote to Aunt Bessie:

> . . . We are getting very stuck for transportation – no boats except those two tiny ones which couldn't bring enough food to feed the Kennedy family – and now the aeroplanes are to go I hear. What a world, and I think we are in for a good long war. . . . Well, one can only face it and do one's best to keep one's head above water through its ups and downs. . . . We have an English general and ADC here for a week – quite a nice old boy – and today there arrived an American general and 3 officers – very strange tropical uniforms our army have ! . . . If you find 2 or 3 cool dresses at Garfinkel . . . send them along – I can repay you by cheque. I don't think it worth paying over $30 a piece for them and you may find something smart much cheaper. . . . Try and use some of that good taste on me. . . .

She wrote too of how intrigued they were by the flight of Rudolf Hess. 'This mystery is *something*. If only it meant the end of this war. . . .' Some time later, J. Edgar Hoover of the FBI wrote to the State Department that 'the Duke is very much worried for fear of being kidnapped by the Germans and traded for the release of Rudolph Hess'.[16] Captain Montgomery Hyde's security warnings had certainly not been in vain.

The heat rose. The chief topic of the Duchess's letters became the weather. 'We have had wind for the last days so it is cool,' she wrote on 26 May, 'still only 80 and the swimming really heavenly.' The officials and ADCs planned their summer escapes to the mainland. The Duke and Duchess longed to follow them, but were resigned – given the attitude of London – to staying in the boiling colony at least until mid-August. 'We can stick it this year,' wrote the Duchess to Aunt Bessie on 9 June, 'with plenty of fans and the air-cooling if it ever arrives. No official things to do makes it easier than last year when we had to do all that without proper clothes etc.' But she was plainly bored. 'There is no news here – we do nothing, think nothing, say nothing – in fact two monkeys instead of three. We had a very successful Empire Flag Day last Thursday. I don't know where the people get the money on these islands. We had a tropical downpour the other day and it played havoc with the terrace painting. . . .' She prayed above all that they would be allowed to leave before the end of the summer.

Now that the season was over and the merchants back in the House, the Duke was determined – in spite of the scepticism of the egregious Kenneth Solomon – to present his reform programme to the Legislature. In accordance with his speech to the House the previous October, he sent messages to the House calling for a rise in the standard wage to offset the rising cost of living, and a large scheme of public works – road building, tree planting, drainage improvement – to relieve unemployment. Solomon, as Leader for the Government, presented the proposals unenthusiastically. A bill was tabled for the public works, and thrown out at the second reading. The wage question was referred to a select committee, which not only advised firmly against an increase, but even denied the Government's power to sanction one. The Duke was furious, but the greatest blow was to come. It has been seen that nothing was dearer to his heart – especially since the *Rene* trip at the end of March – than the development of agriculture in the Out Islands, with a view to making the Colony productive and self-sufficient. The Duke was determined to give official encouragement and help to private farming schemes, and accordingly, Solomon was instructed to introduce a bill exempting from tariffs all supplies and machinery for agricultural and similar purposes, 'to encourage comprehensive schemes of development'. It was promptly and resoundingly defeated.[17] Bay Street made it clear that the last thing it wanted was a self-sufficient agriculture. Its merchants, who kept the Out Islanders in thrall by keeping them poor, made their money by shipping supplies from the mainland; the House derived its financial power from the duties people were forced to pay on imported foodstuffs.

The Duke felt infinitely frustrated. How could one deal with such people, so narrowly obsessed with their own sectional interests? But some kind of reform was now essential. An ominous situation had arisen among the coloured population. Since the beginning of the war, prices – particularly food prices – had increased by almost fifty per cent, owing to poor dollar exchange, extra war duties, and higher freight charges. The poor were finding it harder and harder to pay for even the most basic essentials of life. As the House had refused to sanction any increase in standard wages, a reduction in tariffs had become essential in order to avoid starvation and a revolutionary mood was growing among the people. So vital was this measure that the Duke personally addressed the unenthusiastic House no less than three times during the summer to demand its enactment:

> I consider that the Colony's financial position is entirely satisfactory, and that the grant of some alleviation from taxation to the poorer classes is now fully justified in order to meet the rising cost of living which is inevitable so long as the war continues. . . . As I regard this matter as one of great importance, I sincerely trust early action will be taken upon it.[18]

Finally, with bad grace, the House passed the Tariff Act, 1941, at the end of the summer. But was the relief enough, and in time? The problem remained, and was to lead to grave events a year later.

Convinced of the urgent need for reforms, the Duke was miserable at his inability to carry them through. Not only was the House a law unto itself, but the Duke did not even have control of his own Council. Solomon, who as Leader for the Government was responsible for introducing all Government measures in the House, rigidly upheld Bay Street interests, sabotaging every progressive proposal. The Duke increasingly disliked and distrusted this hard, narrow, devious, humourless little man. By the summer of 1941 dislike had turned to enmity, and one might say that the principal theme of the rest of the Duke's political administration was the struggle between his own reformist intentions and the reactionary policy of Bay Street enshrined in the person of Kenneth Solomon. If Solomon was bitter and unscrupulous, the Duke waged the struggle with determination and adroitness. He looked for weapons; and in the middle of 1941, one came unexpectedly to hand.

In February 1941 Lord Lloyd, the Secretary of State for the Colonies who had 'hoped the Duke would not do well', died suddenly after an obscure illness brought on by overwork.* He was succeeded by Walter Guinness, 1st Baron Moyne, a Tory elder statesman with an interest in zoology who had been Baldwin's agriculture minister in the 1920s, and was well known to the Duke, having lent his yacht *Rosaura* to the Prince of Wales for a cruise with Mrs Simpson in 1934. Lord Moyne, whose tragic and senseless murder by the Stern Gang in 1944 was to have the effect of discrediting the cause of Zionism in the eyes of such men as the Duke of Windsor who might otherwise have thought it worthy, was a humane man of great intellect and far-sighted perceptions. Although a conservative by instinct, his study of Darwinism had instilled in him a rational belief in the democratic progress of peoples. Just before the war, he had headed the Royal Commission on the British West Indies, and so startling were the progressive recommendations of his report that the Government postponed publication. In short, Moyne concluded – after a

---

* His young Private Secretary Dudley Danby was driven to the funeral in the country by Lloyd's brother-in-law Sir Alan Lascelles, the Assistant Private Secretary to the King. Lascelles spent the whole journey ranting and raving against the Duke of Windsor, to Danby's astonishment.

struggle between reason and sentiment – that black rule was the only future for the West Indian colonies, and that it was the duty of the Imperial Government gradually to pave the way for it:

> Representatives of public opinion should be given more opportunity to influence policy, and – though I do not underestimate the difficulties involved – some of them may perhaps be converted from criticism to co-operation if an arrangement can be made whereby they are more closely associated with the work of the executive.

Although the Moyne Report did not deal directly with the Bahamas, the Duke had read it with great care at the outset of his governorship, and had referred to it in his important letter to Churchill of October 1940.

Unexpectedly finding himself in charge of the Colonial Office, Moyne sought to put his advanced convictions into effect. As a first step, he wanted to break the monopoly of local white oligarchies on the executive councils of governors. Members were appointed for eight years, but the leading, reactionary white economic figures in each colony were customarily reappointed and came to regard their position as one for life. At the end of May 1941 Moyne therefore addressed two letters to a number of colonial governors including the Duke. The first – to be laid before the local legislature at a moment of the governor's choosing – declared that, while governors were to retain their discretion, they should hesitate to reappoint a local member for a second term, and only in very rare and important cases do so for a third term. The second letter, which was secret, confided that the purpose of this policy was to break the exclusive power of the colonial class: 'Governors should bear carefully in mind the desirability of broadening the basis of their executive councils and giving, as far as possible, representation thereon to all important sections of the community.'

Thus it was that, in the summer of 1941, the Duke was given a heaven-sent opportunity to confine the power of Bay Street. Replying to Moyne in July, he declared himself 'in full agreement with the principle laid down', even if 'not decided as to the advisability of appointing coloured persons'.[19] He investigated the state of appointments on ExCo; Moore's second term of office would come to an end in December, Solomon's the following May. The Duke would then have a perfect excuse for dropping his adversary as the leading unofficial member and Leader for the Government in the House. He decided not to publish Moyne's first letter right away, but to bide his time. Soon he would have a Council which was truly his own, one of reasonable men, of reformers.

Summer had come, and with it the burning, mind-destroying temperatures. 'I have not felt the heat so much this year – I suppose I am acclimatized,' wrote the Duchess; 'but it does take every inch of energy from me and makes a grease-spot of the brain. . . . The air conditioning got mixed up with the defence orders so I don't suppose it will arrive till after the war.'[20] They were preoccupied with their desperate hope to visit America and the ranch in Canada at the end of summer, and meanwhile filled the sweltering days as well as they could.

It was the Duke's forty-seventh birthday on 23 June. An embarrassed secretary told Vyvyan Drury that a curious telegram had arrived for the Royal Governor and they were uncertain whether to show it to him; it appeared to come from an old girl-friend and was only signed with her Christian name and initial. The message read: 'All love darling. Mary R.'

The Duke wrote to Aunt Bessie, thanking her for a birthday present:

> The summer heat cracked down on us the first days of June with a consistent low temperature of 80 at night and the usual high humidity . . . but the trade-winds blow here some days which helps and we have lately had plenty of rain which is fine for the rock garden. Believe it or not it is now finished and I am very proud of it as it really looks rather pretty all planted up. We spend most evenings and week-ends at the cabana swimming-pool and away from official work, of which as you know there is always more than enough to keep our minds occupied. Still, we can do with a change of atmosphere and people after nearly a year in the Bahamas, as one does feel very much cut off from the outside world. . . .[21]

That summer, they decided to make an important purchase – a fifty-seven-foot Elko cabin cruiser which they named *Gemini*, after the Duchess's birth sign. He wanted to visit all the islands on his own boat; he loved being with her at sea, far from the world. She, though more of a 'landlubber', was concerned for his pleasure and readily fell in with the idea. The first voyage of the *Gemini* was to Eleuthera. They landed at Hatchet Bay, where they stayed with Austin Levy. From there they drove to Palmetto Point to dine with Rosita Forbes, who has left an amusing account of their visit[22] – which was attended by a domestic crisis caused by a negro servant going into a trance at the arrival of 'de Lawd'.

> They had motored 26 miles from Hatchet Bay over the earthquake-in-road semblance. The Duchess still looked delightful. They were both very entertaining. We dined upon a porch with an unexpected view of the pantry refrigerator. The Duchess said nothing could be more inspiring in such a temperature. . . . The culinary exploits of my friends had made possible the success of the party. The Duchess's wit ensured it.

While the model agricultural developments of Eleuthera continued to flourish, another Out Island scheme had been nipped in the bud. The Duke had been doing all he could to advance the sale to Wenner-Gren of Crown land on Grand Bahama. Before agreeing to this transaction, the Colonial Office decided to consult the American Government, as Grand

Bahama was close to the mainland and a possible site for a base. At a conference in the State Department, the naval intelligence representative declared that, while 'there is nothing definite on which he can base an opinion', and the nearest US base would be 200 miles away, 'he would be much happier if the British turned down Wenner-Gren's proposition'.[23] This view was duly communicated to the Foreign Office, who informed the Duke that the deal could not go through.

The Duke was perplexed and annoyed. He wrote to Halifax, asking him 'to find out what it might be that the United States Government had against Mr Axel Wenner-Gren'.[24] Halifax went to see the Under-Secretary of State Sumner Welles, who could only tell him that, although he 'knew of nothing specific against [Wenner-Gren]', the Swede's 'activities during the past two years could only be regarded as suspicious in view of the world situation'. This was no reply at all, and Halifax wrote to the Duke to say that he was unable to obtain any information.

The Duke was angry, and sincerely sorry for Wenner-Gren, for he well knew what it was to have political bureaucracy down on one for no apparent reason. Wenner-Gren took the disappointment calmly. In July, he left the Bahamas on board the *Southern Cross* to spend the summer in Peru, where he was financing an archaeological expedition and had also been invited by the Peruvian Government to undertake various important economic projects. On 4 September he telegraphed the Duke via Havana:

> Knowing of Your Royal Highness's interest in Peru, land of the Incas, I am happy to inform you that we have just encountered two lofty ancient fortresses that guard the entrance valley to 'the city above the clouds'. This is the fifteenth ruin complex discovered by our expedition till today. Life here in the high sierras of the Andes is so marvellous that I hardly see how I can return to so-called modern civilization.

The last line was to prove curiously prophetic.

In Nassau, the Duke and Duchess had few guests that summer. Alastair Mackintosh, eternally optimistic, turned up full of schemes for a new hotel, 'none of which will probably come off as it seems a strange time to develop Nassau when I feel no American will put a foot in a boat once war is declared,' wrote the Duchess. (For they felt America's entry into the conflict could not be too far distant.) And Vincent Astor arrived on board his yacht *Nourmahal*, with a charming and talented young Englishman who had taken American nationality and had met the Duke and Duchess at Lady Cunard's before the Abdication. Jason Lindsey – now famous as the author of such dramatic soliloquys as *Empress Eugénie* – was then working in Hollywood as a designer of clothes and sets. During those few days in Nassau he designed two dresses for the Duchess and found himself quite often at the Duke's table. He vividly remembers the delicious food; on one occasion lunch began with iced pumpkin soup with fresh cream and grated nutmeg stirred in at the last moment, and the Duchess practically forced the Duke (who did not eat lunch) to taste it. Above all, Lindsey was extraordinarily struck by the personality of the Duchess. She was immensely patient when it came to being fitted:

> . . . She could stand immobile for half-an-hour at a time. But she was not idle even then. She could dictate and give orders to as many as eight or nine people without once moving her body or turning her head. She had the same faculty for doing this that Napoleon had. Never once was it necessary for her to return to someone in the group and say: 'Now, where was I?' She always knew. Her talent for organization was extraordinary. . . .
>
> The Duke was always more comfortable with a single person. He could never successfully carry off more than one conversation at a time. The Duchess had the agreeable gift of being able to talk intelligently with a whole roomful at once, as well as the ability to make *you* feel that if *you* had not come, the entire evening would have been a complete fiasco. It was the most remarkable talent of that kind I've ever encountered. She knew how to greet total strangers as if the one thing she had been waiting for all day was to sit down and have a friendly chat with *you*. Even people who only met her once, and casually at that, never forgot it. . . .
>
> The Duchess was a great (and demanding) perfectionist and she had every right to be, for she had no peer when it came to three extremely important things: she had impeccable taste in clothes, she knew everything worth knowing about food, and she was superlative as an organizer – an organizer of anything – a bandage-rolling party, a ball, an invasion. She could have been the first woman on the moon if she had put her mind to it, and I'm sure the only reason she was not the first person to climb Everest was that it didn't interest her.
>
> It is a great and enduring pity that the pure 'cussedness' of the Queen Mother robbed England of the Duchess's talents as a working member of the Royal Family. . . .[25]

Confined to the role of governor's wife in Nassau, the Duchess directed her indefatigable organizational powers to her war work. Her Bahamas Assistance Fund, designed to bring relief to the Out Islands, took off like a rocket. Thousands of cans of milk were shipped out to nourish the young. Sick Out Islanders were brought to the General Hospital in Nassau, while medical supplies went out to parts which had none. She 'adopted' an island – Harbour Island – and sought to make its social condition a model for others. In Nassau itself, she set up a second infant welfare clinic and herself found the money for a nurse and a car. She was infuriated when she read in *Picture Post* an article which began: 'The war is still very far away from some parts of the world. Further, perhaps, from the Bahama Islands than anywhere else in the British Empire.' Did they not know, she wrote to the editor, that the Bahamas Branch of the British Red Cross had just raised £2,739 17s 10d on Empire Flag Day in aid of HRH the Duke of Gloucester's St John's Fund? That they had sent the Old Country 80,510 knitted garments? That £26,500 had been raised for the RAF and £12,000 for Citizens' War Relief? 'I venture to suggest', she protested, 'that your article gives a very unfair picture of the life that is being led out here and is a completely false interpretation of what is actually going on in the Bahamas.'[26]

So the Colony was trying to 'do its bit', and the Duchess had thrown herself heart and soul into organizing the bit. But the Bahamas did seem very far from the grave events of the war in the first half of 1941. England's survival was magnificent, but otherwise the news was appalling. The Germans overran Yugoslavia, Greece and Crete; Rommel wiped out Wavell's gains in North Africa. But in their own minds, the Duke and Duchess were convinced that these events would soon be overshadowed by one much greater; they believed that the United States would soon enter the war on the side of the Allies. 'I do not know what the conditions of travelling will be if the US comes in,' wrote the Duchess to Aunt Bessie on 9 June. 'I think their minds would be ready for war before the summer is over.'

Great Britain was indeed to have a powerful new ally that summer, but it was not the one expected. On Sunday 22 June the Duke and Duchess were having lunch at their beach cabana with the Eric Hallinans – the Attorney-General and his wife. An urgent telegram arrived. It announced the German invasion of Russia. Hallinan recalls: 'The news took us entirely by surprise, and I remember distinctly that we were all excited and thrilled, the Duke especially. He said that Hitler had done a mad thing which would cost him the war, that England was saved, that an alliance with the devil was not too high a price for victory. There was no mistaking his delight.'

When the news had sunk in, it provoked a mixture of relief and unease. The involuntary new ally which had arisen to take the burden off Great Britain was decidedly an odd and dangerous ally. 'What about the Stalin kiss?' wrote the Duchess to Aunt Bessie on 7 July. 'Now we must get used to Communism. If he has to leave Russia will he set up his Government in London with all the rest of the boys and girls? I think the Russian gesture is the end of Germany however.' The Duke wrote to Aunt Bessie: 'The war has taken a queer and unexpected turn hasn't it and I guess we must all be prepared eventually to adopt "the hammer and the sickle" as our national emblems.'[27] But he was heartened by the Atlantic Meeting in the second week of August – forwarding as it did his own great dream of *Pax Americana* – and wrote to Beaverbrook (who as Minister of Supply had attended the conversations): 'Everyone is thrilled at yours and Winston's meetings with the President at sea, and the momentous goings-on are very encouraging. I am too far away to make any comments, and can only say that we are all with Winston and full of admiration at the wonderful job you and he are doing together.' He looked forward to letters from his old supporter, 'for we are very starved for inside news here such as you could give us.'[28] It always saddened the Duke, during such great events, that he was able neither to play a useful part in them nor even to know what they in reality consisted of, beyond the brief propaganda communiqués of the Ministry of Information.

The second half of August saw the anniversary of the arrival of the Duke and Duchess in Nassau. There were a fair number of tributes. The *Nassau Guardian* published a special issue devoted to the Duke's achievements; it carried the suggestion that the Colony had been amazingly lucky to have his and the Duchess's services for a year, and could hardly expect to keep them for much longer. In London, Sir Charles Petrie in *Empire* praised the Duke's desire to make the Bahamas self-sufficient and his 'endless efforts towards revived enterprise', while the *Imperial Review* wrote in an editorial:

> He has reason to be well-satisfied with a solid twelve months of achievement. A list of his activities, legislative, social, sporting, and of those devoted to industry and commerce, give proof of the fact that the King's brother is one of the hardest worked of His Majesty's servants. . . . The charm which won Ottawa, Washington and New York twenty-two years ago has in no way diminished, and to the Bahamians he is still Prince Charming of the winning smile.

That week, the Governor Duke received his first official visitor from the Colonial Office in London. G. H. (later 1st Viscount) Hall had gone down the pits at the age of twelve; since 1922 he had been Labour Member for the Aberdare Division of Merthyr Tydfil. In May 1940 he had become Parliamentary Under-Secretary at the Colonial Office, where he was later to be Secretary of State under a Labour Government. In the summer of 1941 he made a tour of the West Indian colonies, and spent three days in Nassau where he stayed at Government House and fulfilled a heavy schedule of meetings and receptions. The Duke sent a delighted telegram to London about the success of the visit.[29] They were not strangers to one another. Hall had been with Edward VIII in South Wales in November 1936, and could never recall without emotion the great hope the King had brought to the unhappy people of the valleys. Now, in a curious way, their roles were reversed, and it was the Duke's turn to be grateful to the Minister – whom he valued enormously – for bringing messages of inspiration from embattled Britain to the people of one of her more distant colonies. Hall's son, the present Lord Hall, recalls:

I happened to be in London on leave from the Royal Navy when my father returned from the West Indies. . . . Although it was forty years ago, I well remember his enthusiasm for HRH and happiness at the success of his governorship, matched, if not surpassed, by his admiration for the captivating charm of his wife. He praised their qualities endlessly. My father was quite clear in his view that both should be borne in mind for some other colonial contribution, but I know not what. . . .[30]

So – with Hall singing the Duke's praises to deaf ears in Whitehall, and such favourable articles in the reviews – it was not without accolade that the first year of the governorship came to an end. That week, across the ocean, Churchill was explaining the Atlantic Charter to the British people, while German tanks pushed on to Moscow and Rommel pressed against the gates of Egypt. And in Nassau, as the vermilion poinciana blossom died in the intense summer heat, the former King of England presided as usual over his Council of three officials, two ex-bootleggers, a sharp lawyer, a grocer and a drunkard. And they discussed the need to improve the poor-house,[31] and the possibility of employing native women to weed roads,[32] and whether ice should be sold on Sundays.[33]

11
Going North
September–November 1941

———

'We have written to London about a trip to America,' wrote the Duchess to Aunt Bessie on 7 July 1941, 'and it now remains to be seen if the naughty boy is allowed to leave Nassau.' It was the latest episode in an anguished saga which had been going on for a year. In July 1940, bowing to official insistence that he proceed to his post without passing through New York, the Duke had asked Churchill: 'May I have confirmation that it is not to be the policy of His Majesty's Government that I should not set foot on American soil during my term of office in the Bahamas?' Churchill had given assurances; but the Duke's fears proved all too justified. 'I rely on you,' Halifax had written to Lothian that October, 'to dispel any erroneous ideas about our view of a visit by His Royal Highness to the United States.' He was told he could not leave his Colony until after the presidential elections; they came and went, and he was allowed only a brief mercy trip to Miami on the supposition that it would cause him to miss the meeting with Roosevelt on the *Tuscaloosa*. Then came the season – the only season during which the Governor of the Bahamas did not appear (because he was not allowed to) on the mainland. After the season, it was the same story; the plan to visit the Duchess's family and a CCC camp in early April was vetoed without any reasonable justification whatever.

By the summer of 1941 they had spent a strenuous year doing their best at an unfamiliar job in a claustral climate, and were desperate to get away. The Duke pined for his cool ranch in Canada, the Duchess for her family in Maryland, and they longed to be, however, briefly, back in the cosmopolitan centre of things in Washington and New York. This time, they did not see how their request could be refused. It was universal for West Indian governors to take leave during the hot season; the ADCs and overseas officials were all going away; and where could one go but America? Besides, the Duke had some Colony business to transact on the mainland. Apart from the continuing need to promote Nassau as a safe wartime resort, there were the bases to discuss and the growing problem of communications. He hoped to be able to study the Civilian Conservation Corps with a view to finding a similar solution to the Out Island and unemployment problems. And at the same time he was as convinced as ever that, given the chance, he and the Duchess could aid Britain's image in America. They had already won Florida and aided the British cause there. Why should they not win the rest of the United States?

Ideally they hoped to get away during late August and September, escaping the worst of the Nassau heat on the ranch and perhaps witnessing the advent of the New York autumn before returning. They had another reason for wanting to make the trip soon; it has been noted that they both believed the entry of the United States into the war to be fairly imminent. 'We can't plan anything definite for the summer yet and can only hope that nothing will prevent us from getting away at the end of August to America and my ranch in Canada. . . .' wrote the Duke to Aunt Bessie in July. 'We will let you know as soon as our plans mature, dearest Aunt Bessie, and if they ever do seeing you again will be amongst the "high spots" of our trip.'[1]

As ever, London viewed the prospect of the trip with grave concern. It has been seen that it was part of British policy in the United States to prevent the Duke and Duchess shining there. It was not that they were considered unpopular or ineffective as an instrument of wartime public relations. On the contrary, it was their very popularity, their value as potential war propaganda – in short, their capacity for acquiring prestige – which provoked alarm on the part of official (and especially royal) circles. At the Foreign Office, Anthony Eden declared himself against the trip.[2] At the Palace, Sir Alexander Hardinge expressed the King's displeasure. But at the Colonial Office, Lord Moyne did not see how it would be possible to veto the trip altogether. There was no urgent business to keep the Duke in his Colony in August and September. Besides, he was getting restless, and it was doubtless wise to let him have a brief continental fling – provided it was kept under rigid official control. 'It would no doubt be possible to ask the Duke of Windsor to defer his holiday,' wrote Moyne to Churchill, 'but I expect his patience will be rather strained. . . .'[3] Finally, Churchill made his pronouncement, in a personal minute of 16 July addressed to the Foreign Secretary and Colonial Secretary:

I see no reason why the Duke of Windsor should not towards the end of September visit Canada and the United States if he so desires. Such a request would not be denied to any Governor of Nassau. The itinerary must be exactly prescribed and agreed. I presume he would go to New York where he would stay at a hotel rather than with Society people and do any shopping which the Duchess may require. Thereafter they would go to the EP Ranch of which I expect they would soon tire and after that return via Washington where the

President has promised to give them a luncheon. . . . There is no reason why this tour should not be worked out and everything done for the comfort and honour of the former King-Emperor and his wife. But all must be planned beforehand.[4]

Churchill had kept his word.

There followed two months of feverish negotiation between the Duke and the British Embassy in Washington about the details of the proposed tour. It was decidedly to be a release on parole. The first question to be settled was that of dates. It was revealed that the Duke of Kent was also to visit Canada and the United States in the late summer. The two brothers had always been devoted to each other and longed to see each other again; they had only narrowly missed each other (alas, by no mere coincidence) in Lisbon in the summer of 1940. But the British Government could not allow the Duke of Windsor to 'interfere' with Prince George's drum-beating tour, and the Palace was determined that no meeting should ever take place (particularly if it included the Duchess). Even the Duke of Windsor's plea to see his brother alone in Florida for a few hours was instantly rejected. On 23 July the Duchess wrote to Aunt Bessie:

Permission for the trip has been granted, but the usual family complications have arisen as Kent is to be in Washington in the first week of September. This is an official secret, so put it under your gay red hat. That family of my husband's is always going to snub me so one has to face up to the fact, and face up to these humiliating situations which will forever give the American press a chance to belittle us. . . . I do not mind having to wait until Kent has had his fling, but I do resent their attitude most heartily. . . .[5]

Finally a timetable was arranged. They would leave Nassau on 23 September, a safe two weeks after the Duke of Kent's return to England. From Miami they would go to Washington, and spend one night there (being received for lunch at the White House) before travelling to Canada. After ten days on the ranch they would return to the United States, and spend several days in Maryland and a week in New York – but the New York visit was to receive a minimum of advance publicity. By the end of October they would be safely back in Nassau. 'We have to write to Halifax about every breath we are to take on the trip,' wrote the Duchess to her aunt. 'We won't be allowed much playing around America, so we must confine everything as much as possible.'[6]

The next problem to be surmounted was of where the Duke and Duchess were to stay during their tour. In New York, the Duchess wrote,

. . . we have been advised to stay in a hotel rather than in a private house or on Long Island. . . . There seem to be too many jealousies awakened the other way – so Winston thinks, and also Mrs R. The world is funny – but not so funny as England's royal family. . . . What do you think of the Waldorf Towers? I understand the entrance is small and not a lobby like the St Regis – lobbys [sic] are v. difficult for us as people can collect. . . . [7]

As for the overnight stop in Washington, during which the Duchess looked forward to being reunited with Aunt Bessie, 'I can't give you very definite plans, because the powers that be do not give them to us. This far we have heard – we are to spend the night at the Embassy. (A great surprise. The family can't have heard.)'[8] Then came the news that Halifax himself would not be there (throughout the war it was remarkable how often his official absences coincided with the Duke's visits); '. . . but we are still to stay at the Embassy with Ronald Campbell, who Halifax says is going to give a *small* dinner for us. I bet it's small! . . . Needless to say in Canada we do not go anywhere near Government House, because that charming family the Athlones is there. . . .'[9]

The Duchess wrote daily to Aunt Bessie with increasing excitement, relating their hopes and plans and the problems they were encountering, and asking a multitude of questions about conditions in the United States and what to do and not to do. 'You didn't tell me about *climate* in Wash around the 25th – and what it's like in Balto and N.Y. in October,' she wrote on 20 August. 'The clothes question has to be answered from a long distance and lapse of memory makes me need your advice.' She kept wondering if the trip was really going to be worth the effort, and confided to her aunt her mounting fears and anxieties. 'The cost of the journey with so many people is appalling,' she wrote on 23 July, 'and I wonder if it is worth it as one is stared at and still has to be civilized and can never really enjoy shopping and dining like ordinary people.' And on 5 September:

The complications attendant on travelling hardly make the trip worthwhile. One is worn out before starting and upon arrival can't do what one wants – and the official stew about the haughty ex-King is always tremendous – and there is always the US press. That is why France was such a perfect place for us. No officials – always free to come and go as we pleased. . . .

On 10 September she wrote: 'I can see plainly that this trip is not going to be a holiday and that until Balto or even N.Y. I shall not be seeing family or friends. . . .'

She asked Aunt Bessie to arrange medical appointments for them both in Baltimore and New York, and charged her with another, more delicate mission. In Maryland, the Duchess longed to stay with her uncle, General Henry Warfield,* on his farm in the Harford hunting country. He was her

---

* So-called as he had once been Adjutant-General of Maryland. The youngest of the Duchess's four Warfield uncles, and the only one still surviving, he had married a Baltimore woman (Aunt Rebecca) and had one daughter.

nearest relation on her father's side, and she wanted the Duke to see the clan of forthright gentlefolk from which she came. But she had never been very close to her uncle, who had written some wounding words to her in 1936. Would he be keen to have them to stay? 'I don't suppose there is any way Uncle Harry could put us up?' she wrote hesitantly to her aunt on 12 September. 'Could you go and see them and discuss the situation and see if they have any ideas? . . . You could explain to them that we do not want them to give any parties for us – simply a family visit – and we would be away in 3 days. Anyway, sound it all out. Aunt Rebecca will yell her head off . . . but I think they could manage and I'm sure it's definitely the best thing.' In her next letter she added: 'Darling, I have broken the ice for you with Uncle Harry by writing and as good as saying that they *must* take the Duke and myself. . . .' A week later she wrote ecstatically: 'I have heard from Uncle Harry and they *are* going to put us up! You can go over and explain a few details – among them the use of "Sir", because to call him "Duke" is *not* done! . . .'

Meanwhile the Duke was in constant communication with the Embassy about the smallest details of the trip. He was issued with the strictest instructions on what public statements he might make and what meetings he might have with the press. The instinct of the Duke and Duchess was to avoid personal publicity as much as possible; but they realized they were likely to be the object of enthusiastic curiosity and did not want to disappoint their public; and they wanted to ensure that what publicity they did receive was favourable both to them and the Anglo–American cause. 'The implication will be played up by the Isolationists that Your Royal Highness's visit is another "propaganda effort", and I am sure you will agree that it is important no ammunition should be given them in this respect,' the Embassy wrote on 10 September. 'That being so, in view of the non-official nature and brief duration of your visit, I would suggest there should be no press conferences, especially since if any such were held I have no doubt embarrassing questions would be asked by our enemies.' In Washington he could deliver a short, prepared statement; otherwise on principle he was to say nothing. The Duke was naturally unhappy at these orders, which he felt were principally designed to keep his profile low and deny him a 'goodwill role'; but he saw no alternative to accepting them. 'It is important that the press be carefully handled,' wrote the Duchess to Aunt Bessie, 'so we must sacrifice ourselves. The British Press Officer arrived today and everything sounds a beating. . . . Perhaps once the US has seen the middle-aged couple all the fuss will die down. . . .'[10]

The American press might have to be 'handled', but the British press was being told quite clearly how to react. Just before the start of the trip, the British Press Service in New York issued a report for the guidance of

English newspapers which declared that the American press had covered the forthcoming visit 'in an unfavourable light . . . and . . . evidently intend to capitalize to the fullest extent on what they interpret as a difficult situation existing between the Duke and Duchess of Windsor and the British Government, as well as what they present as the Administration's embarrassment in adapting its attitude to fit this implied situation.'[11] It was a cruel distortion, with the implication that the Duke and Duchess were unreasonable in insisting on coming, and themselves responsible for a wave of anti-British publicity.

Finally the moment of departure arrived. The Bahamas gave them a happy send-off. The *Nassau Guardian* wrote:

> His Royal Highness and the Duchess of Windsor . . . are leaving for their first real holiday since they arrived. . . . All of us who appreciate their tireless efforts on behalf of war charities and other local undertakings in addition to their ordinary fully-occupied life at Government House will wish them a pleasant journey . . . which we hope will be beneficial and refreshing to them after this summer heat which they have borne so uncomplainingly.

On Monday 22 September, the eve of their journey, the Duchess wrote to Aunt Bessie:

> . . . I am completely worn out and wish we had never planned the trip. Everybody is too kind and we are beset on all sides by invitations and if you go to one you must go to all – so we are refusing *everything*. It's too bad but it's the only way. . . . I'm sure we won't have a friend left after this trip – besides the press complications. . . . We are public characters, and what a price ! . . . The complications only *begin* at Washington – they are everywhere along the line. . . . Uncle Harry is all set. He doesn't know that a *hurricane* is arriving !
>
> In haste,
> love,
> WALLIS
>
> P.S. Am dreading the plane tomorrow as usual.

Washington, 25–26 September

They started off in Miami, where their popularity was always assured. They were met by the Consul James Marjoribanks and the Mayor Alexander Orr – both confirmed admirers – and a wildly cheering crowd of 5,000. The Duke broadcast a few words to the nation: 'I can speak for all my countrymen when I express to America the heartfelt thanks of Great Britain for all the moral and material help you are giving her in her hour of need.' The Duchess was 'glad to be back in my own country'. They lunched with Arthur Vyning Davis on board his yacht *Moja*, after which the Duke visited the University to inspect 300 RAF cadets undergoing advanced flight-training with Pan-American instructors there. The next day they were given a tremendous send-off as they boarded the train for Washington. Their train was luxurious, having been put at their disposal by their friend Robert Young, the President of the Line; but for the first two hours – to the delight of journalists – the Duke sat with the driver in his cab and talked of geography and machinery. This part of their trip at least had been an effortless triumph. But would the Washington crowd be as welcoming as the familiar Miami one? Would the Embassy and the Administration show anything of the delighted enthusiasm of the friendly Consul at Jacksonville and the Miami City Commission?

Meanwhile embarrassing press rumours were rife in the capital, where the scheduled presidential lunch for the Duke and Duchess at the White House had been called off on account of the grave illness of Mrs Roosevelt's brother. The papers were agog with speculation. Was this the real reason for the cancellation? Journalists might be forgiven for such thoughts, for it was becoming hourly more apparent that the Administration, taking its cue from the Embassy, would be giving the Duke and Duchess a less than outstandingly cordial welcome. However, while the royal visitors were on their way Mrs Roosevelt's brother died, thus ending speculation.

When the ducal train arrived at the Union Station at half-past seven on the morning of Thursday 25 September, its reception made an appalling impression on the observers and reporters present. The Chargé d'Affaires was not there to greet his former sovereign. The small group of minor Embassy officials and State Department aides stayed on the upper level of the station until the very last moment before the train pulled in; when they finally descended to meet it, their coolness contrasted vividly with the wild delight of the crowd outside, which in spite of the early hour already numbered 10,000. The dismal performance was noticed throughout the press. 'It was a sad show to watch,' wrote the *Times Herald*. 'The British and American officials giving the brush-off to a man who, with all the weaknesses one may accuse him of, was still a king once, and is still the idol of the labour classes in England. . . . Fortunately the people of Washington took matters in their hands and cheered the Windsors, showing that even though the ruling class in England may frown, the American people have not lost their traditions of hospitality and gallantry.'[12] They were obviously much heartened by the public welcome, and by the sight of Aunt Bessie who was there to greet them.

In spite of the official chill, their thirty hours in the capital were a hectic popular success. 'The Windsors came, saw and conquered Washington yesterday,' reported one paper.[13] The crowds were unheard-of, and jammed the traffic wherever the Duke and Duchess happened to be; they were larger than the crowds which had greeted the King and Queen in June 1939.

At the Embassy they were received by Sir Ronald Campbell, who as Minister at the Paris Embassy in 1938–9 had become well-trained in the art of treating them with icy reserve. (He is not to be confused with their friend of the same name who was Ambassador in Paris, 1939–40). While the Duchess stayed at the Embassy with Aunt Bessie and her old friends the Hermann Rogers (photographers being ordered to take no pictures of her which showed any part of the Embassy buildings), the Duke went with Campbell to call on Secretary Jesse Jones at the Commerce Department and Secretary Cordell Hull at the State Department. The Duke was in fact a figure of considerable fascination in Washington, and members of the Administration had been vying with each other for the favour of a visit during the day or an invitation to the Embassy dinner in the evening. Then the Duke and Duchess went to pay their respects and condolences to the President, who received them warmly and insisted that they return to the capital later during their trip so that he could give them the promised lunch at the White House.

In the afternoon, at the National Press Club reception, the Duke made a speech which attracted great attention. He had actually written it (in a long series of telegrams) in collaboration with Winston Churchill,[14] and it contained many Churchillian as well as ducal touches. He began by explaining his own position.

Of course, when London and other cities were bombarded and Great Britain was threatened with invasion, I could not help wishing, like every Briton in every part of the world, to share in the fortunes of my country at home. In wartime, however, one serves where one is told, and although it is a very different post to the one I held in the First World War, I have applied myself to the administration of the Bahamas to the best of my ability.

He declared the Bahamas were 'proud to have become a link in the chain of American bases in the West Indies', and announced that the island of Great Exuma had been selected for a naval base.

The British neither fear nor envy the greatness and power of America. On the contrary, they rejoice with every increase because they know that the ideals . . . which have guided the United States are the same as those for which the British Commonwealth of Nations are fighting. May America ever remain 'the land of the free and the home of the brave'.

He was glad to have seen the President again, and 'would like to pay tribute to his generous heart, and to his strong hand which is uplifted against tyranny and aggression.' The concluding sentiments were his own – his dream of European reconstruction under the *Pax Americana*. The speech was reported throughout the American press and very favourably received.

That evening at the Embassy there were thirty guests to dinner with the Duke and Duchess, including the Vice-President Henry Wallace, the Speaker Samuel Rayburn, the Treasury Secretary Henry Morgenthau, the Under-Secretary of the Navy James Forrestal, and the Canadian, Australian and South African Ministers, together with their wives. It was an excellent evening which formed several friendships, notably between the Duke and Duchess and the Morgenthaus. The next morning the Duke, accompanied by the Military Attaché, went to see Henry L. Stimson, the Secretary for War, to discuss the role of the Bahamas in the United States Defense Programme. He stopped off at the Lincoln Memorial to read the Gettysburg Address. That afternoon, the Duke and Duchess set out on their long journey to Canada. It was reported that 'a minimum of officialdom saw them to the station. But the people were there, thousands of them, jamming sidewalks, shoving at barriers, roaring farewell.'[15]

Middle West, 26–29 September

Nothing illustrates the official attitude towards the Duke and Duchess more clearly than the route which the British Embassy had chosen for them to travel from Washington to Canada.[16] To reach Alberta they would normally have headed north across the border to Montreal and then followed the Canadian railway-system west, passing through Ottawa and Winnipeg. The alternative was to enter Canada 'through the back door' from North Dakota, after travelling south of the border across the Mid-West. The disadvantage of the first route in the eyes of London was that it would take the Duke and Duchess through three of the principal Canadian cities where their transient presence would be certain to excite great public interest. The second route also had its dangers, however, for the Mid-West was notoriously 'isolationist' and anti-British; indeed, the Embassy warned that the Duke might well be snubbed by a hostile population and exposed to a most unfriendly press. Faced with these unpleasant alternatives, the authorities had no hesitation in choosing the second of them. The risk of anti-British publicity in America was less important than the risk of a personal success for the Duke and Duchess in the populated centres of Canada.

As it turned out, the journey across the Middle Western States was nothing short of a triumphal progress. Huge crowds turned out to cheer them everywhere. They were forever waving to their admirers from the whistle-stop platform at the back of their train. At Fort Wayne, Indiana, the Duke joked with the delighted throng in friendly repartee, assuring them that 'the Duchess of Windsor is what I like about America'. At Chicago – home not only of isolationism but of the violently anti-British *Chicago Tribune* – the Duke was so heartened by the popular welcome that he made an unscheduled tour of the lake-front; even the *Tribune* endorsed 'the whole-souled tribute of Middle Western Americans to the Duke and the former Mrs Wallis Simpson' – though it could not help noting that the American crowd was 'less divided in its greetings' than the delegation of British career men.[17] At St Paul, the state capital of Minnesota where isolationist sentiment was even stronger than in Chicago, a staggering multitude of 20,000 turned out to greet them as they walked up to the Capitol. In North Dakota alone it was estimated that they made thirty-five waving appearances; the bird-shooting season had just started there, and they were overloaded with gifts of pheasant and prairie chicken.

They entered Canada on 28 September at North Portal, Saskatchewan, and the Duke's ex-subjects 'roared their welcome' there and at Moose Jaw. At the border they were joined by Colonel C. H. King of the Governor-General's staff, who brought with him a letter of welcome (which does not appear to have included the Duchess) from the Prime Minister of Canada, W. L. Mackenzie King (who had told the British High Commissioner that July that 'he would prefer that the Duke of Windsor should not come to Canada'.) 'Many thanks for your letter of greeting on my arrival on Canadian soil,' telegraphed the Duke in reply. Early the following morning they arrived at Calgary, Alberta, where a further message awaited them from the Lieutenant-Governor of the Province, extending 'a most cordial welcome to you Sir and Her Grace the Duchess'. 'We are delighted to be here,' replied the Duke.

Such was the size of the crowd at Calgary that they had to put off a planned tour of the town. They continued their journey by car. It had been raining, and the roads were muddy; herds of cattle blocked their path; water ran over the running-boards as they forded creeks. After three hours they finally reached their destination – the EP Ranch at High River in the Pekisko Hills, 'the only home I ever owned'.[18]

The Canadian Ranch, 29 September – 8 October

The Prince of Wales had bought his ranch on the spur of the moment during his first visit to Canada in 1919.[19] Originally he owned some 2,000 acres of cattle-grazing prairie, with the Rockies rising picturesquely to the west; the ranch house was a simple one-storey building with a red roof. He went there for short visits in the summers of 1923, 1924 and (on his last visit to Canada, in the tedious company of Mr Baldwin) 1927. Apart from the joy of having an estate in the wilds, he had a definite agricultural purpose as ranch-holder; having become interested in stock-breeding as practised on his Duchy of Cornwall lands, he wanted 'to make available the best English and Scottish blood in Shorthorn cattle, Clydesdale horses and Hampshire sheep to the farming of Canada'. By 1930 he had spent almost $250,000 on the Ranch and had built up (with the help of W. L. Carlyle, a professor of agriculture) the finest breeding-herd in the Dominion; he now looked forward to getting some return from the property. But this was not to be. The world depression had cast a blight over Canadian ranching; nowhere was it profitable. Not without regret, the Prince prepared to sell the Ranch, which only seemed to promise an indefinite drain on his resources. But the Canadian Government begged him not to do so. It had become important in Canadian farming; it had captured the imagination of Canadians; it had become a factor in the imperial links between Ottawa and London. To induce him to keep it, they made him a present in 1932 of several thousand adjacent acres of Crown land, and gave him the right – rare among Canadian land-owners – of controlling the mineral resources of the now enlarged estate. As the Duke wrote to his Canadian lawyer in September 1941:

> The annual accounts of the Ranch have always been 'in the red' and on more than one occasion I considered disposing of this liability but refrained from doing so because, until I abdicated in December 1936, I was consistently assured by the Canadian Government that my owning this Western property was a valuable asset in the relations between the Dominion and Great Britain.[20]

After the Abdication, the Ranch caused the Duke of Windsor endless worry. He would have liked to go there with the Duchess – it was now his only property anywhere in the world – but the Canadian Government absolutely refused to allow this until the King had consented to his return to British territory. Meanwhile the losses mounted, and made alarming inroads into the Duke's now precarious finances. Again he thought of selling, but could not find a buyer. In 1938, with a heavy heart, he sold off most of the magnificent cattle herd of which he was so proud but which had cost him so dear. 'I feel sure, Sir, that you are pleased to know that your object has been abundantly achieved,' wrote his loyal agent and fellow-rancher Alick Newton in a consoling letter, 'and that the people of Canada are indeed grateful to Your Royal Highness for the generous assistance you have given to the livestock industry.'[21] But even the now denuded Ranch continued to lose money, if on a somewhat smaller scale – in 1939 it lost $3,000 – and the Duke continued to be prevented from going there. His hopes were raised, but only fractionally, by the discovery of oil in the nearby Turner Valley. 'The chance of the EP Ranch proving productive of oil is slight,' wrote Newton, 'but this chance is the only possibility of recovering the large sums expended by Your Royal Highness on the livestock and property.'

During the early months of the war, the Duke's London lawyers continued to make desultory efforts to sell this great white elephant of an estate which he was not even allowed to see. These efforts met with no success, though Allen wrote just after the fall of France that 'it did occur to me that it was not altogether unfortunate that you still had an estate in Western Canada which you could use as a residence from time to time if need be'.[22] But when would he be allowed to go there? He longed to stop there on the way to take up his post in the Bahamas; but London firmly vetoed all such schemes. 'I had been anxious to discuss various matters with you and see the place again after thirteen years,' he wrote disappointedly to Newton.[23]

At the end of 1940 the American polar explorer, Lincoln Ellsworth, offered him $40,000 for the property. The Duke was no longer sure that he wanted to sell, 'because I regard it as a great asset in these difficult and uncertain times'[24]; but Sir Edward Peacock, when they met in Palm Beach in April 1941, strongly advised him to accept the offer. He was unlikely to receive a better one, and his finances were such that he simply could not afford to keep the property much longer. Sadly, he planned what he thought would be a farewell trip to the Ranch before getting rid of it; he wrote to Newton that he hoped to go there with the Duchess in August or September, and prepared for the visit in his usual meticulous way. 'Is the Ranch habitable and is all in good order including the electric-light plant, water and sanitation? Although we are quiet prepared to "rough it" up to a point, we would expect the clean, if modest, comfort which the house provided the last time I occupied it. . . .'[25]

The Duke was in the midst of these preparations for what he imagined would be a sentimental *voyage d'adieu* when, at the end of June, he received a letter[26] which changed all his ideas about the Ranch. His correspondent, the Albertan Minister of Mines, N.E. Tanner (whom he happened to know), wrote that government geologists had 'examined many promising areas in the Province and have recommended that drilling operations should be encouraged in the Pekisko area as the structure gives every indication that oil would be found'. Since such prospecting 'would be undertaken definitely in the interests of the prosecution of the war', would the Duke consent to withdraw from the special lease of 1932 which gave him control of all mineral rights on his land? This unexpected and abrupt request excited the Duke in an almost juvenile way. He immediately wrote to Allen[27] that 'I am sure you would advise me against consenting to withdrawal, for in view of the large sums of money expended on the EP Ranch, from which I have as yet had no return, I do not consider it fair to ask me to withdraw . . . the first time it looks like a part of the property becoming a source of revenue to me. While I am naturally anxious to help the War Effort, one has to think of the future. . . . I may have to rely on the Ranch as an important asset,' concluded the Duke, thinking of the loss of his possessions in France, and the gloomy picture of his finances recently painted by Peacock.

This was the complicated background to the visit to the Ranch which began, rather later than the Duke had hoped, on 29 September, and lasted nine days. He had written to his slightly sinister old manager Professor Carlyle that he was looking forward to it 'for reasons both of business and pleasure'.[28] The isolation of the Ranch certainly gave him and the Duchess their first interlude of total rest and quiet for many months, free from journalists and crowds. It was refreshing to be in the cool air (it was in fact already rather cold, for autumn arrives quickly in the Prairie Provinces) less than a week after the blistering heat of Nassau. They enjoyed their rambles around the estate in the soft autumn colours. They had, and wanted, little company. Apart from Gray Phillips, Colonel King, and a few servants and ranch hands, there was only Dougie, the young naval-cadet son of Alick Newton, to whom the Duke had taken an instant liking and invited to the Ranch for a week's holiday – 'the best holiday I ever had,' as Dougie wrote afterwards to the Duchess. He was a lively and engaging lad, and would go off alone with the Duke on long duck-hunting expeditions. (Some months later, when Dougie fell ill on active service, the Duke's distress was acute.) The Duke was greeted by the chiefs of the Stony Indian Tribe, who still knew him, as in his days as heir to the throne, as Chief Morning Star. The Duchess met local women; she refused to answer questions about clothes, and talked to them instead about her infant welfare projects in Nassau.

In the course of this pleasant holiday, however, the Duke had to make pressing decisions about the future of his property. He summoned his agent Newton (devoted and loyal but always immensely cautious) and manager Carlyle (a brilliant agriculturist but a devious intriguer). Both of these disparate characters confirmed that the Ranch was now useless as a practical farming proposition, and that Ellsworth's offer was the best that was likely to come. But for three months the Duke had possessed the knowledge that the Albertan Government thought his land might bear oil. He was determined to explore this possibility for himself, especially after an encouraging visit to the nearby Turner Valley Oilfield on 1 October. ('Workers remarked on his constant flow of pertinent questions and sharp interest in anything that caught his attention,' wrote the *Albertan*.) On the 4th he wrote to Ellsworth agreeing to his offer of $40,000 (though a mere fraction of what the property had cost him down the years), on condition that he could reserve to himself a half-share in future oil rights. What he did not yet know was that Carlyle was secretly in league with Ellsworth, and would urge him to hold out for all the oil. Nor could he foresee that a chance meeting in New York three weeks later would cause him to abandon the idea of sale altogether and toy with risky and expensive notions of prospecting for oil on his own land. As naive as he was enthusiastic in matters of business, and mesmerized by the dream that 'black gold' might transform his financial liability into an economic panacea, the Duke was set on a path which would lead him towards ruinous disappointment.

'Our short stay here', wrote the Duke to a Canadian parliamentarian and neighbouring rancher on 7 October, 'has indeed been a refreshing interval in the midst of all the stress and strain of this grim period through which the world is passing.'[29] But their idyll was shattered the same day by the news that a hurricane had hit the Bahamas. Nassau had escaped lightly, but the disaster had taken a heavy toll elsewhere in the Colony, particularly at sea, and Cat Island had been practically devastated. Immediately they offered to return – but Heape assured them he could cope. They sent off messages of sympathy, started a relief fund and spoke to the press of their concern.

The following day they left the Ranch, which they were not to see again for over ten years. Having stopped at two air-bases so that the Duke could present wings to RCAF pilots – 'I wish you all good fortune wherever and in whatever capacity you may serve, and a safe return to your homes' – they returned to Calgary for the long journey south. The *Albertan* said of their farewell:

> An excited, enthusiastic crowd of 3,000 Calgarians, alternately singing 'For He's a Jolly Good Fellow', 'Home on the Range', and 'There'll Always be an England', cheering and crying 'Come back soon !', saw the Duke and Duchess of Windsor off. . . . The West roared a welcome when the couple arrived. . . . A larger crowd that howled with even more friendliness came to shout goodbye. . . . 'When are you coming back ?' they wondered. 'Christmas,' joked the Duke. 'It was fine, but a little cold,' he said. His wife declared, 'I like it very much.' Then the crowd broke into 'For He's a Jolly Good Fellow', and the Duke and Duchess laughed with pleasure. Quietly, suddenly, the train moved. . . . Dashing up, an airman was the last to shake His Royal Highness's hand. . . . Then the train gathered speed and cries of 'Come back soon !' echoed on the platform. . . .[30]

To the people of Alberta, he was Prince Charming still – probably to the rest of Canada too.

Baltimore, 13–15 October, and Washington again

The couple returned to the east coast by the same route, again cheered everywhere, and made for Maryland. The Duchess's homecoming was of great psychological significance for both of them. She wanted him to see something of her solid, worthy, Southern background; he longed for her to have the tribute that was due to her from her 'ain folk'. General Warfield – 'Uncle Harry' – met them with a cheering crowd of 5,000 at the little station of Timonium in the Dularey Valley. The Duchess was visibly moved and thrilled, 'waving and talking and looking all at once', while the Duke seemed 'almost boyishly eager that the General like him'[31]. They spent a quiet family week-end on Uncle Harry's farm.

Monday 13 October was the Duchess's day – their official reception in Baltimore. The city had never seen anything like it. Wild, passionate, tearful crowds – estimated at a quarter of a million – were everywhere as the Duke and Duchess drove with the beaming Mayor in open cars from the City Hall to the Baltimore Country Club, where 800 people had been invited to meet them. There the Duchess greeted countless childhood friends. She was close to tears when the famous operatic soprano Rosa Ponselle sang *Home Sweet Home*. The Mayor expressed the hope 'that your visit here will be the source of much gratification and joy to you. The Duchess belongs to a family long distinguished for public service to this city and state. It is a source of great pride to us all that this Baltimore family is now connected by marriage to the Royal House of England. . . .' It was an intensely dramatic and emotional occasion. Even Lord Halifax admitted to the Foreign Office[32] that the Baltimore visit 'was by all accounts a great success'.

The day after the Duchess's triumph, the Duke – leaving her to consult doctors in Baltimore – travelled down to Washington and called upon the Ambassador. Lord Halifax wrote in his diary:

> After luncheon the Duke of Windsor came to see me, and stayed from 2.45 until 5.30. First of all much general talk, some about the Bahamas, and much about himself and his own position and all the difficulties. He took much the line that I would have expected of rather injured innocence, to which I replied that all that might be all right, but I hoped he would not ever make the mistake of underrating the real and deep feeling that still persisted, and that was not friendly to him or the Duchess, and that did not need much to blow it into a flame. He let me talk very frankly, and was quite sensible about it all, but there is a good deal of bitter feeling I should guess underneath.[33]

Having parted cordially from the Ambassador, who invited him to lunch at the Embassy together with the Duchess the following Friday, the Duke returned to Maryland.

The doctors had diagnosed that the Duchess was suffering seriously from a perforated duodenal ulcer (which had in fact been troubling her since 1928), and might need an operation; but she carried on. On Wednesday they visited (followed by a vast throng) the British relief societies in Baltimore. The Duke talked in his famous way to wounded sailors at the British Merchant Seamen's home. 'They can sink our ships, but they can't break our spirit. Men like you will go on fighting, whatever the odds.' On Thursday they went to see the Governor of Maryland at Annapolis, and the Duke satisfied a long-standing wish and inspected two CCC camps, one white, one black. 'It is a great pity they didn't start something like this in Great Britain,' he said; and lifting lids from kettles to smell food, he declared that the men were better fed 'than when I was growing up in the navy'.

Friday 17 October saw their lunch with the Halifaxes at the Embassy, their fellow-guests being Rear-Admiral V.H. Danckwerts of Admiralty Intelligence, the British Ambassador to Brazil Sir Noël Charles, Sumner Welles the Under-Secretary of State, and Frank Knox the Secretary for the Navy, together with their wives. Lord Halifax (who had only met the Duchess briefly once before) recorded in his diary:

> I was impressed with her general dignity and behaviour, and particularly with her piece of adroit good manners in making Mrs Knox go in to luncheon in front of her. She has got very pretty eyes and forehead, and is extremely well turned out, but the rest of her face is not as good as her eyes, and having once noticed it, I was greatly struck by the commonness of her hands and fingers. In short, I was still left puzzled as to how he could have found her charm so overwhelming as to give up kingship and emperorship for it.
>
> He talked a good deal to Knox about his naval base in the Bahamas, and generally luncheon went very well. They went off about three o'clock. . . . She conversed quite easily about common friends, Baba,* Fruity and Walter Monckton, and never said anything that had any east wind in it – again a mark of wisdom.[34]

They spent the week-end with friends near Warrenton in Fauquier County, Virginia, an old land of space, light and pleasant living far more like seventeenth-century England than anything in England itself, where the Duchess had lived for two peaceful years in the 1920s while awaiting her divorce from Winfield Spencer. 'That was a memorable week-end,' recalled one of her old Warrenton friends:

> They were wined and dined. The Warrenton Hunt met at Oakwood [Mrs Sterling Larabee's house where they were staying] and started from the beautiful lawn in front of the house in their honour, and while they were protected and guarded by all the powers that be as befitted their rank, many saw them and noted their graciousness, natural manner and charm. . . . Wallis was little changed, still the clever, cordial, attractive, unspoiled woman she was when she was here in 1927. . . .[35]

* Lady Alexandra Metcalfe.

New York, 20 October–4 November

Now came the high point of their trip – their week (soon to be extended to two) in New York. They had laid their plans for the great metropolis with the utmost care. Vyvyan Drury (who knew the city and its notables intimately) had already been there for three weeks preparing the ground; after the Washington embarrassment, he had secured the benevolent co-operation of the British Consulate-General. It was indeed a very different arrival to that in Washington. The Duke and Duchess were determined to avoid all personal publicity; they slipped into the city almost unnoticed soon after dawn on 20 October, having taken the precaution of leaving their train at a small New Jersey stop. They took up headquarters at the Waldorf Towers, where Drury's ingenious security arrangements sheltered them from the eyes of a curious world.

They were delighted to be there. It was the most exciting place on earth, and the loveliest time of year to be in it. For eighteen months they had been quite cut off from the world they had known – the world of cosmopolitan, elegant, well-informed people, of politics and society and important things happening; now, just for a few days, they were 'back in the vortex of business and politics' as the Duke wrote to Allen.[36] He told reporters (in the American style he affected and they adored): 'There has been a lot of speculation about why we are here. It's simple. We live in a remote part of the world and are out of touch with things. While we were so close to New York I thought it would be lacking in judgement and enterprise if we didn't come here and make some contacts and look around.'[37] They consulted doctors and lawyers, and received a constant stream of guests in their suite; the Duchess ordered some dresses and hats; the Duke saw various people about the Ranch; and just once or twice they ate in a fashionable restaurant and saw a show.

Perhaps they were enjoying themselves too much? It was at this point that a few unpleasant and inaccurate news stories began to appear – notably in the ultra-isolationist *New York Daily News* – about the unnecessary extent of their luggage and their retinue, the extravagance of 'a floor at the Waldorf' and the Duchess's presumed expenditure on clothes, their being seen 'in café society', the comparison of their leisure with the hardships of England at war. It was a cruel misrepresentation – they were not an ordinary couple, for they were the object of altogether extraordinary public attention; the apparent excesses were dictated for the most part by a desire for privacy and a need for protection. The same stories criticized Churchill for being photographed drinking champagne with De Gaulle, Lady Louis Mountbatten for doing Red Cross work with the Newport social set. To their dismay, the Duke and Duchess also found themselves attacked in a number of journals whose proprietors were known to be out to curry favour with the British authorities, such as *Time* magazine, owned by Henry Luce who was said to be ambitious for the American ambassadorship in London. But such reporting represented only a fraction of the press coverage of their New York visit, which overwhelmingly concentrated on their tireless series of public engagements.

They arrived on a Monday. On Tuesday the Duke called on Mayor LaGuardia to talk of urban housing conditions; the Mayor said the Duke would make an excellent mayor, to which the Duke replied 'You flatter me'[38]. The Duchess visited Inwood House, a centre for unmarried mothers and their babies, and talked of her own infant welfare clinics in Nassau. Wednesday saw a marathon tour of organizations involved in war work: they reviewed mobile hospital units of the British–American Ambulance Corps, inspected 'Bundles for Britain', lunched with the British War Relief Society, played darts with sailors at the British Merchant Seamen's Club, and called at the Union Jack Club and the RAF Benevolent Fund. They were greeted everywhere with a magnificent traditional 'ticker-tape and torn-paper storm', in scenes which 'recalled the Duke's wild reception here as Prince of Wales seventeen years ago'.[39] On Thursday morning the Duke discussed his Colony's affairs at the offices of the Bahamas Development Board, in the afternoon he met municipal officials to talk of the problems of housing the poor. On Friday he flew to Hartford, Connecticut to inspect the production of war planes at the immense United Aircraft Corporation plant. 'Flame gushed from electric furnaces, 2,000 horse-power motors roared in test cells and laden tractors rumbled right past the Duke of Windsor as the former King of England for the first time saw the American defense programme in action.'[40]

In the course of this hectic week there was one chance encounter which was to have unfortunate consequences for the Duke. On the Thursday, in between the Bahamas Development Board and the municipal housing officials, he had been taken to the Museum of Natural History by its Chairman, his friend Arthur Vernay. There he had been struck by a charming and erudite old gentleman, a palaeontologist, who rejoiced in the title of Curator of Fossil Reptiles and the name of Dr Barnum Brown, and claimed that, through his intimate association with fossils, he knew how to 'smell oil'. The Duke was delighted by this coincidence, and almost immediately asked Brown if he would go to Canada to survey the oil-bearing possibilities of the Ranch. When the Doctor duly went in late November his diagnosis would turn out to be wildly favourable (and in fact hopelessly optimistic); consequently the Duke would make the fateful decision to drill instead of sell.

The Duke and Duchess spent a quiet week-end with friends – the

Suydam Cuttings at Gladstone, NJ – and then returned to New York. During their second week there the Duke visited the Brooklyn Navy Yards and walked round the east-side slums, talking to the poor; the Duchess helped organize a Hallowe'en Party for needy children. On Tuesday they went for the day to Washington for the promised Presidential lunch. In the morning the Duke discussed the Bahamas' inadequate air links with the Civil Aeronautics Board, while Mrs Roosevelt received the Duchess warmly in her Office of Civilian Defence and offered to write a preface to a cook-book the Duchess wanted to publish in aid of war relief.[41] The White House lunch was a jolly affair, after which Mr Roosevelt took them on a tour of his residence; the Duke recalled his reception by the ailing Woodrow Wilson in the Lincoln Room in 1919.[42]

Detroit, 30 October

Vyvyan Drury had a friend called Byron Foy, a large man who had married a daughter of Walter Chrysler and was a director of the car firm, which was then making tanks for Britain. Foy suggested to Drury that the Duke visit Detroit; the Duke was delighted with the suggestion, and arrangements were hastily made. All was ready for a day visit when, on 24 October, an irate telegram arrived from Halifax in Washington:

> I have just heard that Your Royal Highness proposes to visit Detroit on October 29th. I had not inferred from what you told me of your plans that you had this in mind. . . . I think it is undesirable to depart from your programme without giving due notice in advance. It so happens that I myself have been booked for some months to visit Detroit. . . . If Your Royal Highness would reconsider the question of your visit to Detroit it would be very helpful, and on any future occasion it would be of assistance . . . if you could give me advance notice of your wishes.

It seemed the Duke was not to be given the chance of a success with the workers. Drury has described to the author what happened next.

> The Duke came to me and said, 'I'm sorry Vyvyan, it's all off. We can't go.' He showed me Halifax's telegram. I was furious. This was sheer obstructive nonsense. I went to see Ronnie Campbell at the Embassy. It was the most disgraceful thing I had ever heard of. The thing was all planned and announced. Detroit was looking forward to a visit from the former King. How was the cancellation to be explained? What impression would the workers have of England? 'Too bad,' said Ronnie. 'He can't go, and that's that.' So I told him that, if such was the case, the Duke would give a press conference to explain that he was reluctantly calling the trip off on the orders of the British Ambassador. So in the end we went![43]

As the Duke stood hatless listening to the national anthem on the platform at Detroit Station, 'which moved many of the spectators to tears', a middle-aged man stepped from the crowd and came up to him. 'Your Royal Highness,' he said, 'I just wanted to welcome you; God bless you.' The Duke looked intently at him and asked: 'Where have I met you?' 'In Winnipeg in 1919,' said the man. 'You were a kiltie.' 'A Cameron Highlander, Sir.'[44]

The whole day was like that. The Duke had never been in better form. He inspected the plants of Chrysler, Ford and General Motors, rode in tanks, asked about everything, and astonished everyone with his knowledge and concern. He had tea with Henry Ford at Dearborne; only a few days later Gerald Campbell of the British Information Services in New York wrote to the Prime Minister to announce that 'Ford is ready to make a contradiction of his announcement of about a year ago when he said that he would not produce arms for Britain.'[45] The Duke's speed and energy were breathtaking. 'Pausing only to shake hands with an oil-stained workman or to wave to cheering workers, the Duke, with an engineering background gained from four years as a naval cadet, fired questions at labourers and guides alike.' It was an overwhelming success. Even the carping report of the British Press Service admitted: 'This trip brought back memories of the Prince of Wales in his most popular days. The same enthusiasm, the same extraordinary appearance of extensive knowledge concerning the subject of interest, the same knack of making friends with all types of people were there.'[46] It was the success British officialdom had feared and tried to prevent. When Halifax himself visited Detroit two weeks later he was pelted with eggs and tomatoes, and Irishwomen picketed his hotel with placards which read 'To Halifax with Halifax' and 'Down With England'.[47]

It was a fine note on which to bring the trip to an end, and after a busy week-end the Duke and Duchess left New York on their journey south. Miami again gave them a rapturous acclaim. They were guests at a Workers' Victory Dinner in aid of a hospital for crippled children. Before they left for Nassau on 7 November, the Duke spoke to journalists about their tour. The *Miami Herald* wrote:

> Maybe it all comes under the head of diplomacy, but the one-time super salesman for the British Empire is now doing a bang-up job of beating the drum for America. . . . 'America's war effort is amazingly good,' the Duke of Windsor declared, 'particularly in view of the short time you have been at it.' And he went on to enthuse about the things he had seen at the Brooklyn Navy Yard, the things he had seen in Detroit . . . and the things he had seen and heard in his many conferences with 'the Mr Bigs of the Arsenal of Democracy'. . . . 'I didn't talk to anyone about intervention,' he said, with a disarming grin. 'But a lot of people in your country said some very nice things about my country. . . .'[48]

And, as they flew off, the crowd cheered and cheered.

On their return, the Duke wrote to George Allen, his trusted London solicitor:

> The Duchess and I had a very interesting and satisfactory visit to America and Canada despite the unfavourable and totally inaccurate writings of two or three malicious, mad-dog journalists. Although no vacation, the six weeks we were away from Nassau . . . were both interesting and thrilling. . . . [We] were satisfied that ninety per cent of the American press handled our visit with dignity.[49]

A press survey showed that only four per cent of column inches on the Duke and Duchess had been downright unfavourable, and most of those from a single isolationist newspaper, the *New York Daily News*. But the British Press Service Report[50] gave a very different picture: 'The general impression created was that of a rich and carefree couple, travelling with all the pre-war accoutrement of royalty, and with no thought either of the sufferings of their own people or of the fact that the world is at war.' There was not a word about their ecstatic public reception, the ubiquitous cheering crowds, their well-known desire to avoid personal publicity, their much-reported patriotic statements and endless visits to war factories and relief societies. British officialdom had not been able to prevent the trip being a success; but propaganda could still distort the fact that it had been so.

The Duchess wrote to Aunt Bessie:

> We both simply took to our beds upon arrival and recovered quietly from the strenuous trip, which the papers called a *vacation*! We had 2 days in Miami where I was able to go into a shop with a *fair* amount of peace. The garden is not much worse than it always was – the house the same except for a little more rust and tropical destruction – Nassau like a deflated soufflé after this trip, and it is hard to settle down to our jobs and the neutrality of a village. I have written nearly 200 letters thanking people for flowers etc. while in New York. . . . I have no pain at all – not even brought on by the battle of N.Y. I am sure I am better off on excitement – it's boredom that gets me down. Mother always used to say that about me. . . .[51]

12
The War Ground
November 1941–May 1942

With America behind him, the Duke opened the new session of the House of Assembly on Thanksgiving Day, 20 November 1941.[1] On this occasion he did not propose a programme of economic and social reform to that reactionary legislature. Instead the keynote of his speech was co-operation with the United States. He spoke of 'the immense moral and material support the people of America are giving to Britain in her hour of need', of his efforts in Washington to improve the Colony's supplies and communications, and of the new US air base on Great Exuma. He talked of how alarmed he had been to learn of the October hurricane; he announced that he had persuaded the Colonial Office to send out a farming expert to investigate the revival of agriculture. (The House duly refused to pay the expenses of this official.) Finally he invited the House to consider some mild proposals on slum clearance and the further relief of food prices. These proposals found their way without delay into the waste-paper baskets of Bay Street.

Five days later, the Duke struck.[2] After the weekly meeting of ExCo he read out the letter he had received from Lord Moyne six months before concerning the reappointment of members of that Council. Two of the unofficial members – Kenneth Solomon and Walter Moore – had served for almost sixteen years; Moore's second term was up at the end of the year, Solomon's the following May. The Duke informed them that, in the light of the Secretary of State's advice, he would not reappoint them. The pathetic and bibulous Moore lapsed into acute distress, but was eventually satisfied with a knighthood. But Solomon was outraged. He *was* Bay Street, the most powerful man in the Bahamas; he saw his position in the Executive as his by right. Moyne's letter gave the Governor an exceptional discretion to reappoint 'particularly trusted and valuable counsellors'; did the Duke not consider him to be within this category? There was a violent exchange, the upshot of which was that Solomon resigned at once, making it clear that he was now the Duke's declared enemy, that with his controlling influence in the House he would now lead the opposition to the Duke's administration, frustrating the slightest reform.

The Duke now took a step which showed great imagination. Moyne had suggested that new appointments on executive councils should be on a broader basis than hitherto. In a colony such as Trinidad or Jamaica, a coloured man might well have filled a vacancy; but the social system of the Bahamas virtually ruled this out in 1941. The colour bar was rigid. Fifteen years later Bay Street was to 'depose' a governor who favoured black appointments, and twenty-five years later blacks had only a nominal representation in the Government. Even Hallinan, who was passionately concerned for the political advance of the blacks, writes that to replace the arch-white Solomon with a coloured man 'would have presented an intolerable challenge to the Bay Street boys, out of the question during the war'. What the Duke did was to appoint a white man of broad views entirely outside politics and the Bay Street caucus. Sidney Farrington was a veteran of the First World War, and the representative of Pan-American Airways in Nassau. He was not a member of the House. His charm and cosmopolitan outlook were unusual in a Bahamian. He was on particularly close terms with the American community in Nassau. He was a man of reasonable views, who entirely agreed with the Duke on the need to make the Bahamas productive. The Duke liked him immensely.[3] The other seat on ExCo the Duke left vacant. Thus, in a council of eight (including the three officials), only three – Christie, Sawyer and Collins – were Bay Street figures, and of these Christie, the most lucid and influential, was generally on the side of the Duke whose presence in Nassau did so much for Christie's property developments. A cabinet revolution had taken place. Could the Duke now turn it to his political advantage?

An immense storm was certainly brewing in the House, where the outraged Solomon had placed himself at the head of the opposition to the Government. Bay Street was in uproar at what it saw as the summary dismissal of its champion. There were violent debates. 'I hope', Solomon declared, 'the House will realize what is taking place with regard to their rights and privileges.'[4] The Duke might now have a council which suited him, but the problem of getting reform through the Legislature seemed worse than ever. Government and House seemed set on a collision course. Only the imminence of the season, when Bay Street obsessed itself with the tourist trade at the expense of politics, dictated a sort of truce. In spite of the ever-increasing difficulty of getting to Nassau from the mainland, there seemed, at the start of December, no reason why the coming season should not be as successful as the last.

The Duke and Duchess shuddered at the thought of having to expose themselves to another season, but in the first days of December they had welcome visitors – James Marjoribanks, the friendly young Consul at Jacksonville who had done so much to help make the Florida trips successful, and his wife Sonia. The Marjoribanks immensely enjoyed their leave at Government House, where they were particularly struck by the 'subtly created royal atmosphere' which the Duchess had managed to achieve. Marjoribanks recalls:

> Entertainment was tasteful rather than lavish. We moved happily and easily from scene to scene – the cabana with its lovely coral waters, the golf course where to my embarrassment the Duke insisted on accompanying me, highlighting by his straight drive and well-controlled approach shots the inadequacy of my own performance. On one occasion I remember seeing the Governor rushing across the course in the middle of our game pursued by detectives and cairn terriers in a (vain) attempt to prevent a baby fall out of its pram while its Bahamian nanny had all eyes for the Duke.[5]

On the morning of Sunday 7 December the Duke and Duchess were down at the cabana with the Marjoribanks, the Arthur Vernays and the Vyvyan Drurys, when the stunning news was telephoned through of the Japanese attack at Pearl Harbor. 'There was a sudden tension, many fears and forebodings,' remembers Marjoribanks, although Drury recollects[6] that the Duchess was thrilled by the news. The United States declared war on Japan, and the following day Germany declared war on the United States. The war had arrived in the Far East – and in the western hemisphere. On Tuesday 9 December came the terrible news of the sinking by the Japanese of the *Prince of Wales* and the *Repulse*, which (as Marjoribanks recalls) threw the Duke into a state of intense personal suffering. One of the ships had been named after him; its loss occurred almost on the fifth anniversary of the Abdication. He hated the Japanese with a passion which was rare for him; he called them 'the Nipponese hordes', and saw them as a yellow disease spreading across the colonial east.

The United States' entry into the war had a revolutionary effect upon the history of the Bahamas, the Duke's position as Governor, and not least upon the attitude of the Duchess. Their autumn tour had shown that, while she had made her home in England in 1928 and had not seen her native continent between 1933 and 1940, she remained profoundly American at heart. When war broke out in 1939, she accepted it as a war which had embroiled her husband's native country (which had treated him shabbily); and, while determined to 'do her bit' in Paris and Nassau and do it well, this (she sometimes felt) was not *her* war. In moments of exasperation she would write to Aunt Bessie of *this* war, even *their* war – though she would also write of her longing for the United States to enter the fray. Pearl Harbor changed all that. *Her* country had been treacherously attacked, *her* people were now engaged in mortal struggle, and she threw herself passionately, almost joyfully, into a conflict which had at last become her own. If she did not openly demonstrate these feelings, it was because she was inclined to make light of her emotions when they were most exercised. Her letter to Aunt Bessie on 16 December was bright, almost flippant.

What can I say about all that has happened, except that I am glad we are going to be *in* the war, which is better than being on the outside. This place is going to become isolated – no boat and only a sea-plane now and again – and everything will be very curtailed. Anyway, from the start of this war it has been a question of the complete re-adjustment of our lives. I think it is wise of them to play at war in Washington – especially with *you* as air-raid warden! . . . I can't believe however that the East Coast is apt to be attacked. The Russian news is good and the Germans seem to be running there as well as in Africa. Xmas will be dull and sad. I have 2 children's parties – Xmas eve Nassuvians and Xmas day English evacuees. I am enclosing you a cheque for $200 which I hope will bring you some sort of cheer on the 25th and I hope you will not be afraid to come here later on when the war settles down. . . . I have had 2 letters from Aunt Rebecca but I simply can't read a *word* she says but imagine I am not missing much. Do write me everyone's reactions. Ethel Bush arrived today saying the country was united and behind Mr R. and all the youth fighting to enlist. Just think what a real fight it is going to be after the peace. That is where the so-called upper classes will fight a losing battle in my mind. Our trip seems a dream but a nice one. We must be here for the duration I fear. And at this rate I shall waddle out – and not speaking to a Bahamian if possible – they get more *difficile* every day.

All my love.

What the Duchess did not write was that two ships had been sunk off the Bahamas by Italian submarines, and that she was working with all her might organizing care for the survivors. Soon troops would be arriving, and she would have to arrange entertainment for them. Here at last was scope for her energy, her organizing genius, a campaign to claim her completely. (Had not a young Englishman the previous summer compared her to Napoleon?) The one thing which saddened her was that, at this moment when the war became so real to her, her husband's talents were so wretchedly under-used.

But for the Duke things had changed too; overnight he found himself transformed from mascot of a tourist playground to lord of a far-flung battle-line. As he wrote to George Allen on 13 December:

With Japan's unparalleled treachery and the entry of the United States into the war, the Bahamas winter tourist season dies a natural death. This Colony will have to revise its financial and economical set-up both drastically and swiftly, and will for the first time be made to feel that there is a war. It is bad luck that the blow should come so late in the day and so near the winter season, for there is no doubt it will cause hardship among the shopkeepers and merchants and unemployment among the coloured population. . . . However, these are only local hardships and easy to bear as compared to the lot of most other countries. . . .

The Duke now found himself in the role of a man of action. With the coming of war to the western hemisphere, an economic disaster had overtaken the Colony – one that he had quite clearly foreseen and warned against. Now that the cult of the rich winter resident had vanished, there was almost nothing of economic value left. Nassau reverted to being an isolated backwater of barren coral upon which existed 30,000 hungry people, with hardly anything to sell abroad and scant resources off which to survive at home. For more than a year the Duke had been ignored as he protested that the islands could not survive indefinitely on the precarious profits of tourism alone; that they needed to find a vigorous and productive course; that the Out Islands had to be rescued from their state of poverty and neglect; that agriculture had to be reborn. And now he was proved abundantly right. 'The normal life and business of the Bahamas has been but little interfered with until now,' he declared in a New Year's broadcast, 'but with the coming of hostilities to this side of the Atlantic, the situation has changed appreciably. . . . [W]e must face facts and realize that we can no longer regard these islands solely as a tourist resort until the ultimate success of our Arms and those of our Allies bring peace to the world again. . . . It will be a privilege to help you readjust your finances and economics to the changes of which we have but slight indication today.'

In this crisis the Duke did not spare himself. Before December was out he had set up a Government Board of 'all the talents' – known as the Economic Investigation Committee – to search for every means of employment and production, relief and revenue. When they could not agree on a chairman, the Duke appointed himself to the post and took personal charge. (It was the closest any Governor had got to the field administration of the Colony, and the idea was a great success. In various guises the Committee was to exist for the next twenty years under the Governor's personal control, and was to prove the main vehicle for the development of the islands.) The leading members were Harold Christie, George Murphy (another ex-bootlegger who was interested in agriculture), the fiery newspaper editor Etienne Dupuch, and another enterprising man of mixed blood, Roland Symonette (who was to become the Colony's first premier when it received responsible government in 1964). All that winter, under the Duke's guidance, they devoted themselves to a passionate search for original solutions. An agriculturist was brought over from Jamaica, various schemes of self-sufficiency were mooted and a

Department of Agriculture was planned. One scheme the Duke himself propounded with some passion. He wanted to set up in the Bahamas something akin to the CCC camps that he had seen in Maryland the previous October – a public project which, like the several admirable private projects on Eleuthera and elsewhere, would both relieve unemployment and teach the skills of the land. But in order to achieve this it would first be necessary to set up a Labour Department – and that, back in the autumn of 1940, had been the proposal over which the Duke had first run into serious opposition from the House.

It might have been thought that, in this critical situation, the House would have begun to co-operate wholeheartedly with the Government. Nothing of the kind occurred. The battle which had begun with Solomon's resignation before Pearl Harbor continued unabated. In an urgent message of 22 January 1942, the Duke – returning to his original request of fifteen months before – asked the House to vote just £538 to set up a 'Labour Bureau', with Hughes doubling as Labour Officer. He pointed out that, with the sudden collapse of the tourist season, unemployment had become unusually serious.[7] The House threw the measure out, voting instead a mere £100 for a 'register of the unemployed'. The Duke was thoroughly exasperated by this intransigence; but Hughes – to the Governor's delight and Bay Street's fury – nobly agreed to undertake the duties of Labour Officer all the same, even though he received no extra pay and was virtually without facilities or assistants. The makeshift nature of his essential office was to have grave consequences a few months later – consequences for which Hughes, with terrible injustice, was to be blamed by the vicious oligarchy of Bay Street.

The House then proceeded to withhold funds for defence purposes. (This was an old Bahamian tradition; the Legislature had refused to pay up for defence in all of the eighteenth-century naval wars.) The Government reacted sharply, and reminded Bay Street that, under the Defence Regulations, the Governor could if necessary raise funds without the House; he also always had the power to dissolve the House. The current seven-year parliamentary term was in fact due to come to an end in the middle of 1942; the House had imagined that it would be extended (as in the Old Country) for the duration of hostilities, but was now informed that the Governor would require elections for a new Assembly after all. The members were furious. They promptly passed two extraordinary bills – the first giving them the right to veto any regulation made by the Governor, the second purporting to prolong the life of the House, in spite of the Governor's decision. Acting under directions from Hallinan, the Legislative Council – the sedate upper chamber whose main function was to provide a retirement club for eminent Bahamians who were helpful to the Government – vetoed this outrageous legislation. The House vented its rage on the Government in general and the hapless Attorney-General in particular. Kenneth Solomon's brother Eric protested that 'it has been impossible to teach English officials that they are not sent here to govern the Colony but to assist in their small way the government of the Colony'. Amid the acrimonious debate, one man in particular made his voice heard against the Government – a brilliant and unscrupulous young lawyer with a talent for political intrigue and invective oratory, one Stafford Sands. This masterful and amoral grocer's son was to become virtual dictator of the Bahamas in the twenty years after the war, and would lead Bay Street first to dizzy heights of wealth and power, then to disaster in a welter of scandal and corruption. In February 1942 he declared in the House that 'the time is not far distant when the House and the Government will reach a showdown'. He was not wrong.

The Duke was disappointed but not disheartened by the continuing opposition of the House. He was hopeful that a combination of careful Government tactics and sheer force of circumstance would eventually win Bay Street round to the economic reform of the Bahamas. On 9 February he wrote to his American friend, the eminent traveller and broadcaster Lowell Thomas:

> . . . What a change the war situation has undergone since we met in New York last fall! Although confident in the ultimate success of the combined forces of our two countries, the news from the Pacific is disturbing and not too encouraging from other fronts at the present time. It is going to be a tough struggle and we don't yet know the half of the sacrifices we shall have to make to wage total war on dictator lines.
>
> Although but a small pebble on the beach, the Bahama Islands are beginning to feel the pinch. . . . It is now my difficult, but at the same time interesting, task as Governor to help these people save what they can from the ruins of a policy whereby the welfare of a large portion of the population was sacrificed to the benefits accruing to a few such illicit and fickle industries. However, I am confident that once the local bosses realize the seriousness of the unemployment situation, and its possible consequences, I shall be able to convince them that a long term policy based on greater self-sufficiency, and even some exports, will be sounder in the end and possibly save the Colony's finances from getting into the red. . . .

In retrospect, the crucial phrase here is seen to be 'the seriousness of the unemployment situation, *and its possible consequences**. . . .' The Duke was one of the few to anticipate that the increasingly desperate economic situation of the blacks might eventually drive them (sleepy people though they were) to some form of disaffection – though he could hardly have foreseen the unusual circumstances under which a violent reaction was in fact going to take place.

* Author's italics.

In the midst of all these political and economic difficulties, the Duke had to face a trauma which affected him both in his public and his private life. This was the blacklisting of his friend Axel Wenner-Gren.

A brief review may be useful of Wenner-Gren's tale. Having made altruistic but slightly absurd efforts as international peacemaker – in the course of which he had been in touch with the Duke of Windsor, though they had not met – he had left Europe before the war to establish himself in the Bahamas, where he finally met the Duke in October 1940. The two men got on excellently, and Wenner-Gren (who initiated a number of philanthropic schemes to relieve local unemployment) had become a valued adviser to the Duke in his administration. But the State Department showed itself increasingly hostile to the enterprising Swede, sabotaging his important proposals (much encouraged by the Duke) for the economic development of Grand Bahama. When the Duke asked Lord Halifax 'to find out what the United States Government had against Mr Axel Wenner-Gren,' Sumner Welles told the Ambassador that he *'knew of nothing specific against him*,* but that his associations with high members of the German Government were obviously intimate [apart from his two interviews with Goering, they were in fact non-existent], and that . . . many of Mr Wenner-Gren's activities during the past two years could only be regarded as suspicious in view of the world situation.

The State Department only had a mass of rumour to suggest that Wenner-Gren might be a threat to the security of the United States, and their real reason for disliking and opposing him was that they regarded his economic ambitions in Latin America as a fierce threat to American commercial interests. He was acquiring what they regarded as a dangerously powerful financial stake in Mexico. 'American capital as represented by big investors and banks', ran a later intelligence report, 'was apprehensive concerning the investment and control of over $100,000,000 by one individual in Mexico. With this sum of money . . . [Wenner-Gren] could have secured control of almost every phase of economic life . . . and driven out any reasonable possibility of foreign development such as might emanate from the United States. . . .'[8] In July 1941 Washington was deeply alarmed when Wenner-Gren set sail from Nassau for Peru, whither he had been invited by the President and Government of that country. The journey was ostensibly for the purpose of inspecting the Andean discoveries of his archaeological expedition; but clearly the Peruvians – as well as other South American governments – were hoping to secure him as a massive foreign investor. The State Department received increasingly worried reports of the Swede's growing influence from United States businessmen in Latin America. These reports naturally did not fail to repeat the rumours of Wenner-Gren's pro-Nazi

* Author's italics.

leanings – and some also suggested that he might be dealing secretly with German money and conniving at the Nazi economic penetration of the continent, an idea which (though backed by no evidence) was taken seriously in Washington. In November the *Southern Cross* was banned from the Panama Canal. Requesting this measure, the State Department explained to the War Department that they were trying to prevent Wenner-Gren bringing off a merger of South American mining interests, and that it was 'quite possible that, though a Swede, he is in reality endeavouring to secure a foothold for combined German and Swedish interests in Mexico and South America.'[9]

On 7 December 1941, Wenner-Gren was at sea on his way back to Nassau when he heard the news of Pearl Harbor. He decided to return to his base in neutral Mexico to wait upon events. These were not long in coming. On 14 January he was placed on the State Department's so-called 'Proclaimed List of Blocked Nationals'. This came as a terrible shock to him; no reason for it was ever given. It effectively made him an outcast in the western hemisphere. It meant that he could no longer go to the United States or do any business with Americans; that his assets there (the Electrolux empire) were sequestered for the duration; and that he was branded for life as a man who had been in league with the nation's enemies. At the same time Washington exercised a formidable pressure on the Mexican Government to deny him access to funds and make him a virtual prisoner in that country. A few weeks later, with some reluctance, the British Government followed suit in blacklisting Wenner-Gren; this meant the winding-up of all his enterprises in the Bahamas and the impossibility of his returning there during the war. Meanwhile, an American press campaign of unexampled ferocity had been unleashed against Wenner-Gren, which he was powerless to counteract in any way. The wildest rumours – his 'intimacy' with top Nazidom, his key role in German economic espionage, his deadly work in guiding Nazi submarines to their targets, the U-boat base he had constructed on Hog Island to await his 'friends' – were repeated as if established fact. The columnists who freely denounced him as an enemy agent did not hesitate to stress – with every kind of sinister inference – that he had been a friend of the Duke of Windsor in the Bahamas (and, said some, long before).

The blacklisting of Wenner-Gren placed the Duke in a terrible predicament. He had not heard much from the Swede over the autumn. After Pearl Harbor Wenner-Gren had written to say that he would be staying in Mexico for the time being; the Duke telegraphed in reply on 5 January: 'The Duchess and I are so sorry to hear you are not returning but hope you will have a pleasant time in Mexico.' The irony was that, with the economic disaster which had struck the Colony after the United States' entry into the war, the Duke more than ever had need of

Wenner-Gren, the main private economic support to his governorship; and now – thanks to United States hostility – he was not there. Then came the American listing. The Duke regarded this as a terrible injustice, but as Governor was hardly in a position to stand up for a man who had just been officially branded an enemy of the United States. However, he did what he could to hold up the British blacklisting. When that came, it brought with it the catastrophic closure of Wenner-Gren's projects on Hog Island and Grand Bahama which the Duke had done so much to foster, throwing some 1,200 natives (almost five per cent of the total adult male population of the Colony) out of work.

'The Wenner-Gren affair is giving the Duke no end of trouble with all his enterprises closing down,' wrote the Duchess to Aunt Bessie. 'The gossip here as you can imagine is terrific with all sorts of wild stories about the Hog Island estate. In fact Nassau seems the centre of espionage in their minds!'[10] As Governor, the Duke tried to dispel rumour by means of a public announcement:

> As a result of continuous rumours to the effect that there are various forms of secret facilities . . . available to the enemy on the Wenner-Gren estate on Hog Island, the public is officially informed that a most thorough search which has been made of the property has failed to reveal the existence of anything of a suspicious nature.

What was less easy to dispel were the outrageous American press stories hinting that the Duke and the spy Wenner-Gren had been conspiring together in the interests of the enemy. When the Duke protested to Washington about these, he was told to his astonishment that they had been traced in part to *German* propaganda sources! Resignedly he accepted official assurances that the stories would cease; but the damage had been done, and the Duchess could barely contain her feelings. To an influential American friend she wrote:

> You will not have failed to notice that the real news value of *l'affaire* Wenner-Gren was that he was 'Windsor's pal' etc., and one article went so far as to say that he was chiefly known in the world not as one of the great international financiers but as the friend of the Duke and Duchess of Windsor. Has it ever occured [sic] to you from what source such harmful insinuations might eminate [sic]? Ever since 1936 the Germans have taken advantage of the widely known and unbridgeable gulf that exists between the Duke and his family (and in consequence any British Government), and have *used* us along these lines with the knowledge that all adverse and damaging news of the Windsors creates dissention [sic] and disunion among the people of Britain. It is a clever and subtly thought-out piece of fifth-column work because these stories fly fast and are eagerly absorbed by willing British ears. The Wenner-Gren story is just the latest example. I am sure no American journalist would, in spite of his avidness for news, willingly want to play this game, but 'theirs not to reason why, theirs but to print or die. . . .' I have no desire for explanations

or denials of any sort; that is not the way to counteract this type of propaganda, and the truth is always there to be investigated when the desire to seek it out is genuine. . . .

The Duke and Duchess were convinced that the charges against Wenner-Gren were utterly false and the result of sheer war hysteria. But they were powerless to act against a tide of calumny which had the implicit approval of the official world. Instead they were forced to minimize their links with two who had been their friends. It pained them to have to do so – but such were the perils of an official position in war. A governor had no choice but to repeat the 'line' of the Imperial Government, even when it went against his every instinct and he knew it to be rooted in lies.

Though the FBI proceeded to carry out the most rigorous investigation into Wenner-Gren's past activities, not a shred of solid evidence was ever discovered against him.[11] Yet his name remained on the blacklist throughout the war. When he demanded to know the reason, none was ever given. When the Swedish Minister to Washington tried to assure the State Department (June 1942) that Wenner-Gren was 'quite loyal and anti-Axis', he was fobbed off with a list of 'suspicious circumstances', ranging from 'his attempt to negotiate between Goering and Chamberlain' and 'his appearance with the Duke of Windsor in the Bahamas' [sic], to 'his intervention in South American economics at the same time as German economic penetration was being attempted'.[12] In 1944, Wenner-Gren's friends in America managed to have his case re-opened, with the help of the eminent lawyer Warren Grimes; but just when it seemed that his name was about to be cleared, the State Department stepped in to prevent this, Stettinus declaring that he was 'potentially still a very dangerous person and a security risk for the USA'.[13]

Until his death in 1962, Wenner-Gren was haunted by what he saw as the monstrous and humiliating stigma which had been attached to him; and what distressed him most of all was that his friend the Duke of Windsor, by association, had also come to suffer from the effects of that stigma. They never met again (though Wenner-Gren returned to the Bahamas after the war and resumed the projects on Hog Island and Grand Bahama which owed so much to the Duke). But they corresponded from time to time, and the Duke never failed to express his sympathy and indignation for the great wrong which had been done to Wenner-Gren's name; he even offered to provide evidence in the event (which was not to be) of the Swede obtaining leave to vindicate himself before the American courts.

The war news was grim during those terrible early months of 1942. It was reasonably obvious to most intelligent observers that the Allies now possessed a substantial long-term superiority. The question was simply whether they would survive long enough to be able to bring that superiority to bear. The Japanese swept through the Pacific and penetrated deep into Malaya; the efforts to push back the Germans in North Africa and Russia struggled and failed. 'The English don't seem to win anything as yet,' wrote the Duchess to Aunt Bessie on 31 January. 'Most discouraging losing Benghazi again, and Singapore does not look bright.' But she added with prescience that 'it will all come out in the long run – and the deciding factor must be fought in Europe anyway'. On 15 February, Singapore surrendered after brief resistance. It was, as Churchill said, 'the worst disaster and greatest capitulation in British history'[14]; the symbolic blow to British prestige sent a violent shudder through the colonial Empire.

At Government House, Nassau, life went briskly on. The Duchess wrote that 'I never see the Duke – a series of conferences and people dropping from the skies', but that the sudden flurry of activity 'has given pep to this dull job and at last there is something for us to do except complain of being sent here'. She herself had never been more occupied. 'I have been so busy *really* this time,' she wrote to Aunt Bessie on 16 March.

> We have been taking care of men landed here from 3 more ships – a job for the Red Cross – and I am endeavouring to open a canteen for the boys to keep them out of the grape vine ! . . . We have just finished a Red Cross Fair in the garden and raised more than we expected – thank goodness as the outfitting of these seamen is a drain on our resources. It is a grand upheaval and will certainly mean the survival of the fittest – which we will be too old or too dead to see.

The sight of the shipwrecked moved her to great compassion. As she wrote in her memoirs:

> I did what I could to make them comfortable while they awaited evacuation. As that terrible spring wore on we began to receive some truly heart-wrenching cases – men who had drifted for days without food or water under the searing tropical sun. . . .[15]

Occasionally news would reach them of their old friends in Europe; often sad, as with the death at the age of ninety-one of the old Duke of Connaught, perhaps the member of the Royal Family who had shown the greatest sympathy for King Edward in the Abdication crisis; sometimes happy, as when the Duchess's old friend Foxie Gwynne married the Duke's old friend Hugh Sefton.* 'May your happiness be as ours,' wrote the Duchess to Foxie. 'Sorry I haven't written, but when the Duke was

---

* Hugh Molyneux, 7th Earl of Sefton.

handed this double-zero job by the powers that be it took all the heart out of me. . . . Perhaps one day when I tell you the true story of Lisbon you will understand me. . . .' One person from whom the Duchess heard that March for the first time during the war was Ernest Simpson. An awful tragedy had overtaken this well-meaning, reserved and sentimental man of business. After the Abdication he had been ostracized socially and suffered terribly; but his shipping concern prospered, and he had found great happiness with his third wife, the Duchess's oldest friend Mary Kirk. In October 1941 – two years after giving birth to their son Henry – Mary died of a harrowing cancer. The Duchess had heard the news in Baltimore; she wrote to Ernest from her heart. Ernest replied five months later, on 16 March:

> Believe me, your letter with its sympathetic thoughts and kind wishes was a great comfort to me in a dark hour, and for that help I am truly grateful. It was good to hear from you, and especially at such a time. Life is indeed a strange thing; and, as you say, it is not given to us to know the whys and wherefores of what happens. At one moment I seemed to have so much, at the next the skies seemed to have crashed in around me. My little boy, however, remains to me, and he is an unmitigated source of comfort and encouragement. He is the dearest little fellow, and we have been drawn so close together, a fact which by some strange intuition he seems to recognize as much as I do. Now, however, alas, I have had to leave him, for I am on my way to join the forces overseas.

Ernest said that his old regiment – the Coldstream Guards – had refused to take him back, but that he had managed to get a commission in the Royal Army Ordnance Corps.

In the weeks following Pearl Harbor, the Duke was much concerned with the security of the Bahamas. He had been warned in March 1941 by Captain H. Montgomery Hyde that Nassau was totally exposed to a U-boat attack, and that there was nothing to stop a snatch-raid on Government House. He had taken the warning to heart, and done what he could to rectify this appalling state of affairs. The local defence force was strengthened and improved; controls were introduced on people leaving and entering the Colony; the GH guard was tightened up. Before America entered the war it was hard to do more: Bay Street begrudged every penny spent on defence, the more so as security measures discouraged tourists, and England could not be expected to give armed assistance against a hypothetical threat in the colonies when she was fighting for her life. But now the war had come to the western hemisphere. The Duke telegraphed London about the 'possibility that enemy submarines are sheltering among unoccupied cays and that air-patrol is necessary.'[16] With the Prime Minister's personal approval, he made a brief trip to the Key West base off the Florida coast for a conference with the American naval authorities on 28 February.

The Duke got on splendidly with the Americans.[17] He explained to them with eloquence and urgency that there was little to prevent the U-boats which were currently devastating US shipping from either establishing secret bases in the Bahamas or launching an offensive against the Colony, which was 'totally undefended against any scale of attack, except perhaps of a minor landing-force from a single plane in the vicinity of Nassau. . . . The general state of the Bahamas at present is that there are no guns in the island larger than machine-guns and only two of these.' Immediate measures were necessary; the United States naval base on Great Exuma would only be ready in the autumn. At a second conference held in Nassau on 18 March, the Americans – much impressed by the Duke as a wartime governor – agreed to set up at once air and sea reconnaissance stations in New Providence and a string of intelligence posts throughout the islands. A squadron of fighters and bombers would be on call in Florida in the event of an emergency. Thus it was that, largely through the personal initiative of its Governor, the Bahamas became part of the home defence system of the United States.

March also saw the arrival of a company of Cameron Highlanders (which had been occupying the Dutch oil island of Aruba) in Nassau, soon to be supplemented by Canadian troops. Half of this force was for the general defence of the town, the other half for the protection of Government House and its occupants. The Duchess – who busied herself in setting up a canteen for these forces – recalled with some amusement in her memoirs:

> With commendable zeal they promptly set up barbed-wire entanglements and posted sentries around Government House. More interesting still, the company commander insisted on staging mock raids from different directions. Usually these took place at night, and David and I, watching from the veranda as the stealthy figures slithered past the unsuspecting sentries, came to the conclusion that the Captain's offensive talents far overbalanced his defensive skill; for he invariably succeeded in penetrating his own lines, and his delight was to burst into Gray Phillips' room while he was asleep and declare him a prisoner.[18]

But the threat of being taken hostage was a real one of which the Duke was always conscious, and it was Churchill in person who had ordered the troops to be sent. As the Prime Minister wrote later that year in a personal minute to the Secretary of State for the Colonies:

> Am I not right in thinking that the only attack against the Bahamas possible is by a party landed from a U-boat? If so, Government House seems to be the obvious quarry. A U-boat would not have the facilities for finding out where the Duke of Windsor was if he were not there or were moving about. The right rule is, one may always take a chance but not offer a 'sitter'. I am therefore in favour

of putting an electrified fence round Government House and the other places mentioned, but not interfering with HRH's liberty of movement otherwise than by informing him of the dangers. It is essential that the seat of government should be protected against a U-boat raiding force, and for this purpose additional platoons should be sent.[19]

The fortification of Government House was only one example of the massive intensification of 'security' which accompanied the United States' entry into the war. Nassau was soon bristling with American agents, while the British networks based in Bermuda and New York grew vast and vigilant. Given that the Duke's immense popularity in the United States was still somehow thought to constitute a threat to England, it was inevitable that a close official eye should be trained on him in Nassau. But there is always something slightly ridiculous about wartime security.

One affair which considerably occupied the energies of British intelligence and indirectly involved the Duke was nothing if not curious. The Bermuda censorship intercepted an envelope posted before Pearl Harbor in Sacramento, Cal. and addressed to an Italian gentleman in Rome. The letter within transpired to be the work of one Mrs Harrison Williams, and seemed to be purely affectionate. (Mona Williams – now the Countess Bismarck – had managed the American side of the *Colis de Trianon* in 1939–40, and seen the Duke and Duchess in New York in October 1941.) Attached to it, however, was a further envelope addressed to Prince Rodolfo del Drago, which was found to contain a picture postcard of Government House, Nassau, of a type normally reserved for the use of the Duke and Duchess and their guests. This was signed with various endearments by 'Grigio'. British security was thrown into an intense flurry. Who was Grigio? How did he know Rodolfo? Why Nassau? Where did the Duke come in? Here might be intrigue indeed. Copies of the compromising missives were made and circulated to London, Washington and New York; in New York they engaged the attention of the legendary spy-master 'Intrepid'; at the Colonial Office they were scrutinized by the new Secretary of State, Lord Cranborne. (The unfortunate Lord Moyne had fallen with Singapore.) Weeks passed, and the identity of 'Grigio' remained elusive; and in April 1942 it was finally decided to write to the Duke enclosing the documents in the case, pointing out that while there seemed to be 'no harm in the letter itself', it nonetheless might amount to 'an attempt to evade the censorship and to communicate through an unauthorized intermediary with persons in enemy territory' which 'might evidently cause embarrassment to Your Royal Highness were it to happen again'.

The Duke knew perfectly well who 'Grigio' might be. As he wrote to a senior British security official:

. . . I am writing to inform you that I have established the identity of GRIGIO as being Major E. Gray Phillips, a member of my personal staff in Nassau.

Major Phillips has made a full confession of his blatant infringement of the regulations . . . the seriousness of which is aggravated by the fact that . . . my name should become connected with the incident.

. . . For my part, I am entirely satisfied with his explanation of this incident and that his endeavour to communicate with an Italian was in no way prompted by any sinister motive. . . . Having known Major Phillips for twenty years, the last three of which he has held an important position of trust as my Comptroller, I can vouch for his integrity. I hope, therefore, that under the circumstances BRITISH SECURITY CO-ORDINATION will . . . overlook the serious breach of security regulations which he has unfortunately committed. . . .

This letter is interesting for two reasons. It shows how loyally the Duke protected the men who served him, and how seriously he took the minutiae of wartime security. He quite realized why such an apparently ridiculous incident might so trouble the official mind. It also says something for his sense of discretion that he appears to have typed the letter himself.

On 30 March the Duchess wrote to Aunt Bessie:

I believe I am in the unique position of being owed a letter by you! We are without visitors though for two days had a combined assortment of American Army and British fly in looking things over. Everything is quiet again. The subs have either moved or been sunk as we have not had survivors in ten days – and I think the troops look quite bored with Nassau and its few diversions. The war seems to have no end in sight yet. Beaverbrook is in Miami and I hope will come here. We might be able to get a line on whether we are here for the duration. . . . The weather has been rather cool and damp – the longer that lasts the better for us. I can't see getting away *at all* – dismal outlook – but we might be worse off. It is not a becoming climate for a long time and no aids to beauty here. I really do wish we could move somewhere inhabited at least by our own class. These awful people day in and day out – it is as though you associated with the shop-owners of Washington. The Bishop is leaving. I shall miss him – have sent lots of endearing messages to Canterbury by him! My clinics are a success so far. . . .

The departure of the Bishop of Nassau provided the occasion for the Duchess's single and celebrated letter to her mother-in-law Queen Mary, whom she had twice met momentarily upon being presented on Court occasions, and with whom she had never exchanged a single word. John Dauglish was one of that legion of persons who, determined to dislike the Duke and Duchess before he had actually met them, ended up by being utterly captivated by them. In August 1940 he had refused (on Church advice) to be present in Nassau to greet them; his friends were soon astonished to receive letters from him protesting his enthusiastic devotion to them.[20] As he had confirmed the future King George VI at the

Royal Naval College at Osborne, he was certain to be received by the old Queen at Badminton (where she had been living since the autumn of 1939 with her retinue of fifty-five), and he gladly offered to carry the Duchess's missive, and even to put in a word about her success as Governor's wife. The Duchess's letter was a masterpiece of nuance, yet not without tact. Its text, first published in her memoirs,[21] is worth quoting again here.

Madam,

I hope you will forgive my intrusion upon your time as well as my boldness in addressing Your Majesty. My motive for the latter is a simple one. It has always been a source of sorrow and regret to me that I have been the cause of any separation that exists between Mother and Son and I can't help feel that there must be moments, however fleeting they may be, when you wonder how David is. The Bishop of Nassau is leaving in a short time for England, having been appointed by the Archbishop of Canterbury, Dr Lang, as Secretary to the Society for the Propagation of the Gospel, an advancement over his post here. I thought if you wished to hear news of David you might send for him. His name is the Right Reverend John Dauglish. He is a delightful man and has been of the greatest help to us here, not only through his understanding but his knowledge of local conditions on this tiny isle. He can tell you if all the things David gave up are replaced to him in another way and the little details of his daily life, his job, etc., the story of his flight from France leaving all his possessions behind. The horrors of war and the endless separation of families have in my mind stressed the importance of family ties. I hope that by the end of the summer we will be nearer that victory for which we are all working so hard and for which England has so bravely lighted the way.

I beg to remain

Your Majesty's most humble and obedient servant

WALLIS WINDSOR

As the Duchess wrote: 'In due course I received a letter from the Bishop telling of his audience with Queen Mary. She had shown a keen interest in David's work in the Colony and asked many questions. But when the Bishop mentioned what I was doing with, I judge, some show of appreciation and approval, there was no response. He met with a stone wall of disinterest.' In a subsequent letter to her son, however, the old Queen wrote: 'I send a kind message to your wife', prompting the Duke to exclaim in delighted astonishment: 'Now what do you suppose has come over Mama?' It was only a dozen years later, when the Duchess was writing her memoirs, that he was to learn, to his profound emotion, of the bold step she had taken from such laudable motives and doubtless at the expense of much pride.

Pencil draft of the Duchess's first and last letter to Queen Mary, April 1942.

The Duke found it hard to forgive his mother for her lifelong lack of affection, her contempt for him and failure to understand him during the Abdication crisis, her refusal to receive Mrs Simpson, and her unbending determination to exclude him from his family and country after 1936. When she died in 1953, the Duke wrote to the Duchess: 'I somehow feel that the fluids in her veins must always have been as icy-cold as they now are in death.' The real tragedy lay in the fact that, while the Duke and his mother were divided by an unbridgeable psychological gulf, the Duchess would have understood the old Queen perfectly well. Though Mrs Simpson had never shown that determined desire to be Queen which Princess May of Teck had so vigorously demonstrated by her rapid change of fiancé in the early 1890s, they were both of them strong, alert, single-minded women of high character and breeding who sought to govern their worlds according to strict standards of duty, efficiency and propriety. As a friend of the Duchess remarked to the author: 'She never wished to be Queen, but had she become Queen she would have played the game perfectly.' Mrs Simpson (as her correspondence with King Edward, shortly to be published, proves beyond a doubt) spent 1936 desperately trying to escape from her situation as royal favourite, and would have made any sacrifice to avoid the Abdication. It was the King who wanted marriage, and was inflexible and determined. Had Queen Mary agreed to meet Mrs Simpson, they might well have worked out a solution together; they might have found a way to temper the Duke's desire for matrimony and so keep him on the throne. But Queen Mary refused, perhaps not desiring these consequences. Yet it was not the Duchess of Windsor who held this against the old Queen in future years.

The visit of Lord Beaverbrook to Nassau hoped for by the Duchess in her letter to Aunt Bessie materialized in the second week of April, and coincided with one of the periodic sojourns of the enterprising but pessimistic Arthur Vyning Davis at Government House. 'We got a lot of news from Beaverbrook and some gloomy views from Mr Davis,' wrote the Duchess on 13 April. 'However, a breath of intelligence is welcome in this moron paradise.' The Duke was delighted to see his old supporter, and above all to have news of England and the war from one who had been in the thick of things. They also talked of personal matters. 'Realizing how desperately tired you were,' the Duke wrote to Beaverbrook (then in Washington) on 18 April, 'we felt very diffident over inflicting you with our problems, which are so relatively small as compared to those of many others in the world today. At the same time, we could not resist the opportunity of explaining our position and aspirations to one who has always taken a sympathetic interest in us.' (The 'we' was not the Royal 'We'; the Duke habitually wrote of the common feelings of himself and the Duchess.)

For almost two years they had put up with Nassau – the pettiest and most difficult governorship in the British Empire – without official complaint. The Duke had written to Churchill in October 1940 about the numerous difficulties and frustrations of his task, but he had faced these manfully, and performed his functions as Governor perfectly. She too had done marvellously in her role as Governor's wife. Together they had done all that had been expected of them – and more, and they had never given the slightest hint of the disappointment which they in fact felt acutely. Since Pearl Harbor, they had indeed had a real and challenging job to do; but even so, they would hardly have been human had they not longed for a better post elsewhere, one less petty and frustrating, one more suited to a Prince, to a man of the Duke's abilities and experience. There was no telling how long the war might last; perhaps another ten years. Were they to spend all that time in Nassau, with its nerve-racking claustral climate and provincial population of 20,000, its intractable political and social problems, its powerful bosses who were quite impervious to reason, its utter insignificance in a world at war? The Duke knew there was a job of substance in which he could do great things for Great Britain – in the realm of public relations in the United States. Their tumultuous reception throughout America the previous autumn had convinced him more than ever of this. While Beaverbrook was in Nassau, the Duke resolved for the first time to ask for an eventual change of post. 'I have written to Winston', he wrote to Beaverbrook on 18 April, 'setting out as briefly as possible what is in my mind, namely (1) that I cannot contemplate remaining in the Bahamas as Governor for the duration of the war, and (2) that I feel confident that I could serve my Country best in some technical appointment in America.'

The Duke wanted Beaverbrook to be his ally in London and plead his cause. As he wrote:

> No one realizes better than I do the obvious circumstances and prejudices which weigh heavily in the scales against my being selected for important appointments, and it might well be considered unwise and inopportune to attempt to force the displacement of certain holders of such appointments as Ambassador or Governor-General at the present time. However, successive phases of this war have produced many unexpected changes, and I have great hopes that a timely word from you may eventually result in the employment of my services in a more useful sphere than my present one.

Alas for the Duke, Beaverbrook was just about the worst person to whom he could then have turned for help.* Having resigned from the War Cabinet the previous month after a row with Churchill, he retained no

---

* Beaverbrook replied to the Duke on 29 April: 'I have of course been thinking much about the discussions we had, and of the various points that arose. And when I return to England at the end of the week I will talk with the Prime Minister.' It is fairly certain that he did not do so.

state office and little political influence. His bad relations with the premier were to be made even worse by a provocative speech in America about the need for a Second Front. Even when Beaverbrook returned to Churchill's good graces a year later, and to the Cabinet in the autumn of 1943, he never had any real intention of helping the Duke, in spite of numerous promises and constant assurances. He was just the sort of man to keep the Duke hoping in order to establish an influence which might come in useful in future. And yet the Duke, isolated and uninformed, continued to rely on him more than on anyone in England for information and help. In 1942 certainly there was no hope of a change of post. The Duke carried on as cheerfully as he could. It was to be one year exactly before he asked again.

In April 1942 there did seem to be some useful point in his post in Nassau, minor as it was. The work of his Economic Committee was at last bearing fruit (in the metaphorical if not yet, alas, the literal sense). The House (which for all its hostility was beginning to glimpse the writing on the wall) was persuaded (largely through the efforts of Harold Christie and Sir Harry Oakes) to sanction the appointment of a Director of Agriculture with staff, and to vote no less than £10,000 for the Duke's version of a CCC camp, which at once became known as Windsor Training Farm. An area of useless scrub in the south-west of New Providence was purchased and 300 men sent to work on it at a wage of three shillings a day. Pending the setting-up of the Agriculture Department, there was a slight problem as to who would do the training. But the philanthropic Oakes donated a nearby house to lodge them, the Duke visited them and exhorted them to great endeavours, and after a few weeks it was announced that 'Forty acres have been cleared and thirty have already been planted with cassava, corn, sweet potatoes, peas and various kinds of beans.'[22]

By this time, however, Windsor Farm had been overshadowed by a project of infinitely greater importance. After long secret negotiations between London, Washington and Nassau, in which the Duke had played an active role, it was announced at the end of April that a major RAF base would be constructed under Lend-Lease by the Americans on New Providence, using local labour. It was the Colony's salvation. At a stroke, it promised to solve both the security crisis and the economic crisis. Nassau would now be full of American engineers and contractors just as it had once been full of American tourists; there would be business for the merchants and employment for the people.

Something must be said about this undertaking, the nature of which has been imperfectly understood by previous authors. During the first two years of the Second World War, RAF flight training was gradually (and for obvious reasons) transferred from the skies above England to overseas stations, mostly in Canada. After Pearl Harbor, with the Atlantic War unleashed in its full fury, it was decided (through Lend-Lease) to establish a new pattern of Operational Training Units at key positions all over the Atlantic, not only to train crews for the RAF but also to play a role in the convoy and escort system, and in oceanic reconnaissance and submarine-chasing. The OTU on New Providence was the third to be begun. Although the Unit itself – to be based on the site of Nassau's existing airport at Oakes Field – was to be exclusively British-run, it was to be backed up by an important new base of RAF Transport Command ferrying men and planes out from America and on to Africa and Europe, which would be shared with the Americans. This would involve the construction of a second base, which was to be some miles out of Nassau and to be known as Windsor Field.

The Americans using local labour were to construct both bases. They would employ between 2,000 and 3,000 unskilled and up to 1,000 skilled workers – almost half of the entire male population of the island – for at least six months. As soon as the enterprise was announced, the senior personnel and foremen of Pleasantville Construction Inc. arrived together with a detachment of the US Corps of Engineers under Major Hayes, taking over the British Colonial Hotel just down the slope from Government House (with whose occupants they were always to be popular). Recruitment (with the aid of Hughes in his role of part-time unassisted Labour Officer) began on 8 May, and work on 'the Project' (as it was mysteriously known for security reasons) started on the 20th.

The following day the Duke dissolved the House of Assembly in preparation for the forthcoming septennial elections.[23] In a brisk speech he summarized the massive transformation which had come over the Colony in the half-year since Pearl Harbor – the new defence alert, the collapse of the 'soft economy', the necessary efforts to stimulate craft and agriculture, the war relationship with the United States:

> Instead of the normal winter tourist season, on which the Bahamas had grown to rely in large measure . . ., we have had to face up to the fact that these more comfortable days are for the time being relegated to the past, and that a policy of wartime economy and defence measures must now take their place.

He announced that he was off to Miami and Washington at the end of the month to discuss defence co-operation, the supply problem, and the market which wartime America might afford for Bahamian produce. He would lose no time in causing Writs to be issued for the new elections.

The electoral system of the Bahamas was a delightful relic of the eighteenth century. It was the perennial ambition of the Colonial Office to reform it; but the only reform that 'Bay Street' had any intention of admitting was a substantial rise in the property qualification which, unchanged since 1882 at £2 8s 0d for New Providence and £1 4s 0d for the Out Islands, effectively gave black men the vote. But the balance was somewhat redressed in favour of white power by an ingenious system of plural voting, and only a man of means could be a candidate. In 1939 a secret ballot had been introduced in the eight New Providence constituencies 'for an experimental term of five years'; it was the one great victory of Sir Charles Dundas against Bay Street, and they hated him for it and were determined not to renew the nefarious measure. But it was the Out Islands (in spite of their utter depopulation) which provided the remaining twenty-one seats in the House, and there nothing had changed. Their representatives were all good Bay Street men who never visited their desolate constituencies save at election time, when they would turn up in ships laden with rum and cake and prove their public worth by cutting bundles of banknotes in half – the other half to be distributed after the happy re-election in an open vote. The Out Islanders were kept too poor by Bay Street, were too dependent on them for loans and supplies, ever to think of putting up their own candidates. By means of this entrenched system the white merchants of Nassau were to maintain their hegemony for another quarter of a century. Government House could do little more than press for reform and try to correct the very worst abuses; but it was doubtless no coincidence that the Duke had timed his official absence from the Colony to coincide with the election fortnight in the middle of June.

The Duchess was not enthusiastic about the journey. Normally she would have been delighted by the prospect of a trip to the mainland (her first since Pearl Harbor); but the autumn tour had so exhausted her, the attendant publicity so distressed her, and so occupied was she now with her Bahamas war work, that she was far from keen to leave. As she wrote to Aunt Bessie on 13 April:

> The Duke will surely go, but is it worth while for me to attempt the trip? I get so little pleasure with the endless publicity and being gazed at everywhere. This time it would be better – but would it be *normal*? That is what I long for. Anyway it's hard to persuade the Duke to make a flying trip without me. We shall see.

To her confidante Nina Drury she wrote the same day: 'I have no desire to go until I go for *good*. It is so hard to come back. . . .' But a week later she had relented, explaining to Aunt Bessie that 'as the Duke seems to want me handy to help with the problems he wants me to come with him', and that it would be a good opportunity to see the family in 'Balto' again and her stomach specialist in New York ('though my stomach has not made itself felt all winter'). Still, she dreaded a repetition of 'the luggage stories', and was determined to travel modestly. 'We would not take an

ADC but keep the party *small*,' she wrote on 2 May, 'and I have written to Uncle Harry that I do not want a policeman or anything. Am also travelling very light this time.' To avoid the horror tales of 'a floor at the Waldorf', they would stay with friends in New York. On 15 May she stressed again that she was 'bringing the smallest amount of clothes possible to save the luggage stories and if not enough will get some there', though on the 18th she somewhat apprehensively asked Aunt Bessie : 'Would one regard evening dress as a bit in advance of the season for Washington or NY? I hope we will be left alone by the press. . . .'

That spring, the war news was a continuous tale of disaster. The Japanese drove the British out of Burma and the Americans out of the Philippines. General Arthur left Corregidor, saying 'I shall return.' In North Africa Rommel swept into Egypt, while in Russia the Germans opened their great south-western offensive with the capture of Rostov. Patriotic Nassau was anxious, but nothing appeared to disturb its calm. On 24 May, Hughes in his capacity as Labour Officer reported to Leslie Heape that labour leaders on the Project were trying to put some grievance into writing, but that it was certainly nothing serious. The men seemed glad to be in work. There was an almost carnival feeling of corrupt electioneering in the air: it was a time when Nassau traditionally enjoyed itself. The skies seemed clear when the Duke and Duchess left their Colony for a month on 28 May 1942. But in such skies black clouds can quickly gather.

Part Three

Wars Within Wars

———

13
The Uprising
May–August 1942

The second American tour of the Duke and Duchess of Windsor, on which they set out on 28 May 1942, could not have been more different from their first, from which they had returned less than eight months before. Then their visit had been quite unofficial, a badly needed (but in the event not very restful) change after more than a year in a trying post. It had been made in an unavoidable atmosphere of press sensationalism; and, the United States being neutral, the Duke had needed to impress upon his vast public that he was the former King and loyal servant of a country at war. Now America was Great Britain's ally; the papers had other things to write about; and the Duke, accompanied by a slightly reluctant Duchess, went to Washington in his official capacity as Governor of the British Colony nearest the mainland – a Colony dependent on America for its survival and bound up with the security of the United States. Last time he had received only vague attention from the Administration, and had to attend mostly to the crowds and the press. This time the proportions were destined to be reversed.

Braving the submarine menace, they crossed to Miami in the *Gemini*.[1] There they spent two days while the Duke discussed naval and supply questions. On the morning of Monday 1 June they arrived in Washington, where they were to spend a few nights at the Embassy. Lord Halifax was absent elsewhere in the Union, so Lady Halifax received them.[2] They lunched with the Roosevelts at the White House, where they were delighted to find as the other guests their old friends Hermann and Katherine Rogers, whom they had last seen in the South of France in the pre-flight days of June 1940. It was a thoughtful attention on the part of the President, who had been a friend of Hermann's father. After lunch the Duchess joined Aunt Bessie, while the Duke went off to the British Colonies Supply Mission to begin his official discussions. The press were respecting their desire for privacy, and the visit showed every prospect of being a quiet and successful one.

It was on his return to the Embassy after his afternoon's business that the Duke received the first disquieting telegram from Leslie Heape, who was Acting Governor in Nassau. It was the copy of a despatch to the Colonial Office, and had been sent at about half-past nine that morning:

> This morning about 1,000 unskilled workers have made a demonstration with some disorder against the wages being paid by American constructors of OTU. Police have the matter in hand. . . .[3]

Disturbing and unexpected as this was, the Duke was obviously not being advised to make an immediate return to Nassau; there was nothing to do but await further information, and so he proceeded with the Duchess to dinner with Lady Halifax. The President's chief adviser Harry Hopkins was there, and the Duchess's old friend Louise Macy whom he was soon to marry. In the middle of dinner the Duke was called away from the table by the Ambassador's Secretary. It was another telegram from Heape, this one sent at about half-past four in the afternoon:

> The situation has not improved. Considerable damage and looting has taken place in the business section. The rioters have now been cleared back into the coloured quarter and as the majority are in liquor it is considered advisable in order to avoid bloodshed to confine action by troops and police to protection of residential and business areas. Curfew has been proclaimed with effect from 8 p.m. tonight. Shooting has taken place, to date 2 rioters and 1 military have been injured.

The Duke returned to the table looking worried, explained what had happened, and said he must return to Nassau immediately. Hopkins slipped away, rang up the White House, and arranged for the Duke to confer with the President at midnight.[4] At dawn, a detachment of seventy-five US Marines under Captain Goodwin, disguised as Military Police and armed with sub-machine guns and tear gas, left for Nassau 'at the personal direction of the President . . . to preserve peace and order on United States construction projects and protect United States property'.[5] Leaving the Duchess behind, in spite of her protests, in the care of Sergeant Holder, the Duke himself followed shortly afterwards in the personal aircraft of the Secretary for the Navy. A third telegram received from Heape that morning was not encouraging:

> No attempt made last night to leave coloured quarters but this morning crowds gathered again in various places and had to be dispersed but no shooting. Have refused to negotiate with labour until disorders are over. 2 dead about 50 injured. 7 detained in hospital with bullet wounds. . . .

* * *

In the national mythology of the new Commonwealth of the Bahamas, the June Riots have been invested with all the mystique which the Irish attach to the Easter Rising, or which patriotic Americans used to ascribe to the Boston Tea Party. In Bahamian history they represent, indeed, virtually the sole large-scale act of violent resistance to white rule. (A demonstration in support of a taxi strike in the 1950s has been dignified with the name of 'the Second Riots' – but this, alas, had no martyrs and few possibilities.) Nassuvian politicians still stir audiences with talk of them. Bahamas Labour Day – not in May but June – commemorates the national heroes who fell in the course of them, or were condemned on account of them. The veteran Bahamian labour leader Randol Fawkes, in a passage of doubtful accuracy but Carlylesque vividness, writes:

> When that mob marched on that June morning, they took upon their shoulders the common burden of all Bahamians – those who protested, those who were silent, and those who did not even realize the indignity of their status. This teeming mass of rags, sweat and bones marched for them all; and, in doing so, they marched themselves straight into history. . . . Like a mighty river that had burst its barrier and in full flood comes tearing onward, so did the labouring masses storm the main thoroughfare of the capital city.[6]

This colourful prose tends to obscure the important fact about the June Riots, that they were quite spontaneous and utterly unexpected. Though a few of the men may have been intent on stirring up trouble, and the black candidates in the forthcoming elections had an interest in encouraging black grievances, no one appears to have foreseen them – not Hughes who was in constant touch with the black labour leaders, nor those leaders themselves, nor the American contractors who were employing the men, and certainly no one in Bay Street or official Nassau. If there had been the faintest hint of trouble, the Duke would never have left the Colony; and if he had not left, the situation might never have got out of hand. The disorders in fact developed out of the blue from circumstances which were almost absurd and trivial. But the underlying causes (as Fawkes correctly suggests) were profound. It was indeed the case that the coloured population of Nassau had been oppressed for too long, and in particular had of late been kept far too hungry, by the vicious Bay Street system. It evidently required only a spark to set this material ablaze.

What might seem (and to so many contemporary observers did seem) illogical is that the revolutionary fuse should have ignited when it did. For in the late spring of 1942 the people of Nassau, who since the previous December had been in a desperate economic plight, had suddenly been presented with an unhoped-for miracle of full employment in the form of the Project. The 'spark' was in fact provided by a curious misunderstanding with regard to the wages paid on the Project. Under the Anglo–American Lend-Lease Treaties, projects in British territories were to be constructed by American contractors using local labour at the prevailing local rate. In the Bahamas, the standard rate for unskilled construction work had been laid down by statute in 1936 at four shillings a day; and so this automatically became the basic pay of the newly recruited labour force in Nassau in May 1942. Of course, four shillings had barely been a living wage in 1936 and was no longer so in 1942; the war had led to a rise in freight costs and tariffs and hence to a large increase in prices, especially food prices. The Duke, acutely alive to the dangers and injustices of the situation, had been trying for more than a year to secure either a reduction in tariffs or an increase in wages, but with little success. Only two months before he had failed in an effort to increase the wage to six shillings. But that was not the point; so glad were the men to have work that they would probably have accepted almost any pay to begin with – but for one thing. The Americans employed on the Project belonged to a different scale of pay entirely; and, drinking in the black bar-rooms (as it was almost unknown for white men to do), they spread the false rumour that the American contractors had been willing to pay the much higher American wages to the Bahamians too – but had been prevented from doing so by the Bahamas Government.

On Friday 29 May – the day after the Duke's departure for America – the 'Bahamas Federation of Labour' (founded two weeks before) presented a letter to Hughes expressing the grievances of the men, and asking for a wage of eight shillings a day.[7] Since all of the signatories were actively involved in the coming elections, this was interpreted as a political campaign gesture. On Sunday afternoon there was a peaceful demonstration in support of the higher wages at the site of the Project outside Nassau, attended by a few hundred of the men; Hughes addressed them and assured them that their complaints were being heard and would be dealt with as soon as possible; the crowd dispersed quietly, apart from a group of turbulent youths who finally left after a minor scuffle with police. That evening Hughes held a meeting in his office with the heads of the Labour Federation, also attended by the American contractors, the ubiquitous Harold Christie, and the most eminent black citizen of Nassau, Alfred Adderley. None of them expected trouble, or saw any reason why work should not be resumed normally the following day.

But arriving at the site the next morning – Monday 1 June – the men, ignoring their leaders, decided not to work but to strike. And they resolved to march in procession to the Secretariat in the Public Square to put their views collectively to the Colonial Secretary. (They do not appear to have realized that the Colonial Secretary was *locum tenens* for the absent Governor and so up at Government House, or that his own place at the Secretariat had been taken by his timid white Bahamian deputy, Charles Bethel.) The procession moved off towards town in good order soon after eight o'clock. Some of the men carried scythes or sticks. These facts were at once reported to the Acting Governor, Leslie Heape, and the Commissioner of Police, Lieutenant-Colonel R. A. ('Reggie') Erskine-Lindop.

A few words must be said about the unfortunate Heape and Erskine-Lindop, both of whom were to take much of the blame for what was to happen in the next few hours. Although extremely good at their everyday jobs, neither of them possessed what Jeeves calls 'the art of the unusual situation'. Erskine-Lindop – forty-four, of an Anglo–Mauritian army family and for six years Commissioner in Nassau – was one of those who possess admirable self-control and great physical courage but show themselves incapable of resolution when faced with the unexpected. Similarly Heape, though in many ways an ideal colonial administrator – fair, just, conscientious, a master of patient detail – was the sort of man who requires several hours, if not days, to understand the meaning of complex new facts. War-wounded, he was no man of action, and a slow (if a deep) thinker. His first mistake that Monday morning was to leave, as he was entitled to do, Erskine-Lindop in complete charge of the situation, giving him a free hand and full powers. He then returned to his files.

One must try to put oneself in the place of the bewildered Commissioner. Up to then his work in the colonial police had consisted of the detection of ordinary crime (including a handful of straightforward murder cases), organizing the ceremonial and guard role of his little force, and participating since 1939 in the somewhat makeshift defence and security arrangements for the Colony. Suddenly, learning that an ugly and partly armed mob of more than 2,000 (some commentators – including the American Consul John Dye – put the figure as high as 3,000)[8] was marching on the Square to confront an official who was not there, his main concern (as he later explained) was to 'keep his men together as a force until the situation developed'. He had some thirty men available for immediate duty at the Police Barracks, and could also call upon about 100 other police, the same number of local defence volunteers, and a company of Cameron Highlanders stationed to the east of Nassau. The trouble was that he had no conception of alternative strategies. He could have cut off the strikers' advance (they were coming by the only good road which leads into the centre from the Project field and the black township of Grant's Town, a road which passes by Government House) – admittedly a risky undertaking. Or he could have played safe and awaited the mob in the Square. In the event he did neither, but telephoned Colonel Haig of the Camerons to ask for a platoon to hold the Police Barracks should he (Erskine-Lindop) decide to order out his men. The platoon arrived half an hour later, at a quarter-past nine; and the Commissioner then emerged from the Barracks with his small – but armed – force and headed for the Square. By then the mob had been in possession of the Square for some while, and the real trouble was just about to begin.

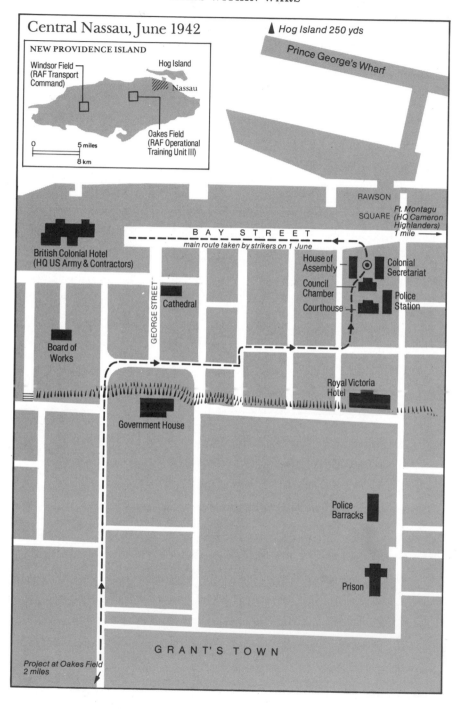

Central Nassau, June 1942

▲ Hog Island 250 yds

Prince George's Wharf

NEW PROVIDENCE ISLAND

Windsor Field
(RAF Transport
Command)

Hog Island

Nassau

Oakes Field
(RAF Operational
Training Unit III)

0   5 miles
8 km

RAWSON

SQUARE   Ft. Montagu
             (HQ Cameron
             Highlanders)
             1 mile

B A Y   S T R E E T
main route taken by strikers on 1 June

British Colonial Hotel
(HQ US Army & Contractors)

House of
Assembly

Colonial
Secretariat

Council
Chamber

Police
Station

GEORGE STREET

Cathedral

Courthouse

Board of
Works

Royal Victoria
Hotel

Government House

Police
Barracks

Prison

G R A N T ' S   T O W N

Project at Oakes Field
2 miles

Even today, with its village quiet lost forever, there is something decidedly quaint about the Public Square of Nassau. Queen Victoria's statue guards its open side, facing Rawson Square and the Harbour. Behind it to the south rises the little ridge on which stands Government House and other landmarks, beyond which Grant's Town lies in the distance. Its avenues are shaded by royal palms, its gardens by a giant silk cotton tree. Its plain, rectangular public buildings, all painted pink, resemble giant doll's houses. (Shared functions in those days indicated that they served a town with half the population of Ramsgate and a territory with one-fifth of the population of Cornwall. The ground floor of the Council Chamber was the Post Office, and the Secretariat also housed the Treasury.) It is a long square, all of 150 yards from the Octagonal Library in the south to the thoroughfare of Bay Street in the north. And by the time the Commissioner and his thirty-four armed men arrived there on the morning of 1 June 1942, it accommodated without difficulty an angry mob of between 2,000 and 3,000 people.

The first elements of the crowd had arrived some half an hour before, and had been furious to find that there was no one in the Secretariat who would see them. Bethel, the Assistant and now Acting Colonial Secretary, was scared to distraction and positively refused to come out.[9] At the Treasury the earthy Taylor had lately been replaced by Herbert Letraille, another somewhat retiring man who declined to face the mass. Eventually Hallinan (a fearless man, as he was later to prove as Chief Justice of Cyprus) went and addressed them from the Secretariat steps; but though he was sincerely concerned for the advance of the black Bahamian, he had an uncertain effect upon them. Tall and distinguished-looking, remote in manner, precise in speech, he seems to have overawed them for a moment but not to have defused the human bomb that had been lit. He told them to choose representatives to go up to Government House, where their complaints would receive prompt consideration. He implied that, if they spoiled the original good impression they had made, the contractors might rely instead on American labour. Having concluded his remarks, he descended the steps and passed unmolested through the crowd on the way to his office in the Courthouse, at the same moment as the Commissioner was entering the Square with his little, rifle-bearing force, which halted before the Police Station.

For a moment nothing happened. Then a section of the mob suddenly surged into Bay Street, which runs for 400 yards west of the Square up to the grounds of the British Colonial Hotel, the smart façades of its prim wooden buildings symbolizing the social, political and economic supremacy of white Nassau. A young white witness, a member of the local Volunteer Defence Force (but not yet called to arms), later wrote to his parents in Trinidad about what then occurred:

. . . [The labourers] thought they had a good case so decided to strike and go to the Colonial Secretary's office in a body and put the matter up to the local authorities in that way. All might have been arranged satisfactorily if the better type of workman had not been accompanied by several hundred of the opposite type – a bad lot. It all started out fairly quietly, but by the time they had all reached town . . . the looters, who were armed with sticks, bottles and cutlasses, had worked themselves up to quite a pitch and started to destroy everything they could lay their hands on. They broke practically every shop window in Bay Street, and looted the merchandise, destroying and stealing quantities of goods from inside the shops as well. They smashed the window of the Red Cross and pulled out a priceless print of some sort which was to be raffled for Red Cross funds, leaving it in the gutter. . . . Two or three cars were damaged and a Coca-Cola truck was looted, all the bottles being swept off and broken in Bay Street. Glass was everywhere. The mob swept up and down and did all this damage in a very short time, before the police and forces could bring pressure to bear. . . .[10]

During this orgy of destruction, where were the Bay Street whites? Some were barricading themselves in their besieged premises; their leading figures, for whose blood the mob was indeed howling, were either seeking sanctuary in the Prince George Hotel, or rushing for their boats and heading for the open sea; and still others, the men of action among them, had fled to the Square where they were attempting to rouse the police.

And where were the police? In spite of the entreaties of outraged citizens, the Commissioner refused to deploy his force for almost half an hour. His men with their rifles remained lined up in front of Queen Victoria's statue. Obviously aware of the inadequacy of his little force, he neither called upon the military for assistance, nor sounded the siren which would have brought the Volunteers to the scene. Nor did he ask the Magistrate to read the Riot Act, nor even inform Heape of what was happening. He merely talked to that part of the crowd which remained in the Square, trying to persuade them to go home.

Eventually, at about a quarter to ten, an agitated Bethel came out of the Secretariat and told Erskine-Lindop that he would have to do something about the situation in Bay Street. The Commissioner then assembled his men in a phalanx and – showing considerable courage – proceeded down the street, meeting a hail of bottles and stones. The rioters dispersed up side-streets as the force advanced, only to return once they had passed. The force then divided into two, one part clearing the street, the other standing picket at street corners to prevent the mob from coming back – until the news arrived that rioters were attacking the Board of Works offices to the west of Bay Street. Most of the force went off to investigate and the mob recovered possession of the thoroughfare.

It was not until a quarter past ten that Heape, who had heard nothing from Erskine-Lindop but had received desperate appeals from citizens, asked for the help of the military in Bay Street. Twenty Camerons under Lieutenant Millar rushed to the scene. Shots were fired in the air and the rioters began to disperse. By eleven o'clock the battered but still lively mob had been forced back 'over the hill' to their township of Grant's Town. All these proceedings were watched with incredulity by the Americans from the windows of the British Colonial Hotel, where they had shut themselves up in their headquarters at the first sign of trouble.

Back in Grant's Town the mob, in the best tradition of riots, broke into the bar-rooms and reinvigorated itself with drink. It was pursued after an interval by the Commissioner and the Nassau Magistrate, accompanied by some twenty Camerons and police. The mob, emboldened by liquor, had now reassembled in force by the Cotton Tree Inn. The Magistrate approached as near as he dared and read the Riot Act. The mob replied by furiously attacking the party with stones and rocks. A Cameron fell in a pool of blood. Showered by missiles and surrounded on all sides, the forces opened fire. By the time the crowd had dispersed, at least seven rioters had been hit – two fatally – and some forty others injured in the affray. The Commissioner assessed the situation, somewhat sanguinely decided that all was calm and likely to remain so, and retreated with his contingent across the hill, leaving four nervous policemen to maintain order in Grant's Town.

Meanwhile, towards noon, a deputation of furious and overwrought Bay Street men, having come out of their refuges to discover their smashed and ransacked properties, had gone up to Government House to make their views known to the Acting Governor, whom they found in urgent session with his senior officials. Barely articulate and speaking all at once, they declared that the situation would never have got out of hand but for the incompetence and neglect of the Government. They demanded that the disorders be crushed at once and mercilessly, that bloody retribution be wreaked on the rioters, that machine-guns be used, that martial law be declared. When Heape attempted to reply, he was shouted down and called 'a fool'. Hallinan alone retained a perfect composure; discussing and dismissing their hothead proposals with his habitual calm logical precision, he incensed them most of all. Suddenly the sound of shots was heard from the direction of Grant's Town. 'That's the stuff to give them!' shouted one of the Bay Street group. They hurried off, vowing that the House when it met would wreak a terrible vengeance on the officials whom it would hold responsible.[11]

Such were the amazing events on the morning of Monday 1 June 1942 in Nassau, whose black population were known for their sleepy complacency and where nothing in the nature of a riot had occurred in living memory. By lunchtime the town centre was an armed camp. The

Volunteers had been called out and curfew declared. At half-past two that afternoon news came that the Grant's Town mob, having regrouped yet again in a state of thorough intoxication, had attacked and burnt down the township's post office, library, ambulance, fire-station and police-station (the four policemen on duty making a lucky escape). At three o'clock ExCo met at Government House, and decided (on the advice of Erskine-Lindop) to concentrate on keeping the mob out of white Nassau, and not to send the forces of order back into black Nassau for at least twenty-four hours. The policy now was a desperate one of containment. That night, few slept soundly in the little capital. The curfew was only partly effective. A Cameron sentry guarding the road by Government House shot and killed a man who refused to halt. In Grant's Town, a coloured shopkeeper shot and killed the leader of a gang about to loot his shop. The next morning, a crowd of 200 broke out of Grant's Town and ransacked white premises in East Nassau, until driven back by the army. The violence seemed very far from over.

That night, after a long and difficult flight marked by engine failure, the Duke of Windsor returned to Nassau.

The arrival of Heape's first two telegrams had created hardly any stir at the Colonial Office (which at that moment had a bigger problem to worry about – the penetration of the Indian Ocean by the Japanese). The Secretary of State, Lord Cranborne, thanked the Acting Governor for 'prompt information' and merely asked for material with which his Parliamentary Under-Secretary, Harold Macmillan, might answer possible questions in the House of Commons. For the Permanent Under-Secretary, Philip Rogers minuted: 'This is an unfortunate affair, but should not, I think, develop into anything more serious.'[12] The news of shooting and fatalities, however, and that a section of the Colony's capital had been abandoned to the mob, threw Whitehall into sudden alarm. Even if order were restored immediately, suggested a Foreign Office minute, the outbreak might lead to much Anglo–American unpleasantness in the bases colonies, and to American reluctance to employ British colonial labour in future.[13] The sinister news that US Marines had been sent in in disguise – 'ostensibly to protect US military installations in the Islands',[14] as the Embassy in Washington reported – was greeted with nothing short of hysteria; worried comparisons were drawn with Haiti and Nicaragua, where the Marines having restored order the State Department had ruled in all but name. On the other hand, no further British troops could be spared for the Bahamas, not even from Jamaica; and it was far from clear whether the disturbances were over or were merely beginning. British Military Intelligence in Washington warned that 'Recurrence of violence anticipated', and even that 'Possible subversive group Axis-sponsored may cause riots ashore combined with some form of submarine activity'!*[15]

Amidst this flurry of anxiety, little thought was given to the predicament of the man who was returning to take charge of the situation. Not since the reign of George II had an Englishman born and trained to be King found himself at the head of a Government faced with a breakdown in public order. (It requires but a moment's thought to appreciate the drawbacks under which others of his original destiny – Edward VII, George V, George VI – would have laboured had they, inconceivably, been required to face a similar situation.) Although labour riots had not been unknown in the British West Indies in the 1930s, the Duke was one of the first colonial governors to have to deal with them under the conditions of the Second World War. And, returning to Nassau some thirty-six hours after trouble had broken out, he had to deal with them at the head of an official establishment which had shown itself in his absence to be less than resolute, key members of which had come close to losing their nerve, and which had already made a number of false moves. In fact he had to face not one crisis but four: the emergency in public order; the matter of the men's grievances, which had to be attended to as soon as order was restored; the fact that work had been interrupted on a military project which was essential to the future of the Bahamas and of considerable importance in the prosecution of the war; and finally Bay Street's determination to crucify Heape, Hallinan, Hughes and Erskine-Lindop for what had happened, and so carry its political warfare against the Government into new realms of bitterness.

The physical crisis – the most urgent problem – ceased almost as soon as it was known that the Duke was back in Nassau. Of this there can be no doubt whatsoever. On Tuesday 2 June – in spite of the exhaustion of the hung-over rioters, and the opportunity given to the authorities to reorganize themselves – things were still very far from quiet. In the morning, the mob had rampaged through the white suburbs of East Nassau; Grant's Town remained a 'no-go area', and one man was killed there in the day's brawling. By nightfall, it seemed unlikely that the curfew would be observed. But the news of the Duke's return spread like wildfire, and by the middle of Wednesday almost all disorder had ceased. The Duke commanded a hesitant Erskine-Lindop to send police patrols into Grant's Town, where no policeman had been seen for forty-eight hours; they reported that all was quiet, and the Duke himself then drove down the Grant's Town streets in an open car. No doubt the arrival of the Marines (whom no one was supposed to know were Marines) helped the

---

* General Marshall, US Chief of Staff, was even more specific on this point. 'This may be part of a well-planned subversive campaign particularly on part of Japs who are reported actively inciting sedition among American and West Indian negroes,' he wrote in an order dated 2 June.

situation; though they were strictly confined to the protection of the US Consulate, the British Colonial Hotel and the Project, they thus released local volunteers for duty elsewhere. But the proceedings of the subsequent enquiry show clearly that it was the presence of the Duke – his mere charisma, perhaps – which was the main factor in restoring peace. The coloured people regarded him as their friend, indeed as their potential saviour; they expected little from the remote officials or the hated Bay Street men, but he, they believed, would hear them and help them. As the most articulate of the black labour leaders, the popular local preacher Dr Walker, said to the Duke that Wednesday at Government House:

> . . . Two years ago when the radio waves broadcast the news of Your Royal Highness' appointment as Governor of the Bahamas, the deaf heard, the dumb spoke, the blind saw and the crippled leapt for joy. Your reputation as a humanitarian and King had preceded you. 'Surely', we said to ourselves, 'the Duke of Windsor will not allow us to live amidst social inequalities which sap our self-respect and prevent us from attaining our full status as first-class citizens?' Fifty-four Governors have preceded Your Excellency [sic] but not one ever brought a ray of hope to the poor and oppressed. We believe that you are not just another Governor for one class of people but the Governor for all colours and classes of the people. In faith, believing, I ask on behalf of all my brothers and sisters : 'Art thou he that cometh or look for another ?'[16]

On Wednesday evening the Duke broadcast to the Colony. It was the only public address he did not write himself in the Bahamas, having been drafted before his arrival by Hallinan, the official who undoubtedly had the strongest grasp of the situation. It was brief and unemotive, expressed the Duke's dismay at what had occurred, and said that only when the men had returned to work could discussions begin on the wages question. On Thursday morning over half the men turned up for work on the Project. It was a considerable achievement, less than three days after bloodshed.

Meanwhile the Duke had begun a hectic round of consultations at Government House with almost everyone concerned in recent events. He was determined to win the confidence of all parties, to get the Colony working normally again, to repress recrimination, to find out exactly what had happened and why. But the difficulties of his task were immense; he had to reconcile the irreconcilable. Bay Street, against whose premises the Riots had been directed, refused to contemplate concessions to the strikers, demanded harsh punishments for them, and were out for the blood of the officials whom they blamed for the outbreak. Both they and the Americans insisted on a tough and uncompromising policy for the restoration and maintenance of order. The Duke meant to be tough; but at the same time he recognized that the strikers had a just cause. They now looked to him to help them; and he was determined to be fair to them. What worried him most was that what had started out as a labour dispute had obviously degenerated into a race riot which had aroused strong intercommunal antagonism. 'While riots started regarding wage dispute because it is universally believed by the men that the Americans will pay substantially larger wages if permitted by local Government', the Duke wrote to the Colonial Office on the 6th, 'racial feelings have been aroused on both sides, and it is this aspect of the situation which is causing me most concern.'[17]

As he pursued his investigations, the Duke quickly realized that the Riots had causes far beyond a mere wage dispute. They amounted to nothing less than an uprising against the whole political and economic system of Bay Street, which he had been fighting for two years to reform. It was remarkable that – apart from the half-hearted siege of the Board of Works – the mob in the town centre on Monday morning had spared all Government offices and vented its destructive rage on Bay Street business premises. Bay Street now blamed the officials for what had occurred: but the people really to blame were themselves.

The adviser who most influenced the Duke at this point was Hallinan, who had for some time been the main target of Bay Street bludgeoning and was now singled out for bitter attack. Bay Street wanted an inquest on the Riots which would pin the blame on the officials: if they had their way, the political position of the Bahamian Government would become weaker than ever, and reform would cease to be possible. Hallinan therefore urged the Duke to ask the Colonial Office to set up an independent commission of enquiry composed of judicial and colonial officers who had never served in the Colony. Such a body, it was reckoned, would surely discover and report that the root cause of the outbreak had been the oppressive Bay Street system; that the Governor and his officials had done their best to reform that reactionary system, and that it was not their fault if they had been forced to confront the sudden violent consequences of the obstruction of their attempts at reform.[18] The Duke readily accepted this advice, and resolved to announce at once that he was asking for an independent enquiry.

On Monday 8 June – 'After a whole week's close study of the situation [he wrote to London], and constant discussions with the Government officials, Executive Council, American contractors and negro labour leaders as well as consulting OC British forces and Commissioner of Police'[19] – he made an important broadcast to the Colony, this time very much his own work and in his own style.[20] His aim, as he told the Colonial Office, was to outline a policy which would take account of the just grievances of the malcontents and so prevent a recurrence of violence, 'without giving impression of weakness but emphasizing that further outbreak of disorders cannot be tolerated nor the way to bring grievances to my notice.'[21] His tone was paternalistic; he spoke to the people as beloved but unruly children who had misbehaved, castigating them for their misconduct, hoping they had learned their lesson, but assuring them that he was out to help them as their fatherly friend.

He began on a note of *l'ordre règne à Nassovie*: 'For several days there have been no acts of violence, and the community is slowly recovering from the terrible shock of recent events.' All the men had now gone back to work, as he always knew they would; but he was still deeply ashamed of them for misbehaving as they had. What sort of behaviour was that, after all he had done for them?

> Before the contractors started work on the Project, I and my advisers were everywhere seeking means to find work for the large numbers of our people who were unemployed. The prospect of obtaining work for two thousand men at four shillings a day would, a few months ago, have seemed too good to be true. But this has come to pass – and yet the advent of your good fortune has been made the occasion of an *outburst* unprecedented in the history of the Bahamas in our time.

In the hope that all was now well, he had decided to lift the curfew. 'On these hot summer nights it is uncomfortable, especially for people who live in small houses, to be confined indoors after 8 p.m.' But no further trouble would be tolerated, and other emergency measures – notably a ban on public assembly – would be continued. 'As the community is slow to recover, so must I be slow in relaxing the measures which have been taken to guard against fresh disorders, especially at a time when the armed forces must be ever ready to repel any action by the enemies with whom we are at war.'

With peace restored, he devoted himself to examining the grievances and complaints of the strikers. This was not easy.

> Unfortunately, the disorders of last week have greatly hindered my enquiries, for I now have to sift out and disentangle what may be legitimate grievances from what may be the work of agitators who are, I believe, in great measure responsible for the mob violence which everyone *now* so unanimously deplores.
>
> More especially do I deplore certain actions and statements which have tended to turn what is purely a labour question into an attempt to stir up racial animosity. I cannot denounce too strongly any such attempt to antagonize one section of the community against another in order to disunite the people of the Bahamas at a time when unity is a most essential part of defence. The subtle efforts of these agitators are directed towards replacing the normal atmosphere of Nassau with strife and bloodshed, and by heeding them you are playing into the hands of the enemy.
>
> We are all of us members of the British Commonwealth of Nations, whatever our race or creed. . . .

In these circumstances . . . every decision must be clearly dictated, not by violence or any threat of violence, but by the justice of the case.

He explained that the Government of the Bahamas, contrary to what the strikers had believed, had never had any say in the fixing of wages on the Project. 'I wish to say that the decision to pay local rates of wages . . . was made in accordance with a high policy far beyond the power of this Government to control.' But he *did* see the men's point of view. 'In the course of my preliminary investigations . . . I have discovered that . . . the job is heavy and arduous and that the contractors, in view of its urgency, require that it be pursued with unremitting energy. . . .' Since he knew the men could not easily feed themselves for such work on what they earned, he had persuaded the contractors to give them a free meal on the job; this would start on the morrow. But that was not all; the Duke assured the men that 'the possibility of departing in some respect from the local rate of wages is in my mind'. Since such a departure could not be made 'without reference to higher Anglo–American authorities', he hoped to return shortly to Washington – where his stay had been 'so abruptly interrupted by last Monday's riots' – to raise the matter with those authorities. 'I have good reason to believe that I will not return empty-handed,' he added.

He continued with an appeal for co-operation:

Above all, let us in the Bahamas refrain from seeking to lay the blame for recent happenings on each other, either in speech or in the press. Recriminations only tend to foster that spirit of bitterness which is, unfortunately, only too frequently the legacy of such events as those through which we have passed, and which it should be our duty to heal as quickly as possible. On the other hand I am determined that all those against whom there is evidence to show that they have taken part in acts of violence, wanton destruction and looting will be prosecuted and dealt with according to *law*, and it is the duty of all *law*-abiding citizens to assist the Government in these prosecutions.

Finally the Duke declared that he was asking the Secretary of State for a Commission of Enquiry, to be composed of 'persons from outside the Colony who will be able to pass impartial and unbiassed judgment based on the evidence I know we shall all be willing to give'.

This vivid discourse made a deep and favourable impression on practically all its listeners. It carried an air both of fairness and strength. The Americans were satisfied, realizing that the Duke was speaking softly and carrying a big stick. The coloured population felt both satisfied and chastened. They saw they had not been mistaken in regarding 'de King' as their best friend. They were much moved the next day when he appeared in person at the Project to supervise the distribution of the first free lunch. And yet the Duke had held out new hope to them in such a guarded and subtle manner that even Bay Street was reasonably satisfied for the time being – seeing that he 'meant business' on 'law and order', that he was determined to punish the ringleaders, and that he had saved the Project on which everyone's livelihood depended. The Duke, indeed, had achieved the near-impossible in satisfying practically everyone – for the moment. He telegraphed delightedly to London that 'my broadcast has met with unanimous approval and I am satisfied that the situation is taken care of, pending final adjustment of rates of wages.'[22] So settled was the mood of Nassau that it was decided to go ahead with the elections in the third week of the month, as if nothing had happened.

To be accurate, there was one party to the proceedings which was *not* satisfied, and which expressed its displeasure in no uncertain language. The Executive Council? Far from it: ExCo met every day after the Duke's return, and – although some of the Bay Street members were nervous of an independent enquiry – they supported every one of the Duke's decisions, with almost cringing subservience. The local newspapers? On the contrary: it was one of those rare occasions when the *Guardian* and the *Tribune* joined forces to cover the Royal Governor with gratitude and praise. The officials? Hardly: he was resolutely protecting them from their violent critics, and it was largely for their sakes that he had asked for an outside enquiry. The United States Administration? Absolutely not: when he met them a few days later, they were generous in congratulating him on his handling of the situation, and none more so than President Roosevelt himself.

The reader will by now have guessed who it was that failed to be enchanted by the Duke's speech. While all in the Bahamas were delighted, all in London – or, to be precise, in the Colonial Office, the Foreign Office, and last but not least a certain other institution separated from Whitehall by St James's Park – were horrified. They had been given advance notice of his broadcast, but not in time to stop him making it. What right had he, a mere third-class colonial governor, to say such things without first consulting them? The fact that he had dealt single-handed with a mass uprising and its immediate aftermath – left entirely to his own devices and receiving not the faintest hint of help, advice, or even sympathy from them – did not, in their view, give him any right to start making heroic addresses to the people, promising them all kinds of dangerous things! Who did he think he was?

Two things in particular alarmed officialdom, as Lord Cranborne told the Duke in an irate 'private and personal' telegram of the 9th.[23] First, the proposal to ask Washington for an increase in the men's pay. Where would this dangerous concession lead? An Anglo–American treaty had laid down the principle that Americans would employ local labour at the local going rate. Was the Duke now going to upset that important principle? The other unacceptable proposal was the official enquiry. The Colonial Office regarded this as totally unnecessary. 'Apart from the difficulty under present conditions of composing a Board of Enquiry from outside the Colony, I do not consider that the circumstances of the recent disturbances . . . really justify such a step, or that the causes of the riots, which in the light of your reports appear to be obvious, need further enquiry.' The telegram ended by ordering the Duke not to return to Washington but to remain in Nassau until further notice.

To this uncomprehending wire the Duke replied with the greatest impatience.[24] 'The handling of recent disturbances', he impressed upon the Secretary of State, 'has been greatly a question of timing and psychology.' To have delayed his broadcast would have been 'fatal': as it was, it had produced the best possible effect everywhere. As for the wage question, he honestly believed that the workers were entitled to better treatment, even under the Anglo–American Treaty; the Treaty after all provided for wages current locally for similar work, but in New Providence there *was* no similar work: the Project was more arduous than all previous undertakings. Therefore the Duke had arranged the free meal – 'with which the men appear fully satisfied' – and was now hoping to obtain in Washington a wage increase of one shilling a day. What incensed him most of all was the refusal to set up an independent enquiry, for

> . . . the merchants who have suffered financial loss and dominate the House of Assembly have rightly or wrongly aroused in the white population acute criticism of the Acting Governor for lack of precautions and weakness in handling of rioters. Demand for an enquiry is insistent and, owing to racial feelings which have been aroused, am certain that no unprejudiced board could be appointed locally, and I therefore urge that an independent commission . . . be nominated, for otherwise the House of Assembly, as soon as it is convened after the elections, will make its own enquiries, which would be bound to be strongly biased and result in an impasse between Government and Legislature.

The Duke did not add that all of his senior officials had threatened to resign if an outside commission was not appointed. It seems amazing that the Colonial Office, which was always well aware of the frightful political circumstances of the Bahamas, should ever have resisted so obvious a request.

The Duke's arguments had their effect: he was at once given leave to return to Washington – though told to 'stay his hand' there until he received further instructions through the Embassy.[25]

And so on Friday 12 June – accompanied by Sidney Farrington, the Executive Councillor whom he most trusted – the Duke returned to America, ten days after he had left it to attend to his Colony's troubles.

He was given a hero's farewell, with expressions of confidence from all quarters. ExCo passed a resolution giving their consent in advance to anything the Duke might agree in Washington.[26] Even Etienne Dupuch in the *Tribune* was unreserved in his praise:

> Today, when the balance has been restored, the feature which stands out above all others is the fact that it was eventually resolved into stability by the dominating personality of one man – His Royal Highness the Governor. . . . His Royal Highness approached the gigantic problem calmly and efficiently. He held conferences day and night. He acquainted himself with every possible aspect of the situation. . . . Today, when normal living has been restored, the community realizes that His Royal Highness handled a delicate situation with tact and dignity, resolution and authority. . . .[27]

By deciding to go back to America, the Duke was certainly taking upon himself an awesome responsibility. 'I have good reason to believe that I will not return empty-handed,' he had told his people. 'I am confident that you will deserve the trust I am placing in you to maintain law and order in my absence,' he had added, 'for no Governor can be influenced in his actions by the dictates of an unruly mob.'

'Everything is fine in Nassau now,' the Duke told reporters in Miami. 'Otherwise I would not be here.' Back in Washington, he went at once to report to Roosevelt, whom he had last seen at the White House with Secretary Knox and General Marshall at the midnight conference on 1 June. The President kept him for lunch and for three hours afterwards – the longest presidential lunch since Pearl Harbor, as the papers noted. The Duke later wrote:

> Trays were brought in by a Filipino manservant and the President became the soul of affability. After the coffee, not wishing to overstay my welcome, I made to bid goodbye to the President, saying that I had several other appointments that afternoon. To my surprise, he asked what they were and after jotting the names on a slip of paper, he called in an aide, gave him the slip and directed him to inform the individuals that I would not be coming because the President wanted to spend more time with me.
>
> For hours I listened while he talked on about all manner of things – from his experiences in integrating negroes into the armed forces, through his familiarity with the French countryside over which he had cycled in his youth, to the military reasoning behind the American decision to mass and train troops in Britain for the invasion of the Continent.
>
> He talked and talked. To this day, I haven't a clue as to what he really wanted of me. But from his occasional light questions as to my life, my experiences as King, I rather suspect it was because he, a man who had achieved on his own the highest summit of political power within a man's reach, was curious about the motives and reasoning of a man who could give up an inherited position of comparable renown.[28]

That evening, Lord Halifax found the Duke in a bad mood, and guessed – no doubt correctly – that it was because he had been away from the Duchess for so long.[29] The two weeks they had been apart were, indeed, their longest separation since their marriage, the fifth anniversary of which had found the Duke in Nassau on 3 June.

How had the Duchess fared during that separation? Anxious for him and wishing she could have accompanied him, she herself left Washington immediately after his dramatic departure and went with Aunt Bessie to spend a week with their relations in Maryland. On 8 June she arrived in New York, begging the press and police to leave her alone. ('The Duchess of Windsor is in town conducting an experiment with the dim-out,' wrote Inez Robb, 'but it is her own dim-out, not the City's, that interests the American-born Duchess. She hopes to be able to dim out her own neon personality until it reaches the point of invisibility.'[30]) She found herself among many friends – 'Doc' Holden, Katherine Rogers, Cordelia Biddle Robertson, Lady Williams-Taylor. She visited canteens and hospitals and relief societies. She saw *By Jupiter* – her first Broadway musical since childhood. She invaded the stores of Fifth Avenue and persuaded them to place orders for Bahamian shell-jewellery. But all the while she worried terribly for the Duke. He was able to send her nothing but brief reassuring messages, and the censored American press was allowed to make only a neutral official statement about the situation in Nassau. Detained in Washington by his negotiations, the Duke sent Farrington on to New York to put her in the picture. 'HRH's handling of the whole situation has been nothing short of masterly,' Farrington told reporters after his arrival, 'and there may be many who regret that it is only on such a minor scale and in such a small community that he has been able to display his talents.'[31]

The Americans were pleased with the way the Duke had handled things, and told him so in Washington. They liked his formula for settling the wage-dispute: since the free meal and the extra shilling were to be given in view of the unusual arduousness of the work, they agreed that the 'prevailing local rate' principle need not be infringed. But London, naturally, did not agree. 'I am inclined to doubt whether such a large flat increase as one shilling a day would be consistent with that principle,' telegraphed the Secretary of State, suggesting a maximum rise of sixpence.[32] The Duke replied that everyone, including the Americans, agreed that one shilling was a proper increase, and he doubted if the men would be content with less.[33]

On the 17th the Duke arrived in New York, to rejoin the Duchess at last. After a pleasant few days there, they returned together to Washington on the 23rd, the Duke's forty-eighth birthday. 'I thought he was in much better temper than when he was here last,' wrote Halifax in his diary. 'No doubt due to having been soothed after a week's companion-ship with the Duchess.'[34] The Duke had more than one thing to celebrate, for that same day the Colonial Office had finally given in to his proposal for the full shilling wage rise.[35]

Much to their delight, the Rogers agreed to return with them to Nassau. They all set out from Miami on the 27th, on board the *Gemini*. Their trip, as the Duchess recalled, was adventurous.

> . . . The Commandant of the Seventh Naval District, Rear-Admiral James L. Kauffman, whom I had known as 'Reggie' in Coronado,* had provided us with a sub-chaser as escort across the Florida Straits, and had also asked his air-patrol to keep an eye on us. All this was fine ; however, no sooner were we out of the harbour than a smashing, blinding tropical rainsquall hit us ; so hard did it rain and blow that it was like being in a heavy fog, but one made up of furious stinging particles. The glass windshield was shattered ; green water swished through the bridge-deck. The Captain, David and Hermann struggled to hold the bow up into the sea. Down below, in the cabin, Katherine and I sat on the sofa, clutching the table, expecting the boat to capsize at any moment. It was a dreadful hour. Then the storm lifted as quickly as it had struck. David looked around for our air and surface escort. There was no sign of either. We finished the voyage under cloudless skies and fortunately without further difficulty.[36]

During the Duke's latest absence, relative quiet had reigned in Nassau. There had been only one isolated violent incident, in which a soldier had killed a worker. In the House of Commons Mr Macmillan had made the error of taking questions on the Nassau Riots together with questions on Forced Labour in Nigeria, to be reminded by Heape that the two matters were not variations on the same theme.[37] In the Colony itself the main happening had been the elections, which (rather to the surprise of some observers) had passed off amid the traditional corrupt practices but otherwise without incident. It had not been expected that the new House would be much different from the last (which had been dissolved merely as a reminder that the Governor possessed the final power of dissolution) ; and in fact it was almost identical. If anything it was even more reactionary than the old one, for Bay Street (using 'mean and underhand methods', as the Duke later wrote to Allen[38]) had managed to unseat the most lucid and vitriolic of their opponents, Etienne Dupuch, in Inagua. In New Providence, where the secret ballot was used for the first time in the Colony's history, only four out of the eight seats fell to coloured men (who had previously held three), the new members including the Duke's friend the black jazz musician Bert Cambridge.

* A naval station in California which had been commanded by E. Winfield Spencer.

Yet hardly had the Duke returned than he had to face another local emergency. After the rough trip from Miami, they dined late at Government House in honour of Katherine Rogers' birthday. In her memoirs, the Duchess took up the story:

> . . . We had just finished the birthday celebrations when, from the veranda, we were startled to see flames leap up into the summer night over the centre of Bay Street. As we watched incredulously, the flames flared and spread. 'Good God,' said David, 'the whole town's burning up.' On the dead run he headed downtown, with the rest of us following as best we could. By the time we reached the scene an entire block, between Bay and George Streets, was in flames. Near the centre of the conflagration was my beloved Red Cross headquarters, already smouldering. . . .[39]

Bay Street was built of wood and burned beautifully. Casting aside all thought of self in this emergency, the Duke gave a display of those reckless heroics for which he had been famed in the First World War.[40] Followed by Holder the detective and Marshall the butler, he dashed into the burning buildings to make sure no one was left inside. Holder forcibly dragged him out; Marshall leapt from one burning rooftop to another and fell, injuring his spine. A group of young merchants appeared in dinner-jackets wandering home from a late-night party; they joined the Duke and Duchess and the others who were working 'like slaves in a chain' to save the stores of the Red Cross and the Island Shop. Finally Major Hayes and his men arrived with fire-fighting equipment from the Project; the Duke ordered them to dynamite the houses next to the imperilled Cathedral to create a firebreak. By dawn the conflagration was out. The Duke ordered quantities of fresh coffee to be brought down from Government House for all who had helped, and then, much to the general amusement, wearily sat down on a large box of dynamite.

It was an indication of the still nervous mood in Nassau that, as the Duchess wrote, 'all of us had a deeper fear that the fire was part of an insurrectionary plot . . ., that it marked the onset of another wave of sabotage and rioting.' The exhausted Duke alerted the Camerons for possible action, and summoned an emergency breakfast meeting of ExCo at Government House. But Erskine-Lindop burst in on them to say that the culprit had been caught – a merchant in financial straits who had hoped to collect the insurance by setting fire to his own property. Duly prosecuted and convicted ('one of the few things Bay Street ever thanked me for,' recalls Hallinan), the man was given seven years.

Having recovered from this melodramatic episode, the Duke once more broadcast to the Colony on 30 June to tell his people what he had achieved for them in Washington. He began by saying that 'the higher authorities' had been appalled by the disorders in Nassau, and had emphasized that the question of wages on the Project was not up to the Bahamas Government:

> Under these circumstances, it can be readily understood that my endeavours to obtain some increase in wages met with no little opposition [he tactfully did not say from whom], and at one time I feared that I might have to return empty-handed. However, I am glad to say that I was able, finally, to convince the authorities of my opinion that the unskilled workers on the project should receive five shillings a day instead of the present rate of four shillings. This I can assure you is no small achievement, for in the general scheme of Anglo–American co-operation on such war projects as the one we have here, the authorities are not easily persuaded to depart from the original policy they have laid down.[41]

That night, there was great rejoicing in Grant's Town. 'Sweet Papa HRH' had delivered the goods.

But in other quarters there was no rejoicing. Of the four crises which the Duke had faced in early June, only one remained. The Riots had been quelled. The workers had been satisfied. The Project was going ahead at full speed. But the political crisis with Bay Street was now intractable.

Now that peace and order had been re-established, the new House of Assembly were ready for war. Their previous opposition was raised to fever-pitch by three factors. They resented having been put to the expense of an election. They felt that the Duke, having made such concessions to the workers, had betrayed their interests. Above all, they had neither forgiven nor forgotten how his officials in his absence had (as they saw it) abandoned them to the mob on 1 June. The Bay Street men who had stormed up to Government House that day had sworn revenge upon officialdom; and those same men had just been re-elected to the House. Clinging to a seventeenth-century view of procedure, the House saw itself not just as a legislature but as a court of law, having the right to try Heape and Hallinan, Hughes and Erskine-Lindop, and even (oh dream!) to put them behind bars. The unopposed election of the Duke's arch-enemy Kenneth Solomon as Speaker removed any doubts there may have been as to the temper of the new Assembly.

The Duke as Governor confronted a gathering storm. He did what he could to head it off. He begged the Colonial Office, which had very reluctantly agreed in principle to the independent enquiry, to appoint a judge to head it without delay, so that he might announce it before the House went ahead with its own 'investigations'. But a suitable man was hard to find.[42] The first candidate offered to the Duke was turned down as he had once been Attorney-General of the Bahamas; the retiring Chief Justice of Barbados was then approached, but found to be senile. The Duke suggested Walter Monckton, who declined on the grounds that he

Government House, Nassau.

The Royal Governor at work in his office.

The Duchess's sitting room.

The Duke's bed-sitting room.

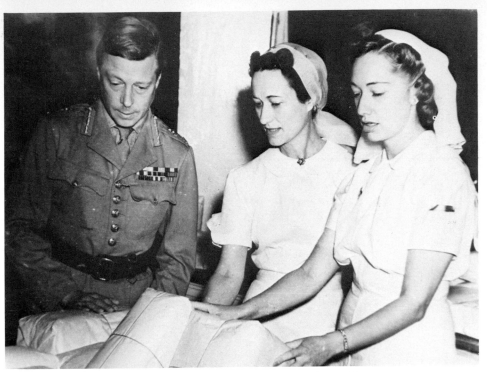

At the Red Cross, with Mrs. Godfrey Higgs.

Aunt Bessie in Nassau.

Miami, September 24, 1941. Going North.

Greeting fans from their train in the Midwest.

On the E.P. Ranch, with the Stony Indians.

Madison Square Boys Club.

Broadcasting after the Riots,
June 1942.

The Duke pours the first bucket of cement at the Project, Oakes Field, May 8, 1942. Behind him stand Sir Harry Oakes (left) and Harold Christie (right), with Sidney Farrington between them in the background.

With Major Hayes of the US Corps of Engineers on the site of the Project, August 1942.

The Out Island Conference, October 1942.

Duck shooting on Andros Island with the Bethell brothers of Bay Street. James Dugdale, the Duke's equerry, is on the right.

With Bahamian Laborers on the mainland.

was too well-known as a friend of the Duke. Bombarding London with largely unheeded telegrams about the urgency of the developing situation, the Duke finally delayed the issue by postponing the opening of the new Legislature until September.

He then took an extremely original step. Among the younger members of the House of Assembly, two clever young Bay Street lawyers stood out as obvious future leaders of their class. One of them, Stafford Sands, was wholly a local product. Fat and expressionless, greedy and amoral, devastatingly brilliant in thought and speech, he gloatingly led the onslaughts upon the Duke in the Chamber and was disliked intensely by the Governor and even more by the Duchess, who knew him as 'the grocer's boy'. The other, Godfrey Higgs, had also hitherto associated himself politically with the opposition to the Duke, but had been won over personally by the charm of the Duke and Duchess, who indeed liked him. Cambridge-educated and a member of the Inner Temple, he was then only thirty-five. This was the man the Duke chose to occupy not only the place on ExCo left vacant by the angry resignation of Solomon the previous December, but also Solomon's position as Leader for the Government in the House of Assembly.[43] 'Much younger than Solomon and better educated,' writes Hallinan, 'he had the smooth, affable, cosmopolitan manners of the well-to-do and moved easily among the rich British and American residents. . . . But he was neither as clever, forceful or influential as Solomon.'[44] Still, it was an inspired choice; and Higgs was to be the Governor's man in a sense that Solomon had never been. For the coming battle with Bay Street, the Duke had acquired the loyal (if slightly reluctant) services of one of the nicest and brightest among them.

Having thus prepared himself for the trials of the future, the Duke returned to the problems of the present. A good idea of these may be gathered from the letters written that summer by the Duchess to her Aunt Bessie.

16 July

Darling,
What a time I've had since our return. First of all the frightful heat which makes writing nearly impossible. . . . [The fire] has added to my work enormously – finding new [Red Cross] quarters etc. . . . The Rogers seem to like it here though there is nothing for them to do and poor Hermann still runs a temperature. They have all the biles and prickly heat. I am now immune to these things. The Project here makes many complications and we run out of things such as milk, ice, distilled water due to the enormous drain, and the island unprepared. Anyway one must expect that. . . . What war news – but I suppose all will be well. . . . I hear Halifax works continually against the Duke even to putting spokes in the wheels of things he tried to arrange for the Colony. . . . Funny people – they better get on with the war and not be so small.

27 July

Dearest Aunt B,

The Rogers left Sat. I am afraid the heat put up Hermann's temperature and rather dragged him down. He had no energy at all poor darling. I miss them a lot. They were no trouble and great company. . . . It's too hot – the island is crowded – everything gives out – we are 2 or 3 days without milk – and so it goes. You can multiply my first opinion of Nassau by 100 now! We have rented a new house for the Red X and open for business tomorrow. I am now busy trying to find a place for a canteen before the school [the RAF flying school] opens. I am glad you didn't come – first the heat and insects and secondly the discomforts in the way of shortages due to too few ships. I hope I can get away – but feel that unless I can accomplish something for Nassau I should stick to the job until the school is going. . . .

14 August

Darling,

This is to say happy birthday on the 19th. . . . There is no news here except that the 'wings' start arriving here next week – they'll get a hot welcome. Our 'kilts' leave at the same time. . . . I am busy with the men's club – which is going to be in the Bahamian Club which you may remember was the local casino in winter. . . . Do take care of yourself. We are rationed on *everything* now and the little car is a Godsend as it goes *weeks* on a gallon.

Reading between the Duchess's jolly lines, one senses that tempers were frayed at Government House that August. As the heat cracked down on Nassau, the town began to feel the first effects of overpopulation, shortages and rationing. The constant fear of new violence combined with the bitter political atmosphere to keep a suffocating tension in the air. The arrival of the advance RAF party to set up their Operational Training Unit at the as yet uncompleted Project was cheering, and gave both Duke and Duchess much to do. But the news from Europe and the Far East was dismal; it was the knife-edge moment of the war. The Germans were poised to fall upon Cairo and Stalingrad; the Japanese stood at the gates of India and Australia; America looked on with anxious eyes.

It was in the last week of that hideous August – when danger seethed under the outward calm of Nassau, and the heat gripped the town like some poisonous miasma, and no one could be sure that 1942 would not see the swastika fly over Leningrad, Jerusalem and Calcutta – that the Duke received dreadful news. Listening in his office to the BBC Empire Service on the afternoon of Tuesday the 25th he heard that his youngest brother, Prince George Duke of Kent, not yet forty, had been killed when the plane he was piloting crashed into a Scottish mountainside. At first the Duke refused to believe it; but confirmation, alas, came all too soon in the form of telegrams from Queen Mary and Lord Halifax.

The Duke was stunned by the blow, for they had been more than brothers. In a life which could never allow him equal friendships with his fellows, it was in Prince George – eight years his junior – that as Prince of Wales he had found his *fidus Achates*. The young Prince was spirited, intelligent, and strikingly handsome. But there was also a wild and desperate streak, and he showed the same recklessness in life as he showed in the air; he had a passion for sensations, and cultivated strange and exotic tastes. It was 'David' who had guided 'Georgie' between the Scylla of nameless desire and the Charybdis of the poppy-seed across the perilous seas of early manhood; and the younger brother in turn had adored and worshipped the elder. 'It can't be true! It isn't happening!' he cried in incredulous dismay, as the new Duke of Windsor left Windsor – for ever. They saw each other briefly twice in 1937, then never again. They might have met at Lisbon in July 1940, had they been allowed to; and they had hoped to meet in America in the summer of 1941, but unyielding hands prevented it. But even in bitter absence they never lost their affection for each other. The loss the Duke of Windsor now faced was the most terrible of his life.

A memorial service took place in Nassau on the 29th in a packed Cathedral, opening with *O God our help in ages past* and closing with *Fight the good fight with all thy might*. All the Government House staff and Government officials were there, and the officers of the newly-arrived RAF contingent and not-yet-departed Camerons. Vyvyan Drury recalled that the Duke 'broke down at the beginning and wept like a child all the way through. It was the only time I saw him lose his self-control like that.'[45] After the service the Duchess wrote to Aunt Bessie:

It is a most tragic death and I think his services will be greatly missed by Great Britain. He was the one with the most charm left at the job – and they made a couple more up with the advances of this world – in spite of the 'turn-coat' to us. We are both greatly shocked and distressed and it is so sad for her and the 3 little children.[46]

As the shock wore off, the Duke found himself plunged into the blackest despair. All the causes of anguish and bitterness which he had tried to forget during his two years in the Bahamas – the exile from his country, the ostracism from his family, the petty persecutions to which he had been submitted by 'Official England' – suddenly came flooding back to him. Even in desperate grief he could not be united with his family; while the death of the one among them who had meant most to him seemed to break the last link with his heritage. He could not face the world or work in the last days of August. The Duchess did what she could for him, and dealt with the letters of condolence which came flooding in. But even she was hardly able to console him. As she wrote in her memoirs: 'The sorrows of a man run deep; and in the soul of every man lie secret enclaves of affection and sentiment that are beyond the probing of a wife's perception.'[47] Intuitively she realized that what he sought in his distress – having lost the man to whom he had been closest – was a form of masculine companionship. Among the RAF officers who had lately arrived in Nassau was an old friend of the Duke, Herbert ('Tony') Pulitzer, the handsome and sophisticated heir to an American–Jewish newspaper fortune who had volunteered in both world wars as a British pilot. The Duchess arranged for him to stay for a while at Government House; and gradually in his bright company the Duke overcame his depression.

He was also cheered by the news that Walter Monckton, who happened to be in the United States as the guest of the American Bar Association, would be coming out to visit him that September. ('How glad we will be to see him and get the low-down,' the Duchess wrote. 'I'll bet it's low all right!'[48]) Monckton had been King Edward's chief adviser during the Abdication crisis; and now, ironically, he was also to be with the ex-King during the second constitutional crisis of his career.

14
Triumphs and Sorrows
of Government House
September 1942–May 1943

On this important occasion of the convening of the Legislature for seven years,
I wish . . . to remind the House that seldom has it been convened at a more
critical time in the history of the Colony. . . . Since I dissolved the Legislature,
the Colony has experienced the unprecedented spectacle of serious civil
disturbances. The true facts concerning the origin and incidents of the Riots
. . . will be the subject of a Commission of Enquiry, the appointment of which
has been agreed to by the Secretary of State. . . . From my three recent
broadcasts . . . the Colony has had an opportunity of knowing my personal
reactions to the whole regrettable incident. . . . Unpardonable as was the
method adopted of voicing possible grievances, and ruthless as must be the
method of preventing the re-occurrence of similar disorders, the events of the
first week of June must have given responsible elements in the Colony much
food for thought.

The date was 1 September 1942, ten weeks after the elections for the
House of Assembly; and at last the Duke was opening the new Legislature in Nassau.[1] He had hoped to delay doing so until the Commission of
Enquiry had begun its proceedings; but the Colonial Office, complacent
as ever, had not yet found a commissioner, and the Duke could delay no
longer. It was only a few days since he had received the shattering news
of Prince George's death; but somehow he had pulled himself together,
and finished the Governor's speech which he was now delivering to the
hostile and suspicious ranks of Bay Street.
  Penned as it partly was in his days of terrible grief, it was an unusually
strident speech. Speaking of the Riots, the Duke went as near as he
dared to placing the ultimate responsibility for them on the oppressive
policy of Bay Street. He deplored the fact that prices had been (and were
still being) kept so high, and wages so low; to the horror of the assembled
merchants, he proposed that tariffs be drastically reduced and revenue
raised instead through an income tax. He accused the leaders of the
Colony of being out of touch with progress and reality, failing in their

insular isolation 'to keep up with the trend of the times with regard to social development and welfare', and spoke of a consequent 'feeling of frustration which I am experiencing – a feeling which is shared by many others who are working for the good of the community'. In language which he had not yet used in his two years as Governor, he demanded reform. He wanted far-reaching administrative changes, he wanted better salaries for officials, and above all he wanted to stimulate agriculture in the now desperately languishing Out Islands. 'In order that these islands be not submerged by the very waves which beat upon their coral-reefs, there must be a drastic change in the psychology both of the legislators and the people to whom they are responsible.'

The Duke concluded:

When in response to my command the Speaker Elect entered this Chamber, he . . . laid claim by humble petition to their ancient and undoubted rights and privileges. To this claim I gladly acceded, for to preserve parliamentary rights . . . is one of the reasons why we are at total war today. But lest the too-rigid enforcement of these privileges ever tends to . . . deny to the people and the Empire some legislation that is not only advantageous but essential at this most critical time, I would remind you of one of the most recent of our eloquent and much admired Prime Minister's trenchant sayings, that 'We have no longer rights but only duties to perform.'

Few present can have had any doubt as to what the Duke had in mind in his reference to 'privileges'. Everyone knew that the House intended, as soon as it got down to business, to unleash a furious onslaught upon the Duke's officials, to hold them responsible for the June Riots, to disgrace them, to punish them, and (in every sense) to make them pay. A constitutional crisis loomed over the extent of the House's powers and how far it was prepared to use them; and the Duke could only hope that his counter-weapon, the Commission of Enquiry, would arrive before that crisis broke out. As he telegraphed to the Secretary of State:

Despite announcement in my speech . . . that official enquiry by judicial officer has been approved by you and should take place very shortly, House of Assembly are likely to appoint deeply prejudiced committee to investigate disturbances with power to call for persons and papers and with definite intention of pinning blame on Government.[2]

He therefore urged the Colonial Office to lose no further time in appointing and despatching the Commissioner.

It was almost too late. On 11 September the Duke wrote in his next despatch: 'Impasse between Government and Legislature . . . has now arisen as House of Assembly has now appointed Select Committee to enquire into Riots with power to call for persons and papers. . . . You will therefore appreciate urgency of request contained in my preceding telegram.'[3]

The Select Committee was made up of seven Members of the House, under the chairmanship of the gross and masterful Stafford Sands. As six out of the seven were Bay Street men, and four of them (including Sands himself) had been among the delegation that had sworn vengeance upon officialdom at Government House on 1 June, it can hardly be said to have been an open-minded body. It opened its proceedings by denouncing the as yet unappointed Commission of Enquiry in advance as a 'whitewash' – thus making it clear that its own advance intentions were to portray certain persons as very far from white.

It then proceeded to command the appearance before it of four officials: Heape, Hallinan, Hughes and Erskine-Lindop. This was the human sacrificial offering that Bay Street demanded from the Governor. These four hapless British colonial officials would take all the blame. What had they done? As Acting Governor and Police Commissioner, Heape and Erskine-Lindop had not, to be sure, shown all the resolution that they might; but then, they had been presented with circumstances which they could not possibly have been prepared for or foreseen. Hughes's great crime was that he had been unable to deal sufficiently rapidly with the labourers' complaints: since the House had refused to pay him a salary or give him any facilities or assistants as Labour Officer, this was hardly surprising. It was harder to find anything of which to accuse Hallinan: his role during the Riots had been merely passive, and after them he had shown vigour in pursuing the Crown prosecutions. But Bay Street was determined not to spare the most resourceful and hated of its official adversaries; and, ignoring the maxim *post hoc nec propter hoc*, its Committee pointed to the fact that it was shortly after the Attorney-General had spoken to the crowd in the Square that the strikers had started rioting in Bay Street.

On receiving their summonses from the House, Heape, Hallinan and Erskine-Lindop reported at once to the Governor.[4] Poor Hughes, who had but a vague idea of what it was all about, was on the point of writing to the Speaker accepting his summons – but was detected in time by Heape and prevented from doing so. The Duke was resolute in shielding his officials; he would not let them go near the House. He wrote to the Secretary of State:

Propose to refuse to make officials . . . or secret papers available to this Committee before Commission of Enquiry has reported, on the grounds that it will prejudice official enquiry and embarrass the Commissioner. Propose, in order to stall the final issue, to take the line that I reserve myself free to review the position after official enquiry has reported.[5]

But through this brave decision the Duke had precipitated the constitutional crisis, echoes of which were to reverberate through Whitehall for the next two years. Since the seventeenth century, the power of the House of Commons in London to 'call for persons and papers' had been virtually absolute. The Imperial Parliament could summon practically anyone other than the Crown in person; but the Crown could not prevent other summoned persons from attending, and any who refused to attend were liable to arrest and imprisonment for contempt. Did a colonial legislature such as the Bahamas House of Assembly, founded in the early eighteenth century on Stuart constitutional principles, have equivalent powers? The Colonial Office was far from sure. The legal authorities were scarce and conflicting. It was not until 1944 that the Attorney-General in London finally gave an opinion on the matter[6]; and even then many points were left vague, so that the British Colonial Empire was dissolved, and its old legislatures became subject to written constitutions, without much further clarification of the issue. The case will no doubt one day provide a rich field for the constitutional historian; but one cannot go into it here. Nor did the Colonial Office wish to go into it in September 1942. 'A very unpleasant situation has arisen,' ran the minute of the West Indian Department to the Secretary of State. 'We feel that the deadlock is more likely to be resolved by personal charm and tact than by force.'[7]

It was as he began to face this constitutional problem of no less complexity (if infinitely lesser magnitude) than the one that had confronted him six years before, that the Duke found himself joined by his old adviser Walter Monckton. Cut off and friendless as they were in the Bahamas, both the Duke and the Duchess were delighted to see him. 'He is in excellent form and is *in love*!' wrote the Duchess to Aunt Bessie.[8] 'But still has to be divorced etc.'* He gave them the first reliable inside news they had had from London for some time. 'He did not seem gloomy about the war,' continued the Duchess, 'but says at least 3 years. I feel I'll scream if one has to hear any more about it!'

The Duke naturally consulted Monckton about the recent crisis. Monckton advised the Duke to remain adamant in refusing to send his officials down to the House, and to rely legally for the time being on that splendid plea which the Common Law makes available to authority in distress, the argument of Public Policy. As the Duke wrote in his next

---

* Monckton was finally divorced in 1947 and married Bridget, Countess of Carlisle. He was dismissed from his post at Court, but reinstated two years later. On 8 December 1948 the Duke wrote to him : 'I wrote to my brother yesterday that I was interested in the announcement that he had reinstated you as Attorney-General of the Duchy of Cornwall. My comment was: "Apart from other considerations, one of my main objections to the official attitude towards divorce in Great Britain has always been the regrettable loss of the services of able and experienced men which are not infrequently incurred thereby." Maybe this subtle reminder of a stupid and untidy situation will not be disregarded.'

telegram to London: 'I consider it prejudicial to Colonial Administration in general, and to the morale of Colonial Officials in particular, that they should be subjected to the inquisition of a prejudiced tribunal.'[9]

On 17 September, after Monckton had left and before the Duke could receive a reply from the Colonial Office which (as he hoped) would back him up, matters were suddenly brought to a head by the development which had been dreaded – a threat from Kenneth Solomon as Speaker to order the arrest of the officials unless the Duke agreed to hand them over without delay. The Duke telegraphed to the Secretary of State: *Immediate private and personal reply urgently required. Can the House take any action against officials if the Crown refuses to order their attendance?*[10] Needless to say, there was no immediate reply to this frantic wire.

Writing to Aunt Bessie the same day, the Duchess did not mention the Duke's political troubles, which were, alas, far from being their only preoccupations.

> I hope Sept. is treating you with cooler weather – it is hot and sticky here – but it is always the worst – there is only a month to go before it improves. This really *must* be our last summer here. I see no reason not to insult us with a new job by June! . . . The cost of living has gone up beyond anything and I can't see how they are going to feed everyone – especially with everyone asking for a rise in wages due to rising prices. The two little boats are gasping for breath – leaping back and forth between Miami and here – and things are difficult to have. Would you send me 2 Virginia hams with the bill? We have no plans, tho' the Duke is pulling at the lead. I do not see much point in coming – the agony of the flight to Miami spoils it all for me. I am certainly no person to be marooned on an island. . . . If the food situation holds out and you are willing to fly I see no reason why you should not come here this winter. . . . Am written out really answering letters for the Duke – such a shock Kent's death.

She was nevertheless deeply conscious of the Duke's latest problem, and found a way to help him. As she wrote in her memoirs:

> One of the advantages of being a woman is that one does not have to become emotionally engaged in the peculiar combativeness that males bring to politics. Mrs Solomon . . . shared my views in this respect . . . and eventually I was able to produce the Speaker and his wife for a quiet, informal dinner. Although David began by being a little leery that a truce could be maintained through the evening, by the time the brandy had been passed and they had lighted their cigars, one would have thought that Crown and Parliament were on their way to becoming one and indivisible. . . .[11]

On 28 September the Duchess wrote to Aunt Bessie: 'Nothing new except that a judge arrives from England tomorrow to investigate the riots – but as his stay is of some duration we do not have to put him up at Government House. Very fortunate with all the white servants away. . . .'

At long last the Colonial Office had managed to dig out a retired colonial judge and send him to Nassau as Commissioner. He was Sir Alison Russell, a shrewd and affable former Chief Justice of Tanganyika and ideal for the purpose; but the Duke was told he would have to find two local men to sit with him. The Duke asked Solomon, now presumably mellowed by Government House hospitality, if he would sit with Russell and call off the House's enquiry; somewhat reluctantly, the Speaker refused. Now in a much stronger position, the Duke persuaded two much-respected Bay Street merchants who were outside the House – Herbert Brown and Herbert McKinney – to join the Commission. In response to public opinion, the Select Committee postponed its proceedings until the Commission had completed theirs. Though the constitutional question remained unresolved, the Duke had won the initiative for the time being. 'HRH seems to have managed this very well,' minuted an official at the Colonial Office. 'There is indeed the possibility of further trouble with the Select Committee when the Commission has reported but this may fizzle out and anyhow we now have an enquiry in due form and a breathing-space.'[12]

The Commission commenced proceedings in the Council Chamber on 5 October. It sat for eight weeks, examining ninety-nine witnesses. The Duke's relief was immense. Since he himself could have no part in the proceedings, he was relieved for eight weeks of the political crisis.

During those weeks he was far from idle. Never, indeed, had more matters claimed his attention. 'The Duke is very busy with this enchanting spot and its complications,' the Duchess admitted to Aunt Bessie on 16 October. 'The work has increased so that the "ballroom"* has become the typists' office and their room downstairs is a waiting-room.'

The issue of government which personally concerned the Duke most was the eternal question of the Out Islands. He was more convinced than ever that therein lay the whole key to reform. Bay Street had kept the islands poor while developing Nassuvian tourism; this policy had lured the increasingly desperate islanders to once booming Nassau, thus making the depopulated islands even poorer and the reliance of over-populated New Providence on tourism even greater. Now tourism had ceased, and Nassau was congested with 'immigrants' who had no cause to return to their own islands, where nothing awaited them but desolation. It was to this fact that the Duke attributed much of the capital's social restlessness: he had been much struck by the fact that most of the 'ringleaders' of the Riots had been Out Islanders. It now became the cornerstone of his local policy to make the Out Islands attractive and productive, not only to change the whole economic nature of the Colony

---

* There had of course been no Government House balls since September 1939.

but also to get the original populations to return there. In order to spread the new gospel of development and return, he summoned a great conference in Nassau of government commissioners, doctors, priests and schoolteachers from the Out Islands, whom he addressed in the gardens of Government House on 23 October:

> For the last two decades, a considerable but false prosperity built up on easy money has attracted . . . too many Out Islanders to Nassau, who have come to look upon this place as a Mecca in every sense of the word. . . . Unfortunate is the fact that all too many Out Islanders who were formerly content with their simple lives on their own islands have gotten [sic] used to the comparative comforts and attractions of the capital. . . . If they are expected to remain in their own homes their lives must be made sufficiently attractive to keep them there. . . .

Soon after, he submitted to the House a proposal for an Out Island Department in Nassau which would plan development along systematic lines.[13] The idea was all his own, and the project the one that meant most to him during his remaining time as Governor.

The Duke's plans for the Out Islands were necessarily long-term. Development would cost money, and the Colony was in debt in 1942. In the short term, what occupied him most in October and November 1942 was the imminent termination of the Project and the setting up at the end of the year of 'OTU III', which was likely to have two consequences of great significance to him as Governor. First, the Colony would be transformed into a major RAF air-base, with an establishment of at least 1,000 officers and other ranks and a rapid flow of trainees. In other words, the Bahamas would for the first time in history acquire an imperial importance. It need hardly be said that the Duke regarded the RAF presence (which had begun in August and increased steadily over the autumn) with delight. He at once struck up a warm friendship with the Commanding Officer, Group Captain Waite – a splendid and spirited figure who was later to mastermind the Berlin airlift. He worked strenuously to sort out initial problems over setting up the Unit, to get the two airfields finished in time, and to create the most efficient and excellent relations between the civil and military authorities, and the British and American establishments. But there was another side to the picture. With the Project near to completion, the problem of local unemployment would once again become serious and dangerous. As the Duchess wrote to Aunt Bessie:

> The negroes are busy *complaining* now that the base is nearing completion and some of them are being laid off. I should not be surprised to see more trouble – but this time one is somewhat prepared and there is enough fire-power on the island to deal with the situation.[14]

How was the coming unemployment to be averted or dealt with? The Out Islands, even if the Duke's schemes were accepted, could provide no work for at least two years. The Duke conceived three possible short-term solutions. First, the RAF might be persuaded to make large use of local civilian labour once the base was operational. Secondly, if OTU III proved to be a great success (as the Duke was determined it should be), it might be enlarged and extended, which would mean further work on the Project. Thirdly, he had hopes of inducing the United States to accept Bahamian labour in agricultural regions which had been stripped of manpower by the Draft. In October and November 1942, the Duke worked strenuously towards these three solutions, in the hope that one or two of them might be realized. In the event, he was to be far too successful – for all three of them were to come about.

Among the many routine affairs to which the Duke had to attend during his eight-week breathing-space from politics was the submission of names of local candidates for the New Year's Honours List. After submitting the local list to the Secretary of State, he could not resist writing to Churchill[15] asking him

> . . . to submit to the King that he restore the Duchess's royal rank at the coming New Year's, not only as an act of justice and courtesy to his sister-in-law, but also as a gesture in recognition of her two years public service in the Bahamas.
>
> The occasion would seem opportune from all angles for correcting an unwarranted step, taken, I will admit, at a time when feeling was still running high with regard to my Abdication, and in Coronation Year, when any action calculated to build up the King's position was considered justifiable, even to the extent of hitting at me where I was most vulnerable, which was to insult the lady who had consented to become my wife. I will be grateful, therefore, if you will make this submission to the King personally on my behalf, and inform me of His pleasure in the matter.

Churchill telegraphed in reply[16] that he had put the matter before the King, who was 'not willing to take action in sense desired. . . . I am sorry not to have more agreeable news but I hope Your Royal Highness will not attach undue importance to this point after the immense renunciations you have made.'

One person who certainly attached no great importance to it was the Duchess. The controversy over what she ought to be called was the very least of her worries that autumn, during which she worked as energetically as ever for the Colony but was not infrequently depressed. The hot, thundery weather continued right into November; and in her letters to Aunt Bessie she expressed repeatedly a feeling which will be familiar to all women who have been brought up in temperate climates and are later made to live in ultra-humid tropical ones. 'The boredom of being here months on end knows no bounds – and I wonder if I won't leave here mentally deficient,' she wrote on 16 October. And again on 23 October: 'I have a feeling I have written to you before to say my mind is going from too long here. . . .' But the Duchess was never one to dwell upon her melancholy, and her reaction was to find some new cause to which she could devote her extraordinary energy and organizational abilities. And one came readily to hand.

Ever since the spring of 1942, the Duchess had been planning to set up some sort of club in New Providence for the armed forces who were coming out to the island, 'to keep them out of the grape vine,' as she wrote to Aunt Bessie. Up to August the only regular troops there were the Camerons, and the US Engineers and Marines, in all about 300; but from August onwards RAF personnel began to arrive at the rate of several hundred a month. The urgent problem was how to feed them properly out of the Colony's limited imported supplies, and how to keep them amused in their spare time – of which they had a great deal, at least until OTU III got going. The Duchess decided to set up a canteen for the men. At first she wanted to do so through a patriotic organization of local women called the Daughters of the Empire; but at the end of the summer there was a terrible row among the women, many of the Bay Street matrons violently objecting to the Duchess's proposal that beer should be served to the men. The result was that the Daughters and the Duchess furiously began two rival canteens, competing in deadly earnest to finish first and do the better job.

Needless to say, the Duchess enjoyed the battle and easily won it. Fred Sigrist contributed premises – a club he owned on Cable Beach which had once catered to rich winter tourists. The Duchess had, indeed, an unfair advantage, since the Duke through his Washington connections could obtain privileged supplies from the mainland; but her speed and energy were nevertheless amazing. On 16 October she wrote to Aunt Bessie that she had been 'getting the canteen started and also working on an Xmas dance for the forces'. On 9 November, barely three weeks later, she announced: 'I am trying my best to get this canteen open – the workmen are supposed to go out today. It is an interesting job and I hope I make a success of it. Preparing for 600 men at a time is quite new to me!'

Her other main news on 9 November was that a hurricane had passed over the Bahamas:

> . . . Everything was battened down but it skipped us and went to Cuba instead. It hit Long Island – but not much damage was done. We are all back to normal and have only lost a few branches etc. and the salt spray had turned the foliage a bit brown. . . . It was sad Halifax losing his son. Do you hear rumours of a shake-up at the Embassy? Some one wrote me that there might be – but then

the world is a mass of rumours. One Ambassador is the same as another as far as we are concerned – the policy being set in 'Buck House'. Perhaps the war will end sooner now that we are able to step out – and then we will be released from this worrisome little island – where the Duke tries *so* hard, but the people are *impossible* to help or be helped.

The Allies were indeed 'stepping out' at last in November 1942: it was the month of crucial victories. In the first week 'Monty' overwhelmed the Germans at El Alamein, capturing 30,000 men including nine generals and 'sending the Germans out of Egypt at an equivalent velocity to the Chosen People but in the opposite direction.'* The following week saw the comparative success of Operation Torch, which brought French North Africa (except for the German stronghold of Tunisia) over to the Allies – and incidentally greatly increased the importance of the aircraft-ferrying role of such bases as the ones about to be completed in New Providence. In the South Pacific the Americans were turning the Japanese advance at Guadalcanal, while the fate of the Germans in Russia was being sealed by the arrival of Zhukhov's offensive and the snow at Stalingrad. 'The news is *so* good', wrote the Duchess at the end of the month, 'that I am *almost* packing my trunks.'

On the 27th came the further news that the French Fleet had scuttled at Toulon. The day before, two events of some local significance had occurred in Nassau. The Commission of Enquiry on the Riots signed their report and so terminated their proceedings. And the Duchess's canteen at last commenced operations.

The Commissioners' investigation had been thorough and they reported in some detail, beginning with an elaborate reconstruction of the events of 1 June. They found an easy victim in the form of Erskine-Lindop. 'We find ourselves reluctantly compelled to come to the conclusion that the Commissioner [of Police] failed to judge the position correctly and failed to issue the necessary orders to meet the position.'[17] He had dithered; when forced to action, he had acted indecisively; and after the final battle in Grant's Town, he had abandoned that township to the mob. 'No doubt the troops and police had had an exhausting morning, but we regret we must come to the conclusion that to withdraw all the forces . . . was an error of judgment.'[18] Erskine-Lindop was shattered by these strictures. He asked to be transferred to the army and sent to a battle zone – but this request was not granted, and so he was still Commissioner in Nassau when, eight months later, the Bahamian Police were for the second time during the war to be confronted with a nerve-racking crisis of large political implications with which they were utterly unequipped to deal.

* Philip Guedalla, *The Middle East: A Study in Air Power*, p. 215.

But the Report did not confine itself to an examination of the Riots themselves. It went on to ask the question: 'Are there any underlying causes which tended to lead to the disturbances?'[19] And it proceeded to a devastating survey of the whole rotten Bay Street system. As Hallinan – and indeed the Duke – had foreseen, by insisting on a post-mortem, Bay Street had put its head in a noose. In the last resort, they were the ones responsible. The Report's final strictures and recommendations were astonishingly similar to those which the Duke had laid before the new House of Assembly less than three months before. It called for the replacement of tariffs with an income tax; for modern labour legislation; for constitutional reform (especially a universal secret ballot); and for the rapid development of the neglected and languishing Out Islands.

The Duke sent the Report to London with his few comments.[20] He felt that Erskine-Lindop had been treated rather harshly, considering that after all he had been obliged to face unforeseen circumstances with a quite inadequate force. He recommended the deletion of a passage on birth-control, since 'while I am personally in favour of birth-control from a humane and social welfare viewpoint, the negroes ignorantly view this beneficial measure as a subtle way of gradually exterminating their race.' Finally he remarked on the Commission's finding that the Riots 'were not due to racial questions':

> ... I personally disagree profoundly. The discrepancy between American and Bahamas wage rates *was* only an excuse to make a vigorous and noisy protest against the local *white* population. I regret to say that the flame of local race antagonism is still fanned by a certain section of Bay Street on the one hand as an excuse for the continuation of a reactionary policy, and by negro agitators on the other hand who, but for the presence of a large military force and considerable firepower, would not hesitate to incite the negro population to further rioting on a larger, better-organized and more dangerous scale.

Meanwhile the Canteen was proving a success, much to the excitement of the Duchess. 'I really think it ought to make the boys quite comfortable,' she wrote to Aunt Bessie on 3 December. 'Life is still the same but much busier, which gives less time to regret that the Bahamas have entered into one's life so intimately!' She sent photographs of the undertaking. 'The different rooms are marked on the back – and there are 3 other reading-rooms of the same order – and a large bar and entrance-hall, showers and dressing-rooms for swimming. It all goes well so long as I can get the food to give at the rate of a ham and a half, 30 lbs of bacon and 35 dozen eggs per day – to say nothing of sandwiches, soft drinks, beer, orangeade and milk!'

On 11 December – the sixth anniversary of the Abdication, as it happened, and exactly two years after their first visit together to the mainland – the Duke and Duchess crossed to Florida for what they hoped would be ten days' holiday. But the Duchess could not relax; she dashed around hectically, organizing supplies for her canteen, buying Christmas presents for her staff, getting the prizes for the various seasonal entertainments she was arranging for the forces. On 30 December she wrote to Aunt Bessie from Government House:

> I have had a busy time since my return and I really was worn out by the shopping. My canteen has taken all my time giving them Xmas cheer etc., and when the hot turkey dinner is over New Years Night I shall be glad and relieved. We had 18 for dinner here Xmas Eve – lunched with the Bushs after the usual round of visits to troops, hospital etc., then at 6 had an Xmas tree party at the Canteen and gave presents from the tree to about 200 lucky ticket holders. I bought all the presents in Miami. . . . So there was the holiday. . . . I hope we can come north some time after Jan. and I really look forward to another summer here with dread. I do think even the Duke ought to take 2 months off – say Sept. and Oct. – and we could go to Hot Springs for a rest from here and from *housekeeping*. I do need it. . . .

What she could not write (on account of the military censorship) was that the Duke had opened OTU III that day, landing at the newly completed base at Oakes Field from a B25. Nassau's RAF station was to prove a tremendous success – as a training centre, ferrying centre and operations centre.[21] Its submarine-chasing and convoy role proved far more effective than expected. Its Transport Command station at Windsor Field became a vital link in the chain carrying men and planes across the Atlantic. It grew rapidly both in size and importance. By April 1943 (when the first trainees returned to England) it had a permanent establishment of 84 officers and 1,300 other ranks, with almost 400 pupils. A year later the establishment was over 2,000, and there were some 750 pupils – including pilots of the Czech, Polish and Dutch air forces. Its success was largely due to the inspiring personality of its chief, Group Captain Waite. But it was in some measure due also to the untiring supportive efforts not only of the Duke, but also the Duchess, who made herself responsible for the comfort of the men. As she wrote in her memoirs: 'One of the military censors confided in me that the principal item of news in the outgoing letters from the troops to their families was their accounts of having just finished a plate of bacon and eggs personally prepared and served by the Duchess of Windsor.'[22]

In the new year, the Duke wrote an affectionate and revealing letter to Aunt Bessie, from which she was distressed to learn that the Duchess had overtaxed herself and suffered a minor breakdown that December:

> . . . While it was mentally good for her to get away for ten days I am afraid she ran herself ragged Christmas shopping for her US canteen* and our large

* Known in fact as the UN Canteen.

GOVERNMENT HOUSE
NASSAU

January 24th 1943

Dearest Aunt Bessie -

I am very ashamed indeed for
not having written you before and hope you
will forgive me - I am delighted with your
Christmas present in the shape of those two
lovely pairs of golfing socks which apart
from your thought of me are very welcome as
a comodity which with many others is
rapidly reaching the stage of non-existance
in Nassau -

Wallis I know gives you our news
such as it is (and by kind permission of the
U.S. Censor!) and enjoyed talking to you from
Palm Beach and Miami last month - While it
was mentally good for her to get away for
ten days I am afraid she ran herself ragged
Christmas shopping for her U.S. Canteen and
our large retinue of servants and hangers-
on who expect presents, wartime or no -
The result was somewhat of a collapse upon
our return and there was no chance of

The Duke's letter to Aunt Bessie, January 24, 1943.

retinue of servants and hangers-on who expect presents, wartime or no. The result was somewhat of a collapse upon our return and there was no chance of resting up with Christmas and New Year's festivities for the troops and their preparation. You know what a perfectionist Wallis is and how she won't delegate much to others when she takes on a job and insists on supervising every detail and indeed doing most of the chores herself. Those wretched ulcer pains always get bad when she overdoes herself but I am glad to say these are better now as she has been taking it easier lately.

I on the other hand had a real vacation to which I felt entitled after more than a year without a 'let-up' and although too short I was able to play golf on those wonderful Florida golf courses and relax and forget all about 'governing'. The volume of work has just about trebled since I came here in August 1940 for apart from the actual administration there are all the wartime headaches such as defence and security and those connected with the presence of large numbers of the Armed Forces. Finally we have the negro problem which has become aggravated since the riots of last June and is not made easier by the attitude of 'some in high places' towards the question of race equality in America ! So one way and another I have no time on my hands although that is fortunate in this place which is picayune in every sense of the word.

As you know Wallis and I get pretty desperate here at times and wonder how long we can stick it out although as it is essential to have a job at the present time and we will never be offered a better one I guess we could do a lot worse and at least we are together which is vital and all-important to us. Besides although the climate of the Bahamas, while healthy, is trying and too warm as an all-year round diet, these islands have the *immense* advantage of being so near the mainland of America. Then as the war drags on one hears the rumblings of the international political clashes which must inevitably succeed the military operations and who knows that we are not fortunate in being able to keep out of the sordid political squabbles that are alas the aftermath of still more sordid war ? So taking it all in all one must be philosophical and not complain for the whole world is 'marooned' some place and when one reflects upon the sufferings of so many millions we should actually count ourselves as very fortunate so far.

We are very sorry you have decided against a visit to Nassau this winter but with the difficulties and discomforts of travelling nowadays I am sure you are right. But the weather has been perfect this month and would be a relief from the extreme cold I know you are having in the North. With much love from us both

Believe me yours very affectionately

EDWARD

The Duchess hastened to reassure her aunt, who had at once written to Nassau in a tone of worried concern. 'I am really feeling better than I have for years at the moment,' she wrote on 5 February. 'Naturally if you have an ulcer and become tired you have an attack – and I got exhausted with all the Xmas things here and tearing around Miami shopping for them besides getting up at about seven a.m. and going to bed about two – but instead of going to bed here for 3 days and curing myself I continued with the job in hand, and was *not* looking or feeling my best. . . . As soon as I got a few days I rested and all was well. I knew exactly what to do and should having had the ulcer since 1928 !'

By the spring she was back in the full flood of war work and domestic problems. 'Everything OK here – lots of work, lots of bridge, lots of servant problems. I don't think any of the white ones will take another summer – and I don't blame them.'[23] The canteen was a wild success and her pride and joy ; but there was much else to do on the home-front. 'I am busy helping the Bishop with a raffle for a fund to aid the leper colony, and also we are requested by England to have another Aid to Russia drive !'[24] She complained about the mail. 'It took *20* days for a letter from Miami the other day and some parcels shipped from NY *Nov* 9th arrived yesterday. Even when we were in Paris and the Germans at the back door the mails were better than that. . . . Perhaps that's why the back door gave way so easily ? But one does expect efficiency in America.'[25] The censorship also annoyed her :

> I know my letters are opened by the US censor even though they are stamped by the Chief Censor here. . . . I begin to think I'm Mata Hari ! Anyway it doesn't make any difference except that it delays everything, and reading the tripe that passes back and forth between my friends and myself must be a great waste of the censor's time – but if the censor is a spinster it might be entertaining as I am being treated to all Mai's love troubles by way of post. It has another drawback for should I want to discuss my stomach trouble with Dr Martin I would feel hesitant at laying all the facts before others than the medical profession. . . . It's not the English censor who opens them – it's my own countrymen that enjoy (?) my brilliant efforts.[26]

She still had not infrequent moments of exasperation and depression. 'We are doing the same things and somehow the time passes. It's like being in jail or a prisoner of war – for this latter is what we really are. I see no relief until the end of the struggle and must try not to worry myself to death trying to be a General Giraud and escape.'[27] But her spirits rose at the prospect of spending May and June in the United States.

The early months of 1943 marked the apogee of the Duke of Windsor's Governorship of the Bahamas. 1942 had been a year of triumph in the face of trial. Up till then, he had done a good job in what was considered by many to be the toughest post in the Empire. But since Pearl Harbor he had saved the Colony from starvation, settled a serious civil disturbance, presided over the smooth transformation of New Providence into a humming war-base, and got the better of his enemies in a bitter political crisis. Nassau in January 1942 had been on the way to becoming a ghost town, bereft of work or trade or resources or any likely future, a place of fears and tensions, a place moreover without defences. In January 1943 its little streets were thronged with American GIs and British airmen, business was booming again and all was calm. When Sir Cosmo Parkinson, Permanent Under-Secretary at the Colonial Office, visited Nassau that month, he did not deny the Governor praise[28]; and if the Duke had been allowed to depart for good in May 1943 to give more worthwhile service elsewhere, instead of being obliged to stay on for two more bitter years, his time in Nassau would have been recognized as one of the most successful episodes in twentieth-century colonial administration.

What made the new year of 1943 particularly triumphant was the publication in the Bahamas of the Report of the Commission of Enquiry, which supported in every detail his own plans for the reform of the Colony. Bay Street was now on the defensive. The House's Select Committee on the Riots (before which the Duke still refused to send his officials) continued its sittings; but in the end it drafted little more than an apologetic reply to the Commission's Report. True, it pinned all the blame on the officials, and claimed that there had been no deep-rooted causes. But then it proposed some concessions (such as the labour legislation which had been current in England in 1900) to stem the tide of reform. As the Duke wrote to London, Bay Street would never have contemplated even these concessions but for the Riots – and there in a nutshell were the deep-rooted causes.[29]

In the winter and spring of 1943 the Duke added a further achievement to his record. For some months he had been addressing himself to the problem of maintaining employment once the Project was finished. Learning from American visitors of serious agricultural labour shortages in the United States, he at once set to work with his contacts in Washington. Mexican labour was being used in California; why not Bahamian labour in Florida? Coert du Bois, head of the Caribbean Office of the State Department, flew out to Nassau in October 1942 to explain to the Duke why it was not feasible; duly won over, he returned to Washington to prepare a draft treaty on the subject, hoping that the labourers would come over in time to save the Florida winter harvests. Such was the origin of the Bahamas Labour Scheme.[30]

It was only when the proposal for the Scheme was communicated to London that the real trouble began. Both Foreign and Colonial Office reacted with alarm to this private initiative of the Duke; there was a strenuous attempt to find serious fault with it. The Foreign Office sent a secret despatch to the Embassy in Washington: could they confirm that the Scheme might cause political controversy in the South? Alas no, replied the Embassy; the labour shortage was desperate and everyone wanted the Bahamians to come. The Colonial Office meanwhile bombarded Nassau with objections. Would this not cause agriculture to be neglected in the Bahamas? It was as yet almost non-existent, replied the Duke, and his own Out Island Development Plan could only slowly absorb surplus labour. Did the terms of the proposed agreement adequately protect the labourers? Bahamians were already working happily in America under these terms, replied the Duke. The Foreign Office then returned to the fray and announced that its consuls could no longer deal with the Scheme as originally hoped; the Duke assured them that his own Labour Officer Hughes could handle the thing. Finally permission was reluctantly granted. The Agreement between the Bahamas and US Governments was signed at Government House on 16 March, and the Scheme announced by the Duke in a broadcast of 4 April. Recruitment began the following day, and by the end of the month some 2,500 labourers had flocked to Florida to pick the annual bean crop.

The Scheme was an immense boon to the Colony.[31] It helped save Southern agriculture during the war (the Bahamians in America, as the Duke had predicted, turned out to be excellent workers); and it certainly saved much of the Colony's population from near-starvation. Altogether, over 8,000 Bahamians were recruited for work in America between 1943 and 1946, priority being given to the inhabitants of the most desperate Out Islands. Earnings were phenomenal by Bahamian standards; and under the terms of the Agreement at least a quarter of the wages earned had to be remitted to savings accounts in the Colony, thus bringing in needed dollars and ensuring the welfare of dependants left behind. Stewart Lack, a young British security officer who arrived in the Bahamas that spring and was involved in monitoring the Scheme, recalls: 'It was an intelligent and imaginative idea, and so far as I know the Duke's own. I think he would dearly have loved to have gone further, but didn't get the support, encouragement and advice he was seeking.'[32]

The spring of 1943 also saw the arrival in Nassau of an extraordinary figure whose influence was to affect the Duke profoundly in the weeks and months to come. Professor J. Henry Richardson of the University of Leeds and the International Labour Office at Geneva, author of such works as *British Economic Foreign Policy* (1936), a world expert on the technique and psychology of negotiation between capital and labour, had lent his services to the Colonial Empire for the war. He had just served with remarkable results as Economic Adviser to the Government of Bermuda; now he appeared in the same role in the Bahamas. This masterful intellectual, with his quick and lucid assessment of the local situation and its inherent hopelessness, quickly became the Royal Governor's right-hand man; the Duke came to rely on his advice on all subjects, and no official had more influence with him. Above all, Richardson explained to the Duke in a thoroughly reasoned manner what he had always believed and most certainly wanted to hear – that he was completely wasting his time in the Bahamas, and had achieved all he possibly could there.[33] And so, from a position of undoubted success, the Duke's thoughts longingly returned to the subject of a change of post.

There were posts for others. Rumour had it that Queen Elizabeth's hedonistic brother David Bowes-Lyon, who had turned up in America on a mysterious mission, was to succeed Halifax as Ambassador. 'I hear H. may leave and the brother of the lady who is so *kind* to me may come in his place,' wrote the Duchess to Aunt Bessie on 18 March. 'Most uncomfortable forces I fear.' In fact Bowes-Lyon had come to take over the political warfare and propaganda work of British Security Co-ordination in New York – somewhat to the dismay of the legendary spymaster Intrepid, who considered the appointment an unsatisfactory one from the point of view of Anglo–American relations.[34] Around this time too the question arose of who was to succeed Lord Gowrie, long due to retire as Governor-General of Australia. The Duke of Kent had been due to do so, but now he was dead. A rumour swept Australia that the Duke of Windsor was being considered for the appointment. The Labour Prime Minister Mr Curtin, who as Leader of the Opposition in 1936 had supported King Edward in the Abdication crisis, was asked at a press conference whether there was any truth in this rumour (which excited favourable comment in much of the Australian press). He replied enigmatically that the appointment of Governor-General required the approbation not only of the Australian Government, but also of the British Crown.[35]

Observing these developments with sceptical curiosity, but filled as usual with the cheery optimism which sustained him through his trials, the triumphant but weary Royal Governor of the Bahama Islands prepared to face Washington once again – for the last time, he hoped, in his present role.

15
No Prizes for Doing Well
May–July 1943

On 9 May 1943 – the day that saw the rout of the last German forces in Africa – the Duke and Duchess set out on their third American tour. They visited Bahamian labourers in their camps near Lake Okochobee in northern Florida and at Swedesboro, New Jersey: the Duke was delighted to see how well they were getting on, and his much-photographed inspections made a great splash in the press. In New York he saw executives of General Foods Inc. about the possibility of their setting up extensive fishing and canning operations in the Bahamas; in Washington he had business with the British Colonies Supply Mission, and attended conferences at the offices of the Anglo–American Caribbean Commission about the progress of the Bahamas Labour Scheme. The British Chairman of the Commission reported back to London that the Duke's tour of the camps had been a great success, and that the scheme had received excellent publicity.[1]

Churchill was in Washington, refreshed after a holiday at the President's mountain retreat in the Catochtin Hills of Maryland. He was in the United States to discuss the next stage of the war with Roosevelt following the victory in North Africa. On the afternoon of 19 May he addressed Congress. The Duke and Duchess went to hear him from the diplomatic gallery; Mackenzie King and Malcolm Macdonald were there, and Churchill's physician Dr Wilson, soon to be created Lord Moran. Moran recorded in his notorious diary: 'As the Duke descended to his seat in the front row, he got as much clapping as Winston, or more, by which we were surprised.'[2] All the newspapers noticed it too, and that Churchill seemed annoyed. The speech was a difficult one, made at a delicate moment. It was in part a victory speech:

The African excursions of the two dictators have cost their countries in killed and captured 950,000 soldiers. . . . There have also been lost to the enemy 6,200 guns and 2,550 tanks and 70,000 trucks – which is the American for lorry and which I understand has been adopted by the combined staffs in north-west Africa in exchange for the use of the word petrol in place of gasoline.

But Churchill spoke as anti-British sentiment was ominously growing in America. There was much difference of opinion not only as to future strategy but also as to division of effort and resources between Europe and Asia. Churchill sought to reassure the Americans that the British had as much interest as they 'in the unstinting and relentless waging of war against Japan. I am here to tell you that we will wage that war side by side with you . . . while there is breath in our bodies and while blood flows in our veins.' The speech received a standing ovation and was judged to have had a most successful effect; but some journalists could not resist remarking that the presence (so loudly applauded) of the Duke of Windsor, 'Great Britain's best advertisement in America', had redounded to the success.

The Duke had two long private meetings with Churchill in Washington that week. They talked much about the war, and they talked of his post. After three years in the Bahamas, the Duke now absolutely wanted a change. He recalled that he had been assured, in July 1940, that Nassau – should he acquit himself well there – would lead to greater things. Had he not done well? Yes, agreed the Prime Minister, he had done well. The Colonial Office thought he had done very well. President Roosevelt thought he had done well. The Duke deserved a change of job; Churchill would do his best.

It is sometimes said that Churchill never had any intention of giving the Duke a responsible position at any time during the war. As Moran wrote of the Prime Minister's attitude: 'It is not Winston's habit to live with his mistakes. He is a very loyal servant of King George and is no longer . . . interested in the Duke.'[3] (This is not the first time one has noticed the curious assumption that loyalty towards the King should involve an element of hostility or at least indifference towards his predecessor.) But reading their correspondence, and considering their close and confidential friendship after the war, it is hard to believe that Churchill had lost his respect and sympathy for his former King, or was insincere in his expressed desire to improve his lot. He honestly would have liked to do something for him. But Churchill was a man of power, and he realized that – increasingly criticized as he was – his power and image largely rested on the continued close personal support of the King and Queen. That support (which had not at first been enthusiastically given) was not without its conditions – the first being that the Court should always decide the Duke of Windsor's fate.

Thus it was that Churchill – having consulted the Colonial Office, the Foreign Office, the American Government, and above all the Palace – returned to the Duke a few days later to offer him the Governorship of

Bermuda, made vacant by the appointment of Lord Knollys as Chairman of BOAC. As in July 1940, he regretted not being able to do better. He required an answer almost at once.

It was a very hard decision. Bermuda was definitely a promotion – but then, since Nassau was generally regarded as the pettiest, the most difficult, and the most unpopular governorship in the service, it was hardly possible to be demoted from it. Bermuda was even smaller and more remote than the Bahamas, with half the population, really nothing more than a great inhabited rock in the middle of the Atlantic; but it was a lush rock in contrast to the barren coral of the shallow seas. The climate was more temperate. The political problem – Legislature versus Government – was similar, but far less acute; over half the population was white (or more or less), so that the powerful local group was not so very unrepresentative. Bermudian colonial history was older and more glorious than Bahamian. Hamilton had the oldest colonial legislature in the British Empire, and had been a bastion of order at a time when New Providence was a haven for pirates. Above all, as the principal Station of the American and West Indian Squadron of the Fleet, it was a historic centre of British sea-power. Admiral Fisher had once commanded there; numerous seafaring royalty (including the future King George V) had served there. In the Second World War it was of great importance as an air and sea base and communications centre. Following the Destroyers–Bases Agreements of 1940–1 the Americans (much resented at first by the local population) had set up massive installations there.

After some days of agonizing reflection, the Duke turned down the offer. It is not hard to see why. As he wrote to his solicitor George Allen: 'Winston does not seem to have got my meaning of a move.' For such a comparatively small rise on the colonial staircase, it was simply not worthwhile starting all over again – getting to know a new set of faces and problems, beginning new ventures, making a new home. At least they were thoroughly familiar now with the smallness and frustration of Nassau, where their regime at Government House had become well-established and accepted. Furthermore, while Bermuda was over 500 miles from the mainland, Nassau (as the Duke wrote to Allen) had 'the immense advantage of close proximity to the United States, which . . . constitutes one of the distinct benefits of life in this otherwise lousy little island upon which we have been marooned for far too long!'[4] The Duchess wrote to Aunt Bessie: 'I am convinced that the Duke was perfectly correct to refuse. . . . I can't see much point in island-jumping. I'm for the big hop to a mainland.'[5]

While the Bermuda offer had the result of resigning the Duke to another year of Nassau, it had another extremely painful effect. As the Duchess put it in her memoirs: 'It was now clear beyond all question that

David's family were determined to keep him relegated to the furthermost marches of the Empire.'[6] As after the death of Prince George, the Duke of Windsor, usually stoically philosophical in the face of the attitude of his family, suddenly gave way to a flash of terrible bitterness and depression. He had done a cruelly hard job in especially difficult circumstances as well as any man, yet even now he was to be allowed no more than a transfer from one remote island to another, even more remote. Such a choice seemed crueller than no choice at all; and the Duke miserably reflected (as he tried so hard not to do) upon the years of petty persecution, the pitiless machinations to keep him out of his country and down, the ruthless protocol which gave the Duchess the unique privilege for the wife of an Englishman of not sharing the dignity of her husband's rank. On 2 June, the eve of their sixth wedding anniversary, he could contain his anguish no longer, and for the first time in three years he drafted a letter to his brother the King,

> . . . in an attempt to bring you to your senses with regard to your attitude towards my wife and myself.
>
> Winston told me that you and he lunched together once a week and he described you as unhappy over this family estrangement . . . and asked me whether there was anything *I* could do towards improving relations between us.
>
> Now I must say that I was *amazed* at this information and especially his enquiring as to what part I thought I could play in this shake-hands-forgive-and-forget act, for no one knows better than you and Winston that I have taken more than my fair share of cracks and insults at your hands and that notwithstanding your belligerence I suffered these studied insults in silence on the supposition that they were a necessary part of the policy of establishing yourself as my successor on the throne.
>
> Granted that the first year or two cannot have been too easy for you – I can see that – but ever since I returned to England in 1939 to offer my services and you continued to persecute [me] and then frustrate my modest efforts to serve you and my country in war I must frankly admit that I have become very bitter indeed.
>
> The whole world knows that we are not on speaking terms which is not surprising in view of the impression you have given via the FO and in general that my wife and I are to have different official treatment to other royal personages. . . .*

Meanwhile, in other official quarters in London, the Bahamas were attracting profound and critical attention. The Report of the Commission of Enquiry – with its damning indictment of the local white establishment and its attitudes – had been published in Great Britain, and read with

---

* The pencil draft (a page of which is reproduced on p. 297) is among the Duke's papers. As with the letter to Churchill of October 1940, it is hard to say whether this letter was actually sent, or whether the Duke merely drafted it (as was occasionally the case) in order to relieve his feelings.

I suffered these studied insults in silence on the supposition that they were part necessary part of the policy of establishing yourself ~~you~~ as my successor on the throne —

Granted that the past year or two cannot have been too easy for you I can see that — but ever since I returned to England in 1939 to offer my services and you continued to persecute and then frustrate my modest efforts to serve you and my country in war. I must frankly admit ~~say~~ that I have become very bitter indeed —

The whole world knows that we are not on speaking terms. which is not surprising in view of the impression you have given via the F.O. and in general that my wife and I are to have different official treatment to other royal personages

Pencil draft of the Duke's letter to the King (second page).

some disquiet by men of liberal views. On 15 April the annual Supply Debate on Colonial Administration in the West Indies took place in the House of Commons in an atmosphere of more than usual excitement. Most of the speakers referred to the Bahamas and, while the Royal Governor received warm praise from both sides of the House, deep concern was expressed about the social and political condition of the Colony. Mr Sorensen, the radical Labour Member for West Leyton, scandalized the Tory benches by suggesting that the riots had been praiseworthy in that they had advanced the cause of reform;* though he added: 'I would like to express my appreciation of the efforts of the Governor of the Bahamas, the Duke of Windsor. Unfortunately his efforts have been frustrated, but I would like to congratulate him on the action he did take and the motives which preceded that action.' Colonel Oliver Stanley, a son of the Earl of Derby and sometime political friend of Sir Oswald Mosley who had succeeded Cranborne as Secretary of State in November 1942, assured the House that the Governor would very soon be inviting the local Legislature to adopt progressive legislation. But as Dr Morgan, the Labour Member for Rochdale, asked: 'What would the Colonial Office do if this high-franchised Legislature declined to accept the recommendations of the Governor?' Would Westminster then change the Bahamas Constitution? Stanley replied enigmatically that the Imperial Parliament always had the power to do so.

The debate stimulated much public and press comment, most of it respectful of the Duke but violently critical of the Bahamian *status quo*. The May issue of Sir Charles Petrie's *Empire* – hardly a radical journal – declared in a leader:

> . . . We share Colonel Stanley's hope, but are still not satisfied that under the present franchise and constitutional arrangements, the 'modern outlook' for which he looks will be forthcoming. Without fundamental changes in the Constitution there will continue, at the door of America, a British Colony based on an undemocratic government, serving the interests of a narrow minority, and impervious to far-reaching reform. . . .

The Duke returned to Nassau from America on 30 June to find awaiting him an extraordinary 'Secret and Personal' letter from the Secretary of State.[7] Dated 12 May and the result of long secret discussions at the Colonial Office, it was sweeping in message and urgent in tone. Colonel Stanley warned that 'there is no doubt that there is a genuine feeling on the subject of politics in the Bahamas, which may well develop into very outspoken criticism unless appeased by substantial measures of reform.' He pointed out 'how the continuance without change of a pre-Reform Bill

---

*This statement – for which Mr Sorensen was made to apologize – was not so very different from the views of the Duke himself! See above, p. 290.

Constitution coupled with a pre-Reform Bill mentality might lead to trouble of the worst kind.' He continued :

> I do not think responsible non-officials in the Bahamas should be in any doubt as to the feeling which is certainly growing up here. Unless they can show, and show fairly soon, that the Constitution which they have inherited is capable of meeting the exigencies of a changing world, then that Constitution, however venerable, cannot be expected to survive.

The Imperial Government accordingly demanded rapid and sweeping reforms. Unless the social reforms recommended by the Commission of Enquiry were implemented in full, the Bahamas would not receive the grants-in-aid which might otherwise be forthcoming under the Colonial Development and Welfare Act. But above all London insisted upon the constitutional reforms which Bay Street were resisting, for 'a refusal to make permanent the vote by ballot and to extend it to the Out Islands seems incomprehensible and certainly over here indefensible, while in the modern world the absence of an income tax law, which has just been introduced even in the West African Colonies, is certainly hard to understand.'

What is so extraordinary about this letter (which appears to have been drafted several times so as to make the language as strong as possible) is that in June 1942 – exactly a year before – the Duke had personally succeeded in getting a Commission of Enquiry appointed in the face of opposition from the Colonial Office and Foreign Office. But now that the Commission had reported – and the Duke was pursuing a moderate and conciliatory policy of gradual reform while trying to calm the political situation – here was the Colonial Office, so recently nervous of stirring things up, suddenly going off the deep end and stridently requiring the Royal Governor to take the offensive against the local establishment and force on the Colony a programme which was little short of revolutionary.

'I know how anxious Your Royal Highness is, and how much Your Royal Highness has done, to avoid a head-on collision between a reactionary Legislature in the Bahamas and a more progressively-minded Imperial Parliament,' continued the Secretary of State ; but 'I do not believe there is any hope of the Bahamas retaining their Constitution unless they put their house in order. . . .' The Government did not want to have to introduce legislation at Westminster to revoke the Bahamas Constitution and thus impose reform by force, 'but if anybody in the Bahamas thinks that such action by the Imperial Parliament is out of the question or so remote a contingency that it can be ignored, they are living in a dream-world.'

In other words, the Royal Governor – who had been brought up to stay away from all contentious politics – was being instructed to have a massive and decisive confrontation with the local powers; and he was wondering how on earth to go about this when, at seven o'clock on the morning of Thursday 8 July 1943, he was informed of the discovery of the charred and battered corpse of Sir Harry Oakes.

16
Violent Death
July–December 1943

The Duke and Duchess had seen a great deal of 'the richest baronet in the Empire' since they had been his guests at Westbourne in the autumn of 1940. This was hardly surprising. Sir Harry Oakes was by far the most important man in the Bahamas. As well as being the Colony's richest resident, he was its principal benefactor and biggest property owner and private employer. He owned a third of New Providence. Having a hand in virtually every productive enterprise in Nassau, he wielded more influence with Bay Street than any other 'outsider'. It was inevitable that the Governor and his lady should be in constant touch with such a key local figure. What was not inevitable, but nevertheless came about, was that they should have grown extremely fond of him. Many people despised Oakes for his bluff, rough style. The Duke, 'always attracted to the pioneering type', was delighted by it, and by the fact that Sir Harry was 'too proud to give up in wealth his plain prospector's ways'.[1] Oakes (perhaps more surprisingly) also came genuinely to admire the Duke, and vigorously supported what he was trying to do for the Colony. The moderate success of the Duke's efforts to make the Colony productive was in no small measure due to Sir Harry's advice and personal enterprise – particularly during the grim economic crisis in the six months after Pearl Harbor, when Oakes did much to soften the hostile mood of Bay Street and to help realize the Duke's plan for an agricultural training camp.

Around this time, however, Sir Harry's life had begun to take a decidedly sombre turn. He was beset by financial worries; as a result of his massive philanthropies his once vast fortune was dwindling away, and could no longer be replenished by the Lake Shore Mine which – once the second richest in the world – was now close to being exhausted. (Hallinan was a little amazed by Lady Oakes saying to him after the murder: 'I don't think anyone realizes how little Harry left: I doubt if his estate will amount to £4 million.') He also had domestic problems, which culminated in the elopement in May 1942 of his daughter Nancy, just eighteen, with

Alfred de Marigny, a Franco-Mauritian adventurer in his early thirties who had become a byword in Nassau (together with his bosom-pal and fellow-countryman, the 'Marquis' Georges de Visdelou Guimbeau) for his dandified charm, his proficiency at yachting, and his heartless philandering. The sweet and innocent Lady Oakes was grief-stricken at the match: the Duchess did what she could to comfort her. Curiously enough, Sir Harry started by rather liking his new son-in-law – had he not at the same age been a species of adventurer himself? – but he rapidly became incensed by what he saw as de Marigny's haughtiness and shabby treatment of Nancy, and there were some fearsome rows. Oakes himself was becoming increasingly bad-tempered and unpredictable; he began to drink heavily, and had long bouts of black depression during which he would relieve his violent anguish by bulldozing trees.

On 7 July 1943 – the last day of his life – he was arranging to leave the Colony for the rest of summer. (His wife and children – including Nancy – were already in America.) Stewart Lack, the security officer who gave him his exit-permit, writes:

> What was Oakes going to do when he left the Colony the following day? Had it any connection with the murder? I think not – rather that, as presumably the murder had been set up, it had to be done before he went. But his projected departure seemed to be a hurried decision: when he and Harold Christie came in to get their exit-permits, he seemed especially keen to get everything done quickly. . . . Had he any inkling of the forces working against him?[2]

However, his other actions that day did not give the impression of a man who expects to die soon. He planted some trees. He took possession of a flock of long-haired sheep just arrived from Cuba, and invited Dupuch to visit him early the next morning to inspect them. In the afternoon he played tennis with Christie at Westbourne. Some other people joined them, whom Oakes invited to stay on to dinner; the last guests left around eleven – except for Christie who asked to stay the night, and was accommodated in the next bedroom but one to Sir Harry's.

That night, the skies above Nassau rose to the occasion in the best dramatic tradition of a Hammer movie. There was a terrific tropical thunderstorm, the likes of which even the tempest-prone Bahamas had not seen for many a month. Rain descended in pitiless, blindingly illuminated sheets, its roar punctuated by deafening explosions of heavy artillery. After it came a howling gale. But at Westbourne, Harold Christie (according to his later evidence) slept soundly. At seven he rose and wandered into the room of his host. 'Harry, for God's sake!' he cried, unable to take in the scene. There were signs of a bloody and violent struggle, and of a fire which had been extinguished by wind blowing through the open window. Burnt and battered, Sir Harry lay dead in his bed.

As the Duchess remarked to a friend later that day, 'Never a dull moment in the Bahamas.'

Here is not the place to try yet again to solve the mystery of the Oakes murder. Some of those still living who were involved in the case – Godfrey Higgs, Sir Eric Hallinan, Colonel Erskine-Lindop – are known to have their private theories, which they are no doubt correct in keeping to themselves. Numerous volumes have been (and certainly will be) written on the subject, some of them (such as the quaint story that Oakes was 'sliced' by the Cosa Nostra for opposing a delightful scheme – apparently dear to the hearts of Christie and the Duke – to set up a gangster-operated casino in wartime Nassau) belonging to the murkier realms of cheap pulp-fiction. What one is concerned with here are the actions and reactions of the Duke.

According to the Duchess, they were woken from sleep and informed of Sir Harry's violent death by Gray Phillips at seven o'clock on the morning of Thursday 8 July.[3] (In fact it must have been slightly later, as Christie asserted that he had found the body just after seven.) Their alarm may be imagined. 'I just couldn't believe it,' wrote the Duchess. 'It seemed incredible to me that anybody could so hate such a good man.' The Duke's first act was to try to impose an embargo on news out of the Colony – an attempt thoroughly justified in view of what was to occur, but was frustrated by the ingenious Dupuch who, due to call at Westbourne that morning to inspect Sir Harry's sheep, had got hold of the news and promptly flashed it round the world. The Duke then summoned Heape and Erskine-Lindop to Government House. (Hallinan was with the police at Westbourne.) The main question was whom to put in charge of the investigation. Erskine-Lindop (a pious but not a decisive man) had a modest doubt as to his own abilities and a greater doubt as to the adequacy of his force. He had been desperate to leave the Colony ever since the 1942 riots; he dreaded getting involved in further local controversy; he had just been gazetted Deputy Commissioner of Police in Trinidad and was anxiously awaiting transfer; in a few weeks he would be gone, and so unlikely to be able to give evidence in subsequent legal proceedings. Major Lancaster, his deputy and successor, had been seconded for temporary security duty with the defence forces. There were in fact no trained detectives available at all, and in the event Major Pemberton, an officer of the merchant marine then serving in the police force, was entrusted with the case. But there was no great faith that he would be able to handle it on his own. The Duke then asked Heape and Erskine-Lindop if they would approve of American help being called in, and they both replied that they would – though neither of them knew exactly what sort of help the Duke had in mind.[4]

What happened next at Government House is revealed by a highly interesting statement which was actually published in January 1965 but then received little attention. A few weeks earlier Etienne Dupuch had written an article in the *Tribune* criticizing the Duke's 'handling' of the case over twenty years before. This provoked a long and critical reply (duly printed) from one of the two doctors who had examined the body at Westbourne on the morning of 8 July 1943.

Dr H. A. Quackenbush – a brisk, articulate Canadian – was known personally to the Duke and Duchess, and had attended Sir Harry Oakes in life. As soon as he had finished his examination, he was summoned to Government House. According to his account, he arrived at the Duke's office around ten o'clock; he may therefore have been the first person the Duke saw straight from the scene of the death. 'What has happened?' asked the Duke as the doctor entered. 'Santa Claus is dead,' replied Quackenbush. He described the condition of corpse and chamber in some detail, and then said something which must have had an immense effect on the Duke. For, in Quackenbush's private opinion, *it was not murder, but suicide made to look like murder*. For he had not touched or moved the corpse; it was only later, when the autopsy was carried out and the skull x-rayed, that it became incontrovertibly apparent that Sir Harry had been fatally wounded by a series of blows from a sharp instrument which could not have been self-inflicted. Early that morning, however, what had most attracted the attention of Quackenbush was a small puncture-hole on the left side of the skull. This looked not inconsistent with a bullet wound, and since Sir Harry was left-handed, it seemed not impossible that he had shot himself. As Quackenbush wrote in the *Tribune*:

> The attempt to burn the house (and all the evidence) was definitely bungled, and could have been an attempt to make suicide look like a murder which could never be solved. Only a few people realized that that particular wing of Westbourne was the original wooden structure.

(Is this to say that Oakes might have said to Christie: 'Tonight I shall die, and when I am dead I want you to burn down the house with my body in it . . .'?) Quackenbush implies that both he and the Duke had good reasons for believing that Sir Harry, given his state of health and mind at that time, would not have been altogether unlikely to have committed suicide – though what these reasons were he (no doubt properly) does not say.

The Duke listened to the doctor's account (so Quackenbush goes on) 'with intent and raised eyebrows', and then asked: 'Don't you think we need help from outside in a case like this?' Quackenbush replied that they did. At Westbourne, Pemberton was making a hopeless mess of things. By removing quantities of furniture in order to take better photographs, he was interfering with vital evidence. The Duke said: 'I think I know how to help', and reached for the telephone. It was then ten minutes to eleven. The only civil flight from the mainland left Miami at noon. As all students of the case know, the Duke rang up the Miami City Police and asked for the services of Captain W. E. Melchen, the head of the Homicide Department, who had guarded the Duke and Duchess during their various visits to Miami and favourably impressed them. Melchen duly brought with him Captain James Barker, his technical and identification expert; there is conflicting evidence as to whether the Duke actually asked for Barker (whom he hardly knew), or whether it was Melchen who suggested him. Wrote Quackenbush: 'All overseas telephone conversations were monitored in those days, so one spoke cautiously. The Duke asked for Miami, and requested that Melchen and Barker be put on the [noon] plane, to come over to help investigate an unusual death, and left it at that.' (Melchen however later recalled that he had been summoned to examine *an apparent suicide*.)

As Quackenbush rose to leave, the Duke said: 'For Lady Oakes's sake, I hope it turns out to be murder; for the Colony's sake, I hope it is suicide.' He then telephoned Westbourne to find out what was happening and tell Hallinan and Erskine-Lindop (who were there interviewing Harold Christie) what he had done. Erskine-Lindop, who knew Melchen, raised no objection; Christie exclaimed (as Hallinan recalls), 'An excellent idea! An excellent idea!' The Duke then sent the following code telegram to the Secretary of State in London: 'Important. Deeply regret to report that Sir Harry Oakes has met violent death *under circumstances which are not yet known.** Hope to obtain expert advice of chief of Miami detectives to assist local police immediately. Will telegraph further.'[5] London sent back its regrets, and merely asked whether it would be appropriate for Colonel Stanley to send a message of condolence to Lady Oakes. The Duke replied that it would indeed be appropriate, and one was sent.

The introduction of Melchen and (more particularly) Barker into the case proved to be catastrophic, and the Duke has been ceaselessly criticized ever since for bringing them in. But that is to criticize from hindsight, and one must look at the situation as the Duke (in constant consultation with his advisers as was his habit) had to look at it on the morning of 8 July. A horrible and violent event had occurred, certain to cause a great convulsion within the Colony, likely to attract endless distasteful publicity, capable of causing terrible embarrassment to the administration. It was of the essence to find out as quickly as possible what had happened. If it was suicide, this would at once have to be established. It was July, a time of intense heat and humidity; fingerprints fade quickly under such conditions, and (to quote Quackenbush) 'a body does not remain fresh for long in Nassau'. The local police were

* Author's italics.

incompetent, and there was no point whatever in requesting short-term help from Scotland Yard CID, 3,000 miles away and staffed on a wartime basis. The only quick outside help could come from America, and the only civil flight left at noon from Miami, a city ten times the size of Nassau where the Duke happened to know the senior detective. As Stewart Lack, who was involved in the security aspect of the case, writes: 'It was an unfortunate decision, although, like so many others, made on the spur of the moment with the best of intentions, using his position and his authority to "cut red tape" – but with, for him, unforeseen and unfortunate results.' But he could not then – no one could – have foreseen the consequences of the investigation.

The events which followed may be related briefly. The detectives arrived on the flight from Miami at two o'clock in the afternoon. They more or less took over the investigation from the local police – at any rate, there was no satisfactory liaison – and immediately established the case as one of murder. Then they got down to 'detection'. While Melchen and Erskine-Lindop interviewed suspects and witnesses, Barker looked for fingerprints. He had not brought a fingerprint camera with him; the Nassau police actually possessed a perfectly good one, but for some reason this was neither offered to, nor asked for by him. Barker later explained he had 'lifted' prints with Scotch tape – a highly irregular practice. Early the following afternoon the Duke made his single and brief visit to the death-scene; his impressions are not recorded. Later the same afternoon, Erskine-Lindop arrested Alfred de Marigny and charged him with the murder of his father-in-law.

Erskine-Lindop has told the author that he believed de Marigny to be guilty at the time of the arrest, but that he did not believe it for long. Since they both came from Mauritius, the Colonel understood the Count better than most, and knew how little violence lurked beneath the fiery temperament.* 'Freddie was not the sort of chap who would have planned to murder anyone,' writes Stewart Lack who knew him quite well. 'He was far too casual and easy-going to bother.' But there was a considerable weight of circumstantial evidence against him. He had a possible motive, he had been in the vicinity of Westbourne at the time of the murder, he had shown considerable agitation the following morning, and the hairs on his arms (according to the evidence of some) were mysteriously scorched. The rakish de Marigny was hated by conventional people in the Colony, who were all too ready to believe he had committed murder – however out of character the act might seem. The Duke also disliked him heartily, but as Hallinan says: 'had he any evidence that

* However, Franco-Mauritian society (as the author is informed by one of its prominent female members) was inclined to believe in the guilt of de Marigny, whom it remembered as a bizarre, highly-strung youth, and regarded (to use its own damning expression) as '*un aventurier*'.

supported de Marigny's innocence, he would undoubtedly have communicated this to me or to the police.'

The following day the Duke telegraphed London:

Alfred de Marigny, British subject from Mauritius and son-in-law of Sir Harry Oakes, arrested and charged with his murder.

Sir Harry was found dead in bed with 4 wounds on the left side of the skull and body severely burned.

After concurrence of Commissioner of Police, whose local force lacks detectives with requisite experience . . ., I was fortunate in securing the services of Captain W.E. Melchen . . . and Captain James Barker . . ., who arrived by plane . . . within 12 hours of Sir Harry's death. Captain Melchen, who has been known to me for 3 years, and his assistant have rendered most valuable service by their relentless investigations, which have in a large measure resulted in the arrest of the accused.[6]

An official at the Colonial Office wrote a minute on the despatch:

The Governor is at some pains to explain why he took the rather unusual step of calling in men from outside, which I must confess I don't very much like. But in the circs I will not question his judgment.

Now, perhaps, was the moment to bring in more experienced help, and indeed, Hallinan, who was becoming increasingly suspicious of Barker's work methods, wrote to the FBI in Washington requesting their expert assistance. But he was informed that, once the police of a US city had been called in, the Federal Bureau would not join an investigation. As the police case proceeded, Hallinan (who as Crown Prosecutor was keeping a close eye on it) was struck by its numerous sinister and eerie features.[7] Vital evidence (such as hand-prints on the walls of the death-room) mysteriously disappeared. The photographs Barker had taken on the first day failed to come out, so that Sir Harry's body, which was being flown to Maine for burial, had to be intercepted in mid-air and brought back again. Above all, few of the witnesses gave the impression of being totally straightforward; many of them (not excluding members of the Oakes family and their advisers) appeared to have something to hide, or even an interest in seeing that no one other than de Marigny was suspected. It is questionable how much progress even Scotland Yard CID (which in fact made a futile attempt to re-open the investigation sixteen years later) would have been able to make under such circumstances.

The committal proceedings against de Marigny opened on 16 July before the magistrate Frank Field, and lasted six weeks. There was an immense crowd. Hallinan led for the Crown, with the black and eloquent Adderley. Godfrey Higgs appeared for de Marigny (in whose innocence he passionately believed) with an eminent coloured junior, Ernest Callender. The romantic possibilities of the case were amply satisfied when de Marigny's estranged wife, the former Nancy Oakes, turned up with the eminent private detective Raymond Schindler to help defend her husband from the charge of having murdered her father. She was followed soon after by Lady Oakes, who had come with the opposite mission of testifying against her son-in-law.

The day following the opening of the preliminary hearing the Duke, accompanied by Captain Dugdale, went to Miami for twenty-four hours 'on private business'* and gave a brief press conference. He called the murder 'a great shock to everybody'. Sir Harry's death was 'a great loss to the Colony, not only in a material way but because he was so very popular'. Asked about the Oakes enterprises in the Bahamas, the Duke hoped they would be carried on. Asked what role he had played in the case, the Duke replied that his summoning of the Miami investigators had been his sole connection with it; and that action had been 'no reflection on the Nassau police'.[8]

'We are endeavouring to keep as clear from this awful case as is possible,'† wrote the Duchess to Aunt Bessie. 'I am afraid there is a lot of dirt underneath and I think the natives are all protecting themselves from the exposures of business deals – strange drums of petrol etc. – *so one wonders how far it will all go*† Most unpleasant as I do not think there is a big enough laundry anywhere to take Nassau's dirty linen. . . .' Her main concern was for Lady Oakes. 'I do feel sorry for her – she is very brave considering everything.'[9]

What was the Duke's position during this time? The Duchess accurately expressed it when she wrote that they were trying to keep as far as possible from the case. It is sometimes said that he 'took personal charge' of the enquiry. In a sense, he was in charge of *every* criminal case, for the police charged with investigation and the Attorney-General charged with prosecution were both directly responsible to the Governor as King's representative. But both Hallinan and Erskine-Lindop emphatically deny that the Duke even 'directed' the case. Rather the problem was that, once the men from Miami arrived, no one knew who was in charge or who was supposed to be taking instructions from whom. With the summoning of the Americans the Duke's personal involvement had ended. And yet, throughout that summer, the affair never ceased to haunt him. It affected him profoundly as Governor in three ways.

Firstly, it created chaos in Nassau. The fact that Sir Harry's ubiquitous private business ventures were closed down pending probate alone caused great economic disturbance. Strong feelings were aroused at a time when the island was playing a significant part in the war and required to be calm, industrious and united. When horror eventually

---

* Concerning the affairs of the EP Ranch. James Dugdale had succeeded Drury as equerry.

† Author's italics.

of dirt underneath and I
think the natives are all
protecting themselves from
the exposures of business deals,
strange drums of petrol etc
so one wonders how far
it will all go – most unpleasant
as I do not think there is
a big enough laundry anywhere
to take Hassan's dirty linen.

The Duchess to Aunt Bessie on the Oakes murder, August 1943.

subsided, it gave way to rumour, recrimination, and violent passions on the subject of the guilt or innocence of the accused. The tension between Bay Street and Government House grew ever greater. Only a few months had passed since the House had tried to pillory the police and Hallinan for their role during the riots; the local establishment was poised to resume the attack, should it again feel itself to have been let down by the forces of order.

Secondly, as Stewart Lack puts it, 'the case achieved enormous publicity of an entirely undesirable kind, involving, amongst other things, a tremendous influx of American journalists and crime reporters and writers, including Erle Stanley Gardner and others – and this embarrassed the administration and dealt a severe blow to the confused Bahamas police, and didn't do anything for the American detectives either.'[10] In their characteristic way, Bay Street shopkeepers and hotel owners were delighted by this whirl of sensational activity; but it was not creditable to the Bahamas to have so sordid a business – which in the long term threatened to ruin Nassau's reputation as a safe resort for rich winter residents – driving the conquest of Sicily out of the American papers. Nor was it reassuring for the Duke and Duchess to realize that the Colony had hit the headlines for the first time since their arrival over so vulgar and vexing an affair.

Yet there was a third reason for the Duke's anxiety. It has been noted that, only a few days before the murder, the Duke had received from the Secretary of State what was probably the most important communication to be received at Government House from the Colonial Office during the war. Colonel Stanley's letter had declared that, following the Riots Report and the West Indian debate in the House of Commons, the Imperial Government were insisting that the Bahamas accept a series of rapid and sweeping socio-political reforms. Chief among the measures required to be introduced were a universal secret ballot, income tax, and full trade union legislation. Until these were brought in, the Bahamas would receive not a penny under the Colonial Development and Welfare Act. And if they were not brought in, the London Government would not hesitate, if it thought it necessary, to amend the Bahamas constitution by Act of Parliament. In other words, the Royal Governor was being instructed to have a showdown with the local powers; and he was wondering how on earth he was to go about this – or rather, how to play the extraordinarily delicate game of inducing London to moderate its demands and the House to accept some of them – when Sir Harry Oakes was found dead in his bed, the Colony was plunged into barely controlled hysteria, the administration was all but paralyzed, and the local tensions became unbearable.

In the four weeks following the murder, the problem of how to prepare the ground for reform, given the local atmosphere, preoccupied the Duke at least as much as the murder case itself. It was obviously out of the question even to broach the subject to the Legislature until the case was out of the way. The Duke replied to Stanley on 10 August, and his letter – which is an interesting example of his style – is worth quoting at length. He refers to the Oakes affair, but the main body of the letter deals with the reform issue. With considerable tact, the Duke infers that he has considered the problem seriously and has a definite plan, but at the same time he gives his correspondent to understand the enormity of the task which has been imposed on him, and the necessity, under the extraordinary prevailing circumstances, of proceeding by careful degrees.

GOVERNMENT HOUSE,
NASSAU.
August 10th 1943

My dear Oliver,
Many thanks for your private and confidential letter of May 12th which I received upon my return from America the last day of June. I have delayed answering it until I had the forthcoming plans of the Legislature lined up, a decision upon which has been further prolonged by the absence of the Speaker from the Colony in connection with the tragic murder of Sir Harry Oakes, Mr Kenneth Solomon being his attorney. . . .

After discussing your letter with my three official members of Executive Council, I have decided that the following tactics are best to pursue. A few days before I convene the Legislature for the opening of the next session in November, I will send for the speaker, Mr Solomon, the Leader of the Government, Mr Godfrey Higgs, and a non-political member of my Council, Mr Sidney Farrington, in whose advice and opinions I place great confidence, and tell them that you have informed me of the feeling that is crystallizing in the House of Commons with regard to Bahamian resistance to certain urgent political and social reforms and that their Constitution is at stake if they continue to pursue this reactionary policy. I can then properly refer to these important issues in my speech at the opening of the next session without these three leading non-official Bahamians being able to accuse me of having slipped a fast one over on them. . . .

Richardson, who is by now thoroughly familiar with the local politics with which I have to contend, is in agreement with my plan of campaign. At the same time, he fully realizes that the resistance to the important measures to which you refer will be intense, for their adoption will without doubt drastically undermine the structure of the long-established Bahamian political set-up.

While the opposition to extending the secret ballot to the whole Colony will come from the more reactionary element in the House of Assembly and this measure has a moderate chance of passing, income tax will be opposed unanimously, for the negro politicians are as fearful of its consequences [i.e. discouraging rich foreign residents] as those of European descent. . . .

Nothing of special importance occurred here during my absence from the Colony in May and June but I had hardly been back a week when Sir Harry Oakes was found brutally murdered in his bed on the morning of July 8th. I had seen a good deal of Sir Harry since my return, who was in excellent shape and more enthusiastic than ever over all his undertakings.

Having satisfied myself that this was no ordinary crime, and that the local police were entirely unequal and unequipped to deal with it, I telephoned Miami and obtained the services of two expert criminal detectives, who arrived in Nassau within twelve hours of the murder and whose investigation led to the arrest of Alfred de Marigny, Sir Harry's son-in-law.

The whole circumstances of the case are sordid beyond description and I will be glad when the trial is over and done with. However legal procedure is slow and ponderous and as the preliminary enquiry is only now being heard before the Magistrate, if the Accused is committed for trial, he will not be tried in the Supreme Court until the October sessions.

What is unfortunate is that, whether de Marigny is guilty or not, local opinion is sharply divided for and against him. In Executive Council, for example, the Attorney-General is Prosecuting Attorney for the Crown and Mr Godfrey Higgs, the Leader of the Government, is defending the Accused, while Mr Harold Christie, the chief witness who was a close friend of Sir Harry and his guest on the night of the murder and the first to discover it, is an unofficial member of over four years' standing. The older and more conservative elements and the whole negro population suspect de Marigny's guilt but above all wish to see the murderer, whoever he is, pay the supreme penalty for so dastardly a crime, which caused the death of a fine old man and great benefactor – and the best friend the Bahamians ever had.

On the other hand, de Marigny, who is a despicable character and has the worst possible record, morally and financially, since his adolescence, has insidiously bought his way with his ex-wife's money into the leadership of a quite influential, fast and depraved set of the younger generation, born of bootlegging days, and for him they have an admiration bordering on hero-worship. This unsavoury group of people would, therefore, like to see de Marigny escape the rope at all costs, whether guilty or innocent – but if the coloured people are ever given the slightest reason to suspect the jury, then the consequences may be grave.

I think it is important that you should know some of the background to this prominent murder case which, although it has probably passed without much comment in Great Britain, has nevertheless aroused considerable sensational publicity in America. . . .

In conclusion, the Duke mentioned that he and the Duchess hoped to be away from the Colony when the trial took place in October. Some writers have viewed this intention as discreditable or cowardly in some way; some indeed, unfamiliar with the practice of heads of government, express astonishment that the Duke was not in the court-room listening to the case. But he could have served no useful purpose by his presence in October; all would cease save for the case, and he had correctly resolved to distance himself from it; given the circumstances 'sordid beyond description' and the atmosphere of sensationalism which would prevail, his prestige might be at stake – and he would need enough of that when he came to present the reform programme to the House on his return. Moreover, it will be remembered that, ever since the Duchess's collapse in the New Year, they had hoped to spend October in the Hot Springs of Virginia. In the circumstances there was certainly no reason for them to change their plan. The Duke was under great strain and far from well. The Duchess wrote to Aunt Bessie on 24 August: 'I really feel that the Duke needs a complete change and no work – we have plenty of the latter in NY always – so this would be different and put a little weight on him – he is still never still [sic] and lunch is a movable feast – anything from jumping into the office to moving trees! It has been terribly humid lately and most people's nerves slightly frayed from the thunder in the air – and perhaps in their hearts.' The Secretary of State expressed satisfaction that they would be absent at the time of the trial.

Meanwhile, the committal proceedings over and de Marigny duly committed, the lawyers dashed off for their holidays before the fearful trial began. The Chief Justice went to Mexico; Hallinan (who was finding the proceedings an unending sinister nightmare, and had hopes of leaving the Colony to become Attorney-General of Jamaica as soon as they were over) to North Carolina. Erskine-Lindop departed for his new post in Trinidad, having been presented with signed photograph and mono-grammed cufflinks by a friendly and grateful Duke. The preliminary hearing had been immensely long, because de Marigny, against the advice of his counsel, had insisted that Higgs and Callender cross-examine all the prosecution witnesses. Fortunately for him this tactic gave the unscrupulous Barker the chance to utter two demonstrable lies, which were later to enable the defence to call into question the authentic-ity of the prosecution's central piece of evidence – a fingerprint pur-portedly lifted at a particular time from a Chinese screen beside Sir Harry's deathbed.

Any fears the Duke may have had that the events of July had exacerbated the tension between Government and Legislature were amply fulfilled when the House reconvened on 23 August for the last four weeks of the session. During the spring, the Duke had had relatively little trouble from the House. It had put up money for the Bahamas Labour Scheme; it had even approved the setting-up of an Out Island Department. Now it was again as difficult as could be – and this was some time *before* it was due to be told of London's clamour for reform. The Government (on Richardson's advice) proposed two urgent but technical measures of wartime financial legislation – a new public loan to reduce the amount of money in circulation, and a revolving credit to the Government to make possible the bulk-purchasing of supplies which might soon become unavailable. Both were thrown out almost without discussion. But the greatest furore was over the creation of a Labour Department, that perennial question. Twice – at the outset of his governorship, and in the dark days after Pearl Harbor – the House had refused the Duke's urgent demands to provide money for the Department. For eighteen months now Hughes had acted as part-time Labour Officer without a Department; he had done his best, he had fulfilled his impossible role almost heroically, but the utter inadequacy of his position had been demonstrated by the hopeless labour relations which preceded the riots – and the vicious assaults of Bay Street which came after them.

By the middle of 1943 the need for a proper Department had become utterly critical for three reasons. The immense work involved in running the Labour Scheme required a full-time officer with assistants; the creation of an Out Island Department meant that the Chief Commissioner could no longer carry his post in conjunction with any other; and the exasperated Hughes, who had been given hell by Bay Street, had finally had enough and was resigning. The Duke therefore once again sent down an urgent message to the House asking them to provide for a full-time Labour Officer. The House – no doubt bitterly recalling how it had failed in its attempt to secure the arrest of poor Mr Hughes – again refused, offering instead to employ two temporary clerks for a Labour Department which (it had slipped their minds) did not yet exist.

It was a time for action. The House had obstructed an essential measure. In two months' time the Duke would be putting a far more controversial measure – electoral reform – before it; now was the moment to show his power. He consulted the sagacious Richardson, who encouraged him in his plan. On 14 September, in his speech closing the session, the Duke struck:

> Whether from a lack of understanding of the basic necessity for a Labour Officer as set forth in my Message, or whatever the causes, it is obvious that those who have made an adverse decision in this matter have entirely failed to appreciate the amount of work now involved. . . . I am, therefore, forced to provide for the salary of a Labour Officer from War Measures. . . .[11]

This announcement caused uproar in the House. Using his Emergency Powers under the Defence Regulations, the Duke was raising money without the consent of the Legislature. Positively Stuart as the Bahamas Constitution was, the Royal Governor looked as if he were behaving like Charles I. But it was clear that London would back him up, and Bay Street was shaken. 'Although my patience has been sorely tried on several previous occasions,' wrote the Duke to Oliver Stanley with a certain schoolboyish pride, 'this is the first time in my three years' administration that I have actually used my big wartime stick. . . .'[12] Richardson was well-pleased with the effect of the little *coup*, and wrote to the Duke in America a few weeks later that it 'has had a most favourable influence on the political situation' – meaning, no doubt, that the shock would help break down Bay Street resistance to reform.

In the rest of his speech the Duke talked of the extraordinary prosperity which had come over the Colony since the grim days after Pearl Harbor, and how well the war was going 'with the spectacular and encouraging news of the unconditional surrender of Italy' and other 'encouraging signs which point the way to the sure frustration of the enemy's plans for world conquest and its ultimate submission.' Resuming his seventeenth-century tone, he warned the House (in a veiled reference to the political battle of the previous autumn):

> While I recognize that legitimate criticism provides a tonic for Government Officials lest they ever become lethargic, I wonder if the critics of Governments, political and otherwise, realize to what extent administrations assume responsibilities towards the community and how much their continued efforts to meet their responsibilities are undermined by those who sometimes irresponsibly and inaccurately seek to misrepresent both the motive and the substance of the measures which are of necessity and after much deliberation recommended for the good of the people?

On one subject it was impossible to stay silent: 'The Colony has recently suffered the severe shock of as dastardly a murder as has been recorded in the annals of crime, the horror being intensified by the fact that the victim was Sir Harry Oakes. . . .'

On 18 September 1943, four days after this stirring oration, the Duke and Duchess set out on the fourth of their American tours. From Miami they went (passing through New York) to Boston, where Aunt Bessie lay in the Faulkener Hospital with a fractured hip. Large enthusiastic crowds greeted them, which the newspapers were quick to compare to the somewhat subdued reception Winston Churchill had received there two weeks before. In the intervals of hospital visiting, Boston was a royal progress. They visited art galleries, service canteens and navy yards. They went to Harvard to see the University and inspect the military units training there. They went to Bunker Hill, where colonial troops had been told to hold their fire until they could see the whites of American eyes. They visited a British sailors' club, to be greeted by a girls' bagpipe band and a crowd of cheering tars; the Duke was as charming with the sailors as he had been at Portsmouth in November 1936. They opened an exhibition of aerial photographs of bombed German cities; pointing to an obliterated metropolitan landscape entitled *Essen*, the Duke cheerfully remarked: 'Amazing! We spent a whole day there.' They went on to Newport, Rhode Island, where they dined with Admirals and the Duke reviewed naval troops. The Duchess had last been there as the wife of Lieutenant E. Winfield Spencer, and had lived in a boarding-house; now she stayed with Mai Douglas and dined with Mrs Cornelius Vanderbilt.

While they were in Newport, a rather touching incident occurred. It has been seen how, in the autumn of 1941, Ernest Simpson's third wife – the former Mary Kirk Raffray – had tragically died two years after having given birth to a baby boy, Henry. Ernest had sent Henry to be brought up by an old Baltimorean friend of both Mary and the Duchess, Mrs Morgan Schiller (formerly Elizabeth Lloyd). Mrs Schiller was at her summer house in Maine, when she heard that the Duke and Duchess were staying in nearby Newport; she rang up and asked if they would like to come and see her, and hear news of Mary's last days, and Ernest and little Henry. They gladly accepted. Alas, on the appointed day there were furious storms and flooding, and Mrs Schiller had to advise them not to come.[13]

On 28 September they arrived in Washington, where they spent three nights at the Embassy with Sir Ronald Campbell. The Duke had long talks with the War Food Administration and the British Colonies Liaison Mission. His line of reasoning was that, since Bahamian labourers were now growing food in the United States rather than their own islands, the Bahamas was entitled to privileged supplies; this argument largely succeeded. There was a further round of royal inspections. They were shown round the FBI Museum by J. Edgar Hoover; they visited canteens and hospitals. 'You should see some of the soldiers at the White to cheer you up,' wrote the Duchess to her still-suffering Aunt. 'Never have I seen such leg injuries.' There was a rumour that the Duke was consulting a neurologist. He certainly looked nervous, pale and tired.

On 1 October they headed west out of Washington into Virginia, up past Warrenton (shades of 1926 and 1941) into the Blue Ridge Mountains. At the Homestead, Hot Springs, surrounded by the extraordinary colour and light and rolling spaces of old Virginia, and breathing the finest and most bracing air in the world, they revived their 'tropically exhausted minds and bodies', as the Duke wrote to Allen, and had their first real holiday since their trip to Canada two years before. Old friends joined them – Milton 'Doc' Holder, Gladys Scanlon and Mai Douglas. 'There are quite a few people we know, perhaps too many,' wrote the Duchess to Aunt Bessie, 'but the hours are early, the food simple, and very little liquid refreshment. The Duke loves it and has good golf every day – so it has all been a great success and really a rest.'[14]

On 17 October – the day before the murder trial opened in Nassau – they left 'the Hot', spending the next week in Washington, the following three weeks in New York, never far from Embassy or Consulate-General from where the Duke (absent from Government House as he was with official permission) could keep in constant touch with the news and his officials. During that hectic month he did not neglect the interests of his Colony in America. He had further talks on supplies and the Labour Scheme; he visited Bahamian labourers in Delaware; he tried to win the support of the Rockefeller Foundation for a new public hospital in Nassau. He wrote to Winston Churchill that he was 'going to try to persuade the President to come to Nassau to inaugurate the two airfields, the nearest Lend-Lease project to the mainland of America. I know how more than fully occupied his time is . . . but he would be performing a ceremony well worthwhile to Anglo–American relations.'[15] He also gave some attention to his private affairs. In the second half of 1942 a Texan geologist named Blackburn had made a sub-surface survey of the EP Ranch and reported that there was certainly oil under the Duke's land and a good chance that it existed in commercial quantities. The Duke, believing that by striking oil on his property he would both benefit the war effort and restore his own highly uncertain financial prospects, now looked around for partners in this initially very expensive venture, and managed to interest two rich New York acquaintances – Charles Cushing, an investment broker and society figure, and Elisha Walker, senior partner of the banking house of Kuhn, Loeb & Co. On 28 October the three of them signed a partnership agreement and set up an oil company called 'Ecushwa' (for Edward, Cushing and Walker). Ecushwa was not however destined to commence drilling operations in 1943, for it found itself enmeshed in hellish and absurd bureaucratic complications which delayed the task for which it was created for almost a year. One cannot go into the details of this amazing (and to a later reader of the files somewhat tragi-comic) tale; but there is one extraordinary episode which is worth recounting, as it concerns the Duke's relations with his family.

The matter arose in the following way. Under the lease which the provincial Government of Alberta had granted in 1931 the Duke was entitled to the mineral rights on his land; but what would happen – the Duke's partners naturally wanted to know – if during the term of the partnership he unfortunately died? According to the wording of the lease (which was marvellously imprecise and kept lawyers and civil servants busy for weeks) it was to continue for ninety-nine years so long as the Ranch was farmed by the Duke *or a member of the Royal Family*. As the Duke's sole heir was the Duchess, the question as to whether the lease would survive him therefore seemed to depend upon whether or not the Duchess was 'a member of the Royal Family'. However, there was no legal definition of the phrase 'member of the Royal Family'; so all seemed to hang on whether or not the King regarded his sister-in-law as a member of his family. On 27 October the Duke somewhat hesitantly telegraphed Allen asking him to approach the King about this. 'As the

Prime Minister has informed me that The King is not yet inclined to give the Duchess her rightful rank', wrote the Duke, 'I do not press for the restoring of the appellage of "Her Royal Highness" at this juncture. On the other hand, I do expect The King to make it known . . . through the High Commissioner of the United Kingdom in Canada that, although the Duchess's royal status is not officially recognized, she is, as my wife, to be regarded legally as a member of the Royal Family.'

The Duke's enquiry caused consternation at Court, and threw the Palace into a terrible dilemma. They had no intention of conceding to the Duchess the faintest suggestion of royalty, but the last thing they wanted (since there was no precedent in English history for a wife not sharing the rank of her husband) was that the Duchess's status should be tested in law. After a brief audience with the King, and somewhat chilling interviews with the new Private Secretary Sir Alan Lascelles, and the royal legal adviser Sir Claud Schuster, Allen was told to his surprise that the expression 'member of the Royal Family' probably only included the King and his wife and his close blood relations – in which case it would exclude not only the Duchess but the wives of all princes. In any case, the King refused to make a formal decision on the matter. The Duke's Canadian lawyer Heward then had a new idea; why not bequeath the Ranch in name to someone who was incontestably 'a member of the Royal Family' (e.g. the Duke of Gloucester), while reserving a life interest (including oil rights) to the Duchess? 'Have carefully considered proposal,' Allen replied by telegram on 23 November, 'but judging from my past and recent experience am satisfied personalities involved would decline.' After causing much nervousness in Palace circles, the problem was finally disposed of by a ruling of the Lord Chancellor that, under English law, the reference to the Duke in the lease might be interpreted so as to include his executors and successors.

The Duke and Duchess were consoled for the icy wind from Buckingham Palace by the warm breezes of American public opinion. During that month in Washington and New York, against the uneasy background of the murder trial (which attracted near-hysterical publicity), something extraordinary happened. They had always been popular in America, and on their three previous tours had received ample proof of their popularity. But this time they positively seemed to have achieved the status of national figures; the Duke began to be treated, by official and non-official alike, as one of the Grand Alliance's elder statesmen. Newspapers questioned him closely about Anglo–American relations and the progress of the war. There had long been general sympathy for the idea that he be given an important post in the United States; many Americans had hoped he would succeed Lothian (which he had so little desire to do); there was even a society entitled 'Friends of the Duke of Windsor in

America', from which he maintained a proper distance. Now, he was almost a national issue. Public figures and eminent newspapers openly declared themselves 'Windsor supporters'. Walter Lippmann, the most influential political journalist in America, and Henry J. Taylor, the top current affairs broadcaster, loudly praised his (and indeed her) good effect on Anglo–American relations. During their week in Washington, the newspapers there were insistent in their demand that he should have some kind of appointment or brief in the capital. An article in the *Star* carried the not untypical headline 'Windsor Appearance Again Accents Their Importance to England in America'. The *Times Herald* wrote: 'Why not use the Duke and his American wife as Anglo–American propaganda? Relations between the United States and Great Britain have struck their lowest level since the war began. . . . Mr Churchill should dispatch the former King and his American wife on a personal goodwill tour. . . .'[16]

It was the height of 'the Windsor Lobby'. On 21 October Helen Essary, a socially influential *Times Herald* correspondent who was friendly with the Duchess, threw a great tea-party for what she claimed were their twenty most powerful and enthusiastic allies in Washington. In accordance with the usual practice, she submitted in advance a list of the invitees:

New Under-Secretary of State *Edward Stettinus Jr.*, former Lend-Lease Administrator and US Steel President.
Eric Johnston, exciting US Chamber of Commerce President. Possible Candidate for President of the United States.
Marriner Eccles, Chairman of the Federal Reserve Board, very powerful in the West, President of the Utah Construction Company, helped finance Boulder Dam and other vast enterprises.
Raymond Clapper, Walter Lippmann and *Mark Sullivan*. Mark is an especially great admirer of you and of the Duke and is putting you in the last volume of *Our Times*.
Congressman Fulbright of Arkansas, responsible for present much discussed post-war plan 'Fulbright Resolution'.
Supreme Court Justices *Reed* and *Murphy*, Man-Power Chief *McNutt*.
Presidential possibilities *Vandenberg* and *Taft*.
Mrs Craig, President Women's National Press Club; Society Editor *Hope Ridings Miller*; *Times-Herald* Editor *Frank Waldrop*; *National Geographic* Editor *LaGorce*; successful Washington physician *Dr Morgan*.
Admiral Standley, just back with a 'mad' on from Russia where he was US Ambassador.
Three Essary daughters ![17]

The whole Administration was dying to come, added Mrs Essary; she would make a thousand enemies. The party was a great success, and the

Duke and Duchess utterly charmed their powerful fans. It cannot be doubted that they enjoyed winning people; they were masters of the unexpected courtesy. In New York that November Harry Taylor, the popular author of *Men in Motion* and *Time Runs Out* whose nightly current-affairs broadcast was heard throughout the Union, mentioned that he was about to visit London. Attached to a note 'We shall look forward to hearing of your thrilling experiences!', the Duke gave him letters of introduction to Winston Churchill and the King. 'Nothing more stimulating could have happened to me than to have received such encouragement as these letters from Your Royal Highness as I leave on my trip abroad,'[18] wrote the delighted Taylor – who, if he did get to see the Prime Minister and Sovereign, would most certainly have pleaded the Duke's cause.

One may picture the emotions of the Duke and Duchess at this time. A thousand miles away in Nassau (where the prosecution case against de Marigny effectively collapsed on 25 October) all the pettiness, frustration, corruption and incompetence of their little Colony was being exposed before the world's eyes on a high and lighted stage. There was so little more they could do there; but America loved them and wanted to keep them. The Duke knew he could do great things for Anglo–American relations, if only he were given a brief. United States opinion of England was always a little equivocal, but the Duke of Windsor was a hero. The British Empire was always more or less unpopular; but the former King-Emperor who now had the strange experience of being one of its successful if extremely minor proconsuls might spread its virtues abroad. He did not want the Embassy, rather 'a sort of roving commission' as he described it to Allen, whereby he might be to America what his grandfather had been to Europe, a wise and charming Prince who might make Great Britain popular in the drawing-rooms and boardrooms of power. He knew how much he could help and longed to, and she longed for him too.

He longed for it – but could he hope for it? The Colonial Secretary in 1940 had 'hoped he would not do well'; for three years British officialdom had been working to do him down in America; and the Duke no doubt recalled the cruel incidents of the past – the efforts to frustrate the *Tuscaloosa* meeting, Lord Halifax's narrowly foiled attempt to prevent his visit to the cheering workers of Detroit, the campaign to make good publicity look bad for the British press, the Foreign Office determination that his Labour Scheme should not achieve excessive success. . . . That his popularity (and hers) had in fact continued and grown was a dangerous fact in the eyes of the Government and Court, the best reason for excluding him from an American, or any, post. For to them it was more important to ensure that the vivid present image of the elder brother should not supersede the dim and absent image of the younger one than to improve the standing of Great Britain in America. That November, he learnt that his brother Harry, the Duke of Gloucester – renowned neither for brilliance nor sobriety – would be sent out to Australia as Governor-General. For him and the Duchess (as he wrote bitterly to a friend) there was only 'the prospect of continuing to rot indefinitely on a semi-tropical island'.

On the evening of 11 November the trial of de Marigny came to an end in circumstances which promised to create immense trouble.* Some days later the Duke and Duchess returned to the Colony. At Miami they were annoyed to learn of newspaper rumours that they meant to retire to an estate in Maryland if the Duke were not given a bigger post. 'I don't know where that report could have started,' the Duke told journalists. 'It is very wrong. I am quite satisfied and very interested in the Colony.'[19]

It is now necessary to give a brief resumé of the drama which was being enacted in Nassau while the Duke and Duchess were in Washington and New York.

'The murder trial of the century' – followed by the eyes of a fascinated world – opened on 18 October before the Chief Justice, the genial and able Irishman Sir Oscar Daly. In the first week, the circumstantial evidence produced by the prosecution (Hallinan and Adderley) looked devastating. A series of witnesses testified to de Marigny's appalling relations with his father-in-law, his frequent threats to smash in Sir Harry's head, his chronic financial difficulties, his 'suspicious behaviour' after the murder. Harold Christie gave evidence; Hallinan was (and remains) convinced that he knew more than he was saying, but he stuck to his original story and, by expressing sympathy for the accused, strengthened the case against him. The scandalous revelations began with the cross-examination of Melchen on the 25th. The attention of the Court was now directed to the prosecution's one item of real evidence – de Marigny's fingerprint which Barker claimed to have 'lifted' from the Chinese screen in the death-room. The defence (Higgs and Callender) drew from Melchen the astonishing admission that Barker had only told him of this crucial 'discovery' a week after it had purportedly happened. When Barker went into the witness-box, Higgs rounded on him, forcing him into a series of damning admissions – and proving in effect that the print could not possibly have come from the screen at the time alleged. (This was later confirmed by an independent fingerprint expert which Hallinan – with scrupulous fairness – had introduced into the case.) The Crown's

---

* On the morning of the same day – the twenty-fifth anniversary of the 1918 Armistice – Lord Halifax called on the Duke in Washington. 'We talked about the Oakes Case that is electrifying Nassau,' wrote the Ambassador in his diary. 'He and the Duchess had lived in the Oakes house for a while when they first went there, and were therefore completely au fait with the geography of the murder. He said the general opinion was that de Marigny . . . would not be convicted.'

central evidence therefore collapsed amid the suspicion that it had been a forgery perpetrated by Barker. Melchen was as astonished as anyone.

In theatrical contrast to the brazen Barker, there followed the pathetic evidence of Lady Oakes, delivered between sobs in a low, broken voice. Her account of the distress which Nancy Oakes's marriage had caused her parents actually helped de Marigny, who was the next to testify. He made a strong impression; in the face of long and fierce questioning by Hallinan, he never lost his nerve or deviated from his story or his tone of wronged innocence. But there followed a dangerous corner for him – the examination of his confederate and house-mate, the 'Marquis' Georges de Visdelou Guimbeau. The whole affair had reduced this nerveless exquisite to a shuddering wreck, and he was liable to say anything at all. But Adderley (rather typically) over-reached himself in taking advantage of this weak and hysterical witness, and was sternly rebuked by the judge. Finally Nancy Oakes made a determined and convincing stand in favour of her husband.

Higgs summed up briefly for the defence and called the prosecution case 'a combination of statements of an irrelevant nature and deliberate lying by police officers whose duty is to protect the public'. Hallinan summed up for the Crown, and talked of 'a rising crescendo of enmity between de Marigny and the Oakes family' which had driven the former to murder to get his hands on the family fortune. (The trial had been a nightmare for the highly principled Hallinan; he was all too aware of the dubious nature of the fingerprint evidence, of which he had taken care never to exaggerate the value.) Then Daly summed up for over five hours, strongly in favour of the defence. 'Barker made statements incredible for an expert. One would think an expert would be more careful. . . . You have heard many rumours over recent months. Rumour is always a lying jade. Keep the refrain of reasonable doubt running constantly through your minds. . . .' (Adderley is said to have remarked to de Marigny: 'I don't know why you bother to hire counsel while you have this Chief Justice.') The jury deliberated for two hours. They disagreed, and so de Marigny was discharged after a 'not guilty' verdict. Amid the wild scenes which broke out, few heard the concluding remarks of the foreman – expressing the jury's regret that Erskine-Lindop could not have been brought from Trinidad to give evidence, and their unanimous recommendation that de Marigny and de Guimbeau be deported forthwith from the Colony.

When the dust had settled, Heape wrote to the Secretary of State in London:

The general opinion is –
>   (i) . . . the Chief Justice could only sum up in his [de Marigny's] favour on
>   the evidence produced in Court.

    (ii) Melchen and Barker, the two American detectives, ruined the case for
the prosecution.

    (iii) The local police stood back when the Americans came in and no one knew
what the other was doing. An example of two many cooks.

The police will be savagely attacked when the House meets. My own view is
that they only did badly because they didn't know what the Americans were
doing and also that a murder of this complexity would be beyond the capacity of
any small police establishment such as we have here.

Eric Hallinan has had an awful time. He has in my view fought a losing battle
with great determination.

Nothing matters if we can get de Marigny and de Guimbeau out of the
Colony, and I sincerely trust that by the time you get this, RAF Transport
Command will have taken both these beauties back to Mauritius.[20]

The outcome of the Oakes Case has been the subject of much
sensational writing, and one must take care to put it in its proper
perspective. It is true that the result was thoroughly unsatisfactory, that
public opinion in the Bahamas felt let-down and cheated of a victim, that
the Colony's ever-present tensions increased, and that the political
atmosphere became worse. The evil of the unsolved crime lived on. The
shock and horror sent through the Colony, writes the Duchess, 'were
never quite dispelled during the remaining time we were there'. But it is
important not to exaggerate the *local* reaction. As Hallinan writes: 'The
main feeling of both Bay Street and coloured Bahamians was just "what a
pity de Marigny got off". However angry and disappointed, I don't think
they really blamed anyone or believed that the police and prosecution
could have done much more to secure a conviction.'

The real disaster arising out of the affair was the immense and
distorted publicity it received in the American 'yellow press'. The Hearst
empire and similar organs portrayed the failure of the prosecution as a
terrible blow to official prestige (as well as to the Duke's reputation), and
the conduct of the case as nothing short of an official frame-up. This was
absurd. While in America the prestige of the police and prosecution is
often at stake in criminal proceedings, this is not so in British courts,
where their business is not to secure convictions but to present the
evidence against the accused in a proper manner. The trial of de Marigny
had been scrupulously fair, Hallinan giving no undue weight to the
dubious fingerprint evidence, Higgs having no trouble in exposing
Barker's perjury. But the picture breathlessly served up by the
American press to the American public was of a corrupt and incompetent
establishment which had failed and been disgraced. The damage was
compounded when an exhausted Hallinan declared he was 'calling it a
day'. He merely meant to say that there could be no question of further

proceedings against de Marigny, in spite of the jury's disagreement; but it sounded as if the authorities were merely giving up.

As for the Duke, the press (encouraged by Dupuch) quickly seized upon the fact that it had been his action (indeed his only action) that had brought Barker into the case. What had been no more than an innocent indiscretion on his part, done with the approval of his advisers, was to be magnified by a whole generation of scandalous writers into an act of sensational bungle and sinister intrigue. Hallinan writes:

> Those who disliked the Duke and those writers who have made a living out of vilifying him have sought to make him responsible for Barker's grave misconduct and the failure of the prosecution, and would like us to believe that his reputation was ruined by the Oakes Case in the eyes of the Colony and the world. In fact his reputation only suffered *after* those writers had spread their venom. At the time, I don't think anyone inside the Colony regarded either the Duke as Governor or myself as prosecutor as having behaved discreditably.[21]

However, although the trial itself did not redound to the discredit of the Duke and his administration, it was immediately followed by another crisis which did threaten to do just that. Having been cheated of de Marigny's blood, vengeful public opinion in the Bahamas – both black and white – demanded that the Government at once implement the jury's somewhat unconstitutional recommendation that de Marigny and de Guimbeau be deported. A deportation order required the approval of ExCo. There was a furious meeting on the 15th, at which the order was violently resisted by Higgs, who was scandalized that this measure should be taken against his client just after he had been vindicated; he never forgave Hallinan, whose job it was to draft the instrument. But the majority approved the order, a curious document which stated that, if the two Mauritians should be 'invited' to leave the Colony and failed within a certain time to do so, then they could be compulsorily repatriated to their place of origin, i.e. Mauritius. The 'invitation' was at once issued; and the complications at once began. The two rakes had no desire whatsoever to return to *'le cher petit pays'*, where they would hardly be welcomed; but where else could they go? The US Consul made it clear that they would not be allowed on US territory, other American countries followed suit, and Pan-American Airways regretted that they could not carry them. Heape begged for a military aircraft to fly them off to the Indian Ocean; London replied that this was out of the question. In total despair, Heape telegraphed the Duke in New York, who in turn telegraphed Stanley on the 19th in his most imperial manner:

> In view of the immense volume of worldwide publicity surrounding the murder trial, and the recommendations of the jury that Marigny be deported following Deportation Order made by Acting Governor in Council, I do press

very strongly for reconsideration of the question of RAF transport being used to carry persons named back to Mauritius. I am convinced that failure to deport them would constitute a deplorable evidence of the impotence of the local government and have a very serious effect on the reputation of the Colony throughout the world.[22]

The matter caused much commotion at the Colonial Office. Stanley felt that 'we must do our best to meet the Duke's wishes' and wrote to Sir Archibald Sinclair, the Air Minister, requesting favourable consideration of the case. Sinclair (who had led the wavering Liberals against Edward VIII in 1936) insisted the thing was impossible; space on transatlantic flights was at a premium, for strict war purposes only. If 'undesirables' were to be carried around the world at RAF expense, where would it end? Would not every sick soldier ask to be flown home, every bereaved official want to fly back to a funeral? There was a war on. The Duke refused to admit the justice of this reasoning. The plane was required to execute an act of high public policy in a Crown Colony playing a significant role in the war. The following week, having returned to Nassau, he telegraphed again:

Although I would be loth to worry the PM at this time, I feel so strongly on this question that I would not hesitate, as a last resort, to approach him direct, because I am convinced that unless the Bahamas Government is armed with the power to move both deportees, the British colonial administration will be subject to derision in the United States, and the relations of the Government with the local people strained to breaking-point.[23]

Much to the relief of all, the colourful and unwitting subjects of this anguished correspondence finally solved the problem by managing to remove themselves from the Bahamas – de Marigny to Cuba, de Guimbeau to Haiti (where, much to the alarm of the Home Office, he succeeded in obtaining an entry-permit to Great Britain). De Marigny lived with Nancy for a while before resuming his life of predatory and promiscuous romance of which he wrote with such entertaining frankness in his memoirs *More Devil Than Saint*.

Heape had feared that Bay Street would take the offensive following the trial; but in fact no immediate trouble materialized. The local whites (with so much to hide) had been as shaken as officialdom by the whole business. Their desire to attack Heape and Hallinan was overborne by a greater one to exorcize the spectre of the case; and they were infinitely relieved to learn that the investigation was not being immediately resumed and that de Marigny would be deported. The Duke's return was greeted with further sighs of relief. It was like the dispelling of a bad dream, as if the affairs of the Colony could simply be resumed where he had left off and all that had happened in the two months of his absence be forgotten.

But had the case affected politics? Just before leaving the Colony the Duke had given a dramatic demonstration that he was prepared to overrule the Legislature using his wartime reserve powers if they tried to obstruct what he considered to be a vital measure. Alas, he was now hardly in a position to repeat such an act of Caesar; and he approached the hard task of unveiling London's reform demands before the House from a position of undoubted weakness. Back in Nassau, he shut himself away for a week to write his speech with the help of Richardson and the officials; they struggled to make the tough meat of reform palatable to the acidulous political digestion of Bay Street.

On Monday 30 November the Project was declared officially completed, and the Duke ceremonially opened the two great airfields which had been under construction for eighteen months and already in use for a year – which indeed were now declining in military importance. That same evening he opened the Legislature.[24] He began by extolling the Project and consequent Bases for their immense benefit to the Colony and important part in the war. They had much cause to be thankful to the Americans. (The Duke had actually tried to get the OBE for the American managers of the Project, but London threw this out.) The Project had provided employment for an average of 2,400 men over two-and-a-half years; it had been a great vocational training for Bahamians (alas too quickly forgotten); the contractors had spent over £1 million in the Colony; the foundations had been laid for a great peacetime role in civil aviation. The Duke passed onto the continuing good economic fortune of the Bahamas and the increasing success of the Labour Scheme. Dealing with the growing deficit of the Colony he deftly mentioned the need for direct taxation, and then passed on to Out Island Development; his Economic Investigation Committee had worked out an extensive long-term programme which would soon be presented to the House. The Duke had been speaking for over an hour, and he now introduced the crux of his address to his lulled audience with a clutch of those rolling sentences that were so typical of his style:

> Those Bahamians who have lately been able to take advantage of the slight and welcome relaxing of Exchange Control Regulations and travel to America, cannot fail to have been impressed as I have how social-minded people have become beyond our shores. In all democratic countries special attention has been directed during recent years to improving social conditions and political thought has gained momentum in this direction as a result of the drastic changes in the social structure brought about by total war. The Bahamas . . . can no longer afford to lag too far behind the forces operating in the world outside.

Should my surmise in this respect be a correct one then the Legislature may well be expected to approach certain political and social legislation that it will be invited to deal with during the coming Session in a constructive rather than a reactionary spirit. . . .

Before the Speech, the Duke had taken Higgs and Solomon aside and explained that the measures he was about to propose were those which the Imperial Government absolutely demanded. This did not prevent the anticipated outcry from the House. A mixed chorus of horror and derision was their reaction, to the accompaniment of scathing editorials in the *Nassau Guardian*. A few days later the Out Island Development proposals on which the Duke had set his heart were laid before the House, requiring £400,000 to be made available over eight years. Members boasted that they would use the prospect of favourable consideration of this as a bribe to dissuade the Governor from the anathema of electoral reform. The Duke was disheartened. 'The House becomes conveniently dumb over the clearest and most explanatory of messages that I send them from which they do not see an immediate financial gain to themselves,' he wrote to Stanley.[25]

That December, the Duchess wrote to Aunt Bessie: 'I am busy planning "something for the boys" for their Xmas treat – not easy with limited cash and supplies.'[26] She worked furiously 'preparing for 1,000 men', and the men went wild with delight on the day as their punch was ladled out by the Royal Governor's lady. To cheer themselves up the Duke and Duchess invited the two gravest pessimists of their acquaintance to spend the festive season with them – Jack Warner and Arthur Davis. It was all a great success. On New Year's Eve the Duchess's American secretary Miss Jean Drewes, of whom she had become very fond, was married. (Congratulating her on her engagement, the Duchess had earlier said: 'If you want an example of a perfect couple, there's one living right here at Government House.') 'We are *not* very impressed with the groom,' wrote the Duchess to her aunt, 'but she is radiant. I lent her the house for a small reception afterwards. Gray gave her away loathing every minute of it. She looked very sweet having prepared herself in New York for the event. He is a rather soft-looking person – just an aircraftman. However, he has painted a great canvas of his status in London and she is now Mrs Brian Hardcastle-Taylor – adores the hyphen.'[27]

So life was not without its charming episodes, and they could still laugh a great deal. But they were putting a cheerful face on what seemed to them to be an increasingly desperate outlook, making the best of a bad job which got worse and worse. 'When will we be released from this life?' was the Duchess's parting comment in her Christmas letter to Aunt Bessie. The second half of 1943 had brought the siren call from America and made their position in Nassau more difficult and painful than ever. The Duke (influenced by the sagacious Richardson) knew how much he could do in the United States but felt there was absolutely nothing more he could achieve in or for the Colony. The stain of evil left by the Oakes affair made it ever more uncomfortable and ungovernable; now that the U-boats had been driven from the Caribbean and the fate of Germany sealed in Europe, it was no longer even important in the war. The people had shown themselves ever more incapable of being persuaded for their own good; peaceful reform had seemed just possible before, it looked a distant prospect now. The Colonial Office wanted a bully-boy dictator as Governor, and the Duke – who had done his best, who had done well – simply could not be expected to carry on in this role. He had finally had enough. He thought increasingly of escape.

17
The Search for Escape
1944

Escape! It sounded so simple. The problem was mildly complicated by the fact that there did not yet appear to be anywhere to escape to. No other appointment was likely to be forthcoming; they would definitely not be welcome elsewhere on British soil; Europe was still *Festung Europa* from which they had fled in 1940; and (even assuming they would be allowed the necessary dollars) they could hardly retire jobless to the United States right in the middle of the war. But as they dejectedly saw in their fourth New Year at Government House, the lack of a haven almost seemed a minor complication – they just had to get away soon. 'I really feel that neither of us can stand this place either physically or mentally for another year,' wrote the Duchess to Aunt Bessie – and perhaps for the first time she really meant it. Indeed, she was working harder than ever – at the Red Cross, the Canteen, the Infant Welfare Clinics; but she no longer worked with the joyful passion that had seized her after Pearl Harbor. Work, hard obsessive work, was now a grim anodyne, an escape from nightmare; she was burning herself out. Her stomach pains were almost constant now, and she had become a prey to all those ills born of overwork and misery that flesh (particularly exiled flesh) is heir to. As always, she tried hard to hide the strain; but for the first time, the Bahamas saw she was a sick woman.

The Duke suffered agonies watching the evident moral and physical decline of his wife. He might have hoped that his own official hell would abate as the war receded; but nothing of the kind occurred. Politics were worse than ever. It was hard to tell which was ghastlier, the Colonial Office with its relentless uninformed insistence, or Bay Street with its blind unyielding stubbornness. London continued ever more loudly to demand the reforms to which the local establishment would never agree. The Duke, having laid out the basic reform programme in his November speech, swallowed his pride and opened negotiations with his grim old adversary Kenneth Solomon, still master of the House. He pointed out 'that the attention of the British House of Commons was focused upon the backwardness of the Bahamas in electoral and social matters and that their constitution might well be in jeopardy if they did not mend their ways.' The Speaker, however, remained 'a reactionary die-hard and blindly averse to all change in principle'; he would, wrote the Duke to the Secretary of State, 'seek every excuse for resisting reform'. After endless discussion, all Solomon would agree to was some further labour reforms – on the condition that the Government ceased to insist on extending the secret ballot to the Out Islands. To that the House would *never* agree! The Duke communicated this unpromising information to the Colonial Office, suggesting that they might limit their immediate proposals to those measures which had some chance of being adopted – new labour laws (which would enable the Colony to qualify for aid under the Colonial Development and Welfare Act); a bill to make the secret ballot permanent in New Providence; another one, perhaps, to extend it to one or two of the more developed Out Islands, such as Abaco and Eleuthera with their substantial white populations. Why press for something certain to be refused when a part of the whole might be accepted? The rest could be introduced with better hopes at a future session. As he wrote to Stanley:

> . . . Were I ever able to get agreement in Council over sending a message to the House inviting them to extend the secret ballot to the Out Islands, which I very much doubt, then the measure would certainly be lost in the House. The whole question is most delicate and fraught with difficulties, and is one which if I take too firm a stand is likely to produce a clash not only with the House of Assembly but also with the unofficial members of my Executive Council. This is a risk which I would personally deem it imprudent to run at the present juncture. I need the support of the Legislature in certain important measures which have been laid before them, such as my long-term Out Island Development Scheme which if adopted will be a very definite step in the right direction, and one which will have the most far-reaching practical results in improving the welfare of two-thirds of the population who are at present living under the most primitive conditions, and whose livelihood is precarious, to say the least. . . .[1]

In other words, it was more important that the Out Islanders should eat than that they should secretly vote. But the Colonial Office was not convinced, and countered in this extraordinary political chess-game by declaring that the Out Island Development Scheme might have to wait; for it was not certain that the administrative staff required – though their salaries had actually been voted by the House – could be spared by the Service. The Duke was furious. He sent off a classically thundering telegram.[2] Had he not told the Secretary of State on numerous occasions that the 'main essential problem' of the Bahamas was the need for Out Island Development? Was he now to tell the House that the Government was incapable of carrying out its own proposals? But the message was clear. The Duke would not get the scheme that meant so much to him unless he also pressed for the universal secret franchise. Sadly, he prepared himself for the long and unhopeful task of persuading ExCo of the Colonial Office view and cultivating sufficient members of the House to get it through. But in a letter to Allen he confessed that 'I am about at the end of my rope here', and that he had threatened to resign in the event of Colonial Office policy requiring the dissolution of the House of Assembly and a governor's dictatorship after the secret ballot had been thrown out, as it was almost certain to be.[3]

The Duke was not the only one to have become finally exasperated with the administration of the Bahamas, which Rosita Forbes had so aptly compared to an ingrowing toenail. His two senior officials, Heape the Colonial Secretary and Hallinan the Attorney-General, had also had enough. They, at least, were escaping. Both had arrived just before the Duke, and both, to their infinite relief, now obtained their transfers. 'It was a source of amazement to the Colonial Office that we had stuck out a whole four years in the Bahamas, where appointments were notoriously regarded as the most trying in the service,' says Hallinan, who remembers his years in Nassau as 'the most difficult and unhappy of my whole career'. The Duke was well-served by these men, representative members of the old Colonial Service, an adequate appreciation of whose work has yet to be written. The able and civilized Hallinan had become a target for the caucus of Bay Street, hating as he did a regime which kept the black people in perpetual ignorance and subjection. Sensing that behind a pleasant if somewhat remote manner lay a determination to outwit them, they attacked him frequently and with venom; but he beat them at their own game when he used their most vicious attack upon him to produce the Riots Report which denounced them. Heape, his great friend, was not brilliant, perhaps rather limited, but possessed sterling qualities of uprightness, thoroughness and dedication. He had been in charge at the ghastly moments of the Riots and the Oakes trial; he never panicked, and he withstood the tidal wave of criticism manfully. Both he and Hallinan were much concerned for the welfare of the coloured people of the Colony, and did all they could to bring some coloured men into the Nassau administration; many in the Bahamas remember them to this day with gratitude and affection.

These two faithful servants immensely liked the Duke, who had so tenaciously protected them in their adversity; and, while he was happy for their sakes that they were leaving (for they had long wished to escape), he was sorry to see them go. 'I have recently been robbed of my best administrative officers and do not know when I can expect them to be replaced,' he wrote to an American acquaintance. 'A British Colonial Governor's position is no sinecure in these uncertain times!' Hallinan stayed on a few more months before departing for Trinidad; but Heape left in January 1944 to become Acting Governor of British Guiana. It hardly seemed possible to replace the experience of this slow but meticulous administrator, with his soldierly air and passion for minutes and correspondence. A prop had been removed, and the Duke felt more exposed than ever. It would be several months before Heape's successor could arrive from West Africa, and meanwhile the Governor, with the help of minor officials, had to face the immense task of preparing Bay Street for reform while carrying on the smooth administration of the colony. Nor could he leave Nassau, even for a short time; and he had to cancel a long-planned trip to visit the Bahamian labourers in Florida during which he had hoped to get in a few days' shooting near Tallahassee with Mrs George Baker. 'It does seem hard', wrote the Duchess, 'and yet we must remain here under any circumstances they see fit to impose on us.'

As life proceeded desultorily at Government House, the Duchess continued to write her weekly letter to Aunt Bessie in an increasingly agitated hand. RAF officers were leaving and new ones arriving – 'one hopes there will be more adonises and Don Juans in the new lot.' Lady Oakes turned up with a great army of lawyers 'and is really looking much better and quite lovely as the result of a philosophy she has worked out'. The climate was dreadful that winter, 'hot and sticky so that one has no lift'. The Duchess struggled to sound snappy and cheerful, but was clearly depressed. 'This is still an awful place,' she wrote on 6 February, 'and some days I feel I can't resist slapping everyone in the face.'

The war too was going through a dispiriting phase after the steady successes on land of 1943. Allied armies inched painfully forward in Italy, Russia and Burma, and people began to wonder whether there would ever be a Second Front. The West Atlantic was fairly clear of U-boats now, and Nassau's main role was no longer as a reconnaissance or training station but – under the aegis of Transport Command – as a staging-post for transatlantic flights. The town was always full of servicemen on their way to somewhere else, and generals and politicians were constantly passing through and expecting to stay without notice at Government House. On top of all her other preoccupations, the Duchess found herself more than ever cast into the role of hotel-keeper that winter. Her transitory visitors never failed to be impressed, for she was strenuous in her determination never to lapse from her vigilant high standards as a hostess; but she rather hated it all, and it took a further heavy toll of her health and strength. 'I am so fed up with housekeeping and all the cares,' she wrote to her Aunt Bessie; and she had to use all her ingenuity to retain her white servants 'who are naturally as discontented as we are. . . . G.H. with only a coloured staff would put me in my grave!' In March four British Members of Parliament turned up to stay, and were much impressed by their reception and the Duke's administration. The Duke took them on a flying trip to Eleuthera to explain his plans for the Out Islands, and at a public dinner for them made a witty speech on Bahamian political problems which brought smiles to the dourest faces of Bay Street.

So, in spite of everything the Duke and Duchess had lost none of their touch, and were perfectly capable of controlling their anguish and giving a first-rate performance. But that March was painful and lonely for them, for everybody else seemed to be leaving. 'It is hard to keep from being the last survivor here,' remarked the Duchess, as the last of the evacuees returned to England. Katherine Rogers had come for a few weeks to bring her some cheer, but now she was going, and so too were Rosa Wood and all the winter visitors; the fortunate Heape and Hallinan had been re-posted, and now they were being followed by that trusted adviser and confidant Professor Richardson. The Duke's great friend Tony Pulitzer, who had consoled him during the dark days after the Duke of Kent's death, suddenly announced that he was departing for the mainland. *'You see 4 years is really too long,'* wrote the Duchess. *'No one can take it. How to get out is the question.'*

From what has been said of the Duke's ever-mounting exasperation, of his constant private hope that he would be relieved of his awful post and offered something better, it might be imagined that he had been perpetually complaining about his situation and threatening to throw it up. This was far from the case. Outwardly he and the Duchess concealed their disappointment perfectly. They spoke of it intermittently to some intimate English and American friends; but no one in Nassau, not even the high officials or the equerries, was much aware of it. Officially as well as socially they were reticent to a degree (in contrast to the Bahamian establishment, which never concealed its astonishment that the Royal Governor was being kept in Nassau). Only three times in three years had the Duke made some discreet protest to high authority. The first had been when Beaverbrook had visited him in April 1942, the second when he had seen Churchill in Washington in May 1943 (whence the offer of Bermuda), the third when he had indicated to the Colonial Office that he would resign rather than dissolve the House and rule as a dictator. By March 1944, however, he was in a state of utter desperation, and in the grip of this mood he drafted an outright letter of resignation to Churchill. He never sent it; his sense of duty reasserted itself. Longing as he did for flight, in war he had to serve. But he sent a copy of the draft to Allen, 'as an indication of what has been in my mind for some time past'; and it may usefully be quoted here:

My dear Winston,

It may seem inopportune to broach the subject of this letter which you will receive in the midst of all your present serious preoccupations, but the time-factor must eventually assert itself.

By August 17th. next, I shall have completed no less than four years in the appointment of Governor of the Bahamas, a post I have conscientiously filled notwithstanding my lack of experience and training in Colonial administration.

But he who is wise senses when he has outgrown his usefulness in any given job, official or otherwise, and without any claim to great wisdom, I am fortunate in being able to detect that this has now happened in my own case. It has been a gradual process and whilst I can say that I have been proud to serve the British Commonwealth in the novel role of Colonial administrator, and that I can look back on the four years I have spent in the Bahamas with some degree of satisfaction in the light of having done one's best for the people of this Colony under the difficulties of wartime conditions, other considerations now enter the picture.

Although still reasonably active in my fiftieth year, so long a spell of official responsibilities in a tropical climate has taken considerable toll of my energy, and your offer of another island governorship last year was further proof, if it were needed, of the limitations placed on my capabilities. These limitations I do not seek to challenge in any way; that is entirely a matter of opinion. Nor do I wish to refer to the circumstances created by my family, which make it impossible for me to return to Great Britain.

In tendering my resignation which will be forwarded through the usual channel of the Secretary of State for the Colonies, I have one request to make of you. That is that the United Kingdom Exchange Control Authority be directed to allow me sufficient US Dollar funds in order that I can live in dignified simplicity in America until such time as I have been able to make some arrangements for the future.

Believe me,
Very sincerely Yours
EDWARD

The Duke explained to Allen: 'You will notice that I have scrupulously avoided any mention of the Duchess in this draft letter, but it is largely her state of mind and health after four years in the tropics that has brought things to a head; that and the difficulties of explaining to the outside world the "whys and wherefores" of our continued exile on these islands. She should just not have to take it any longer, and you know me well enough to understand that when I say I am fearful and reluctant to I have very good reasons.'[4]

Near as she was to a breakdown in her health, the Duchess certainly did nothing to discourage her husband from his now determined course. Her letters grew increasingly exasperated, even shrill. 'I do not think the Duke would hesitate to throw in his hand for this is certainly no place for him and to think he is dumped here solely by family jealousy!' She cursed as never before the climate, the worries of housekeeping, the strictures of the censorship (though no longer the local people, it is interesting to note). Writing to Aunt Bessie on 5 April she ventilated her anguish in a wild little tirade:

> . . . There is no sign of getting elsewhere and some days we feel we simply cannot carry on any longer but everything presents a problem nowadays and it is hard for us to know what best to do. . . . The war looks to be longer now than it seemed in the autumn. . . . I doubt if we will ever see our things again. What a really good mess it all is and it will never become straightened out in our time. How one longs for liberty once again! Being shut up here is like being a prisoner-of-war only worse, as there are trying responsibilities whereas it is the host's responsibility if you are a captured prisoner-of-war. Who would have believed that it could have gone on so long and what will we have got in the end? When you read the war books of those who have seen the horrors, one prays the sacrifices are not in vain. I hope you can read this scribble and will not think I have entirely lost my sense of humour. I am rather tired and I use up a lot of energy hating the place. . . .

So worried was the Duke that he begged her to go alone to the mainland to rest while he continued to await the new Colonial Secretary; but after reflection she concluded: 'I can't bring myself to leave him alone in this awful hot depressing hole.' On 13 May she wrote: 'I dislike this coral rock more every day; but the Duke's patience with the community and England's treatment is really inspiring, and I should not complain in the face of such a good example.'

Life went on. The Duchess reported that she had had 'all the French temperament the chef could muster', but had still managed to entertain 'an endless stream of military all nationalities'. The heat rose sharply until interrupted by 'a terrible storm, a small cyclone' at the end of April. The Duke managed to convince the unofficial members of ExCo of the desirability of extending the secret ballot to the Out Islands, and deftly laid his plans for the House. He was anxious about the coming of the Second Front. 'All these rumours of the impending invasion create an atmosphere of the lull before the storm,' he wrote to Charles Cushing on 30 April; 'but if we are committed to this ghastly frontal attack upon the coast of Europe, which is I am afraid bound to be terribly costly in lives and casualties, it will be a sort of relief to know that the battle is on.' Rosita Forbes returned to the Bahamas with her husband, and there was a great welcome and a highly successful dinner-party for them at Government House. The Duchess confided her growing anguish to Rosita. 'They only murdered Sir Harry Oakes once. They will *never* stop murdering the Duke of Windsor. . . . It is his own family who are against him.' Rosita was full of sympathy. 'You touched me deeply. . . . I should feel equally despairing if my husband were attacked as unfairly. . . . I want to help.'[5] In her war memoirs which she was then writing, she said of the Duchess:

> . . . Infinitely vital and effective, she is definitely a person and real because her faults are the defects of her qualities. Even in a crowded station waiting-room she could not be overlooked. The Duchess of Windsor has a mind and uses it. So many make use of other people's. She has instant wit and wits. She has plenty of courage, although, like the rest of us, she does not always employ it. . . . She loves baubles. But so do we all, in one way or another. It is the last fragment of childhood left in us. . . . The Duchess gives pleasure. She also gives excellent counsel. In the delightful and difficult, the near to impossible Bahamas, I have seen many people fail. I have seen the Duchess succeed.[6]

The calm, efficient façade which the Duke always showed as Governor now belied a state of raging inner turmoil. As in the autumn of 1936, his mind was torn between irreconcilable desires and emotions. One part of him longed for release and nirvana, another side for service and authority. The thoughts which he revealed in his intimate letters to Allen were a mass of paradox and contradiction. On the one hand he wrote, 'with my experience of official treatment since 1936, which includes five years of re-enlistment in the British service and ample proof of the continuity of the hostile official attitude towards myself, my one desire is to return to private life.' Yet it was unthinkable 'to retire at this most critical part of the war, with the most momentous military operations in history impending'. He desperately craved 'an appointment worthy of my experience'; yet he could write that 'I have now become almost resigned to the fact that family jealousy would oppose any suggestion of such an appointment'. The piece which tipped the balance was America. With his popularity there as high as ever, the Duke never ceased to hope that he would be offered the work there for which he knew he was ideally suited.

One man who strongly encouraged the Duke to hold fast in his determination to seek a proper job was Professor J. Henry Richardson, the brilliant and wily economist whom the Duke had secured as economic adviser in April 1943 and who had rapidly become his *éminence grise*. 'He has become my right-hand man and his advice to me is invaluable,' the Duke admitted to Oliver Stanley in August 1943, while to Allen he described the Professor as 'a loyal and trusted friend of mine' whose 'advice to me personally has been the greatest possible help in my administration'. An expert in the psychological technique of negotiation with labour, Richardson knew exactly how to deal with Bay Street; he had urged the Duke to 'speak softly and carry a big stick', to be understanding in discussion and moderate in his demands, but always to make the House aware of his power. It was Richardson who had explained to the Duke the best possible strategy of reform; he had been behind the *coup* of September 1943 when the Duke had used his war powers to force through various measures against the opposition of the House – a demonstration which alas became unrepeatable after the murder trial. Richardson had come for two months and stayed for over a year; the Duke kept him on and reposed the utmost confidence in his advice; and Richardson was only too happy to play the role of genie over the gubernatorial throne. The Duke discussed his most private thoughts and affairs with him. As he wrote to Allen: 'From the moment Richardson arrived, he has been of the opinion that I was wasting my time here, and we have therefore discussed my position in a general way. . . . He is in agreement that America is our best bet. . . . I believe him to be completely sincere in his personal loyalty to me. . . .'[7]

Much to the Duke's sadness, this trusted friend and counsellor – having represented the Bahamas at the Barbados Conference on the Future of the Caribbean, and published a fat and pertinent work (to be entirely ignored) on the economic problems and post-war prospects of the Bahamas – was now being recalled to London with a view to his being posted to the Gold Coast. But when he set out at the beginning of May, it was also with an extraordinary commission as the Duke's secret emissary. For in the lull before the Second Front the Duke, encouraged by Richardson, had at last decided to launch a swift and discreet campaign to obtain for himself the appointment which he craved. Richardson was to make contact with Allen in London, and together they were charged with nothing less than the fashioning of an active party of supporters of the Duke in the Cabinet, the Civil Service, and at Court. They were to make soundings and enlist support, while the Duke tried to rally his influential friends in America. On receiving the word from Richardson, he would demand a change of post.

The plot may seem a little naive, redolent of that touching frankness which characterized, and generally compromised, his more elaborate (but always well-intentioned) schemes both during and after 1936. There is something almost faintly comic about the coded telegrams (in which the King is 'Number One' and Churchill 'Number Two') by which the affair, which they called 'the Sounding-Out', was conducted; but it began hopefully. On 17 May, Allen and Richardson went to see Beaverbrook, who was 'cordial and friendly and fully appreciative of your sterling work and conceding that you had been in Nassau long enough and were entitled to a change.'[8] The Lord Privy Seal (as Beaverbrook had been since re-entering the Cabinet in the autumn of 1943) did not like the 'roving commission' idea, which he thought would overshadow the role of the Ambassador in Washington; but Halifax was due to retire at the end of that year, which might present certain opportunities; Mackenzie King was then in London and Beaverbrook would have a word with him about the Governor-Generalship of Canada; and if all else failed he would at least hope to secure for the Duke the Governorship of Newfoundland. Encouraged by this apparent success, Richardson and Allen approached Walter Monckton, who was curiously powerless to help; and they sought out Philip Guedalla, the leading personality at the British Council and the Duke's faithful supporter, only to find him languishing with meningitis. But they found a powerful friend in the official world in the person of Bernard Rickatson-Hatt, Ernest Simpson's old wartime comrade, formerly Editor-in-Chief of Reuters and now in charge of public relations at the Bank of England, who revealed an important piece of suppressed news. The Colonial Office had plans to federate the British West Indies, and all the local feeling was that this ought to be done under the aegis of the Duke of Windsor.* Indeed, Rickatson-Hatt had received a letter from Jamaica explaining that the negro leaders there would accept *only* the Duke as Governor-General of a Federation! (Federation was duly delayed, taking place under the most disastrous circumstances fifteen years later.) Allen took this letter to the Colonial Office, where the responsible official told him: 'It doesn't surprise me at all. He is widely regarded here as the best Governor in the service.' Allen expressed the hope that this view was known to the Prime Minister.

It remained to find an ally at Court. This was all-important. For Churchill depended for the oft-imperilled supremacy of his position upon the personal support of the King and Queen, and part of the price was that they should always have the last word when it came to deciding the Duke of Windsor's fate. But Churchill did not conceal his personal sympathy for the Duke, and if only one could find an advocate *within* the Court, hostility might abate sufficiently to get an appointment through.

The quest for a suitable sympathizer of the Duke at the Palace was an exceedingly complicated and delicate affair. Some members of his family – such as Princess Alice of Athlone and the Duchess of Beaufort – were very much for reconciliation, but they were not in a position to put in a word for him during the war. The ex-King's close personal friends in the Household, such as Lord Brownlow and Sir Godfrey Thomas, had been thrown out after the Abdication in a swift and violent Palace revolution. Of the two friends who somewhat precariously remained, Monckton could not or would not at that moment help, and Sir Ulick Alexander, whom Edward VIII had made Keeper of the Privy Purse and who would probably have liked to have done something to help his old master (whose wedding he had tried to attend), was sick with gout. In these circumstances the Duke, through his two indomitable agents in London, made a

---

* In the printed index to the archives of the Foreign Office Political Department for the year 1942, the following curious file reference appears under the Duke of Windsor's name: 'Proposed Governor-Generalship of British West Indies if raised to Dominion status.' Needless to say, the file in question (ref. A8975/8975/14) is not available for general consultation in the Public Record Office.

disastrous error of judgment. Up to July 1943, the King's Private Secretary had been Major the Hon. Sir Alexander ('Alec') Hardinge, who hated the Duke of Windsor, was known to have intrigued against him during his reign, and executed the subsequent royal policy to ostracize him uncompromisingly and with relish. When Hardinge was forced to retire through ill-health his place was taken by Sir Alan ('Tommy') Lascelles, who had been King Edward VIII's Assistant Private Secretary and had also served him as Prince of Wales, and whom the Duke of Windsor imagined would be relatively sympathetic to him. It was a cruel illusion, for (as the Duke was later to realize) Lascelles, too, detested and despised his former master and had rejoiced in his fall and, if anything, was even more determined than Hardinge to exclude the Duke from any position of influence and prevent his return to England.[9] Being as yet ignorant of this animus, it was into Lascelles' poisonously prejudiced ear that George Allen and Professor Richardson communicated the Duke's intense desire for an appointment 'worthy of his experience'. The reply was brusque. No one at Court would intercede for the Duke before the King. Nor would the Court allow any other person to do so. The Duke, unsupported, would have to write to the King himself.[10]

In other words, the Duke, who had received no communication of any sort from his brother since July 1940, nor obtained a response to his own anguished missive of a year before, was being invited to beg. Allen urged the Duke to swallow his pride and write all the same. The success of their efforts seemed so near. 'I feel that if you could bring yourself to do this it would be a sagacious step to take. Your letter to the PM will of course be communicated to the King and discussed with him, so that it would be better, don't you think, that he should be warned in advance of what your wishes are . . . rather than be confused and neutral?'[11]

Back in Nassau, the Duke and Duchess waited anxiously for Allen's and Richardson's report. June came, and with it the summer humidity – 'like writing in a boiler factory', the Duchess assured her aunt. A horrified legislature was asked to provide £532 to replace Government House furniture eaten through by termites; there were dire warnings and bitter complaining, but the measure got through. The Chief Magistrate, the affable but dim Bancroft, succeeded the incisive and happily departing Hallinan as Attorney-General; and the new Colonial Secretary, Duncan Stewart arrived, a man of thirty-nine who was judged by the Duchess to be 'really nice, also bright, and the complete opposite of the last one.' (He was to be murdered five years later by a fanatical native in Sarawak.) The third of June was their wedding anniversary. 'We had a nice party here to celebrate our 7 years of bliss – just think, 5 of which have been war years and 4 in the Bahamas – not as planned!'

On 4 June came the news that the Allies had entered Rome; and the following day the Duke received Allen's letter about the 'Sounding-Out' in London. His spirits rose. At last there seemed hope of a post, although he wondered if he could bring himself to write the 'begging letter' to the King upon which the Court were insisting, as 'too much stinking water from the Palace has passed under the dam in the last eight years' for him to be able to crave favours which might so well be refused save at the expense of much doubt, hesitation and pain. But the following day changed everything, with the launching in Normandy of the Second Front. Once again it had become entirely inopportune for the Duke to press his suit; and now the conclusion of European hostilities was in prospect, which would at least solve the problem of his wartime employment.

'We all have our ears glued to the invasion news and have our thumbs crossed,' wrote the Duke to Allen. 'As old timers of the last war, we naturally realize the plight of the first waves of the attacking troops engaged and the probable casualties, but I guess these are unavoidable in such stupendous military operations. There is evidently no other way to terminate the seemingly endless state of war of which the whole of mankind must be as heartily sick as we are.'

But there was work to do in Nassau. Now that there was once again a Colonial Secretary in the Secretariat, the moment had arrived for the Duke's great confrontation with Bay Street over the secret ballot. For months he had schemed and brooded (with Richardson's clever advice) over the apparently doomed proposal which London wanted forced through; and he had devised a devilishly cunning plan. He had no hopes that the extension of secret voting to the Out Islands would get through the House, but he was confident that they would pass a measure making it permanent in New Providence (where the five-year trial period envisaged by Dundas's Act was coming to an end); and beyond that he meant to make use of the Legislative Council, that faintly ridiculous, powerless, rubber-stamping upper chamber which he always had nicely under control.

One of Hallinan's last duties had been to draft an electoral reform bill for Higgs to put before the House. But the Duke concluded that this would be courting disaster, and instead sent down a message to the House asking for the two specific reforms (extension to the Out Islands and permanence in New Providence) and adding: 'His Royal Highness has the honour to inform the House that the passing of this measure is expressly desired by His Majesty's Government.' The matter was referred to a committee headed by the masterful Stafford Sands. On 29 June, as expected, the Committee reported (Higgs and the negro Toote dissenting) in favour of a permanent secret ballot in New Providence but firmly against the extension to the Out Islands. On 3 July – the day the

House was to debate the report – there was a large coloured demonstration against it, addressed by Adderley. That night, the report of the Committee was adopted by seventeen votes to eight. A bill was then introduced to make the secret ballot permanent in New Providence, and passed its first reading. A week later it went up for rubber-stamping before LegCo. LegCo duly rubber-stamped; but it did more. It publicly deplored the fact that the House had not passed an Out-Islands measure for the legislative councillors to approve. It then passed a Resolution for transmission to London denouncing the intransigence of the House. It was over half a century since LegCo had last come up with such a Resolution. The House shuddered. It almost looked as if London was being invited to put its worst threat – forcible revision of the Bahamian constitution – into effect.

The Duke's aim was to give Bay Street a salutary shock to encourage them to drop their resistance to electoral reform at the next session. If anything, the device was far too successful. The fiery Dupuch – 'dangerous and unpredictable', as the Duke warned London – hailed the Resolution as heralding the imminent collapse of the local political establishment; a hint of unrest ensued. Nor was London particularly pleased. The Colonial Office hated having to take responsibility. How on earth, it asked the Duke, was it to reply to the Resolution? But that the political deadlock had been broken there was no doubt at all; for the rest of the summer, the House behaved itself beautifully. Within a fortnight of the Resolution it approved what the Duke considered to be the finest legislative achievement of his governorship – his Out Island Development Plan, under which £400,000 was to be made available over eight years for the systematic improvement of settlements.

On 23 June the Duke was fifty years of age. It is the time of life when men of his character and temperament are generally at the height of their powers, and have the surest touch. But it is also the moment when one looks ahead to the remaining opportunities which life may have to offer. The Duchess had been exhausted by her long months of official entertaining, and Government House received only one house-guest that summer. On 22 June she wrote to Aunt Bessie: 'I have a Squadron-Leader stopping here for about a week. He had a bad jeep accident – was driving it and it overturned and killed one of his best friends and injured 2 others badly. I thought it would be a change of scenery and diet for him to come here after he left hospital. He is nice and no trouble.'

By mid-July the new Colonial Secretary was sufficiently in harness for the Duke and Duchess to be able to leave the Colony for the first time in eight months. On 16 July – the day the Allied armour smashed the German line at Caen and poured across the Orne into the great plain of France – they arrived in New York, where the Duke got down to official and business conversations. Beaverbrook was there, though as the Duke wrote to Allen, 'I just couldn't be bothered to pursue my quest or penetrate the veil of mystery with which he surrounds his every movement.' In May, Beaverbrook had promised help for the Duke and even suggested possible jobs, but it was evident that he had done nothing for him. On another front, however, there was a momentous development; the Duke conferred with his Ecushwa partners Cushing and Walker, and they finally made the great and expensive decision – in the face of numerous risks and uncertainties, but with fair prospects of success – to drill for oil on the EP Ranch.

The Duchess meanwhile consulted her doctors, who confirmed that her health had deteriorated considerably, that her stomach illness was now serious, that she now also appeared to have appendicitis and that surgery could not be long delayed. With magnificent courage, she had made light of her conditions and given an impression of almost robust vivacity; but she really needed help now. In August they stopped at Washington (where the Duke negotiated an increase in the Colony's petrol quota), visited Bahamian labourers in their camps on the Eastern Shore, helped Aunt Bessie celebrate her eightieth birthday on the 19th, and spent their week-ends quietly with old friends – the Knight Woolleys at East Hampton, and Mai Douglas and the Robert Youngs at Newport. A widely published photograph showed them both looking anxious, tired and ill. At the end of the month the Duchess was admitted to the Roosevelt Hospital, New York, for what the public were to know as the first of many successful operations for the removal of her appendix. It was in fact infinitely more serious, a surgery necessitated by an ulcerous growth in the duodenum which was developing a distinct suspicion of malignancy.

It would be unchivalrous to dwell upon the sufferings of the Duchess, who went under the knife on 31 August, or upon the acute distress and anxiety of the Duke, who maintained a bedside vigil. Their friends stood by them and helped in every way. When an atrocious press canard flew out to the effect that the Duke and Duchess had engaged ten rooms at the hospital, repainted them in pink and blue, installed a dozen portable telephones and retained a regiment of nurses, Hermann Rogers of the press censorship and Fred Bate of NBC saw to it that the story was swiftly and publicly corrected. The operation was a success, and the Duke was pictured in the newspapers exuding joy and relief and jauntily wearing a boater. Yet he hardly left her side for the twelve days she remained in hospital.

By midday on 11 September the Duchess was well enough to leave (her departure coinciding with the arrival of Madame Chiang Kai-Shek). Five hundred boys at two nearby schools had somehow got hold of the news; foregoing their lunch, they dashed to the scene. As the Duke and Duchess emerged a resounding cheer went up, followed by yells of 'Hiyah Duchess !' and 'Ray for the Duchess', and the surge and press of a wildly enthusiastic adolescent male mob. The Duke nervously danced forward in an effort to calm the crowd, but the Duchess (dressed in pink and black) was thrilled to bits, and surrendered herself to a little orgy of autograph-signing while the press photographers captured her radiant with spontaneous delight. As they drove away the boys laid siege to the car and swarmed over the running-boards, still madly cheering. 'Minus her appendix but none of her charm,' wrote the working-class *New York Sun*, 'the Duchess of Windsor took her leave of the Roosevelt Hospital amid an unscheduled fanfare that made the occasion seem truly momentous.'

But she was weak and needed to convalesce. The Hot Springs of Virginia once more awaited them, and they made their way there by stages, taking Aunt Bessie with them. The days passed quickly and pleasantly there. The Duke wrote to Allen: 'The Duchess, I am glad to say, is fine after her operation, and gaining strength every day in this lovely mountain resort. It is doing me lots of good too, for I shared in the operation, which was naturally an anxious time for me.' Recovery was aided by excitement, for on 22 September came the news that the drillers at the Ranch had found traces of oil in the coal sandstone at 1,500 feet.

Only a few days after their arrival at 'the Hot', Churchill telegraphed to say that he was staying with Roosevelt following the Second Quebec Conference and would like to see the Duke, who duly travelled to Hyde Park in late September. When Roosevelt was wheeled into the entrance-hall to greet his visitor, the Duke got a shock:

> He had grown very thin since our last meeting [wrote the Duke twenty-two years later] and the skin of his face had taken on a strange transparency. I must have made an involuntary gesture of surprise which the President was quick to notice. 'Ah,' he exclaimed, 'you find me thinner. Well, the doctors wanted me to lose some weight and I feel all the better for that.' On being conducted to another room where Winston was working on some papers, I asked him what he thought about the President's condition. 'What do *you* think?' Winston countered. 'He looks to me like a very sick man,' I replied. 'Oh, no,' he insisted, 'it is only that he is tired, very tired.' At luncheon later on, when I sat next to Mrs Roosevelt, there was Winston in great form growling clever things while at the other end of the table our host sat in silence, a frail, almost feeble figure. . . .[12]

It was in this dying state that Roosevelt was to be re-elected a few weeks later for his fourth Presidential term and then go off to meet Stalin at Yalta, 'that ghastly piece of folly by my view [wrote the Duke] which had the effect of sanctioning the entrance of Soviet power into the heart of Europe.' In the Duke's opinion, 'Roosevelt's failing health left him incapable of perceiving the menace that he was agreeing to let into

Europe.' It was the last time that he saw the President, with whom he had developed such a curious friendship since the *Tuscaloosa* meeting less than four years before.

At Hyde Park that September the Duke discussed his personal affairs with Churchill, and reported to Allen 'a long and satisfactory talk – in so far as it went, which was not very far.' The Prime Minister agreed that the Duke had done excellently in the Bahamas; that there was nothing more for him to achieve there; and that he should be allowed to give up Nassau whenever he wished, and return to his home in France as soon as this was possible. (Leclerc had entered Paris on 24 August, and the very same day de Lattre was freeing the coast around La Croë; but France was still plunged in chaos and agony.) However, when the Duke asked if he could serve in another and more responsible post at least until the end of the war, Churchill looked unhappy and became evasive and switched to another and extraordinary subject. As the Duke wrote to Allen:

> The only thing he did say of interest, and which amused me a whole lot, was to emphasize the alarm and discomfort it would cause the Palace if I were to indicate any intention of taking up residence in Great Britain. . . . I did express surprise at his remark and that, after eight years' absence, I was still considered so formidable a menace to the solidarity of the monarchy; especially so because hardly a day passes by that British propaganda does not stuff us with the extent to which the King has established himself in the hearts of the people.[13]

So the Duke had at last obtained his release from his painful post – on condition that he was to stay out of England and not expect any alternative official employment of any kind. Yet a part of the Duke never ceased to hope that one day he would be offered a proper job. It seemed to him almost impossible that the vendetta should go on for ever, that his training should be wasted, that his public popularity should count for nothing. In October he tried again, and wrote to Churchill from Hot Springs:

> Whilst I realize that the German war has yet to be won before the situation in Europe can crystallize into anything recognizable, and that it is still too early to visualize which job, if any, there might be for me on that continent, I would not wish to remain unemployed if there was any sphere in which it was considered my experience could still be appropriately utilized.[14]

So passionate and sincere was his desire for service that he even offered to do undercover work for the Foreign Office in liberated Europe – work that would never have brought any public recognition; but this offer did not receive so much as an acknowledgement.

Despite these bitter (but hardly unexpected) disappointments, the

Duke and Duchess thoroughly enjoyed and profited by their stay at Hot Springs, doubtless fortified not only by the cool mountain air but also by the knowledge that their forthcoming return to Nassau would probably be the last. (Though there would be no hurried or undignified departure; the Duke's 'release' would be kept secret, and they would see out another Nassau winter.) Pictures of them that autumn show them looking fit and hale. In mid-October they returned to New York, visiting *en route* several of the plantations using Bahamian labour. Now that the Bahamas were less important as a war-station, the Duke's labour scheme was essential as never before; the autumn and winter marked the greatest extent of Bahamian labour in the United States, 6,000 people (or about fifteen per cent of the Colony's adult workforce) working on American plantations who would otherwise have been miserably unemployed. The Duke was photographed picking fruit with negroes, and told reporters how glad he was to see them flourishing and how proud of their record there – Bahamians were already thought to be the best imported workers on the mainland. He also hoped that they were learning agricultural skills which they would practise when they returned to their islands – but this was wishful thinking.

The second half of October in New York was a time of intense excitement, for it really seemed that Ecushwa was about to make a big oil-strike on the Ranch. The story of Canada's first and last privately owned oil-well is complex and fascinating, and has all the ingredients of a first-class comic novel with a brilliant cast of highly unlikely characters. As the autumn proceeded, the drillers encountered pocket after pocket of oil, news from the Ranch became ever more enthusiastic, and the Duke and his partners, aware of the risks but lured by a sort of gambler's fever, committed greater and greater funds to prospecting ever further down. By the end of October, when the Duke left New York, the well was at 2,710 feet and there seemed to be a considerable showing of oil in the Fernie Shales. By the end of November the bit was in the lime at 3,335 feet; the moment of truth had arrived; the next stage would finally reveal whether oil was present in commercial quantities or not. The Ecushwa partners held their breath; and . . . there now arose technical difficulties which suspended all drilling operations for two months. In February 1945 the drill continued its thrilling progress, and on the 14th oil at last began to flow – only to turn into water, like a miracle in reverse. The Duke took the news philosophically and telegraphed to Walker: 'A great disappointment for all of us but thank you and Charlie for fine co-operation and faith in project.' He himself had committed about $100,000 to the enterprise, a substantial part of his private fortune. Had oil been struck (as it so nearly was) it would have obviated those pressing financial problems which (contrary to what is usually supposed) were never far away during the remainder of his life, and which obliged the unfortunate former King of England to give television interviews, lend his name to historical films, write magazine articles on men's clothing and gardening, and seek the company of men who were supposed to understand the Stock Market.

But it was full of hopes for a financially secure future that the Duke and Duchess left New York (where all the talk was of the reconquest of the Philippines and the impending presidential election) at the beginning of November 1944. ('While it looks like the New Deal will be re-elected [sic],' the Duke wrote to Allen, 'it will I believe be a close fight.') In Miami they had to occupy themselves with a matter which caused them much regret – the sale of their yacht *Gemini*; 'all very sad [wrote the Duchess] as the boat really helped us to bear Nassau, and I had begun to love fishing and our week-ends aboard. However, we were advised that the market was good now – so amidst tears we left crew and boat.' Discretion prohibited her from mentioning the ulterior reason for the sale, that they would soon have no use for the craft because they would not be there. For the Duke's resignation was to remain a close secret until the end of winter. While he was still Governor, he meant to govern.

'A rough trip,' wrote the Duchess to Aunt Bessie after her return.

I found everything the same only shabbier, and Marshall more irritable ! We found that we had an air marshal and wife, a brigadier-general, and a wire from Edith Lindsay asking to come for the week-end. I managed to arrange it all. . . . It is very *flat* like the island to be back and as you say rush agrees with me – mother always said no one could look uglier than I am when bored.

The Duke resumed the government of the Colony on 8 November. There was a brief scare as German U-boats, thought to have been long since driven from local waters, suddenly began a new long-range offensive. There was a brisk correspondence with London on the supply of ping-pong balls to the Duchess's canteen. Telegrams flew back and forth on the subject of Anglo–American oil exploration in the shallow seas (oil obsessed the Duke that month). There was an effort to obtain a bigger fertilizer quota in view of the increased tomato crop. There was a West Indian Governors' Conference to prepare for, and a visit from the Secretary of State in the New Year. It was necessary to decide whether to reappoint the headmaster of the Government High School or find another one. The Colonial Office wanted to know what progress was being made on the Secret Ballot. The Duke assured them he was returning to the charge.

He closed the Legislature on 20 November and opened it again on 4th December. He spoke much of the war :

On no previous occasion when I have addressed the Legislature, has the war situation been as propitious as it is today. . . .

After five anxious years with but a narrow strip of sea separating them from a relentless foe, for a time in imminent danger of invasion, and always vulnerable to devastating air attacks, it is not unnatural that the people of Britain are more immediately concerned with the progress of the advance into Germany because it lessens the danger to their families and their homes. . . .

But however much we may despise the principles for which the Germans are fighting, we must not minimize the extent of the stubborn defence they are offering along the frontiers of Germany. In the same way it would be wrong for our hatred of the Japanese to allow us to underestimate their capacity for resistance not only in Nippon itself, but in China, where their hordes have overrun so much territory.[15]

Turning to politics, the Duke deplored that the House had not yet introduced the electoral reform or the labour legislation required by London; he urged them to do so in the coming session. He talked of the great success of the Labour Scheme; and added, on a favourite theme:

Sooner or later the bulk of these 6,000 Bahamians will be returning and it is their re-absorption into the life of the Colony that will eventually become a pressing and far more difficult problem than many anticipate. . . .

But are these returned workers going to be as content with their old life and environment as before? Will their perspective not have changed since they have been away, and have not education, the radio, and the printed word made even those who have stayed at home restless for something better?

He strenuously advocated reforms in agriculture, in education, in the health service, and concluded 'that my insistence on the necessity of certain fundamental changes in your outlook is prompted solely by my sincere interest in the Colony's welfare, and by my desire that you shall not find yourselves unprepared to face the new conditions of a fast-changing world.'

The Duke was now without hope that he would be offered another post during the remainder of the war. (Though once it was over he would try to serve again, and in fact the real saga was only beginning.) The Court remained bitterly opposed to his being accorded any further work or honour; it was utterly determined to keep him and his detested helpmeet in lifelong exile. But the Duke continued to harbour one cherished hope. At some point – probably during 1945 – he and the Duchess would be passing briefly through England on their way back to Europe. After all that had happened, it was unimaginable that the Royal Family should suddenly extend the hand of friendship to them; nor, after all they had endured, would they be quick to accept it. Palace doors would not – would never – be flung open to them. To that the Duke was painfully resigned; but something he could not endure was the thought that the world, with scornful laughter, should see them continuing to be cast out by his family and excluded from his country. He longed for some little official act, some minor, formal recognition from the Palace, just to put rumour at rest so that the public and the press might feel that, the war being over and the Abdication part of history, she and he were no longer 'despised and rejected' by Official Britain. As the Duke wrote to Churchill:

> Were the King and Queen to behave normally to the Duchess and myself when we pass by England, and invite us merely to tea at one of their residences, a formality which as a matter of fact is prescribed by Court protocol in the case of Colonial Governors and their wives, it would avoid any division of feeling being manifested. . . . It would never be a very happy meeting, but on the other hand it would be quite painless, and would have the merit of silencing, once and for all, those malicious circles who delight in keeping open an eight-year-old wound that should have been healed officially, if not privately, ages ago.[16]

Did not Winston think this 'the best cure for an evil situation'? He begged the Prime Minister to persuade the King and Queen 'to swallow "the Windsor pill" just once, however bitter they may think it is going to taste.'

Churchill replied on New Year's Eve. He had pleaded with the King for the single meeting, as had General de Gaulle and others. But George VI – and his wife and mother – declared that never, under any circumstances, would they receive the Duchess. 'I do not see any prospect of removing this difficulty,' wrote Churchill. 'I have not concealed my regret that this should be so.'

18
Capax Imperii
January–September 1945

And so 1944 ended, and the curtain rose on the last act. For the second time in his career, the Duke of Windsor prepared to cease to rule. The circumstances of the renunciation – and the thing renounced – were not remotely comparable. But once the decision had been taken, he was motivated by much the same feelings as before. He wanted to go with dignity, to make things as easy as possible for his successor, and to exercise his responsibilities right up to the moment of discharging them. Nothing in his governorship became him like the ending of it.

His first task in 1945 was to receive Oliver Stanley, the Secretary of State for the Colonies, who called officially at Nassau on New Year's Day in the course of an overseas tour. Stanley marvelled at how well the Duke had done. They discussed the date and manner of the Duke's departure; it was decided that his resignation should be announced on 15 March, to take effect at the end of April. Were he not to resign, his five-year appointment would come to its natural end on 9 July, unless extended. He was therefore laying it down exactly ten weeks ahead of time. By offering to do so, he occasioned great relief in the Colonial Office and the Government. Had he not done so, they would have had the embarrassment of announcing that his post had terminated and there were no plans to give him any other.[1]

The Duke did not trust Stanley enough to discuss with him his other plans. As he wrote to Allen, 'he is far too close to the Palace to give our hand away to. He is a personal friend of the King and Queen as I am led to understand and therefore dangerous.'[2] The Duke was obsessed with the mysteries of what was going to happen to him, and brooded upon his future in long introspective letters to his faithful solicitor. But the immediate problem was quite simply that of where he and the Duchess were to go after leaving the Bahamas. Their wish was to return to France as soon as possible to see what was left of their houses and possessions; but all depended on the war. In the summer of 1944, with the German armies cracking in France, Italy and Poland, it had seemed possible that

349

the European war might be over by Christmas; but this was not to be. At the end of the year the Allies were repulsed in the Ardennes, while the Germans still held on the Gothic Line and the Vistula. 'It is obvious that someone in the Allied High Command had blundered terribly,' wrote Allen,[3] who kept the Duke in touch with the background to the military developments. Churchill meanwhile advised that liberated France was 'in a very troubled state', that the Duke should not think of returning there before the summer, and that in any case he ought to pass a few months in the United States before crossing the Atlantic – passages were not easy.[4] The idea of spending the summer in New York, if somewhat uncomfortably, suited the Duke quite well. He needed a respite to assess his position and plan the next stage of his future.

There remained, however, four months before his departure. This was a frantic period for the Duke, who was determined to advance all of his as yet unrealized initiatives as Governor, as well as beginning a few more. He hardly had time to attend to his oil-drilling enterprise in Canada, which now reached its climax,[5] or to the regiment of guests who stayed at Government House that winter, spear-headed by Aunt Bessie who arrived for Christmas and, to the Duchess's delight, stayed the whole season.

He asked the House for £77,000 towards Out Island development in 1945. This was agreed to on 22 January with remarkably little fuss.[6]

On 27 January he repeated to the House the Colonial Office demand for the extension of the secret ballot to the Out Islands.[7] Bay Street, further softened up by a talking-to from the Secretary of State,[8] was almost ready to give way to this.

He continued to stress the need for social reform. His last Message to the House, on 30 April, brought to their attention the conclusions of the International Labour Conference at Philadelphia on 'minimum standards of social policy in dependent territories'.[9]

He formulated plans whereby the facilities of Transport Command could be used after the war as the basis of a great new future in civil aviation. This was the subject of his last official telegram to the Colonial Office on 1 May.[10]

He considered the future of his Bahamas Labour Scheme, which had saved the islanders from destitution while draining their islands of manpower. In ExCo it was resolved that, while the existing mainland labour could continue for so long as both labourers and US Government wanted it, no further recruitment should be permitted.[11]

ExCo also discussed that winter 'whether the time was ripe for a major attempt to combat the sandfly nuisance',[12] and pressed the Duke to lend his name to the proposed new hospital which he had persuaded the

Rockefeller Foundation to finance.[13] (He modestly refused, and it is now the Princess Margaret Hospital.)

Finally – his farewell achievement – he secured a reform which was a century overdue and upon which he had long been determined. With its habitual meanness, the House had always hitherto refused to reimburse Governors and their overseas officials for travelling expenses incurred in getting out to the Colony; nothing had done more to make Bahamian posts unpopular. Now at last it was persuaded to pass legislation to cover such expenses[14] – thus earning the Duke the gratitude of all the Colony's future British administrators. The first to take advantage of the new measure was his successor, one William Murphy. Murphy – an experienced colonial servant quite without allure – did not however present the Bahamian Government with much of a bill, since he only came from Bermuda where he had been Colonial Secretary.

The Duke's resignation – announced as planned on 15 March – had been a well-kept secret and occasioned some surprise. The official reason given for it was that, 'having directed this British Colony's war effort, it is only practical that I should hand over to my successor, who will be responsible for post-war policies, before those problems descend upon him.' The justice of this was incontrovertible. But the Duke admitted in a letter of 19 March to the newspaper magnate Roy Howard, who had become his friend and supporter, that it

> . . . all derives from the fact that the Court and Cabinet in London won't let bye gones be bye gones, even in the greatest crisis that has overtaken mankind. I have a perfectly clean record in the matter, for I have done everything within my power to heal the breach, but to no avail.
>
> Any immediate future official war activities of mine therefore must be determined by the value the British Government places on my services which are always available. On the other hand, I see no good reason why I should continue to rot indefinitely on a semi-tropical island or accept some other exiling job, just because the British may not offer me a worthwhile appointment. . . .

The announcement made, the Duke was resolved to end his governorship on a cordial and conciliatory note, with past struggles forgotten. From his delicately worded farewell messages it would have been hard to gather that there had been much political conflict surrounding his administration, let alone continuous internecine strife. Addressing the Legislature for the last time on 3 April, he merely remarked:

> Under present disturbed world conditions there must be times when the Legislature finds it difficult to appreciate the full implications of certain measures that are laid before them. Such occasions have, fortunately, been very rare during my administration, and for my part I shall carry away with me only recollections of harmony and understanding.[15]

It must be remembered that these words were addressed to an assembly which had done its best to frustrate his every reform, which had long tried to withhold funds for essential defence purposes, which two-and-a-half years earlier had tried to arrest the Duke's officials, and whose general behaviour, roundly condemned by the Riots Commission, had been such as to cause the Colonial Office seriously to consider abrogating the Bahamian Constitution. But the Duke had some cause to feel that he had won the political fight, and he wanted to be magnanimous in victory. He wrote to Allen that, in spite of the

> ... difficulties I have had to contend with owing to the attitude of the reactionary white element who rule the local House of Assembly, and their stubborn opposition to the progressive measures I have invited them to adopt ..., it would be most unfortunate if my final bow to Nassau should be tainted with any hint of recrimination. As a matter of fact, although this reactionary white element has often proved itself an irritating obstacle in my administration, they have actually voted funds for most of the important schemes I have initiated, even if they have voted them reluctantly and with bad grace.[16]

He had learnt with some concern (he told Allen) that Reuters had commissioned Dupuch to write a series of articles about his governorship. As Bay Street's most outspoken opponent, Dupuch might play up those aspects which the conciliatory Duke now sought to play down. 'While I of course agree to suitable articles being written, and that Dupuch is by far the best man to write them ..., [any] attempt on Dupuch's part ... to use me as the stick to beat his political adversaries must be avoided at all costs. ... As it will generally be known that I have given these interviews, it would be deeply resented in responsible white circles were they to feel that I had used the medium of Dupuch to get even with them, so to speak, which, as a matter of fact, I have no desire whatever to do.'

Given the Duke's anxiety to depart in an harmonious atmosphere, he cannot have failed to be pleased by the local reaction to the news of his going. 'We were astonished and stirred', wrote the Duchess, 'by the genuine regret with which our imminent departure was viewed.'[17] The ordinary coloured people of the Colony felt that they were losing the best friend they had ever had. Even the toughest of his Bay Street adversaries found themselves touched by affection and gratitude, while his arch-opponent Kenneth Solomon unbent to express the appreciation of the House. The Duchess was given tremendous farewells everywhere, especially by the Red Cross and the RAF. 'We all feel like orphans,' wrote Alice Hills Jones, the nurse in charge of the infant welfare clinics.[18] At the Duke's last ExCo meeting on 25 April,[19] Godfrey Higgs proposed with unanimous approval that the Council

> ... place on record the very real loss which the Colony has sustained by the resignation of His Royal Highness the Duke of Windsor KG as its Governor.

During his administration the world has been engaged in the most gigantic conflict of all time, which has greatly increased the burdens of all Governments and has accentuated social, political and economic problems. Yet, due to the unceasing and untiring efforts of His Royal Highness and the wisdom, foresight and ability which he has shown throughout his term of office, not only has the financial position of the Colony been fully preserved but salutary improvements have been effected in political and social life.

Higgs meant this sincerely, and would stand by every word of it today.

The Colonial Office too had much unofficial praise for the Duke – though there was not to be the slightest mark of official recognition either for him or for her. The Secretary of State had congratulated him informally in the new year. The next Secretary of State to visit the Bahamas, the Fabian socialist Arthur Creech Jones, actually declared in public that the Duke's administration was 'the best the Bahamas had had in recent times'.[20] Brigadier Daly, Officer Commanding North Caribbean Defence Area, thought the Duke the best of all the governors he visited.[21] Sir Philip Rogers, who was Private Secretary to the Permanent Head of the Colonial Office during the war and visited the Duke in Nassau,[22] recalls:

We in the Colonial Office regarded the Duke of Windsor as a good Governor of the Bahamas. Naturally he was unfamiliar with the routine of administration and he rightly left this largely to an excellent Colonial Secretary. In the broader field of political relations, however, he had a sure touch in a Colony that was notoriously difficult politically. In his views on the social colour bar he inclined somewhat overmuch, in my personal view, to the views of the dominant white commercial community but it was politically inevitable that any Government of the Bahamas at that time should pay considerable regard to their views and certainly not feel able to cut right across them. Quite apart from his social or ceremonial duties, which were considerable for such a small place and which, of course, he and the Duchess of Windsor handled superbly well, he presided over his Executive Council with a sure touch and kept his hands well on the political reins. He was also very good in dealing with the Americans, both military and civil, at a time when their presence in the Bahamas was of considerable military importance. . . . I do not think a really experienced Colonial Governor would have had any more success than HRH in these respects and overall he might not have done so well in the circumstances of the time. It was . . . occasionally embarrassing to us to have a Royal Governor in a place with such notorious political problems but it is a tribute to HRH that such embarrassment never became acute. . . . In short, given wartime circumstances and the political circumstances in the Bahamas (including its very odd Constitution), our feeling in the Colonial Office was that he did a good job.[23]

Given such plaudits, how can it be that the popular image of the Duke and Duchess in the Bahamas depicts them leading there a purely selfish and hedonistic existence? How has the legend evolved that they gave but perfunctory attention to their duties and devoted themselves to languid pleasures? What is the origin of the widespread belief that the Duke failed as Governor? A gossip-column work which briefly appeared in the United States in 1953 summed up the governorship thus:

> Despite the Duke's work, the entertainments, the constant visits from the representatives of famous dressmakers, golfing, swimming, playing double solitaire, the banjo and the bagpipe [sic], the Windsors became a little bored with Nassau.[24]

Twenty years later, the same theme was taken up by Lady Donaldson, who in her life of the Duke – which is curiously regarded by some as his official biography – writes:

> He had neither the training nor any understanding of the discipline required of His Majesty's representatives in the Colonies. One of the small complaints made against him was that whereas other Governors had made it a duty to patronize 'any attempt at art' such as concerts, picture exhibitions and so on, he resolutely absented himself from this kind of thing, which bored him, while he was seen to raise his opera-glasses from the front row of seats when a strip-tease act was performed. The Duchess was the more unpopular. . . . It may or may not be true [sic] that she visited Miami every week to have her hair done,* or that while she was in Nassau her purchases from New York averaged a hundred dresses a year at an average of $250 a dress, but these things were generally believed. . . .

and are still believed on account of their malicious repetition. Lady Donaldson devotes the rest of her chapter[25] to recounting nasty stories about the Duke deriving from that lively but hardly impartial source, Etienne Dupuch. But this assessment is kindness itself compared to a venomous volume which appeared in April 1981 and was serialized in the *Daily Express* (which has since apologized to the Duchess of Windsor and paid her an undisclosed sum).[26] As this expresses it:

> The Duke had failed. . . . His sense of constitutionality was too vague. . . . He could, at any point, have suspended the House of Assembly for the duration of the war and simply forced his plans on the islands [!]. He chose not to. . . . At the end of the war, they left the islands quickly . . . in utter disgrace. . . . They left exhausted, thin, defeated. Their reforms had never happened and their authority had dissolved. . . . The matters of treason, riot and murder were forgotten in their glossy social life. . . .

* One of the many myths is that they spent most of the governorship in America. Up to May 1943 their trips to the mainland only amounted to ten weeks over nearly three years – the lowest ratio for a Governor of the Bahamas this century. In the last two years they spent about a quarter of their time in the United States; this was dictated by a mixture of health reasons and important official reasons. Throughout the five years the Duke stopped at Miami fifteen times and the Duchess thirteen (including the start and finish of their five mainland tours), their longest stay there being in December 1942 when they went to buy stores for the Duchess's canteen.

What lies at the root of so much scandal? There is a simple answer. By sending the Duke and Duchess to the Bahamas, the Court had pushed them into a publicity trap. They were manoeuvred onto a stage where it was impossible to perform well unless one performed with a certain public style; yet that very style condemned them to the taunts and sneers of a malicious world. The Duke had written to Churchill in October 1940 that 'it goes against the grain to play the part of "greeter" amidst all the horrors and misery that this war inflicts and which we have seen with our own eyes, a role that has never been in our make up and a form of publicity which, while helping these islands, would obviously react very badly on ourselves at this time.' Never had a fear proved more justified. Most of the American press wrote about them fairly and even enthusiastically; but there was a 'yellow press', its archpriest William Randolph Hearst, which thrived on scandal and was always unpredictable, while the illustrated weeklies with their vast readerships were likely to write anything which sounded sensational. Even a fairly serious monthly such as the *American Mercury* could publish an article in 1944 alleging, among numerous absurdities, that the State Department footed the bills for the ducal trips to America and that the Duchess kept a signed photograph of Ribbentrop on her bedside table.[27] The Duke's resignation provoked a flood of idle speculation. An article in *Time* magazine carried the title 'Abdication from Elba'. Press summaries of his governorship tended to concentrate on the supposedly idyllic character of its *mise en scène*. Such publicity distressed the Duchess for the Duke's sake; she wrote of her distress to her friend Rosita Forbes. In her reply of 3 April, Rosita got to the root of the problem:

. . . the general public does not know about Windsor Field or Transport Command on NP. So it has no idea of HRH's achievements. It still regards Nassau as unpleasantly rich, comfortable and safe. I myself shall be criticized – in spite of Arthur's desperate illness – for having escaped the war for 16 months on LONELY, DULL, HARD-WORKED Eleuthera in North America. Thus *anyone* is bound to be criticized who, in wartime, is connected – by malicious or fadish gossip in the yellow press – with travel (especially 'as a caravan' – your own laughing words), with special accommodation in trains or hotels, with much baggage, with jewels or clothes or entertainment, indeed with anything that is not a definite and enduring war purpose. All royal publicity . . . has one apparent purpose, to show that Palace life is exactly like everyone else's, that in wartime kings and queens use no more heat, light or water than their subjects, that they have the same rations and the same couponed clothes and never travel without a war purpose. Queen Mary is always represented giving lifts to servicemen – wherever she motors. . . . All this may be just propaganda, but it is popular in Europe and more and more so among Americans. . . . I believe there is still, among very many people, a deep and warm regard for

HRH, but America, or rather a silly section of the yellow press, has misrepresented or at least mistakenly emphasized the Duke's and your activities. Instead of describing your work on the Project, the Red Cross, the infinite efforts HRH has made for these recalcitrant isles, there has been so much nonsense about 'a floor at the Waldorf', 'party of ten visits Boston', '37 trunks', 'night-club friends', 'beach life' and 'millionaires'. You will notice that whereas wealth used to be glamorous, it is now definitely unpopular. I think it is terribly difficult to realize what the war has done to England unless you live there . . . the deep bitterness and resentment against anyone a little privileged in the way of comfort or security, or reputed 'out of it' because of a special job. . . .

Rosita concluded that the Duke and Duchess had suffered from bad publicity, and would go on suffering, because – unlike the Royal Family in England and people similarly in the public eye – they had no public relations machine to organize and protect their public image for them. They were therefore helplessly exposed to the malice of a suffering world. She suggested that they retain the services of one of the big American PR organizations, as the leading American families did: 'Note the Rockefellers' complete immunity from criticism.' What she did not know was that they simply did not have the financial means to do this. The only PR organization which might have helped them (and it was one of the best in the world) was the Lord Chamberlain's Office in London – and it never did.

The Duke of Windsor formally ceased to be Governor of the Bahamas on 30 April 1945, the day Hitler committed suicide. He and the Duchess sailed from Nassau without ceremony at dawn on 3 May, the day Lord Louis Mountbatten entered Rangoon. It would be quite wrong, however, to imagine that their departure marked the end of their association with the Colony. To begin with, they took away with them a permanent reminder of the Bahamas in the form of Sydney Johnson.

Sydney was a nineteen-year-old youth from Andros with an angelic coffee-coloured face who had done various jobs at Government House and sometimes deputized for the Duke's American valet Mears. He was an excellent servant, utterly devoted and possessing an almost voodoo-like intuition. He recalls that the Duke and Duchess sent for him in their private sitting-room two or three weeks before their departure.[28] Having posed various questions about his family, the Duke asked whether he would like to come with them to America and Europe. Sydney was too overwrought to reply. He had never thought of leaving the Bahamas in his life. 'Think it over,' said the Duke. 'If you decide to come with us, give it a year or so to see how you like it. The winter after next we will bring you back here, and then you will know whether you want to stay in Nassau or carry on with us.' Sydney never regretted his decision to join

DATE OF ARRIVAL		NAME	DATE OF DEPARTURE	
1945			*1945*	
March	8th	John Brett Robey	March	10th
March	12th	Alastair Mackintosh	March	17th
March	23rd	Bingley	March	25th
March	24th	Arthur V. Davis	March	28th
March	28th	H. Dunbar Maconochie	April	4th
April	4th	Julian Jefferson	April	9th

Last Government House visitors, 1945.

them. He remained the Duke's valet until his master's death, and stayed on with the Duchess for some time after that. They cherished him, and he worshipped (and still worships) them.

As they had promised Sydney, they came back during the winter of 1946–7, staying with the Arthur Vernays. They were surprised how much affection they had kept for the islands, and for the next ten years they came back for a few weeks most winters, enjoying the company of such old friends as the Vernays, the Sigrists, the Killams, Arthur Davis, Austin Levy, Bishop Burton, Rosita Forbes, Lady Oakes and Lord Beaverbrook. The Duke liked his golf there. They tried to keep these trips as quiet and unpublicized as possible, and rarely went near Government House. After the mid-1950s, and the deaths of Sigrist and Vernay, they visited less often.

They did not try to forget their reign in Nassau. Rather they regarded it with something of the nostalgia which many prisoners-of-war later feel for their camp days. Since (through no fault of their own) it was virtually all they could look back on by way of service, they looked back on it with a certain quiet pride. And since success in this small difficult job was all they had been allowed to achieve, they held on to their sense of achievement. In public, they always spoke and wrote happily of their years in Nassau – *Five Fruitful Years*, as the Duchess entitled the Bahamas chapter in her memoirs (although readers between the lines wittily substituted 'frightful' for 'fruitful'). 'I look back with pleasure and satisfaction to my five years in the Bahamas,' wrote the Duke in 1966. 'I worked hard and tried to do a good job as Governor.' Their feelings about the Colony's numerous shortcomings and frustrations they kept largely to themselves, as they had at the time.

They surrounded themselves with souvenirs of the Bahamas. At the French mill-house which the Duke converted into his country residence in the 1950s there was a cosy room filled with Bahamian books, maps and native work. In 1959 he was pleased when the Legislative Council of the Bahamas, having hung a portrait of King George VI in their Chamber, also commissioned one of himself dressed as an admiral.[29] Later that year he was less pleased when he was personally attacked in the House of Assembly during an acrimonious political debate concerning the possible re-opening of the Oakes murder case. His traducer apologized.

He was always glad to see his old Executive Councillors and other eminent Bahamians when they passed through Paris, and hear the latest news. He followed the Colony's political progress with keen interest. Less than a year after his departure, the secret ballot for the Out Islands at last went through. But in the continuing struggle between Bay Street and Government House, it was Bay Street which seemed to be winning over the next twenty years. The greedy and amoral Stafford Sands – the original of Ian Fleming's *Goldfinger*, the 'grocer's boy' whom the Duchess so disliked – wielded vast authority through his control of the Finance Committee of the House and the Bahamas Development Board, and led the corrupt local oligarchy to dizzy heights of wealth and power. The Out Islands were once more forgotten in an upsurge of now not always very exclusive tourism. But there was a difference, for a fierce coloured opposition to the Bay Street hegemony was growing, with articulate leaders; the principal item of its folklore was the riots of June 1942, invested with something of the romance of the Easter Rising. In 1952, Bay Street got rid of Governor Sir Robert Neville, who had paid serious attention to the new movement and tried to break down the colour bar. In his place came the charming but ineffectual Lord Ranfurly (1953–7), who sought to conciliate the two sides; it was his governorship which saw the beginnings of a Bay Street plan to sell semi-sovereign rights in Crown land to a development company – an affair which the Duke viewed with much head-shaking concern, sensing the corruption and political trouble to which it might lead. 'One *can't* just sign away a piece of territory like that,' he remarked to Grace Dudley. The late 1950s and early 1960s saw some social reform and the coming of responsible government – but with

Bay Street hands still firmly on the reins. The first local Cabinet, installed in 1964 with Symonette as Premier but Sands as Finance Minister and the real mastermind, was a government by Bay Street for Bay Street. But the oligarchy over-reached itself, and was brought down amidst the noises of the Grand Bahama scandal. In 1967 the moderate negro nationalist Pindling became Premier, winning a majority of seats in the House the following year. A distinguished retired judge, one Sir Eric Hallinan, now arriving to fill a vacancy on the appeal court, was amused to hear coloured people declare: 'It's our turn now!' A wind of change was blowing through the Bahamas. The Duke, believing as he did in the Empire and its benevolent paternalistic role, was not without a twinge of nostalgic regret.

In April 1968 the Duke and Duchess, accompanied by Sydney, paid their last visit to the Colony, staying with their friends Lord and Lady Dudley who lived at the Killams' former residence Graycliff, a lovely colonial mansion next to Government House. They were received with all honour by the Governor, the New Zealander Sir Ralph Grey. The Duchess, accompanied by Lady Dudley and Lady Grey, revisited the scenes of her old welfare work. The infant welfare clinics were still there, and there was a brand-new Red Cross. 'What a change !' she exclaimed. 'We had one room for wrapping bandages and another which we used as a small office.'[30] There was a party for them at Government House, to which the Duke asked that Godfrey Higgs and Sir Etienne Dupuch (as he had now become) be invited – a generous act, for Dupuch (who had fallen under Lord Mountbatten's influence) had written somewhat disparagingly of the Duke in his memoirs published the year before. Higgs recalls that none of their charm had faded ; they were all attention towards their guests, and had forgotten nothing of their Bahamas years. Two years later they thought of coming back again, but the Duchess was unwell. (The fact that Lord Mountbatten was expected in Nassau may have been an additional disincentive.) The Duke wrote from Palm Beach to the Governor, Sir Francis Cumming-Bruce, to express their disappointment at not being able to meet him at Government House 'where we resided for five pleasant and interesting years during the war. I was looking forward to a golf game with you at Lyford Cay. . . . I shall hope for another opportunity as well as hearing from you how the old Colony is faring. Things, I am afraid, have changed a good deal since my time. . . .'[31]

But there was to be no further opportunity. On 28 May 1972 the Duke of Windsor died of cancer of the throat at his house in Paris. A little over a year later the Bahamas ceased to be a British Colony, and the flag came down for the last time over Government House. Perhaps it was as well that the Duke did not live to see this. As his friend Lady Mosley has written in her delightful book on the Duchess :

The Duke was thankful that it did not fall to his lot to preside over the decline in British prestige, power and prosperity. He was well aware that he could have done nothing to halt it, but the pulling down of Union Jacks all over the world would not have come easily to him.[32]

One must return however to May 1945, when so little of this future could have been foreseen. Having slipped away from Nassau at dawn on the 3rd on board the *Jean Brillant*, the Duke and Duchess spent a quiet week with friends in Palm Beach. It was there that they celebrated VE Day on the 8th. On the 13th they arrived in New York where they stayed for the next four months, having been advised not to return to Europe until the autumn. They were pleasant months during which they saw much of their friends, but they were months filled with uncertainty for the future. In the second half of July they took a short holiday, going to New Brunswick for the fishing (their first visit to Canada since 1941) and to Newport, Rhode Island. A projected visit to the Ranch was cancelled on account of wartime travelling restrictions. They made a number of trips to Washington, where they kept in touch with the Embassy and met President Truman at the White House on 13 August – the day the Japanese agreed to surrender. Otherwise they lived quietly at their flat in the Waldorf Towers, where the press respected their desire for privacy.

It was a busy summer for the Duke. There was the aftermath of the Ecushwa disaster to sort out, their return to Europe to arrange, his whole future to plan. He spent long days locked in consultation with his legal and financial advisers. Allen came over from London to help him.

One question predominated. Having ended his career (unique among royalty) as a colonial governor, what was he to do now? 'Official Britain does and always will regard me as a problem,' he wrote to Roy Howard,[33] 'and as I see no point in prolonging the impasse, I must from henceforth plan my life along unofficial lines.' But idleness was anathema to him. 'Although I have passed the half century, I still retain considerable energy and a very real interest in world affairs, and I feel sure that I shall eventually be able to fit myself into some useful occupation despite the official British stigma.' He even toyed with the idea of a business career in America, visiting Cleveland, Ohio at the end of June to study the industrial methods of his friend, the railway tycoon Robert Young.

There were two matters that summer which particularly affected the Duke's thoughts upon his destiny. First, he was made aware of the extreme precariousness of his personal finances. There is a widespread myth that the Duke and Duchess were fabulously rich and possessed that form of avarice which is peculiar to millionaires. The truth was exactly the opposite. They were almost always in financial difficulties, and rarely able to live within their income. That they usually managed all the same to lead a comfortable and elegant existence, and to entertain extremely well, was due in part to such short-term financial expedients as the writing of their memoirs; in part to the housekeeping genius of the Duchess, who could decorate a room or give a dinner-party at a fraction of what it might cost another hostess; in part to the generosity of the French Government; and in part to the free travel, special hotel rates and other favours offered by kind friends (or less disinterested parties), favours which they were never in a position to refuse. But this pleasant optical illusion of their post-war prosperity was only to be achieved after much planning, and in the summer of 1945 their circumstances looked peculiarly bleak. The Duke's capital had been depleted during the war by imprudent investments, the great personal expense to him of running Government House in Nassau in appropriate style, and the Ecushwa calamity. All he could rely on was the modest allowance he received from the King, which showed no signs of being increased (and never was) and which at least once during the war it had been threatened to terminate. One result of these circumstances was that the Duke appeared to be faced with the necessity of earning his living somehow after the war. Another was that the possibility of their living in America was ruled out for the time being. 'I think the Duke has the US firmly in his mind,' wrote the Duchess to Aunt Bessie in October 1945, 'but we could not keep up with the friends we made and pay the income tax as well.'

The Duke can hardly have been surprised at the news of his parlous financial state, which had caused him intermittent anxiety throughout the war. The other news which affected his future, however, flabbergasted him as it did practically everybody. On 15 June the United Kingdom Parliament which had sat since November 1935, and therefore throughout the reign and abdication of King Edward VIII, was dissolved by King George VI on the advice of Churchill. When the votes in the subsequent General Election were counted on 25 July, the Labour Party was found to have overthrown thirty years of Conservative dominance in the House of Commons with an absolute majority of almost 200 seats. An astonished Mr Attlee, 'a modest little man with a great deal to be modest about', became Prime Minister. New York reporters were not slow to corner the Duke. 'Would you care to discuss the change in British politics?' The ex-King replied: 'It is a tradition in my family that we never discuss politics in public.' But in private, he did give some indication – at least of his surprise. To his friend Duff Cooper, now British Ambassador in Paris, he wrote on 1 August:

> The outcome of the British elections certainly was a surprise to me as it must have been to you and Winston and all your colleagues. The reaction in America is, in the main, one of disappointment, but they seek consolation in the fact that the post-war problems which confront the new Socialist Government are so

gigantic that it is almost impossible for it to live up to all its commitments. However, American opinion is profoundly disturbed over Attlee's pledge of closer co-operation with the Soviet, and the disappearance of Winston from power as the last bulwark against the spread of Communism in Europe.

It would be wrong to suppose that the Duke was disappointed in the new Government. Though he feared that Socialism might make Europe riper for Communism, he believed (as he wrote to Allen on 30 July) that 'Great Britain herself . . . is well able to control the extent and tempo of the new political experiments with sanity and moderation.' Some of his old friends had lost office (such as Walter Monckton, briefly Solicitor-General); but so had many enemies (such as Somervell and Simon, Baldwin's eager legal lieutenants during the Abdication). On the other hand, the new Secretary of State for the Colonies, under whom he would have served had he remained in the Bahamas three months longer, was his old friend and admirer George Hall, the miners' MP who had accompanied him to South Wales in 1936, and tried after visiting him in Nassau four years earlier to get him a better job. The new Dominions Secretary, Lord Addison, was also a friend. The new President of the Board of Trade, Sir Stafford Cripps, had been 'a King's man' in 1936. The new Lord Chancellor, William Jowitt, had written a legal opinion for the Duke in 1938 arguing that it was unconstitutional for the Duchess to be denied royal status. The new Chancellor of the Exchequer, Hugh Dalton, was the son of the Duke's earliest tutor at Windsor and his comrade from the Italian Front in 1917–18; as Chairman of the Parliamentary Labour Party in 1936, Dalton had at first been inclined to take the King's side in the Abdication crisis, though he eventually suppressed this inclination in view of what he considered to be prevailing public opinion. Apart from the more austere nonconformist elements, and a few such as Harold Laski who had not forgiven the two weeks in Germany in 1937, Labour politicians as a whole tended to be friendlier towards the Duke than Conservatives. Many among them recalled his concern for the British working man, or were indignant at how he had been treated by a Conservative establishment.* Against this, however, there was the need to take account of working-class public opinion, which since the Abdication, and especially during the war, had been subtly indoctrinated into regarding the Duke and Duchess, insofar as it had been encouraged to think about them at all, as a spoilt, sly and sybaritic couple deserving of little consideration.

Nevertheless, the new Government filled the Duke with hope. Since

* Opposing himself to a proposal to erect a statue to Stanley Baldwin in the House of Commons, Mr Michael Foot, leader of the Labour Opposition, declared on 4 March 1982 that he had been 'a King's man in 1936' and had never 'forgiven' Baldwin for the Abdication of Edward VIII.

the Abdication it was Conservative England, so closely tied to the Court, which had persecuted him and frustrated his desire to serve. When Churchill had intimated some months before that there would be no recognition for the Duchess or work in England for the Duke, he had been speaking for the *ancien régime*. The new guard could be no worse; it had no axe to grind, and the Duke fervently hoped it would welcome him back to England and give him, his wife at his side, the real service for which he longed. That service would not now be war service, for August saw the dropping of the atomic bombs and the capitulation of Japan. But the task of post-war reconstruction would be quite as challenging as that of victory; he desperately wanted to play a useful part in it; and perhaps his family, unyielding in war, would find the heart to make peace with him now the world was at peace?

Such was the mood in which the Duke of Windsor set out from America on his way back to Europe in September 1945 – exactly six years since he had set out from France on his way back to England. On both occasions he put behind him the frustrations and persecutions of the recent past. On both occasions he clung to the hope that, under the aegis of a reconstituted British Government and in the atmosphere of changed world conditions, he – and his wife – would be reconciled with his family, and so enabled to return to his country and serve it appropriately. And on both occasions he was wrong.

The Duke and Duchess were indeed alive to the possibility that bitter history might repeat itself; and it was for this reason that she begged him to return to England without her this time. Her presence, if contemptuously ignored as before, could only make things harder for him. He had not seen any member of his family for over eight years – except for the single interview with the King in 1939, and the irritating encounters with the Duke of Gloucester in France. Perhaps, alone with them, he could effect a reconciliation which might embrace her later.

They therefore sought to return to France without stopping in England, whither the Duke would make a solitary trip after they had reinstalled themselves in Paris, where their rented house in the Boulevard Suchet, they were delighted to learn, had survived the occupation intact. After unsuccessfully trying to catch a boat to Marseilles, they finally sailed from New York on the 15th on the SS *Argentina* bound for Le Havre, which did in fact stop briefly at Plymouth, though they did not go ashore.

Back in America, their news was eagerly awaited by Aunt Bessie, who had seen much of them over the summer and heard their hopes and plans. On 22 October, exactly a month after their arrival in France and just after the Duke's five-day visit to London alone, the Duchess wrote to her aunt from the Boulevard Suchet:

Darling Aunt B.,

So much to tell you that the plane which carries my unexciting news will drop. We were quite comfortable on the boat and the food awfully good. We had foggy weather and quite a roll. . . . Everyone was very efficient at Havre – army-lorry to take our things and the Embassy car for us. . . . I found the house looking really lovely and after five years away I would not have changed a thing. Fernand has aged but certainly has taken wonderful care of everything. The great blow fell when we were informed that the house had been sold. . . . House prices here are such that I cannot describe and hotels are the top and scarce as the US Army is all over Paris so . . . we have to move from here . . . (I must now continue by candle light. The electricity is off for half an hour and on half an hour – quite an irritant to the nerves. I had a dinner of 18 under these conditions for the Duff Coopers – not too good – but luckily we have our pre-war candles to help.) We have to start packing December First. You can't imagine how I hate to leave and feel I shall go mad if we do not finally settle somewhere. . . . The Duke's London visit passed off most pleasantly even though their attitude regarding me is the same and they prefer we do not live in G.B. as it would be too much competition for the brother – which seems weak. Also they do not want him to find work outside as the idea is you can't give a King a job. Wonderful people aren't they. . . . What do you think of it all? I would not feel so down about the future if we could remain here in this lovely house – but it is finding a place and beginning again which is so dreary. . . . Do write soon even if I have been so late, but you can imagine what it's been here under the circumstances.

All love

WALLIS

Upon his return to France from England, the Duke wrote to the King:

Dear Bertie,

I was very glad to see you in London after so long an interval and to find you looking so well and vigorous after the strain of the last six years of total war.

No one realizes better than I do all that you have had to endure along with the people of Great Britain in the front line against the Germans, and my admiration for your fortitude knows no bounds. On the other hand, although in another sphere and under quite different conditions, my life has not been easy-going either, and without any desire to seek praise I am satisfied that the job I undertook as your representative in a third-class British Colony was fulfilled to the best of my ability.

. . . Now that all the shooting is over and postwar problems emerge in all their complexity, . . . [my] desire to offer my services to you is sincere and genuine. . . . I suggested the field of Anglo–American relations . . . because . . . I am convinced that there can be no lasting peace for mankind unless the two countries preserve a common approach to international politics. Having spent more than one year at intervals out of the last five in America, I have

364

made many useful contacts in that country and I believe a number of converts among convinced isolationists. . . .

While I am frank to admit that I was sorry when your answer was in the affirmative to my question as to whether my taking up residence in Great Britain would be an embarrassment to you, I . . . am . . . prepared to put your feelings before my own in this matter. On the other hand, don't forget that I have suffered many unnecessary embarrassments from official sources uncomplainingly in the last nine years, but I have reason to believe from the spirit of your recent two long talks with me that it is now your desire that these should cease.

The truth of the whole matter is that you and I happen to be two prominent personages placed in one of the most unique situations in history, the dignified handling of which is entirely yours and my responsibility, and ours alone. It is a situation from which we cannot escape and one that will always be watched with interest by the whole world. I can see no reason why we should not be able to handle it in the best interests of both of us, and I can only assure you that I will continue to play my part to this end.

I spent a very interesting week in London and accomplished a great deal in a short time. I saw Winston, Attlee, Bevin and George Hall in that sequence and found odd spare moments to visit old haunts in the West End or what is left of them. It was wonderful to find Mama looking so young and well, and she took me for a long drive through the bombed areas of the East End docks' section and back across the Thames through Kensington on the Sunday. . . .[34]

Yours ever,
DAVID

To these conciliatory lines the King replied a month later[35] that he was 'very pleased' the Duke realized he should not return to live in England; that there was no question of official work for him in peacetime; but that everything would be done to facilitate any plans he might have to leave Europe for good and spend the rest of his life in America.

Notes to the Chapters

The author has had the privileged use of various papers from the archives of the Duke and Duchess of Windsor, including a number of their private correspondence files, certain confidential reports, the whole of the Duchess's wartime correspondence with her Aunt Bessie, and their press-cuttings and photograph albums, visitors and engagement books. It may be assumed that any quotation in the text for which no source reference is given in the following notes derives from this material, which has not yet been catalogued and indexed and may not be available for public consultation for some time to come.

In these notes, *Duchess* refers to the English edition of the Duchess of Windsor's memoirs *The Heart Has Its Reasons*, first published in 1956, and *Duke, 1966* to an important article by the Duke of Windsor on the subject of his wartime career, which appeared in a number of American newspapers – notably the *New York Daily News* – on 13 December 1966, and shortly afterwards in England in the *Sunday Express*. WO, FO, CO, CAB, PREM and AIR refer to the classes with those designations at the Public Record Office at Kew.

1. The Return That Never Was

1. Review by Rebecca West under the title 'Uneasy Lay the Head' in the *Sunday Telegraph*, 16 December 1979
2. Duchess to Aunt Bessie, 20 July 1939
3. Dina Wells Hood, *Working for the Windsors*, pp.128–46
4. *Ibid.*, pp.138–9
5. Lord Birkenhead, *Walter Monckton*, p.169
6. *Duke, 1966*
7. James Lees-Milne, *Harold Nicolson*, II, p.108
8. Duke to Philip Guedalla, 25 July 1939
9. *Duke, 1966:* 'Like a private reprieve the war came. . . .'

10. Harold Nicolson, *Diaries* (1980 edition), p.167
11. Hood, p.144
12. *Duke, 1966*
13. *Duke, 1966*. 'When . . . old friends suggest, as they sometimes do, that the war might have been prevented had I stayed on the throne, my answer is, "nonsense". My brother, I am sure, tried as hard as he could to stop it. In these grave matters it is always the Government rather than the throne which calls the tune.'
14. Birkenhead, p.171
15. *Duchess*, pp.320–1
16. Hood, p.151
17. Duchess to Aunt Bessie, 16 September 1939
18. Duchess to Aunt Bessie, 10 September 1939
19. *The Times*, 9 September 1939
20. *New York Times*, 15 September 1939
21. *Duchess*, p.322
22. *Duke, 1966*
23. Lord Louis Mountbatten to King Edward VIII, 7 December 1936
24. *Duchess*, p.323
25. *Ibid.*
26. For slightly differing accounts of this arrival, see Lady Alexandra Metcalfe in Frances Donaldson, *Edward VIII*, p.348; Lord Mountbatten's reported words in Richard Hough, *Mountbatten*, pp.113–14, and J. Bryan III and Charles J. V. Murphy, *Windsor Story*, p.402; *Duke, 1966*; and *Duchess*, pp.323–4
27. *Duchess*, p.324
28. *Daily Mirror*, 14 September 1939
29. *Daily Express*, 14 September 1939
30. *New York Times*, 12 September 1939, p.10
31. Mollie Panter-Downes, *London War Notes*, p.17
32. Donaldson, p.349
33. Walter Monckton's notes in Birkenhead, p.172
34. Edited extract from George VI's diary in Sir John Wheeler-Bennett, *King George VI, His Life and Reign*, p.417
35. *Duke, 1966*
36. *Duchess*, p.324
37. Birkenhead, p.172
38. *Duke, 1966*
39. *Ibid.*
40. R.J. Minney (ed.), *The Private Papers of Hore-Belisha*, pp.236–8
41. *Ibid.*
42. R.H. Liddell-Hart's diary for 1 October 1937 in his *Memoirs*, II, p.32
43. *Hore-Belisha*, pp.238–40

44. *The Times*, 19 September 1939, p.6
45. Lady Alexandra Metcalfe in Donaldson, p.349
46. Duke to Sir Samuel Hoare, 22 September 1939: Templewood Papers, RF3
47. Donaldson, p.349
48. *Duchess*, p.325
49. *Ibid.*
50. Sibyl Colefax's diary for September 1939, in possession of Michael Colefax
51. Nicolson, pp.167–8

2. Phoney War

1. Brigadier Davy's notes
2. Lord Coleridge to the author, 23 February 1982
3. Roland Vintras, *The Portuguese Connection*, p.25
4. Sir Harold Redman to the author, 1 December 1981
5. Vintras, p.25
6. Sir Harold Redman to the author, 28 November 1981
7. Ministry of Defence to the author, 21 September 1981
8. Brigadier Davy's notes
9. Despatch 492/S of 19 September 1939 in French Military Archives at Vincennes, 7/N/2817
10. WO 106/1653/19
11. Alanbrooke Diary in Liddell-Hart Centre for Military Archives, 18 October 1939
12. Brigadier Davy's notes
13. Brigadier Swayne's diary, WO 167/40
14. WO 106/1678/1A
15. Donaldson, p.353
16. Duchess to Aunt Bessie, 13 October 1939; interview with General Olivier Poydenot, 20 November 1981; Count de Salis to the author, November 1981; Swayne Diary, 5 October 1939
17. Vintras, p.25
18. Lord Coleridge to the author
19. Vintras, p.25
20. WO 106/1653/54
21. Pownall Diary in Liddell-Hart Centre, 8 October 1939
22. Donaldson, pp.353–4
23. *Ibid.*
24. Swayne Diary, 8 October 1939
25. WO 106/1678/2B
26. *New York Times*, 27 June 1940

27. WO 106/1678/2A
28. Sir Harold Redman to the author
29. WO 202/3/32A
30. Vintras, pp.25–6
31. WO 106/1678/2B, pp.5–6
32. WO 202/3/25A
33. Interview with General Poydenot, and letter from him to the author of 26 November 1981
34. *Ibid.*
35. *Duchess*, pp.327–8
36. WO 202/3/28A
37. Pownall Diary, 18 October 1939
38. Noble Frankland, *Prince Henry Duke of Gloucester*, p.143
39. Alanbrooke Diary, 18 October 1939
40. *The Times*, 1 November 1939, p.12
41. *Duchess*, p.329
42. *Ibid.*
43. WO 106/1653/88, 29 October 1939
44. Bruge, *Faites sauter la Ligne Maginot!*, p.97
45. WO 106/1653/88
46. J.R. Colville, *Man of Valour*, p.169
47. Donaldson, p.356
48. *New York Times*, 7 December 1939, p.8
49. *Duchess*, p.328
50. WO 106/1678/3B
51. *Ibid.*
52. Beaverbrook Papers (House of Lords Record Office), Series G, Box 23, Folder XVI
53. Duke to Philip Guedalla, 18 December 1939
54. Undated letter from Duchess to Sibyl Colefax, in possession of Michael Colefax
55. Letter in possession of Michael Colefax

3. Sensing Disaster

1. Interview with General Olivier Poydenot, 20 November 1981
2. Interview with General Pierre Billotte, 8 October 1981
3. Interview with General Billotte
4. *Daily Express*, 25 January 1940
5. Donaldson, p.356
6. Duke to Ironside, 16 February 1940
7. Article by Philip Jordan in *News Chronicle*, 9 February 1940
8. *Hore-Belisha*, p.239

9. *Journal des marches et des opérations du VII Armée* in French Military Archives at Vincennes, 29/N/352
10. WO 106/1678/4
11. Ewan Butler, *Amateur Agent*, p.17
12. Appendix X to Report on VII Army, WO 106/1678/4
13. *Ibid.*, Appendix C
14. *Ibid.*, Appendix Y
15. Memoirs of General Loizeau in French Military Archives at Vincennes, 1/K/213
16. Frankland, p.149
17. WO 106/1678/5
18. Diary of Harold Nicolson (unpub.) for 11 March 1940; letter to his wife of 13 March 1940 (Sissinghurst Papers)
19. Letter in the author's possession
20. Oliver Harvey, *Diplomatic Diaries, 1937–1940*, p.336

4. Whence All But He Had Fled

1. Swayne Diary (WO 167/41): 12 May, 13 May, 15 May 1940
2. HVO 215/2 of 13 May 1940 in WO 106/1655
3. J.R.M. Butler, *Grand Strategy*, II, p.182; *Duchess*, p.330
4. Harvey, p.358
5. Churchill, *Their Finest Hour*, p.42.
6. Colville, p.187; Butler, p.187
7. Harvey, p.359
8. *Duchess*, p.330
9. *Ibid.*
10. *Ibid.*, 331
11. Duchess to Aunt Bessie, 4 June 1940
12. Frankland, p.155
13. Harvey, p.365
14. On the 28th Reynaud told Spears that Paris was 'no longer in danger' since the Somme bridges had been destroyed. Sir Edward Spears, *Assignment to Catastrophe*, I, p.260
15. *New York Times*, 7, 8, 9 June 1940
16. *Duchess*, pp.331–2
17. Malcolm Muggeridge (ed.), *Ciano's Diary*, p.273 (2 July 1940)
18. *Duchess*, p.332
19. Spears, II, p.313; see also Sir Ronald Campbell's telegram to Lord Halifax of 19 June in FO 800/326/180–2
20. Of particular interest for the decision to leave France are Geoffrey Bocca, *She Might Have Been Queen*, pp.187–93 (apparently based on the accounts of the chauffeur Ladbrooke and Rosa Wood); Lord

Templewood's 'A Deep-Laid Plot' from *Spain in the Second World War* (Templewood Papers, XXIII); and Consul Dodds' report in FO 800/326/193

21. Sir James Marjoribanks to the author, 26 September 1981
22. 'Record of conversation between Lieut.-Col. G. de Chair and HRH the Duke of Windsor at 14.15 hours, 18 June 1940 at Bordeaux', WO 208/609
23. *Duchess*, p.334
24. Interview in the *New York Times*, 26 June 1940
25. FO 800/326/193
26. FO 800/326/185
27. Bocca, p.192
28. FO 800/326/183
29. *Duchess*, p.335
30. Adela Rogers St Johns' syndicated article (e.g. in *Atlanta Journal*), 20 November 1940
31. FO 800/326/187
32. FO 800/326/184
33. War Cabinet Conclusions 174/40, 21 June 1940
34. FO 800/326/190
35. FO 800/326/191
36. FO 800/326/195

5. Spanish Interlude

1. Lord Templewood, *Ambassador on Special Mission*, p.49
2. FO 800/326/185 is Hoare's telegram to Halifax to say he has just learnt of the Duke's presence in Spain. It was sent at 8 p.m., after the Duke had crossed the frontier.
3. Templewood Papers, Box RF3; Duke of Windsor, *A King's Story*, pp.259, 339–40; Templewood, *Nine Troubled Years*, pp.215–24; *Duchess*, pp. 246–52
4. Published in America as *Franco: The Complacent Dictator*
5. Templewood, 'A Deep-Laid Plot' from *Spain in the Second World War*: TS in Templewood Papers, Box XXIII
6. 'A Deep-Laid Plot', p.9
7. *Duchess*, p.338
8. *Foreign Relations of the United States*, 1940, III, p.41; see also 'A Deep-Laid Plot', p.11, for Hoare's report of this conversation. 'The words, harmless and understandable in themselves, might have been used . . . to make trouble.'
9. *Duchess*, p.339
10. 'A Deep-Laid Plot', p.18

11. Templewood Papers, XIII/16/29
12. 'A Deep-Laid Plot', p.11
13. See e.g. *New York Times*, 26 June 1940, p.5
14. FO 800/326/196
15. FO 371/24491 ; Sir Walford Selby, *Diplomatic Twilight*, pp.120–2
16. *Dez anos de politica externa*, VII (Lisbon 1971), pp.156–7: Minister of Foreign Affairs to Portuguese Ambassador in London, 21 June 1940 (translated by Dr Toby Bainton)
17. FO 800/326/197–8
18. H/XLI/18–21 in FO 800/326
19. *Duchess*, pp.340–1
20. *Duke, 1966*
21. Templewood Papers, XIII/20
22. Templewood Papers, XIII/16/37
23. Templewood Papers, XIII/16/29
24. *German Documents on Foreign Policy, Series D*, Vol. X (1957)
25. Walter Schellenberg, *Memoirs*, pp.127–43
26. *German Documents*, D/X/2, 9
27. Templewood Papers, RF3
28. 'A Deep-Laid Plot', p.12
29. *Ambassador on Special Mission*, p.36
30. FO 371/24407/74
31. 'A Deep-Laid Plot', p.12
32. The episode is discussed by Templewood in *Ambassador on Special Mission*, pp.52–3, and in some more detail in the unpublished *Spain in the Second World War*.
33. Templewood Papers, XIII/20
34. *German Documents*, D/X/86
35. FO 800/326/202
36. FO 800/326/203
37. Templewood Papers, XIII/16/37, 5 July
38. The Hon. Neil Hogg to the author, 6 April 1982
39. FO 371/24490
40. The arrangement to accommodate the ducal party at the villa at Cascais was made for the Embassy by the manager of the Palacio Hotel at Estoril. Sir Walford – who was uncertain about Espiritu Santo's sympathies – was not very happy about it, but felt 'that it would do more harm than good if an attempt were made at that late stage to put things into reverse.' (Ralph Selby to the author, 15 March 1982)
41. Selby, *Diplomatic Twilight*, pp.42–3, 58, 66. 'The Austrians were unquestionably grateful to HRH for his presence in Vienna at a time when they were under so much pressure from Hitler.'

42. *Duchess*, p.340
43. The original text of this telegram remains classified, but a description of it may be found in the index to Lord Halifax's diplomatic correspondence at FO 800/327 under reference H/XLI/23
44. FO 371/24249/148–50
45. *Duchess*, p.342
46. FO 371/24249/155
47. Templewood Papers, XIII/20, 8 July
48. Duchess to Aunt Bessie from Cascais, postmarked 15 July 1940

6. Leaving Europe

1. See Compton Mackenzie, *Windsor Tapestry* (1938), pp.528–34
2. See chs. 7–8 below.
3. Sir Philip Rogers to the author, 14 April 1981
4. Interview with Sir Leslie Monson, April 1981
5. Interview with Dudley Danby, March 1982
6. Diary of Sir Ronald Storrs in Library of Pembroke College, Cambridge
7. *Ibid.*
8. The Hon. Sir Bede Clifford (1890–1969) was the younger son of the 10th Baron Clifford of Chudleigh. He married Alice Devin of Cleveland, Ohio. He was an old friend of the Duke of Windsor, whom he had accompanied on his Australian and South African tours. See his memoirs *Proconsul*. The Hon. Sir Charles Dundas (1884–1956) was the fifth son of the 6th Viscount Melville. He married Anne Hay of New York.
9. Michael Craton, *A History of the Bahamas*, p.273
10. Sir Charles Dundas, *African Crossroads*, pp.196–7
11. FO 371/24249/159
    The FO 371/24249 series (henceforth referred to as the *Lisbon File*) probably contains most of the correspondence which passed between the Lisbon and Washington Embassies and the Foreign Office with or on the subject of the Duke in July 1940, though in considerable disorder and with significant omissions. It begins (at f.147) with the following extraordinary unsigned handwritten minute dated 1963: 'The attached folder came to light when I was clearing through ancient folders we keep of reference pages. I really do not think American Department is the right place for what appear to be the originals of the telegrams on the appointment of the Duke of Windsor to the Bahamas during the war. Should it not now go into the archives?'
12. *Lisbon File*, 166

13. *Lisbon File*, 163A
14. *Lisbon File*, 206
15. *Lisbon File*, 209
16. *Lisbon File*, 205
17. *Lisbon File*, 210
18. *Lisbon File*, 161
19. *Lisbon File*, 181
20. *Lisbon File*, 184
21. *Lisbon File*, 187
22. File in National Archives, Washington, 844E/001/52
23. *Lisbon File*, 186
24. *Lisbon File*, 188
25. *Lisbon File*, 233
26. Schellenberg, pp.135–43
27. *German Documents*, D/X/159
28. *Lisbon File*, 190; Birkenhead, *Walter Monckton*, pp.179–82
29. Press statement by Walter Monckton, July 1957
30. Duke of Windsor to Lord Templewood, 14 August 1957: Templewood Papers, RF3
31. *German Documents*, D/X/277

7. The Worst Post in the British Empire

1. Craton, p.12
2. Quoted in Craton, p.134
3. Sir Alan Burns, *Colonial Civil Servant*, p.269
4. *Ibid.*, p.272
5. *Ibid.*, pp.89–90
6. Sir Bede Clifford, *Proconsul*, p.194
7. Dundas, pp.146–62, 182–98
8. Rosita Forbes, *Appointment with Destiny*, pp.107ff.
9. Interview with Valeria Moseley Moss, February 1981
10. CO 23/703
11. Sir Etienne Dupuch, *Tribune Story*, p.48; CO 23/708
12. Interviews with Mary Teegarden Holder; the *Knickerbocker News*, 28 August 1940
13. Interview with Vyvyan Drury, May 1981

8. Making the Best of a Bad Job

1. FO 371/24249/200
2. *Nassau Guardian*, 3 September 1940
3. Interview with Vyvyan Drury, May 1981

4. Adela Rogers St Johns in the *Atlanta Journal*, etc., 18 November 1940
5. Bocca, *She Might Have Been Queen*, p.204
6. Dundas, p.147
7. Clifford, p.188
8. Interview in the *Bahamas Handbook*, 1963
9. St Johns articles, *loc. cit.*
10. FO 371/24249/200
11. Minute in FO 371/24249
12. FO 371/24249/195–6
13. FO 371/24249/201 (24 August 1940)
14. Sir Ronald Storrs' diary, 14 July 1940
15. Duke to Churchill, October 1940: 'I will admit to having been apprehensive of the possible effect of this difference in our official status on our position in a small community like this British Colony; but somehow I felt that in view of the gravity of the war situation, this chronic insult to my wife might well be overcome if not entirely lost in the vast changes that are taking place before our eyes.' See below, pp.147–8
16. Telegram 414A of 1940, Bahamas Record Office
17. American Consul Nassau to Secretary of State, 1 November 1940, National Archives Washington, 844E/001/60
18. Bocca, *The Life and Death of Harry Oakes*, p.89
19. *Nassau Guardian*, 24 August 1940
20. *Nassau Guardian*, 3 September 1940
21. Telegram 436 of 1940, Bahamas Record Office
22. Sir Eric Hallinan's notes
23. Forbes, *Appointment with Destiny*, p.197
24. Sir Eric Hallinan's notes
25. *Ibid.*
26. Forbes, p.197
27. Interview with Godfrey Higgs, March 1981
28. Sir Eric Hallinan's notes
29. *Ibid.*
30. *Ibid.*
31. *Ibid.*
32. *Ibid.*
33. *Ibid.*
34. Minutes of Executive Council in Bahamas Record Office
35. Dupuch, p.35
36. Interview with Vyvyan Drury, May 1981
37. Adela Rogers St Johns, *The Honeycomb*, 1969
38. FO 371/24263

39. Instalment 7 of 23 November
40. Interview in the *Bahamas Handbook*, 1963
41. Interview with Valeria Moseley Moss, February 1981
42. 15 October 1940
43. Telegrams 480B and 484 of 1940, Bahamas Record Office
44. Interview with Vyvan Drury, May 1981
45. For example on 13 July 1940, just after the announcement of the Duke's Governorship, the *New York Press Survey* sent to the Foreign Office saw fit to report comments only from the following portentous journals. '*Milwaukee Journal* definitely hostile. *Cleveland Press* described him as the manager of a high class winter resort and hoped he would not do any intriguing under the Nazis. *St Louis Post Despatch* satirized the ease of an Empire salesman's life.' (FO 371/24249/224)
46. *Votes of Legislative Council 1940–1941*, pp.2–7
47. National Archives Washington, 844E/001/60
48. 21 November 1940
49. 7 July 1941
50. Sir Eric Hallinan's notes
51. Charles Bedaux's papers: letter to Solbert, 23 August 1937
52. Gunnar Unger, *Axel Wenner-Gren*, pp.133–48
53. Telegram 151 of 14 May 1940, Bahamas Record Office
54. Marguerite Wenner-Gren, *Flight in Fantasy*, 1960
55. Telegram 414A of 30 August 1940, Bahamas Record Office
56. Fulton Oursler's article in *Liberty*, 22 March 1941
57. Telegram 422 of 4 September 1940, Bahamas Record Office
58. Telegrams 528 and 532 of 1940, Bahamas Record Office
59. See Philip Goodhart, *Fifty Ships that Saved the World* and Burns, *Colonial Civil Servant*, p.171ff.
60. Sir Eric Hallinan's notes
61. Meeting 31 of 30 October
62. Meeting 34 of 27 November
63. Meeting 36 of 11 December
64. *Ibid.*

9. Pax Americana

1. FO 371/24263/234
2. FO 371/24263/235
3. CO telegram of 4 December 1940, Bahamas Record Office
4. Minute in FO 371/24263
5. Telegram 595 of 5 December 1940, Bahamas Record Office
6. See especially FO 371/24263/245, which gives the vital clue as to who was in fact responsible.

7. Sir James Marjoribanks' notes (communicated to the author in June 1981)
8. *Ibid.*
9. Interview with Jahn Dahllof, March 1981; interview with Vyvyan Drury, May 1981
10. Sir James Marjoribanks' notes
11. Interview with Vyvyan Drury, May 1981
12. Nicolson, *Diaries* (1980 edition), p.88, 13 December 1935
13. 15 October 1940
14. PREM 4/10/4/320–1
15. Telegram 616 of 16 December 1940, Bahamas Record Office
16. Lord Beaverbrook, *The Abdication of King Edward VIII*, pp.108–9
17. *Duke, 1966*
18. Interview with Vyvyan Drury; Telegram 641 of 30 December 1940; *New York Times*, 14, 15, 16 December 1940; Fulton Oursler in *Liberty*, 22 March 1941
19. Oursler, *loc. cit.*
20. Duke to Wenner-Gren, 21 December 1940, 1 January 1941
21. Duke to Aunt Bessie, 7 July 1941
22. Oursler, *loc. cit.*
23. *New York Times*, 26 December 1940

10. The Play Ground

1. *Nassau Guardian*, 16 August 1941
2. Sir Eric Hallinan's notes
3. Forbes, *Appointment with Destiny*, pp.192–3
4. Interview of Nurse Alice Hill Jones by Maxine Sandberg, 1962
5. FO 371/24263/233
6. *New York Times*, 12 January 1941
7. FO 371/24263
8. FO 371/26191/156ff.
9. 31 March 1941
10. File on the security of the Bahamas, 1940–1, including correspondence, report of March 1941, and items intercepted by Bahamas censorship: Archives of H. Montgomery Hyde
11. American Consul Nassau to Secretary of State, 28 November 1940: National Archives Washington, 811/34544/202
12. Forbes, pp.108–9
13. *Nassau Magazine*, Anniversary Number 1942, p.10
14. Sir James Marjoribanks' notes; *New York Times*, 19, 20, 21, 22, 24 April
15. Telegram of 27 March in Bahamas Record Office

16. National Archives Washington, 740/0011/EW1939/21295
17. *Votes of the House of Assembly*, 1940–1: Message No.36 of 1 May 1941; Second Reading of Bill on 21 July
18. *Ibid.*: Governor's speech to House of 24 February, 30 June, 28 July; Message No.53 of 10 July; Bill introduced 8 September
19. CO 23/715
20. 7 July 1941
21. 6 July 1941
22. Forbes, pp.208–9
23. National Archives Washington, 800/20211/Wenner-Gren, 28 May 1941
24. *Ibid.*, 22 June 1941
25. Jason Lindsey's notes, communicated to the author August 1980
26. Duchess to Editor of *Picture Post*, 18 August 1941
27. 6 July 1941
28. Duke to Beaverbrook, 15 August 1941
29. Telegram 580 of August 1940 in Bahamas Record Office
30. Viscount Hall to the author, 30 April 1981
31. Meeting 21 of 20 August 1941
32. Meeting 23 of 17 September 1941
33. Meeting 22 of 3 September 1941

11. Going North

1. 6 July 1941
2. FO 371/26191/19
3. PREM 4/10/4
4. FO 371/26191/25
5. PREM 4/10/4/279–83
6. 26 July 1941
7. 6 August 1941; 20 August 1941
8. 4 September 1941
9. 5 September 1941
10. 10 September 1941
11. British Press Service Report 620/1941, 22 September
12. Igor Cassini in *Washington Times Herald*, 26 September
13. *New York P.M.*, 26 September
14. FO 371/26191/67
15. *Time*, 4 October 1941
16. PREM 4/10/4/286–7
17. *Chicago Tribune*, 28 September 1941
18. *New York Times*, 30 September 1941
19. See e.g. Townsend, *The Prince of Wales* (1929), p.175ff.

20. Duke to C.G. Heward KC, 14 September 1941
21. 3 April 1939
22. 11 June 1940
23. Duke to Alick Newton, 7 April 1941
24. *Ibid.*
25. *Ibid.*
26. 12 June 1941
27. 30 June 1941
28. Duke to W.L. Carlyle, 7 August 1941
29. Duke to Hon. George Hoadley, 7 October 1941
30. *The Albertan*, 8 October 1941
31. *Baltimore News Post*, 12 October 1941
32. FO 371/26191/70
33. Lord Halifax's diary at Garrowby (by kind permission of the present Earl), Tuesday 14 October 1941
34. *Ibid.*, Friday 17 October 1941
35. 'Wallis Warfield's Warrenton Days Recalled' in *The Fauquier Democrat*, 14 September 1950
36. Duke to Allen, 13 December 1941
37. *New York Mirror*, 22 October 1941
38. *New York Times*, 22 October 1941
39. *New York Times*, 23 October 1941
40. *New York Times*, 25 October 1941
41. Duchess of Windsor, *Some Southern Recipies*; Eleanor Roosevelt's column in *New York World Telegram*, 30 October 1941
42. *Duke, 1966*
43. Interview with Vyvyan Drury, May 1981
44. *Detroit Times*, 30 October 1941
45. PREM 4/26/10/1438
46. British Press Service Report 789/1941 of 24 November
47. PREM 4/26/10/1444
48. Stephen Trumbull in *Miami Herald*, 5 November 1941
49. Duke to Allen, 13 December 1941
50. British Press Service Report 789/1941 of 24 November
51. Duchess to Aunt Bessie, 23 November 1941

12. The War Ground

1. *Votes of the Legislative Council*, 1941–2, pp.2–8
2. CO 23/715
3. Interview with Reginald Farrington, March 1981
4. *Nassau Guardian*, 30 November 1941
5. Sir James Marjoribanks' notes

6. Interview with Vyvyan Drury, May 1981
7. *Votes of the House of Assembly*; Message No.15 of 22 January 1942
8. National Archives Washington, 800/20211/Wenner-Gren, 21 July 1942: totally valueless, being a second-hand report given by a Mexican with an axe to grind to an American businessman reporting to the State Department.
9. *Ibid.*, 24 November 1941
10. 31 January 1942
11. Interviews with Sir Berkeley Ormerod and others
12. National Archives Wenner-Gren file, 18 June 1942
13. Unger, pp.133–48
14. Winston Churchill, *The Hinge of Fate*, p.81
15. *Duchess*, p.347
16. FO 371/30640
17. National Archives Washington, OPD/381/Bahamas, 13 April 1942
18. *Duchess*, p.348
19. Churchill, p.789
20. Interview with Nina Drury; interview with Bishop of Nassau, March 1981
21. *Duchess*, p.356
22. Report in *Votes of the House of Assembly*, pp.60–2
23. *Votes of the Legislative Council*, pp.95–101

13. The Uprising

1. *Duchess*, p.348
2. Halifax Diary (Garrowby Papers). On 1 June the itinerant Ambassador arrived at Harrisburg, Pa., from Columbus, Ohio. He returned to Washington the next day after the Duke's departure, writing in his diary: 'The Duke of Windsor has had to go back to the Bahamas on account of some labour riots. Dorothy's dinner party for them seems to have gone all right last night.'
3. CO 23/731/1–3; FO 371/30644/22–4
4. *Duchess*, pp.348–9
5. OPD 370/61/Bahamas, 2 June 1942 in National Archives Washington
6. Sir Randol Fawkes, *The Faith That Moved the Mountain*, p.24
7. The account which follows is based on the following sources: the Report of the Commission of Enquiry into the Riots; the Commission's *Proceedings* in the Bahamas Record Office; the official correspondence between London and Nassau in CO 23/731 and FO 371/30644; and the reports sent by the US Consulate Nassau to the State Department (National Archives Washington, OPD 381/Bahamas/

1942). Sir Eric Hallinan and Colonel R. A. Erskine-Lindop were also kind enough to clarify a number of points.

8. US Consular Report of 30 June 1942
9. Sir Eric Hallinan's notes
10. CO 23/731/79. E. Brownrig's letter to his parents in Trinidad, intercepted in censorship, 5 June 1942
11. CO 23/731/98. Duke to Colonial Office, 17 September 1942
12. Minute sheet in CO 23/731
13. FO 371/30644/17–18
14. FO 371/30644/25
15. CO 23/731/39
16. Fawkes, p.31
17. FO 371/30644/120
18. Sir Eric Hallinan's notes
19. FO 371/30644/110–11
20. *Ibid.*, ff.132–5
21. *Ibid.*, f.111
22. *Ibid.*, f.139
23. *Ibid.*, ff.137–8
24. *Ibid.*, ff.139–40
25. *Ibid.*, f.142
26. ExCo Minutes, Bahamas Record Office, 17 June 1942
27. *Nassau Daily Tribune*, 13 June 1942
28. *Duke, 1966*
29. Halifax Diary, 16 June 1942
30. Inez Robb syndicated article, 9 June 1942
31. *New York Times*, 16 June 1942
32. FO 371/30644/145
33. CO 23/731/44
34. Halifax Diary, 23 June 1942
35. CO 23/731/45
36. *Duchess*, p.350
37. CO 23/731/41–2
38. Duke to Allen, 12 January 1945
39. *Duchess*, p.350
40. The author has interviewed a number of eye-witnesses of the Bay Street fire, including Vyvyan Drury, Reginald Farrington, Sir Eric Hallinan and Mary Teegarden Holder
41. Report of the Commission of Enquiry, p.37
42. CO 23/731
43. Interview with Godfrey Higgs, March 1981
44. Sir Eric Hallinan's notes
45. Interview with Vyvyan Drury, May 1981

46. Duchess to Aunt Bessie, 29 August 1942
47. *Duchess*, p.352
48. Duchess to Aunt Bessie, 29 August 1942

14. Triumphs and Sorrows of Government House

1. *Votes of the Legislative Council*, 1942–3, pp.2–15
2. CO 23/731/94
3. CO 23/731/96
4. Sir Eric Hallinan's notes
5. CO 23/731/96
6. CO 23/736
7. Minute on CO 23/731
8. Duchess to Aunt Bessie, 17 September 1942
9. CO 23/731/98
10. CO 23/731/100
11. *Duchess*, p.347
12. Minute on CO 23/731
13. *Memorandum on the Establishment of the Out Islands as an Administrative Unit* enclosed in Governor's Message No. 29, *Votes of the House of Assembly*, 1942–3, pp.63–8
14. Duchess to Aunt Bessie, 26 September 1942
15. Duke to Churchill, 10 November 1942
16. Churchill to Duke, 22 December 1942
17. Report of the Commission of Enquiry, p.21
18. *Ibid.*, p.29
19. *Ibid.*, p.40
20. CO 23/731/127
21. AIR 29/689 and the following pieces contain the fascinatingly complete operational records of OTU III
22. *Duchess*, p.353
23. 5 April 1943
24. 4 March 1943
25. 5 February 1943
26. 23 January 1943
27. *Ibid.*
28. Sir Philip Rogers to the author.
29. CO 23/734, Duke to Secretary of State, 24 March
30. CO 23/760
31. Interview with Godfrey Higgs, March 1981
32. Stewart Lack to the author, 17 July 1980
33. Duke to Allen, 3 May 1944
34. H. Montgomery Hyde, *The Quiet Canadian*, pp. 170–1

35. The *Melbourne Argus*, 7 August 1943. Following a row over the appointment of the first Australian-born Governor-General, Sir Isaac Isaacs, in 1931, the sovereign had established the right to a personal say in the nomination of his representative in Canberra, and it was to this fact that Mr Curtin was no doubt alluding when he indicated that the Australian Government did not have an entirely free choice.

15. No Prizes for Doing Well

1. CO 23/760
2. Lord Moran, *Churchill: The Struggle for Survival*, p.97; Halifax Diary, 19 May 1943
3. *Ibid.*
4. Duke to Allen, 3 May 1944
5. Duchess to Aunt Bessie, 24 August 1943
6. *Duchess*, p.355
7. CO 23/734; 23/744

16. Violent Death

1. *Duke, 1966*
2. Stewart Lack's notes
3. *Duchess*, p.354
4. Colonel R.A. Erskine-Lindop to the author, January 1981
5. CO 23/714/1
6. CO 23/714/5
7. Sir Eric Hallinan's notes
8. *Miami Herald*, 22 July 1943
9. Duchess to Aunt Bessie, 24 August 1943
10. Stewart Lack's notes
11. *Votes of the Legislative Council*, 1942–3, p.200
12. Duke to Oliver Stanley, 24 January 1944
13. Interview with Mrs Morgan Schiller, March 1981
14. Duchess to Aunt Bessie, 9 October 1943
15. Duke to Churchill, 6 November 1943
16. *Times Herald*, 24 October 1943
17. Helen Essary to Duchess, 22 October 1943
18. Harry Taylor to Duke, 6 November 1943
19. *Daily Telegraph*, 23 November 1943
20. CO 23/714/42
21. Sir Eric Hallinan's notes
22. CO 23/714
23. CO 23/714/27

24. *Votes of the Legislative Council*, 1943–4, pp.2–13
25. CO 23/744
26. Duchess to Aunt Bessie, 1 December 1943
27. 6 January 1944

17. The Search for Escape

1. CO 23/744; Duke to Secretary of State, 24 January 1944
2. Telegram 6 of 5 January 1944 in Bahamas Record Office. 'Your secret telegram 286 Administrative Staff Out Islands is a great disappointment and an embarrassment to me.'
3. Duke to Allen, 3 May 1944
4. *Ibid.*
5. Rosita Forbes to Duchess, 3 April 1945
6. Forbes, *Appointment with Destiny*, p.209
7. Duke to Allen, 3 May 1944
8. Allen to Duke, 31 May 1944
9. See Lees-Milne, *Harold Nicolson*, II, pp.86–7
10. Sir Ulick Alexander to Allen, 29 May 1944
11. Allen to Duke, 9 June 1944
12. *Duke, 1966*
13. Duke to Allen, 30 September 1944
14. Duke to Churchill, 3 October 1944
15. *Votes of the Legislative Council*, 1943–4, pp.134–48; 1944–5, pp.2–7
16. Duke to Churchill, 3 October 1944

18. Capax Imperii

1. Interview with Mrs Leslie Higgs, March 1981
2. Duke to Allen, 13 December 1944
3. Allen to Duke, 21 December 1944
4. Churchill to Duke, 31 December 1944
5. See above, p. 345
6. *Votes of the House of Assembly*, 1944–5, Message No.8
7. *Votes*, Message No.12
8. CO 23/744
9. *Votes*, Message No.33
10. Telegram in Bahamas Record Office
11. Executive Council Minutes, meetings 1 and 8 of 4 January and 21 February 1945
12. *Ibid.*, meeting 4 of 31 January
13. *Ibid.*, meeting 13 of 21 March
14. *Ibid.*, meeting 7 of 14 February; *Votes*, Message No.21

15. *Votes*, p.61
16. Duke to Allen, 12 January 1945
17. *Duchess*, p.358
18. Alice Hill Jones to Duchess, 7 February 1946
19. ExCo, meeting 16 of 25 April
20. *Duchess*, p.358
21. Donaldson, p.382, quoting Sir John Balfour
22. January 1943
23. Sir Philip Rogers to the author, 14 and 27 April 1981
24. Iles Brodie, *Gone with the Windsors* (1953), p.255
25. Donaldson, p. 383
26. Michael Pye, *The King over the Water* (1981), p.251ff.
27. Helen Worden in the *American Mercury*, June 1944, p.675
28. Interview with Sydney Johnson, April 1981
29. Sir George Roberts to Duke, 13 January 1959
30. *Nassau Daily Tribune*, 2 May 1968
31. Duke to Sir Francis Cumming-Bruce, 8 April 1970
32. Diana Mosley, *The Duchess of Windsor*, p.195
33. Duke to Roy Howard, 19 March 1945
34. Duke to King George VI, 18 October 1945
35. King George VI to Duke, 10 November 1945

Bibliography

Paul Albury, *The Story of the Bahamas*, 1975
Princess Alice, Countess of Athlone, *For My Grandchildren*, 1966
Lord Beaverbrook, *The Abdication of King Edward VIII*, 1966
H. MacLachlan Bell, *Isles of June*, 1934
J. Benoist-Méchin, *60 jours qui ébranlèrent l'Occident*, 1956
Pierre Billotte, *Le temps des armes*, 1972
Lord Birkenhead, *Walter Monckton*, 1969
   Lord Halifax, 1965
Suzanne Blum, *Vivre sans la patrie*, 1975
Geoffrey Bocca, *The Life and Death of Harry Oakes*, 1959
   She Might Have Been Queen, 1957
Ragnar Boman and Ingrid Dahlberg, *Dansen kring guldkalven*, 1975
R. Bruge, *Faites sauter la Ligne Maginot!*, 1973
Sir Alan Burns, *Colonial Civil Servant*, 1949
   History of the British West Indies, 1954
Ewan Butler, *Amateur Agent*, 1963
Maurice Chevalier, *With Love*, 1960
Winston Churchill, *The Hinge of Fate*, 1951
Sir Bede Clifford, *Proconsul*, 1964
J. R. Colville, *Man of Valour*, 1972
Noël Coward, *Future Indefinite*, 1954
Michael Craton, *A History of the Bahamas*, 1962
J. A. Cross, *Sir Samuel Hoare: A Political Biography*, 1977
Frances Donaldson, *Edward VIII*, 1974
Sir Charles Dundas, *African Crossroads*, 1955
Sir Etienne Dupuch, *Tribune Story*, 1967
L. F. Ellis, *Welsh Guards at War*, 1946
David Farrer, *G for God Almighty*, 1969
Sir Randol Fawkes, *The Faith That Moved the Mountain*, 1979
Rosita Forbes, *A Unicorn in the Bahamas*, 1939
   The Prodigious Caribbean, 1940
   Appointment with Destiny, 1946

BIBLIOGRAPHY

Colin Forbes Adam, *The Life of Lord Lloyd*, 1948
Noble Frankland, *Prince Henry Duke of Gloucester*, 1980
Anthony Gibbs, *Gibbs and a Phoney War*, 1967
Philip Goodhart, MP, *Fifty Ships that Saved the World*, 1965
A. Goutard, *La guerre des occasions perdues*, 1956
Philip Guedalla, *The Hundredth Year*, 1940
Oliver Harvey, *Diplomatic Diaries, 1937–1940*, 1970
Dina Wells Hood, *Working for the Windsors*, 1957
Alistair Horne, *To Lose a Battle*, 1969
Marshall Houts, *Who Murdered Sir Harry Oakes?*, 1976
H. Montgomery Hyde, *The Quiet Canadian*, 1962
                           Secret Intelligence Agent, 1982
Charles Ives, *The Isles of Summer*, 1880
Sir Charles Jeffries, *The Colonial Office*, 1956
James Lees-Milne, *Harold Nicolson: A Biography*, 2 vols., 1980–81
B.H. Liddell-Hart, *Memoirs*, 1965
                         The Second World War, 1970
John T. McCutcheon, *Drawn from Memory*
Alfred de Marigny, *More Devil than Saint*, 1946
Ralph Martin, *The Woman He Loved*, 1973
R.J. Minney (ed.), *The Private Papers of Hore-Belisha*, 1960
Lord Moran, *Churchill: The Struggle for Survival*, 1966
Mary Moseley, *The Bahamas Handbook*, 1926
Malcolm Muggeridge (ed.), *Ciano's Diary*, 1947
Nassau Daily Tribune, *The Murder of Sir Harry Oakes*, 1959
H.G. Nicholas (ed.), *Washington Despatches 1941–45*, 1981
Harold Nicolson, *Why Britain is at War*, 1939
                         Diaries and Letters, 1966–8, 2nd edn 1980
Mollie Panter-Downes, *London War Notes*, 1972
Robert H. Pilpel, *Churchill in America*, 1976
James Pope-Hennessy, *Queen Mary*, 1959
Sir Henry Pownall, *Diaries 1933–1940*, 1972
J. Henry Richardson, *Review of Bahamian Economic Problems*, 1944
Walter Schellenberg, *Memoirs*, 1966
Sir Walford Selby, *Diplomatic Twilight*, 1953
Sir Edward Spears, *Assignment to Catastrophe*, 1956
C.P. Stacey, *Official History of the Canadian Army in the Second World War*, 1957
A.J.P. Taylor, *Beaverbrook*, 1972
Lord Templewood, *Ambassador on Special Mission*, 1946
                         Nine Troubled Years, 1954
Gunnar Unger, *Axel Wenner-Gren*, 1962
Roland Vintras, *The Portuguese Connection*, 1974

BIBLIOGRAPHY

Axel Wenner-Gren, *Call to Reason*, 1937
Sir John Wheeler-Bennett, *King George VI, His Life and Reign*, 1958
Duchess of Windsor, *Some Southern Recipes*, 1942
              The Heart Has Its Reasons, 1956
Duke of Windsor, *A King's Story*, 1951
              A Family Album, 1960
Kenneth Young, *Churchill and Beaverbrook*, 1966

Votes of the Honourable House of Assembly of the Bahama Islands, 1940–1945
Votes of the Honourable Legislative Council of the Bahama Islands, 1940–1945
Report of the Commission Appointed to Enquire into Disturbances in the Bahamas which Took Place in June, 1942.

Index

389